No Time to Slow Down

For Roger and Susi
with warmest
Regards.

Bill + Tilly
Ribeau

Dr. William C. Gibson

No Time to Slow Down

UBC Alumni Association
University of British Columbia

Printed in Canada on acid–free paper

ISBN 0-88865-528-2

Canadian Cataloguing in Publication Data
Gibson, William Carleton, 1913-
No time to slow down

ISBN 0-88865-528-2

1. Gibson, William Carleton, 1913- 2. Medical teaching personnel—British Columbia—Biography. 3. University of British Columbia—Biography. 4. University of British Columbia. Faculty of Medicine—History. I. University of British Columbia. Alumni Association. II. Title.

R464.G52A3 1996 610'.92 C96-910130-9

UBC Alumni Association
6251 Cecil Green Park Road
University of British Columbia
Vancouver, BC V6T 1Z1

This book is dedicated to all the

UBC Presidents

1913–1918	Frank F. Wesbrook
1919–1944	Leonard S. Klinck
1944–1962	Norman A.M. MacKenzie
1962–1967	John B. Macdonald
1968–1969	F. Kenneth Hare
1969–1975	Walter H. Gage
1975–1983	Douglas T. Kenny
1983–1985	George Pedersen
1985 (March–October)	R.H.T. Smith
1985–present	David W. Strangway

and to all the

UBC Chancellors

1913–1918	F.L. Carter-Cotton
1918–1944	R.E. McKechnie
1944–1951	Eric Hamber
1951–1957	Sherwood Lett
1957–1961	A.E. (Dal) Grauer
1961–1966	Phyllis G. Ross
1966–1969	John M. Buchanan
1969–1972	Allan M. McGavin
1972–1975	Nathan T. Nemetz
1975–1978	Donovan F. Miller
1978–1984	John V. Clyne
1984–1987	W. Robert Wyman
1987–1993	Leslie R. Peterson
1993--present	Robert H. Lee

TABLE OF CONTENTS

ILLUSTRATIONS

20. At the microscope studying cancer of the liver, Beijing, China, 1980.

21. In the Memorial Room, Woodward Library, U.B.C., 1980.

22. W.C.G. in California (Portola Valley).

23. The Chancellor of the University of Victoria, 1987.

24. Normal School (Camosun College), Victoria, B.C. at Dogwood Tree Ceremony, memorializing J.W. Gibson. September 17, 1986.

25. Accompanying Rt. Hon. Denis Healy at Rockerfeller Study Center, Bellagia, 1988.

26. Chancellor, University of Victoria, 1988.

27. Awarding a prize at Royal Roads Military College, Victoria, 1988.

28. No caption.

29. With Cecil Green (r) and Lord Walton, Oxford, 1990.

30. Ian, Kate and David Gibson, U.B.C., 1993.

31. Dr. William Gibson and his wife Clotilde in Victoria.

32. W.C.G. looking to the future in Mystic Vale at the University of Victoria.

THE HON. NATHAN T. NEMETZ, C.C., Q.C.

I have had the great pleasure of knowing the Gibson family since the early 1930s. Bill's mother and father lived in Victoria, and were a highly intelligent set of parents. I once attended a dinner at their home, but dared not go again, despite their generous hospitality. The reason is that there existed a family tradition that each guest would be expected to speak in the language chosen for discussion on the night in question. Fortunately the night I attended, I learnt that the language would be Latin. Accordingly, I boned up on 5 or 6 words relating to food that might be served that evening. I was lucky, but I decided never to take another chance in case the language to be used might be Greek, or for that matter, Swahili. To have parents like the Gibsons was indeed, a unique experience in the lives of their children.

But my subject matter relates to the member of the family that I know best, William Carleton Gibson. Although I privately still call him 'Billy', he was always 'William' to his mother, and I was warned accordingly.

At the outset I can state without contradiction that of all my classmates, Billy has become the best known alumnus of the University of British Columbia. But it is not only that he is well known - he is respected for the great work he has accomplished, both here and abroad.

After the War, he joined the Faculty of Medicine. Of him, it can be said that when he became involved in a good cause, he never relaxed until he succeeded in reaching his goal.

It was he who sought out our most distinguished patrons, Mr. and Mrs. Cecil Green, thus allowing them to create Cecil and Ida Green House, the Green Lectureship, and the beautiful new Green College.

It was he who developed the Kinsmen Foundation to assist the University in fundraising, It was he who, after many years, finally convinced Puggy Woodward to create the Woodward Biomedical Library. It was he, as Councilman and a member of the Board of Parks and Recreation, who assisted in setting up the present day Park structure that made Vancouver the green capital of the West.

For all these achievements he was granted the degree of Doctor of Laws Honoris Causa.

I had the privilege of working with him shortly after he returned home form his service in the Air Force. It was because of his efforts that the University Club of Vancouver was founded. There are a host of other projects which he helped achieve, and in his book he tells of the work he did.

Recently he was asked "Bill, when are you going to slow down?" He replied truthfully and persuasively "I haven't the time to slow down."

We have remained friends for almost 60 years and I can attest to the proposition that so long as some worthy university objective requires his service, he will always be on hand to achieve that objective. He and his wife winter in Palo Alto, but like his good friend, Cecil Green, his heart remains in British Columbia.

To read this biography is to appreciate how much one person can accomplish in a single lifetime.

PART ONE

CHAPTER ONE

Introduction

It is not everyone who is so rash as to publish his autobiography while he is still alive! As Dr. Johnson remarked, no man is on oath in writing his own obituary. In order that my readers may be as little confused as possible, I have prefaced what is recollected by a brief chronology.

I was born prematurely in Ottawa in September 1913 and, as my mother frequently remarked, I have been "in a rush ever since." I vomited my way to Canada's west coast city, Victoria, in the hot summer of 1914, just as the Great War was declared. The confusion on the railroads as mobilization began did nothing to ease the burden on my poor mother (she was tough and knew the Wilder West, having "washed" gold in Alaska at an early age). She was accompanied to Victoria by my two–years–older brother, James. My father had gone ahead to Victoria to find a house with suitable grounds around it. He had been appointed head of agricultural education by the government of Sir Richard McBride and his dashing minister of education, Dr. Henry Esson Young. In those days, ministers of the Crown Provincial drove to the gleaming new parliament buildings on Victoria's harbour in a coach–and–four.

At the age of six, I began my unusual education at the trim, brick Quadra school and completed my elementary work at North Ward school — thought by my parents to provide the most rigorous training in the province. Its principal, J. M. Campbell, had been a carpenter on Prince Edward Island until the age of 24, when he "saw the light" and became a great teacher. His clan moved across the entire width of Canada to dominate British Columbia's educational scene for several generations.

North Ward school—long since demolished to make way for the Victoria Press building—had the largest proportion of Oriental students in the city. It was there that I learned to respect these students and their families. By 1926 it was time to enrol at Victoria high school where Sir Arthur Currie had taught in pre-war days. The school was an elegant edifice with fine playing fields and tennis courts, all presided over by Ira Dilworth, a talented musician and English teacher who had gone from the Okanagan Valley to Harvard and back in order to try to educate the children of the pioneers.

From 1929 to 1931 I attended the first commerce course at Victoria College, a two-year institution that was affiliated with the University of British Columbia—both having been, early in the century, colleges of McGill University in Montreal. As the Great Depression deepened, a degree in commerce seemed irrelevant. A medical uncle convinced me that I should prepare to go into his profession and as a result I undertook pre-medical studies at the University of British Columbia from 1931 to 1933. I kept up my interest in commerce, taking a first class in money and banking, but compressed every pre-medical course offered, along with scientific German, into two hectic years, graduating with a Bachelor of Arts degree in 1933.

Entering McGill's faculty of medicine in 1933, I found myself amongst a wild group of students, largely American it seemed. Towards the end of the first year, I learned that the five-year course in medicine was to be shortened to four years, to accord with most North American schools. The dean, Dr. C.F. Martin, agreed that I could break off at the end of my first year, take a Master's degree and then return to finish my M.D. degree three years thereafter.

With a research fellowship, I was able to enter McGill's Montreal Neurological Institute on its opening day in September 1934, in search of a Master's degree in research. After a year, the director, Dr. Wilder Penfield, sent me to Oxford to the laboratory of his old teacher, Sir Charles Sherrington, O.M. Dr. J.C. Eccles supervised me for my Doctor of Philosophy degree.

In the spring vacation of 1936, I travelled to Madrid to work in the Cancer Institute with Professor Pio del Río-Hortega and at the Instituto Cajal with Dr. Fernando de Castro. Research travel funds enabled me briefly to visit French and German laboratories in later vacations and to spend a week in the summer of 1937 visiting the laboratory of Professor Lawrentjew in Moscow and the Pavlov dog farm under Professor Orbeli near Leningrad.

With the benefactions of "the automobile king" Lord Nuffield in 1936, the Oxford clinical school was haltingly launched and in the autumn of 1937 eight of us were admitted to the remarkable six-month credit bearing course in the clinics and wards of the Radcliffe Infirmary. Pathology lectures by Howard Florey and Boris Chain adumbrated the great future of penicillin and other antibiotics. It is sometimes forgotten that Osler's predecessor as Regius at Oxford, John Burdon Sanderson, in 1871 recorded that penicillium mould prevented bacterial growth in flasks of broth. By June of 1938 I was granted the Doctor of Philosophy degree for my research on the microscopic structure of the synapses (the points of contact and communication between nerve cells).

McGill generously allowed me to enter the third year of the four–year medical course, and I proceeded happily along until the winter struck. Gradually the long hill up to McGill's medical school became steeper and my joints and chest became more painful daily. I was diagnosed as having rheumatic fever with heart disease. After being hospitalized several times in the Royal Victoria, the professor of medicine, Dr. J.C. Meakins, decided that I must go to bed for a year. As a result, I spent the first three months of 1939 on a little beach near Acapulco, Mexico and the remaining nine months at my home in the lovely city of Victoria, British Columbia.

Graduating with my new class in 1941, I was allowed to intern at the medical branch of the University of Texas in semitropical Galveston. With the bombing of Pearl Harbour I went to join the U.S. Air Force at Randolph Field near San Antonio. I found that in 1941 a Canadian citizen could not be a medical officer in the American forces, but the general in charge arranged for my entry into the Royal Canadian Air Force with no questions asked. The recommendation of Dr. Paul Dudley White, who had seen me in Boston after my convalescence, certainly helped.

At all events, I served with the RCAF high altitude research group and eventually went to Air Force headquarters in Ottawa where I finished the war as deputy director of medical research. Before being properly discharged, I rejoined Dr. Penfield at McGill, completing the first diploma in neurology in December 1947. The ensuing year found me teaching brain pathology at the University of Sydney in Australia, and thereafter I served as visiting professor at the University of California in San Francisco en route home to Canada.

In July 1949 I was appointed director of research for the mental hospitals of British Columbia and, with the opening of the new faculty of medicine at the University of British Columbia in Vancouver, as professor of neurological research. By 1958 I wanted a breather and spent eight months of my only sabbatical year in the clinical laboratory of neurophysiology with Professor Henri Gastaut in Marseille, and four months at the Maudsley Hospital in London with Sir Denis Hill.

From 1959 until my retirement from the University of British Columbia in 1978, I served as professor of the history of medicine and science. Then for five hectic years I chaired a financing body—the Universities Council of British Columbia—spending a great deal of time on trial by the three provincial universities who competed for shrinking funds. On January 1, 1984 I took on the chancellorship of the University of Victoria, as the elected representative of its 20,000 graduates.

This condensed itinerary may help readers to follow the ensuing story more easily.

CHAPTER TWO

Victoria, 1914–1931

Anyone growing up in Victoria, B.C., soon comes to realize the truth of the local saying: "When a dog chases a cat across the street in Victoria they are both walking." The leisurely pace of life, the mild climate and the beauty of the natural setting have turned generations of residents and even visitors into lotus–eaters of a high order. It is suggested derisively by foreigners that a tweed curtain separates Victoria from uncouth neighbouring cities such as Vancouver and Seattle. The truth, of course, is that the entire continent of North America is isolated, not just the tea–drinking, bird–watching and flower–gardening haven of Victoria.

Long before my family arrived in Victoria from Ottawa in 1914, a distinctly British tone had been set by people who came from the United Kingdom. Victoria could have been a quiet provincial town anywhere along the south coast of England, with much of its activity centred about a picturesque harbour and its inhabitants close to being "a nation of shopkeepers." There had been an upper crust since the early days of the all powerful Hudson's Bay Company, in addition to the army and the navy (with its summer visitors from the Bermuda Squadron) and the colonial civil servants.

The town's business area was a mixture of shops: book stores in which much free reading took place, grocery stores, which in some cases sold liquor, and a colourful Chinatown, some of whose residents had been deported from Vancouver in 1887 when serious riots broke out there due to labour strife. The Chinese found quiet employment in the numerous large houses that had been built by early settlers. The Crease family, from the county of Cornwall, named their extensive home and grounds "Pentrelew," meaning "a house on the hill," as it was on Fort Street. Senator Macdonald built a castle reminiscent of Armadale on the Scottish island of Skye. A new landed gentry developed, with some of their holdings running into hundreds of acres. Many settlers had acquired land at one dollar per acre.

As if the post–California gold rush through Victoria to the Fraser River had not been enough for the fledgling Victoria of 1858—with 10,000 men suddenly thrust upon it—there was a second human whirlwind of gold seekers in 1898 heading for the Klondike. They sought, en route, food, boots, outdoor clothes, snowshoes, sleighs and even local dogs to go with them.

Governor James Douglas (1803–77) used his very considerable powers as if he were still running the Hudson's Bay Company, but some of his best ideas were shot down by the Colonial Office in London. He had his hands full with post–Klondike gamblers, drunks, opium dens and upstart Canadians on the mainland of British Columbia who hoped to steal the provincial capital and take it to the rapidly developing deep–sea port of Vancouver. He created a town plan for Victoria, stopped tree cutting on the waterfront and preserved Beacon Hill as a great park between the Strait of Juan de Fuca and the city. The Colonial Office in London was more keen on placing demanding British gentry in such far off colonies as British Columbia than in getting competent and trained people to help Douglas with his enormous task of administering a boisterous area four times the size of the United Kingdom. His unfailing ability to foresee trends in development helped him to locate the temporary parliament buildings on the south side of the harbour, to be followed by the handsome stone buildings designed in international competition by a 26–year–old English architect, Frank Rattenbury.[1]

The opening of the illuminated parliament buildings in 1899 helped to focus Victoria's attention on its protected harbour. Rattenbury's influence on the enhancement of that area increased with the opening of the Empress Hotel in 1908, which he had designed once the legislative buildings were complete. His colonnaded Canadian Pacific Steamships building on the water's edge added to the harbour's charm.

In 1928 Rattenbury returned to England with his second wife, she with her third husband. Seven years later she and her young chauffeur were cited for the murder of the great architect. The mallet–wielding chauffeur was gaoled for life. The wife committed suicide, closing a bizarre chapter in our history.

As a child I imagined that the rest of the world was a garden and that everyone grew up with English skylarks soaring in the heavens, waiting to plummet down to earth in one frightening dive. In summer we trekked to our farm on the slopes of Mount Tolmie and as children ran around with drinks of buttermilk for the sweating men putting up hay. The sunshine had then, and still has, the almost miraculous quality of stinging the skin while, at the same time, a gentle, cool breeze brings pleasing relief. It has always seemed strange that Victoria, an ocean city, should have almost the longest hours of sunshine in the country. The combination of the west wind, the Japanese current via the north Pacific and the absence of mountains on the southern tip of Vancouver Island may be the cause of the lovely, moderate climate. The co–existence of orange–barked arbutus (Madrona) trees with Garry oaks and conifers is unique.

The mountains that we grew up with were the Olympics, 15 miles by sea across the Strait of Juan de Fuca, in the state of Washington. With snow on their peaks much of the year, they were the sentinels guarding the boisterous waters, named so long ago for the navigator who, it is claimed, discovered the fabled but imaginary Northwest Passage.

As children we were warned repeatedly that our homemade rafts, paddled too far from shore, would get us into riptides and offshore currents that would carry us into the open Pacific. Gradually we learned that Pacific was indeed a misnomer and that the towering seas could disable great ships in equinoctial storms. Our favourite liners were the gleaming white Empresses of the Canadian Pacific line, which sailed to Japan. The early diesel ships, the Aorangi and the Niagara, sailed to New Zealand and Australia. Little did I know that in 1949 I would sail on the Aorangi from Sydney to Vancouver.

Childhood memories are often fragmentary and incomprehensible. My first was of a smoke–belching fire engine drawn by four dashing white horses that once passed in front of our house in the middle of the night. For a long time it seemed strange to me that a portable fire on wheels should be rushing to a house fire; but that was in the days of pumpers powered by steam generated as the red creation answered the alarm. Equally confusing to a child was the overnight change from driving on the left side of the road to driving on the right, something long delayed and never fully accepted by some residents of Victoria. It presaged the end of the British Empire and the letters to the editor of the Colonist newspaper were full of shocked disbelief. The tweed–capped, red–faced old boys, who piloted their brass–nosed open Morris Cowleys down the middle of the roads, never changed anyway. Some were remittance men whose families in Britain paid, through banks in Victoria, monthly sums to keep errant sons permanently out of Britain.

The return of troops and of navy ships at the end of the Great War is still a vivid memory. The music seemed to go on throughout the night as "Keep the home fires burning" was replaced by "There's a long, long trail awinding," written by newsman Stoddard King in nearby Spokane. Finally, Sir Arthur Currie, who only today is seen to have been one of the truly great generals of that war, came home to plant (with Marshal Foch) memorial plane trees the length of Shelbourne Avenue near our farm. Unfortunately, in many cases these trees have been butchered to accommodate transmission wires.

The aircraft pilots who came back from that war were the dashing young blades of Victoria. The public was well aware of the "flying coffins" they had flown, because the main floor of the Hudson's Bay Store on Douglas Street was given over to an entrancing display of captured German planes, as well as Allied planes piloted by the harem–scarem Canadians. We became accustomed to a Flying Boat that Eddie Hubbard flew over from Seattle on Saturdays with the last mail for the ships going to the Orient. He was soon replaced in our personal hall of fame by the Eve brothers who imported a gleaming Ford tri–motored passenger plane which, remarkably, was able to take off and land on the Scott farm near ours at Mount Tolmie. Watching from a rocky high point nearby, we were mesmerized by this great metallic bird. It disappeared, alas, into the sea and no trace was ever found of it or its passengers. The Scott farm had seen some unusual planes in its history, including the first Canadian–designed plane, built and flown in 1910 by my namesake (no relative) William Wallace Gibson. Only in Victoria could he eventually collide with an oak tree.

My father, a botanist, was an adviser to Mrs. R.P. Butchart as she struggled to develop the sunken garden in a disused limestone quarry at Tod Inlet, 13 miles from Victoria. Jennie Butchart had a great sense of humour and as children we would greatly enjoy her stories. At one time she had 40 Chinese working at Benvenuto. In contrast, I remember Mrs. Dunsmuir of Hatley Park, the grande dame with 72 Chinese gardeners who wore more diamond rings on her fingers than I had seen before or since. For some reason she was interested in Mrs Emily Crawford's (our cousin) early proposal to build a highway from Prince George at the northerly bend of the Fraser River to the Peace River of B.C. country at that time accessible only from Alberta.

The Dunsmuir story of the discovery of coal on Vancouver Island and the subsequent fortunes made was well known to us as children. What was less well known was the history of their townhouse, Craigdarroch: a turreted castle that still dominates the height of land within the city of Victoria. The legend, probably apocryphal, that we as students at Victoria College grew up on was that on moving to their 650–acre country estate, now Royal Roads, the Dunsmuirs decided to sell off their large holdings around Craigdarroch Castle. The land below them belonged to the long–established families: the Spencers with their department stores, and the Creases of legal fame—Chief Justices and lawyers stemming from Ince Castle in Saltash, Cornwall (today the home of the dowager Viscountess Patsy Guinness Boyd).

To promote the sale of the Dunsmuir city properties, it was arranged that each purchaser of a building lot would be entitled to one raffle ticket on the castle. As luck would have it, a man who had stretched his credit to the breaking point purchased a lot and won the castle. The bank, which held a mortgage on his property, soon discovered this and dismissed him and took over the castle.

This beautiful structure, with views over the sea to the Olympic Mountains, remained unoccupied until near the end of the Great War. It was offered to the Department of National Defence as a hospital and rehabilitation facility for returning soldiers. With stairways reaching up to five levels and three dozen fireplaces as the only heating system, its life was a short one for this totally impractical purpose. The building lay fallow again for years until it was purchased for a song by the Victoria School Board as the home of Victoria College, originally founded by McGill University in 1903. For years the college had been housed in the top floor of the Victoria high school, the fine edifice in which General Sir Arthur Currie had once taught.

Life in Victoria in the 1914–18 war era was, by some standards, still slightly unreal. Thus today slipped noiselessly into tomorrow and there was always time for tea. The 96–year–old medical pioneer Dr. John Sebastian Helmcken, who had arrived fresh from Guy's hospital medical school in London in 1850 to serve the Hudson's Bay Company, was still alive. (His little white wooden house has been preserved near the parliament buildings.) He was the survivor of the physicians who held four of the seven seats on the early Legislative Council of British Columbia. Helmcken and his colleague Dr. Carrall, a McGill graduate, journeyed via San Francisco and Chicago to Ottawa in 1870—three years after the rest of Canada had joined in a Confederation—to propose the terms on which British Columbia would join Canada. The doctors, accompanied by Joseph Trutch (later to be Lieutenant–Governor), had a long list of desiderata, the first in importance being the completion of a railway linking British Columbia (as the far west coast colony was known) with eastern Canada. One of the stipulations was that a marine hospital of sufficient size to serve as a future medical school would be built at Victoria's Esquimalt base of the Royal Navy. Other provisions in the 1871 agreement with Canada included a daily steamship service from Victoria to Olympia (the capital city of the state of Washington), and there was to be a service to San Francisco every two weeks.

One of Dr. Helmcken's patients was the young artist Emily Carr, who has described in *The Book of Small* a typical visit to the diminutive physician with the tall Churchillian hat and the great gold watch chain. An early form of health insurance was developed by the French community in Victoria, with links to the French Benevolent Society in San Francisco. This helped the 20,000 gold seekers who invaded British Columbia after the gold fever of 1849 in California had subsided.

The Royal Jubilee Hospital in Victoria was initiated by such early families as the Pembertons and incorporated the latest innovations of the time (including corridors with several right–angle turns to keep bacteria from spreading!). The pioneer naval doctor, O.M. Jones, destined to be one of North America's outstanding surgeons, introduced the practice of having each hospital patient's relative occupy a bed in the same room in order to give the necessary care at a time when nurses and nursing schools were very sparsely distributed. One of O.M. Jones' discharge summaries concerning a persistent alcoholic reads: "discharged for calling nurse a liar." Aging or chronic patients were cared for at home as in the case of Lady Crease. In 1872 her husband, the chief justice, built a large house named Pentrelew, which incorporated a water–driven elevator for his invalid wife. Until recently this contraption, the width of a wheelchair, operated smoothly and silently, long before electricity was installed. Gas lit the rambling wooden house. Crease, according to his long–lived daughter Susan, planted "acorns gathered in England from trees under which Pitt and Wilberforce had campaigned against slavery" along his frontage on Fort Street. When the local telephone company sought to cut down these sacred oaks, Susan Crease told the company to move its wires across Fort Street.

Victoria's protected harbour was a great discovery in 1849 for the Hudson's Bay Company's fur trade and for the factor whose farm could be reached miles inland by a long arm of the sea. For the first half–century a long wooden trestle spanned James Bay in the heart of the sleeping city. Then Senator Barnard and his friends decided to pump out the bay, to replace the trestle with a fine stone causeway and to have the Canadian Pacific Railway build its Empress Hotel, allegedly on 18,000 hemlock piles driven into the harbour bottom, inland from the causeway. Until then Bishop Cridge had only been able to reach his pioneer church by canoe.

With the fine stone parliament buildings and with the fabled Empress Hotel, the structure of the present picturesque harbour took shape. As if Victoria did not have enough characters of its own, there were many others that came to stay at the Empress, some for the rest of their lives. When Zane Gray, the prolific writer of westerns, arrived, he said it was the only hotel he had ever entered where he felt he must take his hat off at once. In 1970, when I accompanied Lord Mountbatten to a dinner given for him at the White House, I learned from President Nixon that he and Mrs. Nixon had spent their honeymoon at the Empress and that he considered it one of the best hostelries in the world. The same opinion was shared by President Clark Kerr of the University of California and by the campus planner William Wurster of Berkeley.

The Royal Navy's Bermuda Squadron used to spend the summer at their naval base near Victoria in the days before there was a Panama Canal. One duty that they carried out en route up the Pacific coasts of North and South America was to land on the Galapagos Islands off Ecuador to search for shipwrecked British sailors. A barrel on the beach of one island was then, and may still be, the post office into which letters could be dropped for eventual delivery by ships circling the globe.

While the Canadian Pacific steamships no longer grace the harbour in Victoria, their gleaming white hulls remain in my memory. The best known was the Princess Victoria, built at Newcastle-on-Tyne. The legend is that Capt. J.W. Troup, who reigned supreme on the west coast in C.P.R. matters, was visiting Britain to monitor progress on his newest ship when he learned that two battleship engines were available and could power his Princess Victoria. These were fitted quietly and in 1902 Capt. Troup brought the fast ship around Cape Horn. He miscalculated his speed and nearly grounded the craft in front of the Empress Hotel. Troup developed the C.P.R. fleet of 6,000–ton ships, which ranged far up into Alaska and locally provided day and night boats to Vancouver and Seattle.

Longevity has often characterized the residents of Victoria. For the academic years 1926–27, my father was asked to become the acting principal of the Victoria Normal School at Mount Tolmie. Fifty years later, 80 percent of the original 137 students of 1926–27 could be traced and 86 students were still in touch with their alumni association. Sixty years after entering the Normal School, a large contingent attended a tree-planting to honour their much-beloved acting principal.

When I attended North Ward elementary school at age 12, it was across the railroad tracks of the ancient wood-burning Victoria and Sidney Railway. The school boasted the toughest mixture of white and Oriental children in the city. It also had the best teachers and the strictest discipline. One came to have great respect for the Oriental students as they excelled in art work, in athletics and in deportment. Strangely, a perennially bankrupt board would not permit them to join the local YMCA. What they missed thereby was the training and support offered by the great physical trainer Archie McKinnon—today happily memorialized by the naming of the University of Victoria's splendid gymnasium in his honour.

He taught us swimming and gymnastics. We were small fish compared with the Pedens (the 7-day bicycle racers), the Chapmans (national champion basketball stars) and the Patricks (of ice hockey fame). What all of us learned from Archie was fairness in sports: no booing, no dirty tricks and no grudges. Franc Joubin, later Mr. Uranium, was his pupil.

Only twice, in my memory, did Victoria have natural ice to skate upon. One of our fellow students at high school tried to skate on thin ice at Goodacre Lake in Beacon Hill Park and was drowned. Field hockey, cricket, rugby, soccer and outdoor lacrosse flourished. In the harbour, rowing was popular (though far less so than it is today at Elk Lake where the Victoria Rowing Club and the University of Victoria share excellent facilities built on a shoestring with the generous help of the Francis Winspears and the Walter Koerners).

I found music lessons to be torture and I finally gave them up in order to play rugby. Learning to play the piano by ear was much more fun and the piano has been a friend ever since. I spent my time doing things other than studying. I won a medal in a seed-growing contest conducted by the Rotary Club of Victoria and have been collecting seeds of whatever kind each autumn since. An oratorical contest on a peace theme brought me a medal, but the thing I recall most clearly was a senior high school contestant's opening statement. She shouted at the top of her strident voice, "War is Hell!" which merely may have startled her adult audience but caused convulsions among the younger students who sought shelter under the pews of the church in which the contest was being held.

Each year the Kiwanis Club of Victoria sponsored a music festival, with vigorous choirs and soloists. I was a runner for the two British judges who spent long hours listening to the contestants. The distinguished visitors were Plunkett Green and Harold Samuel. The former sang wonderful ditties for the youngsters and the latter showed his brilliance at the piano to enthralled audiences.

The multitude of unique characters who resided in Victoria added to the charm of the area. Robert Service was the poet who once worked in a Victoria bank. There was also the newspaper editor named Smith who changed his name to Amor de Cosmos and stretched a barbed–wire fence across a main thoroughfare that he was sure had encroached upon private property. A Klondike merchant and originator of the still–delicious Rogers chocolates became caught up in the real estate fever that infested the city in 1912. Two city blocks adjacent to the Empress Hotel were lined with offices advertising lots for sale on Long Beach (150 miles away on the Pacific coast of Vancouver Island). One Friday Mr. Rogers, without his wife's knowledge, invested the enormous sum of $19,000 on a lot near the city hall. He could not sleep for the ensuing three nights and early on Monday rushed to his real estate agent's office, begging him to sell it at once. He quickly was given $22,000 and left a chastened man, happy that his wife had not found him out. His risky profit may have helped pay for the excellent carillon that the Rogers installed in St. Andrew's Presbyterian Church as a memorial to their son.

The city trembled in its shoes when a man dressed in a convict's uniform sailed a raft into the harbour. He had made his way there from the leper colony on Bentinck Island (the most southerly extension of the Canadian coastline in the Strait of Juan de Fuca). Dr. Arthur Price, the city health officer, was summoned. He had seen leprosy in his early colonial career and after examining the sailor announced that the man had never had leprosy. That was the end of the leper colony on the west coast. It had been sited on Bentinck Island because the William Head Quarantine Station, where the ships from the Orient had to stop, was close by.

Prior to his experience at Victoria Normal School, my father had just completed his postgraduate studies at Stanford University with such professors of education as Terman and Cubberly, and was fired up with new hopes for British Columbia's school system and its teacher training program. After his year at the Victoria Normal School, he was asked by the minister of education to take on the joint supervision of that school, together with a larger one in Vancouver. After a year he informed the government that in some respects these institutions were academic backwaters that eventually should be closed. His hope was that a department of education would be supported at the University of British Columbia.

The air was blue for several years over this suggestion, with the principal of the province's largest high school railing against the University of British Columbia as Babylon. My father would turn in his grave today if he knew how the post–war universities of the province surrendered large fractions of their budgets to divinely guided educationists, as opposed to educators within their gates.

Education was much valued in my home and my parents laboured mightily to get four children to university. My brother was Rhodes scholar for British Columbia in 1931, taking his Doctor of Philosophy degree in history at Oxford. There, at New College, he had the great pleasure of working under the benevolent gaze of Warden H.A.L. Fisher and of Sir Reggie Coupland, one of the fathers of the plan to separate Pakistan from India.

As will be clear from a later chapter, I was enabled, thanks to Wilder Penfield, to graduate with Oxford's Doctor of Philosophy degree in the physiology of the nervous system. Two sisters also graduated from university and served in the Second World War in their respective professions.

My parents loved music and gave us all a grounding in the piano. Singing at home, at school or in church was thought to be normal in those days. My father had been baptized "John Wesley" and his mother expected him to become a minister of religion. He failed her, but in Victoria was a pillar of the Methodist church until 1925, when that denomination joined with most Presbyterians and Congregationalists to form the United Church of Canada.

In search of something more liberal in the way of a world outlook, our family moved to a First United Church nearby, where a rousing chorus, led by an excellent organist, sang the Scottish psalter to perfection. A scholarly preacher spoke out in favour of the League of Nations and opened our eyes to forces competing for world domination. As he preached he kept one eye on a handsome, black, leather–covered, loose–leaf book of notes. When he closed it with a resounding smack of his fist, the organist could be seen turning on the blower for the pipe organ and we gave a youthful sigh of relief. Strangely, for the 1962 centenary of the founding of the First Presbyterian Church of Vancouver Island, I was invited to preach at the Sunday morning service. I reminded the faithful that in Geneva in 1553, their hero, John Calvin, had Michael Servetus (the theologically trained physician) burned at the stake for what was later recorded as "the crime of honest thought." Only three copies of his work on the lesser circulation of the blood and on the holy trinity have survived, and the large congregation seemed relieved to know that one of those is in Edinburgh!

The summer of 1929 I spent working at Klitsa Lodge—an isolated but beautiful Vancouver Island hostelry for Americans who wanted to get away. Cornelius Vanderbilt Jr., his wife, dog, and fellow New Yorkers found the lovely lake, with snow–capped mountains in the distance, a quiet haven. An army doctor and his wife from Hawaii occupied a nearby island with a house panelled in lemon wood! My duties began at 6 a.m. with the silent cleaning out of ashes from the massive stone fireplace in each lodge and the laying of fresh kindling and logs for a succeeding evening's warmth. Then to the kitchen to carry out the monosyllabic orders of Wong, the chef. Washing dishes by hand took up most of the day, which ended with a fitful sleep in a hot attic — all for $1.00 per day in pay. I looked forward to the ensuing college year as a rest! Before entering Victoria College in the autumn of 1929, I had the good fortune to join an expedition into the Forbidden Plateau, high in the centre of Vancouver Island's mountainous backbone. The stunted and twisted yellow cedars were a revelation in this paradise, and one could see red snow on the glaciers, due, it was said, to a type of algae on the surface.

It was to the historic Craigdarroch Castle that my brother, two sisters and I went for the first two years of our university work. The massive stone structure with beautiful oak panelling served 200 to 300 students in those years. The moving spirit was not the quiet principal, Percy Elliot, a McGill–trained scientist, but rather the wildly enthusiastic Walter Gage—mathematician, registrar, cheerleader and chauffeur—who had come from Vancouver to teach at age 19. A bachelor all his life, he was married to Victoria College and eventually to the University of British Columbia where he served as president for a decade.

Gage was the greatest teacher of mathematical concepts I have ever seen. As we sat on park benches in the mirrored dining room, he paraded back and forth on a dais, jabbing a piece of chalk at the long blackboard, shooting off sparks and calling, in a humorous voice, the full names of students in front of him. As registrar he knew the given names of everyone who entered and would recite these with gusto. At times a stray dog would wander into the dining room only to be addressed by Gage as one of his brighter students.

The Depression that began with the stock market crash of 1929 hit the families of some of the students very hard. Walter Gage repeatedly dipped into his own meagre resources to help out the victims. In the circumstances, the students were forced to produce their own entertainment, so at noon every Friday there was a raucous sing–song or pep meeting. Gage led these in the Dunsmuir blue drawing room with tremendous physical output. He conducted with both arms flailing while I played the piano with both hands flying. The rachitic old table on which he performed was like a parallelogram most of the time, but he steadied himself by grasping the marble mantelpiece behind him. He taught us the songs composed by the students who participated in the Great Trek of 1922 in Vancouver, when students returning from the war demanded that the University of British Columbia campus at Point Grey be developed, as promised since 1912.

The other college professors were less phrenetic, except for Mme. Sanderson–Mongin, who taught French in the Blue Room in a spirited conversational fashion. There were hilarious moments when she would ask a student to translate a saying such as, "Le vin est tiré, nous devons boire." The charismatic lady pounced upon a rugby player and he blandly said, "You can lead a horse to water but you can't make him drink."

Economic history was a very interesting course taught by a serious but amiable lawyer who had lost an arm in an accident. It was said that he had a great future with captains of industry or reigning politicians who, uttering a string of profanity, would say "Get me a lawyer who doesn't say 'on the other hand.'" The little band of seven of us who registered in the first commerce course had tutorial teaching from Walter Gage in the mathematics of finance and investment. He told us that he kept one lecture ahead of us and would often say, looking at the blackboard (which was as covered by chalk as he was), "Surely that can't be right." He gave lectures on the then revolutionary theory of relativity on Tuesdays at 8 a.m., while we sat on chairs in the kitchen. No one from our little college, in that era, was prepared for the shock of going to the University of British Columbia with its 500–acre campus and its 1800 wild students!

Before leaving the subject of Victoria College, I must recount the classic story, still told, of the first principal, Dr. E.B. Paul. He appeared to us as the original "Colonel Blimp" with his walrus moustache and explosive bursts of speech. As a young man he had served in the British diplomatic service in Japan and was said to have learned that language well. One day, while toiling (with the aid of his cane) up to the college on the hill through the oak trees, he crossed the boulevard grass in front of the diminutive Judge Gregory's house. Like a shot Gregory was out of his rocking chair on his sun porch and shouted at the aging principal, "Dr. Paul, could I ask you not to walk on my grass?" Whereupon the stooped and white-haired Paul swung around as if bitten by a terrier and fumbled out his words, "Judge Gwegowy are you addwessing me in your capacity as a supweme court judge or as a pwivate citizen?" "Oh," said Gregory, "just as a private citizen, I assure you." Paul replied, with much saliva flying, "Then, as one pwivate citizen to anover, let me tell you to go to hell."

CHAPTER THREE

University of British Columbia, 1931–1933

Not even the Great Depression in the world's economy could dull the picture and the promise held out by the new campus of the University at Point Grey, Vancouver. The site was the most westerly extension of continental Canada jutting into the Gulf of Georgia. The buildings were only six years old and there was an air of expectancy about the forested 548 acres set aside. In 1909, as an endowment, a reserve had been placed on 2,000,000 acres of lands in the interior of British Columbia by the Minister of Education, Dr. Henry Esson Young. He had been one of William Osler's favourite medical students at McGill and at the University of Pennsylvania. When it was found that the alleged endowment was nothing but jackrabbit country, gravel and rock not worth fencing, a trade was arranged with Canada's Department of Defence, which owned the six square miles of Point Grey on the western edge of Vancouver. (It had been recommended by a site commission under the chairmanship of Dr. O.D. Skelton of Queen's University, later the doyen of Canada's Department of External Affairs.) The federal government, in 1912, transferred this large park-like area to the province of British Columbia for its university; only 1,000 acres has ever reached UBC, the remainder still being held by the provincial government. (In 1988 most of the remaining acreage was dedicated as a Regional Park.)

In 1922 the students of UBC decided that the time had come to move from their tattered shacks on the grounds of the Vancouver General Hospital (left over from McGill College days) out to the "promised land" at Point Grey. The veterans returning from the war had been disillusioned to find that the area committed by the provincial government for the new campus was still forest. Thus, a mass campaign was carefully prepared by such far–sighted young bloods as Ab Richards (later a leader in GATT), Jack Clyne (later a Supreme Court judge), Percy Barr (later a forestry professor at Berkeley), Aubrey Roberts and Jack Grant (later career newspaper men) and several hundred other dedicated undergraduates. In the 1922 summer vacation students throughout the province obtained 65,000 names on a petition to the government demanding that the university be built on its too–long–empty site at Point Grey. (The founding president of UBC, Dr. Frank Fairchild Wesbrook, had called the projected campus site "the loveliest in the world." He died, alas, in 1918 at age 50, in the influenza epidemic that followed the Great War.)

Finally the Great Trek of 1922 took place through downtown Vancouver, with students and faculty parading the seven miles out to the promised land, where stones for a cairn were assembled to mark the spot on which the new buildings must rise. Then student representatives went by the midnight boat to Victoria and presented ten suitcases full of the rolls of the petition, each tied with blue and gold ribbons, to the speaker of the legislature. He could hardly see the legislators through the mountain of papers, and on cue, Ian MacKenzie, a sitting member for Vancouver and an Edinburgh graduate, moved that all should adjourn to one of the large committee rooms to hear the petitioners properly.

The legislators may have thought they were in for a boring session, but so clearly did the students present their case that the members of the House began to worry about the next election. If every electoral area in the province were to be invaded at election time by silver–tongued orators such as these, there could be trouble. The government very quickly announced that the university would be constructed at Point Grey, to open in 1925.

When, therefore, I saw the beautiful campus in 1931, the buildings were spick and span, two being handsome stone edifices and five being "temporary" frame–and–stucco structures. (These five are still in use more than 70 years later.) The only residential accommodation on campus was at the Anglican and United Church Colleges. I followed in my brother's quarters at the latter and for two years enjoyed the spectacular, if distracting, view of the snow–capped mountains beyond Howe Sound and of the distant peaks further to the northwest on our beloved Forbidden Plateau on Vancouver Island. (That massive and twice–blessed island, 300 miles long by 50 miles wide, was originally named "Quadra and Vancouver's Island" to mark the friendly exploration carried out together by the great naval captains in 1792, beginning, actually, off the cliffs of Point Grey.)

Life in residence was never dull: the grave theologians became flustered on arriving from their homes one morning to find a Model–T Ford blocking the entrance to the chapel. The engineering students took credit for backing this antique down a long and narrow hallway without scratching the shiny new walls of the college. The principal, Dr. J. G. Brown, was equally upset when he found that a bedroom had been re–occupied by a graduate of the previous year, who had returned because he was unsure of some points of doctrine (or so he said)!

A path led from the theological colleges to the main campus, passing over a wooden foot bridge dubbed the "holy way" by Freddy Wood, an English professor. (Some years later the once innocent stream became a raging torrent as a freak blanket of snow melted suddenly, washing out a valuable section of the clay cliffs edging the campus. The washout halted at the doors of the Anglican College, but the concerned principal suffered a heart attack and was never the same again.)

The work I undertook was heavy, with money and banking mixed with elementary biology, advanced zoology, organic and physical chemistry, genetics and scientific German in my first year on campus. In my graduating year there was histology, embryology, advanced organic chemistry and biochemistry. There was so little money voted by the depression–ridden legislature that the UBC budget had to be cut back by more than half, and some very talented professors had to seek work elsewhere. As a result, students in our small class in histology (microscopic anatomy) had to lecture to each other under the supervision of the distinguished entomologist George Spencer. His was a far–ranging philosophic mind and I am happy to say he is memorialized today in a visiting lectureship. The fiery Edgar Black—a fish biologist who was to become one of the pioneers in World War II in the oxygen problems of sustained high altitude flight—taught physiology.

Across the campus were two characters: Garnet Sedgewick in the English department and John Ridington, the bearded, pipe–smoking librarian. Sedgewick was a diminutive bachelor who played to a student audience far beyond those registered for his courses. He would strut back and forth upon a high dais and proclaim: "When I get to heaven, as I no doubt shall, I shall play Hamlet." He recognized no authority in the modern world as sacred, and his courses delighted the large number of students who poached on his lectures.

John Ridington, on the other hand, was a self–taught potentate with such regal bearing that he was known as "King John." He may have been a British newspaper man in his youth, but had the good fortune to be on hand when the thousands of volumes, ordered by the bibliophile President Wesbrook, arrived in boxes at the Fairview Shacks (handed over by McGill College in 1913). Wesbrook sent Ridington to Albany, New York, for a six–week course in librarianship! From this King John returned enamoured of the classification system known by the name of an undergraduate at Amherst College who had devised it: Dewey. Wesbrook had already written to the top libraries in North America asking for advice. With one exception, he was urged to adopt instead the Library of Congress method, which he did.

The exception was the University of Toronto, which, in Wesbrook's words, wrote "a kindergartenish effusion" of no value. Ridington quickly fell into line and began the arduous job of sorting and cataloguing the books that had been purchased over–seas by Wesbrook's former colleague, J.T. Gerould, of the University of Minnesota. Poor Gerould had been stranded in Leipzig by the outbreak of the Great War. Although an American citizen, he was put in prison as an alleged spy. The incriminating "secret documents" were the plans for the eventual construction of UBC at Point Grey! The gaolers suspected some coded messages in the thousands of catalogue cards he carried and repeatedly dumped them on the floor of his cell. Eventually he made his way through Switzerland to Genoa and returned to the States by ship. Wesbrook was very relieved, as he had been held responsible by his colleague's family for weeks.

By the time the handsome stone library building opened at Point Grey in 1925, Ridington was putting on further airs, much to the amusement of faculty and students alike. He told our class during an orientation tour in 1931 that we were to walk on the black squares on the checkerboard floor, as there was no money to clean the white ones.

Soon after opening day in 1925, Ridington, with a flourish, put up a notice concerning study cubicles: "Anyone desiring carrell privileges should see me." The editor of the student newspaper, The Ubyssey, was the irrepressible Earle Birney, who changed the notice to read "carnal privileges." Ridington exploded when he saw the amended version and declared the library closed until the culprit was caught.

The next eruption on the placid and spacious campus took place in the poultry section of the faculty of agriculture. The university possessed the most productive hen in the world. She could lay more eggs than any bird in history. Suddenly she disappeared and, for a change, UBC made the front page of the newspapers. Day after day the police tried to locate the chicken. Of course the man who recorded the number of eggs produced was frantic. Suddenly, mysteriously, the famous Hen No. 6 was found back on her nest. Long afterwards, the Hon. James Sinclair admitted to his cabinet colleagues in Ottawa that in his student days at UBC he had entertained the world's greatest egg–layer for a few days at his home in North Vancouver.

Athletics and noon–hour pep meetings in the auditorium were welcome relief from the daily news of a worsening economic depression. I played the piano in the pit for these noisy sing–songs, getting a shower of banana skins and apple cores on my neck when they fell short of the stage. Occasionally the pep meetings had to be used to assemble large numbers of students to hear a local personage, such as a newspaper publisher who had been to Russia and wanted to tell the students all about it. He was given full attention for a reasonable time but then the engineers in the gallery could no longer be restrained and started their inevitable cheers and songs.

The athletic picture was one of intense activity. The women's basketball team journeyed to Prague—thanks to a good friend of UBC—to win the world championship. English rugby was of high quality, with some of the speediest players ever seen in British Columbia, such as Art Mercer and Howie Cleveland. The engineering team was never beaten. The summer session students nobly provided tennis courts, which were used the rest of the year by such champions as classmate Freddy Chu. Two classics professors, Dr. O.M. Todd and Col. Harry Logan, invariably could be seen at the soccer, rugby and track events. I opted for field hockey, but when I scored from centre forward position on my first day, the coach moaned, "You might have passed the ball."

As provincial funding became even further curtailed, discussion broke out in faculty ranks, some feeling that they were being victimized while others had little reduction in budget. One student leader thought he should impeach the president. Years later he told me he felt his student behaviour was so disgraceful that he could never again show his face on campus.

Finally, a commission of businessmen was set up by the provincial government to advise it on methods of weathering the depression. One of their recommendations was that the university be closed forthwith! Students and public alike reacted violently, and the auditorium had a standing–room–only crowd at the Vancouver Institute's Saturday night debate between the unfortunate chairman of the commission of enquiry and Professor Henry Angus, who headed the department of economics at UBC. Angus, born in B.C., Oxford trained, and one of the Angus dynasty in Canada's industrial life, repeatedly had to call the audience to order, asking them to be fair to his opponent. When Angus merely said he was proud to be a native son, the students cheered wildly.

In the meantime the students organized a monster petition to be circulated from door to door throughout the province—10 years after the first one that had sparked the Great Trek. Students returned to their home towns to collect signatures. In downtown Vancouver, Chris Spencer opened the family's large department store to students who sat at tables in the main concourse signing up citizens. The organization of the petition–gathering campaign was the masterpiece of a commerce undergraduate, Winston Shilvock. The 1,700 students were assigned their tasks methodically. Today a retired stockbroker in the sunny Okanagan Valley, he looks back on those tempestuous days with satisfaction. Not only was the university kept open, but the people threw out the government at the next provincial election.

One of the stoutest defenders of the university was Dr. George M. Weir, head of the education faculty. He took on every critic of UBC that he could find and debated with them on the hustings. He soon found himself minister of education and of health. His contemporaries on the hard–pressed faculty included a former president of the Student Union at St. Andrew's University in Scotland, the voluble George Drummond. George would say to his large class studying foreign trade, "If there are any intellectual obfuscations, ventilate yer doubts." He dealt at length with "the better terms of barter trade." The habitually inattentive back row in his class he called "Ye lounge lizards and garter snakes."

Despite the Great Depression, student life occasionally went from the serious to the hilarious. The student paper, The Ubyssey, ran as close to the line as possible. The newspaper offices were a shambles, with the perpetual humorist Hymie Koshevoy writing his "muck page," and a future chief justice, Nathan Nemetz, hanging on to a telephone for dear life as he sat on a windowsill, his feet inside and his head outside the publication's office, as he tried to maintain a conversation with a complaining parent. There was evidently much concern in farm communities that male and female students were said to be "matriculating together." Little wonder that Nathan's specialty became dispute resolution.

The load of pre–medical sciences was so heavy that, except for money and banking, I had to drop out of the commerce course, much to the disgust of Professor J. Friend Day who was supposedly in charge of it. He wore a tattered red sweater and repeatedly told his students of his career in the Kennecott Copper Company. No one knew where the copper empire was, but the stories were legion. During World War II, I was asked by the retired Prof. Day to appear on his radio show. He benevolently told his listeners that this Air Force high altitude researcher they were about to hear was his "old pupil Billy Gibson."

Photographs of the very new but penurious campus showed cows allegedly called in to cut the grass on the library lawns. Transportation was by large, red, lumbering Leyland buses. They were said to have been brought across the Pacific by ship to Canada from Vladivostock, and were the war surplus from the armies of intervention that had sought to reverse the 1917 Russian Revolution. One engineering student thought they were the best transporters in the world because they had four square cylinders. The songs that the students chanted as the buses swayed wildly on their one–mile ride from the tram terminus at Sasamat village to UBC occasionally were not printable even in The Ubyssey.

All students were required at the beginning of the fall term to pay $10.00 as "caution money" to cover any breakages that might occur in the laboratories or elsewhere on campus. At the end of the year one could sign a waiver turning over any unused money in one's account to a fund for the construction of athletic facilities. Since UBC began, students have financed all recreational capital structures. In 1924, a year before the promised land at Point Grey was occupied, students, under their leaders Dal Grauer and John Oliver, seeded an athletic field to be ready for use in 1925. This policy has persisted ever since, with annual fees collected for student building initiatives. Intramural sports have thus expanded to become one of the largest programs in North America. A gymnasium quickly followed the first athletic field, though Sherwood Lett, acting as solicitor for the students, remarked to me that when he signed the document committing $40,000 of future student funds for it he thought he heard the gates of the provincial gaol closing remorselessly on him. The on–campus athletic facilities were supplemented by an off–campus 18–hole golf course on the adjoining University Endowment Lands. There we could play on Saturdays before 8 a.m. for 25 cents! This public course had an habitué, a member of the well–

known Cave–Browne–Cave family. One day he was asked by an American tourist, who had found the rudimentary clubhouse, if anyone could take him around the course. Always the gentleman, our extravert native sprang to attention and said he would be pleased to accompany the visiting golfer. On extending his hand to the Californian, he said, "My name is Cave–Browne–Cave," whereupon the American replied, "And mine's Home Sweet Home."

The summer of 1933 found me in the mountains of Idaho operating my medical uncle's hobby farm. It would be hard physical work, he warned me, and he was right. He left me with Harvey Cushing's two–volume *Life of Sir William Osler* (the great Canadian physician who made Johns Hopkins medical school so famous, and who served Oxford University as Regius professor of medicine from 1905 to 1919). This remarkable biography won the Pulitzer Prize in 1925, and became, for me, a sure guide to medical study, practice and research. I could not have been given a finer introduction to clinical medicine, its history and its contributors. At McGill, in Montreal, it became the touchstone of students and faculty alike.

My family of animals on this isolated farm had to be watered each morning and night by 400 shots of a hand pump over a deep well. To end confusion at the watering trough, I developed a system in which horses and then cows received the first pumped water. Then, through foolproof fences the overflow went by separated troughs to sheep and finally pigs. The chickens flitted about, drinking at will in their queer manner. Though the work day began at dawn, the Osler reading began in the cool of the evening by oil lamp. By autumn, when I arrived at McGill, I was in good physical shape and knowledgeable about its medical traditions.

CHAPTER FOUR

McGill University, 1933–1935

McGill in 1933 was a highly sophisticated university, presided over by Chancellor Sir Edward Beatty, who was also president of the Canadian Pacific Railway, and by the principal, Sir Arthur Currie, the erstwhile school teacher from my home in Victoria, B.C., and one of the most able generals in the Great War. Beatty was a bachelor whose interest in research was known to a very few friends. In 1917 he ploughed one million dollars of C.P.R. funds into metallurgical research at their huge smelter at Trail, B.C., in order to speed up the refining of war metals. Throughout his life in Montreal, for some personal reason, he gave money to support the work of Dr. Clarence Hincks of the Canadian Mental Health Association in its effort to develop a research programme against schizophrenia.

Sir Arthur Currie, on the other hand, was nearing the end of his career, buoyed up by his humorist friend Stephen Leacock. There was no mistaking Currie on campus, with his great height and commanding presence, but Leacock remained for me only a legendary figure. I used to see a slightly stooped man wearing a cap and an old raincoat leaving the campus at the end of the day. As he habitually came from the Arts Building, I thought it must be Bill Gentleman who was described to me as the porter. When, eventually, I saw the real Bill Gentleman in action, with his walrus mustache and tailcoated grey uniform trimmed with red braid, I sadly realized that the old man in the raincoat had been Stephen Leacock. The students wrote a second verse to their raucous song "James McGill": "Stephen L, Stephen L, Though he knows a lot of biz, Nonsense makes him what he is, etc."

Medicine was then a five–year course, with the first year heavily laden with anatomy. The professor was Dr. Samuel Whitnall, an Oxford graduate who affected a monocle on a black retractable ribbon.

He lectured in a black silk Oxford gown in a most perfunctory way. When he deigned to enter the dissecting room he wore a white flannel coat with black pinstripe down to his knees. Late one afternoon the dissecting room was almost empty when "Sammy" Whitnall appeared. Mordecai Etzioni, an enthusiastic student (and later a Vesalian scholar), called out, "Dr. Whitnall come and see this vein—it's an odd one for sure." Sammy walked over, put the monocle in his eye and said: "I am the Robert Reford professor of anatomy, and not to be hailed as one does a taxi."

The meteoric John Beattie taught neuroanatomy with a flare, explaining that nerve cells "talked" to each other by points of contact known by the Sherringtonian name synapse. An antiquated lecturer downstairs in microscopic anatomy thought these structures doubtful. Down the hill in physiology the Scot, John Tait, held forth in a monotone. To prevent students from dozing off he employed a 15–foot–long bamboo pole. Woe betide you if this menacing shaft switched back and forth in front of your nose and you could not answer the professor's question. An eager biophysics student, Kenneth Evelyn, would reach out helpfully and catch the bamboo and answer the question for others. His confederate, Andre Cipriani, was equally helpful. Tait prided himself on never giving a first–class mark in his subject to a first–year medical student, so Evelyn and I had to settle for 79 percent.

At the end of my first year in medicine I learned that McGill was about to change to a four–year medical course similar to that in the United States. I went to see Dean Charles Martin, who had taken an interest in me, to ask if I might drop out for a year to take a Master of Science degree, joining up at the end of it with the first four–year class. He agreed and I immediately sought an interview with Dr. Wilder Penfield, whose Montreal Neurological Institute (M.N.I.) was nearing completion further up Mount Royal. His secretary, Hope Lewis, was a bit doubtful of all this, but put me down for a 10 minute appointment in a few days. With butterflies in my stomach I went up to the attic of the Royal Victoria Hospital and was ushered into an office about the size of a telephone booth. With a broad smile and a firm handshake I was welcomed by "The Chief," who listened to my plan with interest. Before I could complete it he said: "I believe in students dropping out to take a higher degree in research. I did that at Oxford and I did student research at Hopkins." I said that I was aware of that and he said, "You know a lot about me!" In a second he had Dr. W.V. Cone on the telephone and said: "I have a young whippersnapper here who knows how to stain nerve cells with silver. We should put him to work on that corpus callosum problem of macular splitting and sparing in temporal lobe tumours." This was all Greek to me, but Dr. Cone evidently understood it. He agreed.

In August I was putting up hay at my cousin's farm in the Ottawa Valley when a letter arrived from McGill. The little daughter of the house ran out to the fields with it, and to my surprise Dr. Penfield offered me a research fellowship for one year. He said at the conclusion of his letter: "My feeling is that a year by the wayside is not lost but often adds a great deal to one's capacity for absorbing things of value as one goes through one's medical course." I was to report for the opening of the Neurological Institute on September 27, 1934. I quickly arranged to live at Strathcona Hall opposite the Roddick Gates on the lower campus and began work in the McGill medical library at once on my research project.

The opening of the Montreal Neurological Institute was a great occasion, with Harvey Cushing—the father of modern neurosurgery—present, along with the premier British neurologist, Gordon Holmes, of the famous Queen Square in London. Absent was the presiding genius of the Rockefeller Foundation, Dr. Alan Gregg, who had produced one million dollars as an endowment for neurological research and half the cost of the graceful building, to be matched by local private donors. He always avoided praise.

There had been neurological institutes proposed in other parts of the world (probably since time began) but strangely they never quite came off. Under the great platanus orientalis (sycamore) tree on the island of Cos, Hippocrates taught his students the diagnosis and prognosis of brain diseases. Even before that, in Egypt possibly about 2500 B.C. (according to the Edwin Smith papyrus), the results of head injuries were described in detail. After the Napoleonic wars Marc Dax, in the University of Montpellier—the oldest medical school in the world still teaching—described the speech centre in the dominant or left hemisphere in aphasic right-handed veterans who had suffered localized brain injuries.

In 1918 it had been the hope of Dr. Harvey Cushing and Dr. William Salmon that returning American veterans with wartime head injuries might be kept together in a neurological institute in Washington, D.C., for continuing study and research. The proposal never received the support it deserved and the brain-damaged veterans were soon dispersed over half a continent.

In the case of the Montreal Neurological Institute, however, a different and more realistic approach was taken. In the years between 1913 and 1928, Wilder Penfield cogitated on the best method of bringing patients with brain problems together for scientific research. In the physiology laboratory at Oxford he had been introduced to the nervous system by Sir Charles Scott Sherrington, F.R.S., the Waynflete Professor. Oxford had long been a centre for such investigation. Thomas Willis (1621–75) had coined the term neurology and his pupil Christopher Wren had drawn history's finest sketches of the surface and depths of the human brain. Along with Dr. Thomas Millington they formed what we would today call an early brain research institute in Oxford. With Boyle, Hooke, Lower and Warden Wilkins of Wadham College, the groups known as the "Oxford Experimental Clubbe" and "The Invisible College" joined others in London to found the Royal Society in 1660.

As Penfield, the Rhodes scholar, journeyed back and forth to France in his Oxford vacations helping in a volunteer wartime American hospital near Paris, he was seriously injured when the Sussex—on which he was crossing—was torpedoed off the south coast of England. (The gifted Spanish musician Enrique Granados was killed as the torpedo exploded.) Sir William Osler, the Regius professor of medicine at Oxford, learned of the injury suffered by one of his young friends and had him brought to his home, The Open Arms, in Oxford. It is not sufficiently recognized today that Osler was a very creditable neurologist among his many clinical accomplishments, and his attachment to the nervous system certainly rubbed off on Penfield.

After graduating at Johns Hopkins in Baltimore with a medical degree Penfield was awarded a Beit research fellowship at Oxford, thanks to his mentor Sherrington. Part of each week he spent at Queens Square in London, commuting to and from Oxford by bicycle!

He told me that at the end of each week his favourite method was to catch a beer lorry headed west from London and hang on to its superstructure as it lumbered slowly along the highway. On one occasion an old Johns Hopkins acquaintance, accompanied by a bevy of beauties in a Rolls Royce, pulled alongside and recognized Penfield. They stopped for a perfunctory salutation, which of course lost Penfield his beer truck! He never forgot this misfortune — the more so as it kept Mrs. Penfield waiting on the outskirts of Oxford to which she always cycled to welcome him home.

Back to the opening of the M.N.I. on that beautiful day in 1934. Sir Herbert Holt the banker (and the target of every political orator in Canada) and his nemesis Mayor Camillien Houde were in the group of notables crammed into the foyer, or Hall of Fame. High on the walls were the names of the major contributors to our knowledge of the brain. One of these, then little known to the public, was Alzheimer. The central focus of the rotunda was a white marble statue copied from one in the Louvre, "Nature revealing herself before science," the gift of the Reford and Hodgson families.

The revered man in Oxford who was unable to attend because of his wife's fatal illness was Sherrington, the Nobel laureate in medicine of 1932, when he shared the prize with Edgar Adrian.

In a way, the opening of the M.N.I. was a triumph for Sherrington's approach to medicine, energized by a persistent pupil, Penfield. People tend to take any institute for granted once it has been established, but little do they realize what concepts went into it, and what battles had to be fought to implement them. The great challenge, which the young Penfield saw and accepted, was the creation of a self–sustaining hospital with a full commitment to research. In other words, a bastion of medical science for the good of present and future patients.

September 1934 found such a constellation of specialized clinicians, medical and surgical residents in training, and advanced researchers, that a mere medical student felt awfully small. Nevertheless, the give and take in the laboratories was free and open and each helped the other. The researchers had been chosen for basic assaults on our massive (and expensive) ignorance of the brain's functioning and diseases.

One of my assignments in the institute was to teach English to Dr. Jesus Maria Sanchez–Perez from Madrid. In return he was to teach me Spanish: a language in which Penfield had worked in Madrid in 1924. From 5 to 6 p.m. I did my best to give Sanchez–Perez a grounding in English, which he often said "Is a hell of the language." By 6 p.m. he often found himself suddenly "fatigado" so my Spanish progressed slowly. In order to "perfect" his English he used to sneak away to St. Lawrence Main, where he could get "six shows for six cents" in that depressed era. What he learned was not always Oxford English and he often surprised his hostesses in Westmount with his wild phrases.

The institute enjoyed a fine view of the Molson Stadium and on autumn Saturdays one could see the hair–raising runs by George Degnan, the medical student from California. The McGill band played the old favourites: "James McGill" and "Put on Your Red and White Sweater," which sent even the most staid old alumni into a frenzy.

The staining of "boutons terminaux" (synapses) in animal brains proved to be very difficult. The Chief had heard that a researcher at Yale had done this successfully in the spinal cord, so he sent me to New Haven for a month to work in Professor John Fulton's superb laboratory. It turned out that in the cerebral hemispheres of cats, this man at Yale had nothing to contribute to McGill, but in the medical historical field Yale was a gold mine. Dr. Harvey Cushing had retired recently from the chair of neurosurgery at Harvard and had returned to the scene of his undergraduate baseball triumphs in New Haven. We had many good discussions on Sir William Osler's life at Johns Hopkins University and at Oxford. To live in Yale's teaching hospital was an education in itself: it seemed to me that the telephone paging system was always in search of the medical resident Dr. John Lawrence, later the director of the Donner Laboratory in Berkeley, California.

I had an opportunity to visit the rich library of the New York Academy of Medicine to see the Edwin Smith Papyrus: the oldest scientific document in the world. It is a study of the anatomy of the head and neck copied from clay tablets in Egypt as long ago as 2500 B.C. The superb translation of Professor Braisted of the University of Chicago allowed me to study the section on brain injuries. I was happily immersed in this pursuit when a tall, handsome man stopped beside my library desk and said: "Have I seen you before? Is your name Gibson?" I stood up and said that he had my name right but that I had never been in the New York Academy before. He then smiled and said: "I was at Queen's University in Ontario with your father, I'm sure. We played football together." Such was my introduction to Dr. Archibald Malloch, the distinguished librarian of the Academy and surrogate son of the Oxford Oslers after their son Revere was killed in the Great War. He sent his regards to Wilder Penfield, whom he recalled as a patient at The Open Arms after the torpedoing of the Sussex in 1916.

I was sorry to leave Yale but had to return to McGill to get on with my Master of Science degree work. Before I left New Haven, the ever–helpful Professor John Fulton gave me a copy of Osler's last paper "The Old Humanities and the New Science," read to the Classical Association of Great Britain at Oxford in 1919.

On returning to McGill it was decided that the thing most needed was a study of the shapes and sizes of the boutons terminaux in a location where they could be stained readily with silver solutions. Thus, I began spinal cord transections in anaesthetized cats, in the superb sterile operating room on the seventh floor, studying the synapses on the large nerve cells at varying times post–operatively, from 24 hours to 120 hours. For unknown reasons degenerating nerve terminals take up much more silver than normal ones, and the swelling induced by severing the terminals from their cells of origin makes the tracing of nerve fibres a very practical procedure.

As my research picked up speed, more and more people came to look down my microscope. Habitually Dr. Penfield would drop in on his way home to dinner and would sit down in my cubicle to the fine Zeiss instrument provided by one of his early New York patients. With the discerning eye of a neuropathologist he would pick out the minute structures: the dark doughnut–like boutons against the golden background of millions of criss–crossing fibres. Invariably I would have to call his attention to the fact that he was already late for dinner, before he would leave.

By the summer of 1935 the "inmates," as some called us, had dispersed. W. Lister Reid returned to Australia. Bill Stewart, the Oklahoman who developed tuberculosis (the disease that had killed an earlier neurosurgical resident, Wilbur Sprong), went off. This pair had been the greatest trial to Miss Flanagan, the director of nursing. Arriving home in white tie and tails from the Nurses' Ball at the Mount Royal Hotel, they tried to get in the front door of the institute. It was locked, but after a bit of searching in the dark they found the door bell. This they pushed intermittently, but without result. The reason that no one answered for some time was that the circuit had been crossed in construction so that wires went to the fire alarm in the second floor ward. The next day this was rectified with much adrenalin being released.

However, the post–ball problem did not stop there. Reid and Stewart were on time for the 8 a.m. operation next day, when The Chief was to stimulate the cortex of the exposed brain of a patient under local anaesthesia with gentle electric currents. He announced that he would like one of these short–of–sleep assistants to sit down under the sterile drapes to record what was happening to the patient each time the stimulus was applied. Suddenly Reid and Stewart vied to make these vital observations and The Chief said pointedly, "I think one observer is sufficient." Reid won and was relieved to be sitting below the drapes. As The Chief would call "on" when he applied the tiny electrode to the brain, there should have been a response from Reid. Next time, in a louder voice, "On." No reply from the observer Reid. A scrub nurse was asked to see what the trouble was. The fatigued Reid had fallen asleep.

On one occasion The Chief's young son, Jefferson, told his father that a man walking up University Street had been struck by a chute of ice from the roof of the Pathology Institute nearby. The victim had been taken into the Neurological Institute for first aid. Barely suppressing a smile, The Chief remarked: "If the ice had come from the ninth floor roof of the M.N.I. the man would have been taken permanently into pathology."

As the end of the academic year approached I had the assistance of Dr. William Vernon Cone, neurosurgeon, neuropathologist and photographer par excellence, in illustrating my thesis. The large coated plates that he used in the photomicrography division produced the clearest pictures ever published of the degenerating synaptic structures. They must have been the reason that my thesis was graded cum laude and magna cum laude by the McGill judges, and certainly the reason that the Archives of Neurology and Psychiatry in Chicago gave early publication to the work. Fulton's textbook, Neurophysiology, reprinted the illustrations in 1937.

Before the end of the academic year I was offered a summer job as doctor at a summer camp on Lake Minnesing in Algonquin Park, Ontario. I proceeded by train to visit my relations in Ottawa. My paternal grandmother was approaching 100 years of age and still dressed in the Victorian manner. As a child she had endured five weeks of an Atlantic crossing by sail from Northern Ireland. It may have seemed hard, but was nothing in comparison with the cholera–ridden ships that crossed about the same time. The great potato famine drove many to the New World; in my grandmother's case she remembered landing along the Canadian shore of the St. Lawrence River because of impassable rapids and transferring to lake boats that took her family part way to their final destination, Faribault, Minnesota (not far from the present day Mayo Clinic). The Indians there were very hostile and absorbed all of the sugar, flour and salt with which the settlers plied them. Finally, the immigrants had to give up the struggle and they wistfully sought the shores of the St. Lawrence, near Dickinson's Landing, Ontario, which had seemed so hospitable after their Atlantic crossing. Eventually the clan moved northward to the farming country near Ottawa.

My grandmother, whose name was Lucinda, had taught school at age 15, was married at 17, and raised 11 children. She hoped that my father, christened John Wesley, would go into the ministry. Having lost that cause she concentrated on me, asking "Willy–am what is to be yer life's werk?" When I would reply that I was studying medicine, she would retort, "Ach, I mean you real life's werk!" On being taken to a moving picture theatre she called out in her shrill voice, "Those people are moving, with their heads, and talking!"

The many children in the audience called out, "That's old Mrs. Gibson," and could not believe this centenarian's presence. As we left the theatre she remarked: "Today I have fallen from grace. I must see my minister quickly." She insisted that she had seen a "magic lantern" show in her childhood but the people then did not move about the screen. At the general election she insisted on voting for Sir Wilfred Laurier, though he was long since dead.

By taking a local train northwest to Madawaska and walking over a disused trestle, I finally came to the trail into Algonquin Park. As preparation for a long summer in the bush I had had my head shaved. The black flies feasted on my scalp and I arrived after a nine-mile hike in a sad state.

The summer was beautiful and I learned to handle a canoe on long expeditions and to sail a dinghy. In an electrical storm three of us capsized and the sail was struck by lightning. The McGill electrical engineers with me argued all the way back to shore as to whether the "mule kick" we received was by direct action or induction.

The event of the summer occurred while I was fishing with a McGill student named Dan Munn—blind from birth, but a keen sportsman. Suddenly I sighted an excited paddler coming towards us and waving a paper in his hand while shouting at us. We imagined it was an inspector of fishing licenses! But the paper was a cable from Wilder Penfield who was visiting Oxford. I later learned that he had been keen to surprise his old teacher Sir Charles Sherrington at his hotel there so had buried himself in a newspaper at Sir Charles' usual breakfast table. As the dapper little man sat down, Penfield lowered the newspaper and a great smile spread over each face.

Penfield told him that he was on his way back to Montreal from Switzerland where a world neurological meeting had been held. (It was at this meeting that the president, Professor Ascher, referred to the absent Sherrington as "the philosopher of the nervous system.") Soon Sherrington was inviting Penfield to tea to meet his distinguished Australian student J.C. Eccles. Penfield said he really should get back to London but C.S.S. was adamant. At tea later in the day, Eccles asked Penfield if there was anyone who could demonstrate boutons terminaux in the sympathetic nervous system. Penfield replied that he had a young Canadian who could probably do that as a result of his work at the Montreal Neurological Institute! In a few minutes it was agreed, and the cable was sent by Penfield to the wilds of Northern Ontario. It said: "Sherrington offers 150 pounds per year demonstrationship in physiology for research proceeding to D.Phil. degree. Advise acceptance." I wrote an acceptance on the back of the telegram and the messenger in the canoe vanished into the distance. I was soon to be on my way to Oxford.

One piece of unfinished McGill business followed me to Broad Street, Oxford, where I lived with my brother James. Dr. Maude Abbott, Sir William Osler's protégé in congenital heart disease research, was preparing the printed catalogue or bibliography of Osler's writings. She had laboured mightily to bring it all together, but wanted an index prepared before it went to press. She convinced me that I was destined to prepare it at Oxford, where there would be plenty of time! To run ahead of any chronology, all I can say is that I cut up two copies of the galley proofs and arranged the separate little strips in alphabetical order in 26 little cream jugs that I borrowed from the famous Miss Brown above whose Kookaburra Café we lived. Alas, a new maid on the premises threw out all of the "waste paper" that I had laboriously segregated into the jugs. So I had to do it all over again, but this time I pasted the valuable slips on a roll of wall paper acquired from a decorator downstairs. The bulky parcel reached Montreal and was turned into the required index.

CHAPTER FIVE

Oxford, 1935

After a brief visit to my family in British Columbia—made as a guard on a Chinese emigrant train—I retraced my steps to Montreal and then to New York, sailing on the S.S. Majestic. The third-class section of the ship was full of students, including Sam Hughes from Toronto, wearing a bright red tie and threatening to eliminate the establishment in Europe and North America.

I was met at Southampton by my brother James, who was by then a Royal Society of Canada fellow at New College. He had already spent the years 1931 to 1934 studying history there. As the ship approached the dock at Southampton I could see long rows of what I took to be circus wagons. It was not until I got through customs and immigration formalities that I realized that these were English trains. The engines seemed like toys after the Rocky Mountain locomotives, but I soon came to respect English trains, especially those getting into Oxford just in time to make college gate by midnight.

After much clicking of compartment-door handles and waving of flags by the guard, we set out for Oxford. The smooth "takeoff" and running of this English train were a delight. There was none of that thunderous banging and bumping of coaches that goes on in America. Even the countryside was quiet. Little hay cocks in neat rows, sheep grazing on rolling green meadows and half-hidden country estates passed in placid succession. The trip from Winchester to the Thames at Oxford was one succession of green hedges contrasted against the red ploughed earth, sheltered by an autumn sky with those billowy grey-brown clouds, which in England one imagines one can almost touch, they are so close. Now and then we would overtake a freight train. The dumpy little cars linked together by oversize chains were called goods wagons, and as they stopped at some rural halt, their little buffers clinked together like a row of bottles falling down.

As we passed the opening to the underground river—Lawrence of

Arabia's boyhood haunt—I had my first glimpse of the spires of Oxford, recalling Winifred Letts' lines: "The years go fast at Oxford, The golden years and gay." When the train stopped, a frightful commotion began on the station platform. Returning undergraduates burst out of the compartments as if responding to an electric shock. Baggage flew in all directions as bespectacled lads in their late teens rushed to greet their tweed-coated friends with an "Ow–hello." Oxford's station, looking more like a public convenience than a station, was cluttered with popcorn wagons, bicycles and baby carriages. Outside, little grey cabs that could spin about on a farthing were being assailed by students, each one piling more luggage on the roof than the last. Finally, we arrived at our rooms in the Broad, which overlooked Balliol College: Oxford's architectural nightmare, of which a French visitor once remarked, "C'est magnifique—mais ce n'est pas la gare."

An hour before dinner, the Broad presented an animated spectacle of fond parents lifting large trunks off the backs of cars and having college scouts haul them to their little boys' rooms; of a muddy group of players just back from a game of rugger; of thin young men with long hair and blazers looking pleased with themselves after a good tea; and of horses jogging by with the Great West Railway baggage wagon loaded down with trunks from New Zealand, San Francisco, Capetown and even Cambridge.

After settling into our rooms and having dinner with noisy students from many corners of the globe, we went along the Broad, past the Sheldonian Theatre with its Roman "emperors" heads, past the Clarendon Press and into New College Lane. There James pointed out the house outside the college walls where he had been allowed to spend the third year of his Rhodes Scholarship. On the roof was a little green wooden structure that had served as Edmund (Comet) Halley's observatory. Then we strolled along between darkened walls to a narrow oak gate, set in a great pair of oak doors that filled the stone arch of the college. An oak beam, probably the trunk of a tree, barred the heavy doors against forced entry by a mob, something well known to Oxford in the years since New College was founded in 1379. The main quadrangle, with its carefully tended grass circle, was lit by gas lamps. The oak staircases were well worn as undergraduates ascended three floors to their rooms, often the same rooms that had housed their ancestors. Lights flickered in the library over another archway leading to the Garden Quadrangle. The garden, further beyond high ornamental iron gates, was enclosed on two sides by the original city wall of Oxford. Its bastions were provided with slits for shooting arrows and steps up to the battlements for the discharging of hot oil and catapulting of stones. After more than six centuries the perennial garden still radiates soft colours and the birds still sing from the trees high on the mound that rises above dark green lawns.

As dusk descended we walked through the cloisters, passing the memorials to members of the college killed in the 1914–18 war. The inclusion of a trio of German graduates' names had caused apoplexy among the group described by Sir William Osler as philistines. A tablet memorializing John Galsworthy was set in a wall replete with the names of other departed fellows of this ancient foundation. Passing outside the city wall we walked along Holywell to see Magdalen College tower and bridge by moonlight. Towards the stretch of the Thames, where for centuries oarsmen had trained and competed, we looked at the ornate barges that city companies in London had built generations before, and that had been towed to their resting places, for most of them were settling at the river's edge. That was my introduction to Oxford by moonlight.

The next day I entered New College gate and came upon a welter of bicycles surrounding the porter's office. A mail rack, a grate fire and two imperturbable porters greeted me. Alsopp did the honours in chapel and Boulcott ran the telephone exchange, which was strictly for the Warden, the dean, the bursar and the chef. Undergraduates were not allowed telephones in Oxford—with the exception of the president of the Boat Club. All messages had to be taken personally or a messenger on a bicycle would periodically deliver notes from one college to another; this was doubtless a device to limit conspiratorial activity!

The Founder's Quadrangle was enclosed by the Warden's lodgings, the chapel and hall in one roofline, the library, and a block containing some of the more expensive sets of rooms, which opened off a series of staircases. Somewhere on each staircase the scout would have a coal supply and a gas ring for heating water. Plumbing was unknown, so one's ablutions were performed in the bedroom china reminiscent of little hotels in the Wild West. Further appurtenances were located in a stone barn under a dark corner of the college wall. A raucous young lord had bought hundreds of metal letters at Woolworth's and had tacked them on the doors of the dozen stalls to form an erotic set of names.

An ivy-covered archway led to the Garden Quad, whose cobblestones owed their scorched appearance to a record fire in which a victorious crew burned their boat upon "heading" the river. Not con-

Often the longing comes upon us to heave Demosthenes, Cicero, Virgil and Livy into my grate and kindle the pile. Why should man spend these pleasant years in elucidating the obscure and uninteresting and stilted verbiage of the Aeneid, when after all his labour he has grasped mere rubbish?"

December 13, 1925, 1st term Oxford, pg. 121

The sun was now low; it gilded and enamelled the western clouds in a truly glorious fashion, and gave the sky that brilliant light blue colour that is really heaven's blue. Looking through the black tracery of a bare and lonely oak into that unfathomable blue one could see clearly, so it seemed, the lucid interspace of world and world, where dwelt the ancient gods.

December 8, 1926

Pedantry on glossy paper I rate far below accurate scholarship, but the former now floods an expanding and vulgarized market. How useful to remember the caustic epigram coined in Alexandria in wordy, windy times like ours: 'Big book? big nuisance.'

Cattle Boat to Oxford, R.I.W. Westgate,
Walker and Co., New York, 1994

tent with the size of the conflagration, the aforementioned young social cyanotic ordered his piano and window frames cast down upon the fire from his rooms above. Even Heidelberg of 1912 paled beside this!

From one corner of the quad I could hear a babel of voices and a great clinking of glass and crockery. The Junior Common Room was in full swing. Milling around a blazing grate fire were about 200 young ideas, each more vociferous than his neighbour. Between sips of coffee (read: chicory), they shouted at each other about their summer's experiences, their escapades in London and their prospects for the term or the crew. I had come to study the physiology of the nervous system, and here, I thought, was the world's best example of mind over matter: bucketfuls of adrenalin being shot off into the smoke-filled air. In one corner there was the loud plaid gang, "rolling the hot potato" twice as hot as any B.B.C. announcer ever imagined possible. In another group stood the freshmen, overawed by their voluble seniors, but not bound to "fag" for them as they had been at the public schools previously. Near the door stood the lanky transatlantic gang, distinguished by their short haircuts and pressed clothes. They had yet to buy the tramp-like outfit of the Oxford undergraduate: flannel "bags" and a tweed jacket with leather elbows. Considering the climate, no more suitable costume was ever designed. It had spared the impecunious the outrageous prices of three-piece suits, so slavishly worn then in America. It has kept alive a sartorial democracy in a university cursed with a few groups of reputable wastrels and conspicuous snobs.

Beyond the cobbled quad lay one of the most picturesque gardens in England. With velvet lawns and rolled paths, a few great trees and a perennial border, it was a delight to look upon. Already the cats were beginning to prowl across the lawns, in search of the totally unprotected birds. The Warden's wife considered she knew the life of the college cats better than they did themselves—she kept a bell on a white marauder named William. But her chief claim to fame was the annual garden party that she gave at the college, for the Society for Unmarried Mothers of London. To this great event all members of the college were expected to come with a full purse—the better to buy the bushels of children's toys and noisemakers offered for sale.

To leave the college by Holywell Gate was to enter a Dickensian world. The old gabled houses—some with a lurch forward, some with a lurch backward—were painted a variety of colours: white, brown and even pink. What a story these walls could tell! The tin-

1935

All that will be necessary will be to amend the 1925 Agreement by eliminating the Emperor of Abyssinia and substituting the Italian Government as the author of the voluntary concession claimed by Britain. The event should be all the more gratifying to the British Government because it will be no longer necessary for that Government to fulfil its own part of the 1925 bargain. What Britain undertook was to induce the Emperor of Abyssinia to grant to Italy a sphere of influence in Abyssinia such as is now superfluous.

Observer

All sound-thinking Britons will wish Italy well in the great enterprise to which she has set her hand. The day that Mussolini establishes Italian authority over the ancient but barbaric land of Ethiopia will complete the beneficial progress by which Europe has brought law, order, and public health to a continent which less than a century ago was plunged in primitive misery.

Lord Rothermere in *Daily Mail*, July 1935

I have a great personal admiration for Mussolini, who has welded a nation out of a collection of touts, blackmailers, ice-cream vendors, and gangsters.

Letter in the *Saturday Review*

But for us to threaten Italy in defence of a primitive African State whose election to the League we vigorously opposed, and whose citizens could not even get into an English golf club, would be the most fatal blunder ever committed by a British Government.

G. Ward Price in *Daily Mail*, September 1935

kling bicycle bells and quacking horns of little underdeveloped motor cars all added to the strangeness of this narrow thoroughfare. From Holywell I turned into St. Cross Road and strolled along beside the high wall of Magdalen, down to the High. Here, double–decked buses with smelly diesel motors tumbled in and out of the lines of cycles that crossed Magdalen Bridge to Iffley, Headington and Shotover (a corruption of Chateau Vert). Magdalen, sentinel–like with its bell tower, was lapped by the ripples of the Cherwell. An occasional punt or canoe would glide noiselessly under the bridge, passing up to the Rollers or down to the meadows.

Along a cobbled street towards the Thames lay Merton with its row of postmaster's houses, its Mob Quad, and its chapel, grown old before most of Oxford existed. A modern–minded bursar whose calling was physics had not only thrown out all coal–burning appliances in favour of electrical, but he had illuminated the quadrangle with mercury–vapour lamps. Magpie Lane, with its cobbles, window boxes and raucous laughter coming from student's rooms, boasted a lamp post set squarely in the middle of the narrow lane to protect the people of Oxford from wild young men with high–powered racing cars. Past St. Mary's with its bells, All Souls undergoing repairs, the portly Radcliffe Camera and the recently internally lighted Bodleian Library, I made my way back to the Broad.

Late in the day I joined the 75 freshmen assembled in New College Hall to hear the dean read out the rules governing matriculation. We were told to appear "sub fusc" or we should be sent down. I thought some of the lads would go into convulsions when the dean said, "The standard of academic dwess is wapidly detewiowating." When he came to the rule that says, "Boots, if worn, should be associated with dark socks," the freshmen howled!

We were then marched over to the Divinity Schools, where we proceeded to matriculate under the august gaze of the "Socialist" vice–chancellor of Oxford, A.D. Lindsay. Fortunately for Oxford, but unfortunately for England, Lord Halifax, the chancellor, was usually too busy recommending Christian forbearance to the weak, while appeasing the "strutting little braggarts" in Europe and Asia, to attend many university functions. He may have had an unpleasant recollection of arriving at an Oxford meeting where he was to speak on "Opportunities in the Indian Civil Service" to find it packed to the doors not by Englishmen but by Indians!

Following the matriculation ceremonies, I went to Evensong, which, on this particular day, was unaccompanied. Few things in this world rival the singing of England's boy sopranos. The college had a choir

Two Views of History

Universal education is the most corroding and disintegrating poison that liberalism has ever invented for its own destruction. There must be only one possible education of each class, for each sub-division of a class. We must therefore be consistent and allow the great mass of the lowest order the blessings of illiteracy.

Adolf Hitler, *Mein Kampf*

When the history of our English education comes to be written, no single step will be found to have contributed more effectively to the spread of the university idea through England than the decision of the Government in 1918 to allot £8,000,000 to enable ex-Service men to enjoy the privileges of university education. Twenty seven thousand students went to the universities with the aid of these state grants. As I examined every dossier I am in a position to affirm that this large body of students was drawn almost exclusively from families to whom the notion of a university career for one of their numbers would have seemed up to that time, foreign, if not fantastic.

H.A.L. Fisher, *An Unfinished Autobiography*

school of the first order, and gave places to boys from all parts of Britain. The introduction of calculating machines into the college bursary had given more time for choir work to the clerks who sang in accompaniment to the sopranos.

Leaving the chapel, I stopped to re–read two memorial tablets dating from the Great War. One listed the names of students, lay clerks, servants and others of the college who had been killed in action, and read, in part, "Worthy of all they learned here and an example to all who came after them." The other memorial was to the German students of the college, "who coming from a foreign land entered into the inheritance of this place and returning fought for their country and died in the war of 1914–1918." I walked around the quiet cloisters thinking about the two memorials. I concluded that there must have been, at least among some people at the end of the Great War, a greater determination to build a better world. But where was it now? The English papers were full of patent medicine advertisements, dog–racing schedules, the cynical mutterings of casuists like Sir John Simon and encomiums of Mussolini and Hitler by English opportunists who were tired of democracy.

In the evening the Warden addressed the freshmen in the hall. The dim lighting and the dark oak panelling set the stage as the Warden entered, clad in a red academic gown. Stroking his white hair, he spoke first of our Oxford heritage and then called on us to learn to write and speak the English language correctly and gracefully. He charged us to prepare ourselves, in these privileged years, to be of the greatest possible service to our generation, and reminded us of Earl Haig's letter to his nephew: "Prepare for the highest posts. This is not ambition: it is your duty."

Some of us had irreverently placed a wager as to how long it would take the Warden to arrive at his favourite phrase: "Now when I was minister of education in Lloyd George's cabinet…." He did not disappoint us, and before long we were being given the substance of one of the Rt. Hon. J.H. Thomas' minor confessions. As "Jimmie" drove his railway engine nightly through Oxford, he yearned to look in where the twinkling lights burned in the colleges, "to feel the pulse of the great university." (How was the Warden to know that soon Jimmie would be taking the pulse of the stock market and following such bright lights as Newfoundland bonds and budget leakages?) In conclusion, he told us: "Dreams of coming here are now realized. Dreams of doing and achieving, and the making of life–long friendships with these eccentric islanders, must now begin."

Eccentric the islanders may have been, but they had other qualities too. Some were enjoyable; others exasperating. Some knew a lot but gave it out sparingly. Some knew nothing and dilated on "the glory of the Empire," "the finest climate in the world" and "the lower classes." Some frigid–faced old colonels would not even tell you the time for fear of contamination, whereas some of the country folk would confabulate without end, such as the old lady who told the Regius professor at the Radcliffe Infirmary that her father could not have had tuberculosis because "'e was stillborn, 'e wuz."

Every college in Oxford boasted its share of eccentrics and New College not least of all. The modern era began with Warden Spooner, who reputedly told the freshmen each year that what they first needed was a "well boiled icicle." His injunction that if they "tasted a whole worm" they would leave Oxford by the "town drain" is doubtless mythical, but a reputable authority says that the old man once announced the hymn in chapel, "Kinkering Congs Their Tattles Tike." The best apocryphal story concerns a venerable professor of law who once had the misfortune of teaching his subject to an American who knew shorthand. The American, after returning to the States, eventually became a law professor in New York. He proceeded, with the permission of the venerable Oxford don, to have the notes printed for the use of his students. A Rhodes scholar came over with a set of these notes, now serving well into their third decade, and followed them word for word as their originator droned on and on in a barracks–like classroom in New College. After the fifth lecture the student said to himself, "He'll *have* to change his lecture tomorrow—he can't possibly use the same words as he did 30 years ago." But on the morrow the bearded old campaigner began exactly as the original notes read: "Gentlemen, since addressing you yesterday, I have changed my mind."

Another yarn concerns the dean, who, during the Great War, had to be content to have the carpenter, Cross, as his batman in college. One evening, while dining out of the college, the dean was caught in the rain, with the result that he had to have his evening clothes pressed for dinner the following night. Cross did his best with the iron, but as the dean started down for dinner he noticed that the trousers had been pressed along the seams at the sides, with the resultant appearance of a Dutchman's breeches. The porters still delight in describing the dean's anguished call down the stairs, "Cwoss, you have wuined my twousers."

For sheer narrative there was none better than that of Peters, one of the oldest and most respected scouts of my time. It needed only a nod of the head to get him started on his experiences in the trenches during the Great War. At precisely the same place every time he would say: "Then, sir, wot d'you 'spose 'appened? The garage came over." But Peters was not easily fooled. He knew a rumpled bed from one that had been slept in. He also knew when a student was putting up an unannounced guest and would call out as he knocked on the door in the morning, "'ere's water for the other gentleman too, sir."

The college librarian was a bearded and stooped old Greek scholar who imagined he had been some Ionian hell-raiser in early times. Actually, he supplied the British navy in the Aegean in the Great War with meat from his forays on the numerous small islands in the archipelago. It is said that on one occasion he signalled a large French ship to stop for inspection by his one-gunned sloop. After receiving three threatening Morse messages from the sloop, the French vessel signalled back, "Does your mother know you're out?" and sailed on.

Each of the colleges laid claim to some share in the collective nonsense that pervaded the university. One college, with large holdings in local real estate, refused to allow the tenants to hang out washing on Sunday. The same college had a tutor who became so exercised over the General Strike that he formed a mobile squad of students for emergency services of some ill-specified nature and offered them to the government with great ado. After endless preliminary training and checking of details, they marched to the station and boarded an early-morning train for London. They had only gone the few miles to Didcot when one of the party saw a copy of the *Times* announcing that the strike was over!

One college still delights in telling the story of a bumptious midwest American who arrived to find no handshaking party out to meet him. He noisily demanded of the porter the location of his rooms. The porter wisely turned him over to the dean, a wizened old man with half-moon spectacles. The American stunned the old man with his blast of chatter, pulled open a zippered leather filing portfolio and drew out a copy of a letter sent to the college "last spring from my home in Galesburg, Illinois." The dean blinked and finally said: "I seem to remember putting that down on the back of an old envelope. Let me see now. I wonder where it is?" He went over to a table and pulled out a drawer jammed with old letters. He threw it the length of the room. Then he took a second drawer and threw it down in the same direction. He tossed the letters out of a third drawer and, looking over his glasses, said, "You see, young man, we have our filing systems too!"

Hearty young men of the "huntin', shootin', fishin'" type have always enjoyed themselves for a year or two at Oxford. Some have left in time to avoid the examiners, while others have been "sent down." A group of the latter cut were cashiered by their college for ambushing the chaplain one dark night as he was on his way to his rooms, and for jamming a toilet seat down over his head with such vigour that the carpenter had to be called to remove it. Another set of rowdies pinned the unfortunate man down on the lawn overnight with heavy metal croquet hoops. He very nearly died of pneumonia as a result. One prankster at Christ Church kept his tutor in a perpetual state of alarm by creeping up the stairs at about three in the morning to discharge a specially large-gauge shotgun filled with blanks under his door. Ballistics have long played a part in Oxford life, ever since King Charles defended Oxford against the Commonwealth by mounting his guns on the mound in New College garden. Pistols and blanks were half the battle at the rowing races on the Thames, and many an exuberant fan has ridden off the tow path on his bicycle from a combination of too much beer and one hand on the trigger. The great Jowett is reported to have said to a despondent student who came to his study resolved to shoot himself if his paper were rejected: "Not on my nice carpet. Please, not on my nice carpet."

In the matter of natural surroundings, Oxford has been abundantly blessed. Just how the founders of the early colleges chose such a low-lying waterlogged site is not clear, but the same hydrophilia influenced the refugees from Oxford town's terror who migrated eastward to found Cambridge. But once the dampness of Oxford is forgotten, who will not concede the beauties of its environs: of Boars Hill with its unobstructed view out to the Bristol Channel on a clear day, or of Shotover, "The highest point of ground between Oxford and the Ural Mountains?" How many thousands of students have cycled out past the Haldanes' home to the penny ferry on a wire run by the old lady at the Victoria Arms, climbed the stile into Old Marston and hiked on up the hill to Elsfield Manor, the home of the late John Buchan? What student has not loafed along in the spring sunshine past the crocus borders and thatched roofs of Wytham Abbey to end up at the Trout at Godstowe—once a meeting place of pelf and proctors?

For those who definitely wanted to avoid the proctors, there were more distant haunts, far beyond the bounds of the "progs" and "bullers." Beaconsfield, Kingston Bagpuize, Nettlebed and Shillingford with its beautiful bridge were all frequented by students in search of a pint of "old" and a game of darts.

Though pubs were then out of bounds in and around Oxford, a

phenomenal number managed to exist. The proctors, or university police, did a thriving business at the Lamb and Flag, through which Museum Road traffic passed in a constant stream. American freshmen, ardently searching for a souvenir, hoped they would be caught and hailed before the black–gowned proctors for a ten–shilling fine. Thus, a rather sheepish group of young men early in the term could be seen trailing out of the basement offices of the progs any morning at 10:30. For saving all the little boys from the wiles of the town, the noble dons who served as proctors received 450 pounds a year. They drove an old broken–down Austin until Lord Nuffield spread his millions before Oxford, where after these riders of the night drove around in a Morris–8.

In fact, the Nuffield era was a handsome one for Oxford. Having mended Sir William Osler's motor car tires at a little shop years ago, Lord Nuffield set about doing his best for medical science when his Morris car–manufacturing profits became astronomical. He was determined that "Cowley's latin quarter" should not stagnate and generously came forward at a university meeting one afternoon, not with one million but two million pounds.

Lord Nuffield made history in another sphere by drawing up to his plant one day and, in a few moments, arranging for two left–wing propagandists, each named Brown, to go to Russia—to stay! With their way paid, Messrs. Brown set out to see the apple of their eye: the Soviet Union. After a time, one returned to say how terrible life was in Russia. So it was not long before the other returned to paint a glowing picture. The latter was a Scot in his twenties. One night Kerensky, Russia's last prime minister, came to Oxford to address the Liberal Club. After plodding through his written address, word by word, he was asked by this Scottish firebrand if he could honestly say that things were worse in Russia now than in 1917. Kerensky jumped to his feet and shouted, "What does Mr. Brown know about conditions in Russia before 1917?" Whereupon the ever–ready Brown came back, "What does Mr. Kerensky know about conditions in Russia **since** 1917?"

A great part of Oxford life revolves about "the river" (the Thames). It is no rushing torrent, but rather one of those slow, safe rivers more suited to sculls and eights than most in America. For generations a series of ginger–breaded barges served the respective colleges on the Thames. Wonderful indeed were the devices painted on them. Some of the more waterlogged ones would keel over at a dangerous angle as 200 or more roaring spectators on the roof would run to the side to see a close finish. The river being too narrow for racing abreast, the contest was to see which boat could bump the one ahead, all starting from points down the river equal distances apart. "Eights Week" in the spring term was one of England's greatest fashion shows and relatives came from afar to enjoy themselves.

Spring term at Oxford was truly "river term." The sweet laziness of punting on the Cherwell, a tributary of the Thames, was intoxicating to even the most staid students. Spring, the river and the hawthorn trees were the setting for many a moonlit serenade. Gramophones were being displaced by portable radios, but even so one could be sure of hearing some rasping little machine grinding out Dorothy Sayers' favourite "Love in Bloom."

The proctors did their best to see that there was no moonlight bathing, but even they tired of treading the path along the fields half the night. The other half was covered by the silent patrol of respectable university people who, upon payment of an annual one pound and presentation of a letter of good character, were allowed to walk their dogs in the parks after closing time!

Oxford's bathing was done behind board fences: "Dames' Delight" for the women and "Parsons' Pleasure" for the men. Out of term, men were allowed to bathe, suitably costumed, in the women's enclosure if accompanied, but all year round Parsons' Pleasure remained inviolate and old colonels sunned themselves on the lovely grass like basking sea lions on the California coast. I often thought, as I looked at this array of retired old war horses, of Mussolini's view of the British Empire as "A stranded whale from which one could cut blubber with impunity."

I had not been long in my rooms in the Broad before the delegacy of lodgings told me that since I was not 25 and did not hold the B.A. degree of Oxford University, I must move into licensed lodgings. These constituted one of the greatest rackets in Oxford, whereby a landlady had to pay a licensing fee to the university in return for the privilege of taking in students. These students had to be in at a certain hour each evening or pay a fine. Page after page of rules had been set out, all in the same tune, to the effect that no student should have a latchkey to his lodgings. The charges for rooms, breakfast, hot water and coal were exorbitant, making the whole thing one concentric ripoff.

As a result of all these petty annoyances meticulously designed to prevent one working as late at night as experiments in the laboratory demanded, I set about preparing a campaign to blast the delegacy of lodgings. My brother handled the case for me, pleading the cause of science at the hearthstones of the heads of colleges, especially of the women's colleges! At the same time, he kept a caustic pen busy on the delegacy, icily ignoring their little book of rules and as much as telling them that there was no hope for peace in Europe if their supercilious attitude were to pervade England any further. In the meantime, my licensed landlady co-operated nobly and I was able to get some laboratory work done at night. By Christmas the sun shone and a ruling was given to the effect that advanced students, i.e., those doing research for higher degrees, could reside where they liked and keep what hours they liked. So back I went to the Broad, with its passing show. The organ grinder who came to town each Saturday had not deserted me, but he was astonished at the hail of pennies that greeted him from my window the first Saturday after my return. His organ still had asthma and skipped a few of the higher notes in "Santa Lucia."

The first term went well, with the usual bouncing around to find a satisfying sports club, a good bicycle for two pounds ten, some lecturers worth listening to and a good bookseller. The debates in the union had fallen off since the hubbub over king and country in 1934 where Randolph Churchill had played the ass by trying to destroy the society's minute book. The political life at Oxford had begun to atomize, with Liberals, Conservatives, Labourites and Fascists running competing shows. The Labour Club greatly outdistanced the others and boasted over one thousand members. Their Friday evening lecture series drew large crowds to the town hall. The union occasionally outshone the others, however, by pulling Bertrand Russell and Dorothy Sayers out of the hat. But most of its members consisted either of ambitious politicos or real students who came to use its excellent library.

Five hundred clubs waxed and waned in Oxford, though a stalwart 50 or 60 carried the candle most of the time. Besides a club for every known shade of politics and for every imaginable sport, there were those for the "Squires of Oxford" and for the aesthetes, cranks, drunks, iconoclasts and explorers. No foreign language existed that did not have some devotee; no species of tree toad without its admirer. Shakespeare was toasted weekly at one club once the motion had been put, "Resolved that the bard be not read tonight." The Raleigh Club, addressed by the empire's statesmen, drank its toast from a beautiful loving cup, "To the Empire of the Bretagnes." The Railway Society met fortnightly to compare changes in timetables and to have a quiz programme on the number of milk cars No. 343 carried from Piddling Rowbeck to Tiddling Hatcheck on Saturdays.

The lost causes branch of Oxford life was really the hardy peren-

He has invented a very curious and exceeding speedy way of **Etching**. He has started several things towards the emendation of **Water-works**. He has made **Instruments of Respiration**, and for straining the breath from fuliginous vapours, to try whether the same breath so purified will serve again.
He was the first **Inventor** of drawing pictures by **microscopical glasses**. He has found out perpetual, at least long-lived, lamps, and registers of furnaces, and the like, for keeping a perpetual temper, in order to various uses; as hatching of Eggs, Insects, production of Plants, Chymical Praeparations, imitating Nature in producing Fossils and Minerals, keeping the motion of Watches equal, in order to **Longitudes** and **Astronomical uses**, and infinite other advantages."

Description of Christopher Wren by Thomas Sprat in his *History of the Royal Society of London, for the Improving of Natural Knowledge*, London, 1667

The bread to eat in London is a deleterious paste, mixed up with chalk, alum and bone ashes; insipid to the taste, and destructive to the constitution. The good people are not ignorant of the adulteration: but they prefer it to wholesome bread, because it is whiter than the meat of corn: thus they sacrifice their taste and their health, and the lives of their tender infants, to a most absurd gratification of a mis-judging eye: and the miller, or the baker, is obliged to poison them and their families, in order to live by his profession.

The Expedition of Humphrey Clinker, Smollett, 1771

Scribes and Pharisees saying it was inevitable, if only they would say it is horrible. As it is, they are only trying to think of a mild theological formula to cover a cleft that goes down to Hell. For the first time within mortal memory the Government and nation has set out on a definite, deliberate campaign to make the poor poorer. People who are already clinging with their teeth and finger nails to the edge of the chasm are to be formally and legally kicked into the chasm.

G.K. Chesterton on the Means Test, 1936

nial. The anti-vivisectionists, having lost in their fight to keep the Sir William Dunn School of Pathology from encroaching on the parks, had now set about hounding the experimenters. My mailbox was often stuffed with the goriest tales of mad scientists beating the brains out of helpless animals at night. These I read with feeling to my experimental cats as they waited each morning for the operation to begin. They only yawned and sneezed as I read them these "true stories," and thought me a silly ass for wasting their good time. These operated cats swaggered around the animal hospital like well-to-do hypochondriacs warming to an "organ recital." And well might they swagger, considering the electric bedwarmers and special food they received!

The Americans at Oxford formed a microcosm in some ways. A few aped the poorest type of undergraduate and went about slobbering out their words in studied hot-potato fashion. A number of misfits made up "Little America," a spiritual replica of Admiral Byrd's south polar base. These ingrown football heroes stocked their rooms only with American magazines, pined that back in Moronia, Nebraska, you could at least get a milkshake for a dime, and went around moaning about the Oxford weather and the food. However, many more, by putting something into their Oxford sojourn, got something out of it. They introduced electric razors to counteract the hot water shortage and offered barbers anything to get a real hair cut. The usual eight-penny trim was more conversation than anything else, except, of course, for the finale, when the barber hacked off the last offending wisps around the ears with a dry razor and no soap! The Americans (the term also included the Canadians) managed to force their colleges into providing milk with meals. A precipitate food strike at Pembroke brought a definite improvement in the meals in many college halls. A few wild westerners at Balliol had had their fill of paying high prices for dinners in Hall, graced only by an enormous pipe organ long since silent. Collecting the menus for a week, they tramped the town enquiring of caterers their price for providing similar meals. The lowest ebb in Balliol's cultural history was reached when these renegades appeared before the master and told him that Lyons would do it for one-and-six, **with** music!

CHAPTER SIX

Oxford Medicine

The history of medicine at Oxford is the story of a group of exceptional characters, from Christopher Wren to Charles Sherrington. The former, besides being England's greatest architect, was a forerunner in experimental work on blood transfusion and was the first to picture accurately the arteries at the base of the brain, known, after his teacher, as the Circle of Willis. Sherrington was still adding to our knowledge of the functioning of the brain, nerves and sensory organs, more from his matchless pen in 1935 than from the laboratory. The centuries between Wren and Sherrington were packed with the trials and tribulations of science in general, not only medical science, trying to break free of the chains with which superstition in Oxford shackled it. The Invisible College, a forerunner of the Royal Society, came into existence in about 1645 when a group of men met in a London tavern, "for the obtaining of knowledge of the causes of things" (to use Francis Bacon's expression). The original members of the group, including Willis, Wilkins, Robert Boyle and Glisson, were joined by Sir William Petty who had ideas for rocket planes in warfare, and by Christopher Wren whose prodigious intellect was, in time, to be applied to every imaginable thing from Latin verse to blood transfusion, microscopic insects to architecture. Moving to Oxford in 1651, the Invisible College added Pepys, Evelyn and Hooke to its numbers, and was given shelter at Wadham College, where Wren had graduated. He and Wilkins had already turned the college into a veritable laboratory jammed with scientific instruments, models and gadgets.

Wren came up to Oxford at the age of 17. With his interest and proficiency in injecting the blood vessels of specimens, it is little wonder that he should, while at Oxford, investigate the possibility of transfusing living animals. Sprat, in his "History of the Royal Society," records that: "by this operation diverse creatures were immediately purg'd, vomited, intoxicated, kill'd, or reviv'd, according to the quality of the liquor injected."

Having outlined a surgical procedure for the removal of the spleen, Wren joined the mathematicians. In 1656 he solved a problem proposed by Pascal to the Geometers of England; he was even indecent enough to return to Pascal a problem over which the French savant spent four years without success. Wren's first architectural work in Oxford was the Sheldonian Theatre in the Broad, through which endless numbers of raucous undergraduates have since rollicked on degree days; one of them distinguished himself by shouting across to Cecil Rhodes, who was receiving an honorary degree, "Rhodes, don't look so damned bored."

Robert Boyle, the father of aviation medicine, carried out his famous experiments on the laws of gases at Oxford in about 1660. Three centuries later, John Scott Haldane was to put to practical use the many fundamental concepts developed by Boyle. It is a sad commentary indeed that the sciences had to be smuggled in through the side door of theology's mansion house in the latter half of the 19th century in order to be recognized by the university at all. Riding astride the two mules Geology and Genesis, men like Sir Henry Acland succeeded in showing the mentally constipated clerics who ruled Oxford that the goodness of God was truly manifest in the wonders of nature. It was evidently more important for the established church to live on rents from great slum areas, and on profits from breweries and armament factories, than to investigate disease, malnutrition or sanitation. Nevertheless, great discoveries came from the museums in the Parks Road where chemistry or "stinks" was gradually introduced along with other fundamental sciences.

Lord Nuffield's munificence in 1936 caused many to ask if Oxford ever had a medical school and, if so, where was it? For years it was lost among alleyways and execrable old brick buildings behind the Museums. Anyone who thinks that John Ruskin "let himself go" when he designed St. Pancras station in London should cast an eye at the Museums. They were the storehouse for Oxford's tamed fossils and the refuge for several hulking dinosaur skeletons. Expeditions to the ends of the earth brought back all manner of butterflies, fish, shells and scalping equipment. This was all fondly dusted, day in and day out, by a vigorous old boy of 80, who practiced his parts for the Bach choir while he swished his feather broom about. He was a very chatty soul, I found.

Beyond the Museums all was confusion. Medical undergraduates taking their three pre-clinical years before proceeding to London

Sherrington was a great raconteur. His eyes would twinkle as he told of Jean Paul Marat (1743-1793) a prominent politician in the French Revolution. He posed as a physician at times, as well as a lawyer. Sir Charles categorized him as a thief. Evidently Marat visited Oxford and expressed great interest in the Ashmolean Museum. He borrowed from a don associated with it, the keys, over a week-end, the better to inspect its rich collection. Monday came and there were no keys, no Marat, and most of all, no gold collection left. Promptly, by chance, an instant alarm was raised and it was reported than an unusual character was seen riding rapidly in a westerly direction. Finally he was found in Bristol, searching for a ship to take him back to France. At his trial in Oxford, Marat claimed that to steal as little as a loaf of bread from an individual was punishable by death, but that to steal from a public institution was no crime at all!

He met his end in a sitz-bath, where he was immersed up to his neck in the bootlike contraption, in an effort to assuage the itching of a frightful skin disease. While dozing therein he was stabbed in the neck, fatally by Charlotte Corday d'Armont.

formed a boisterous but hard-working group. Their bicycles and toy-like motor cars filled the lanes to overflowing. The old buildings suffered many insults through the years: the postman could push a large bundle of mail under the front door of the physiology laboratory because the stone doorstep had been so worn down. The saving grace of these damp old buildings lay in their view over the parks. Cricket and rugby for the young, and croquet for the old, made up the daily round. I used to wonder, as I watched the bearded old men pounding their mallets on the lawn in a fit of temper, if they realized that somewhere near their circuit two sticks of dynamite lay buried. During the Great War the venerable John Scott Haldane decided that it was, after all, a bit risky to have dynamite sitting on his desk. These two sticks had rolled back and forth for years, too immersed in the Oxford atmosphere to fall off, but with the advent of military airplanes it was decided to bury them. If the dynamite could speak, it would tell of a little, stooped man, who could never find his spectacles because they were pushed up on top of his bald head. And what the spectacles could tell: the old man experimenting on his firebrand son, "J.B.S.," with noxious gases, respirators and deep-sea diving devices. Few men have contributed so practically towards the complex problems of flying, mine and marine salvage, and protection against poisonous gases as did John Scott Haldane. His interests ranged also into the field of philosophy, and he was very much an authority on such historic schools as the humoralists and the mechanists. His memorial service in New College chapel was one of the largest seen in Oxford.

Another member of the Haldane connection who brought medical studies to a high level in Oxford was the long-haired, hollow-faced John Burdon Sanderson. Today he is immortalized in the undergraduates' story of his coming to class and explaining that in order to save time he had dissected out the nervous systems of a pair of frogs the night previously, at home. He said he would pass them around for inspection, and rustled in his pocket for the paper bag containing the frogs. He opened the bag and brought forth … two sandwiches. He turned pale and said, "Gentlemen, I'm sure I have had my lunch." (Incidentally, in 1871 he recorded his observation that penicillium moulds prevented bacterial growth in flasks of broth.)

Still, stranger things have happened, such as the debate in the Anatomy Building between Thomas Huxley and the Bishop of Oxford on the subject of evolution. The crucial point of the debate was whether or not the hippocampus minor in the brain was peculiar to man only, as distinct from the apes. It appeared so, but Huxley used

Spain is republican and will remain so. Neither the regime nor the flag will be changed... Civilians who are now armed will be requested to hand over their arms to the authorities and to return to their schools, their offices and their factories, and thenceforth to give up taking part in politics.

General Franco, August 10, 1936

Believe me the fate of civilization is being decided in Spain. We are defending the heritage of our ancestors. You are about to revive the Spanish Empire, itself also a legacy from the past. Man has need of faith in God and Fatherland.

General Franco at Burgos, October 3, 1936

A military view of life shall shape Spanish existence. Our State will be a totalitarian instrument in the service of national integrity. The system of political parties with all that flows from them: representation by conflicting parties, and Parliament of the well-known type will be implacably abolished.

Phalangist Programme, April 20, 1937

Our aim is the same as that of Germany and Italy: to treat the people as the true citizens that they are.

General Franco, September 13, 1937

Great pleasure is expressed in the garrison at the kindness of Gen. Franco in permitting the Royal Calpe Hunte of Gibraltar to resume hunting in the neighbouring Spanish territory. The Seville newspaper *A.B.C.*, referred to sport as being a necessity to Britons, especially hunting. The newspaper mentioned the fact that the King is patron of the hunt, and it expressed the hope that the British would be more polite to the Nationalists and, in view of the concession, not describe them as Insurgents.

Daily Telegraph, Novermber 13, 1937

a dissection to demonstrate that the hippocampus minor was merely another folding of the grey matter in order to get all man's brains inside his skull, and was not a specific structure found only in humans. This great and ancient debate was immortalized by Charles Kingsley's book *The Water Babies*, in which he dubs the disputed part of the brain, "the hippopotamus major." The debate is commemorated by a brass plate in the Anatomy Gallery. To my surprise and delight, one day in 1935 the gifted professor of anatomy read to us a chapter of *The Water Babies* as his introductory lecture on the nervous system.

I did most of my work in Sherrington's original operating room, now displaced by a "modern one with a plate glass window!" Sir Charles was not a tall man, and the little halo of electric light bulbs that made up his illumination was perilously close down around one's ears. There was no chromium plating or cinema ballyhoo about this little room, and yet—perhaps therefore—Sherrington, by his operations and experiments here, drew from the nervous system many of its most closely guarded secrets.

Few men have had such a transforming influence on one great field of medicine: neurology, which is the study of the nervous system in all its relations. Sherrington began his medical career as a bacteriologist and was sent out by St. Thomas' Hospital, London, to study the cholera epidemic that in 1885 was decimating Spain. There is a doubtful, but delicious, story told of Sherrington exhausting all his resources in trying to take blood from new cases, until he encountered the Ministry of Health in Madrid. The police had refused to allow any investigators near the towns freshly invaded by the disease. The minister saw him and was affable, but adamant. In a moment of utter dejection, Sherrington dropped his hands into his pockets, thereby jingling together several silver dollars. The minister's face immediately lit up, and Sherrington saw him pick up his pen. He could not believe it as he heard flowery phrases in praise of "a few selected medical researchers." He left the office less his silver but with carte blanche to see every case of cholera in Spain if he wished.

In the same year another young bacteriologist, Ramón y Cajal, was dashing about Zaragoza, Spain, studying the cholera germs with that rare new device: a microscope. He worked long and hard on the delicate changes that took place in the blood corpuscles as infection gained ground. When the epidemic was over he went back to his ill-paid teaching post in Valencia's medical school to write a handbook for his students on the magic of the microscope, and on the minute

Oxford

The night is fallen and still thou speakst to me,
what though with one voice sole, with accents many,
tongued turret and tongued stream, tracked pasture fenny,
and cloister spirit trod, and centuried tree,
and, bondsmen loosed in Times's tranquility,
thy bell-discharged hours. If wharfage any
thine 'tis where Age shall, nursing late his penny,
smile at long last to hand him Charon's fee.
And now, below, through shadows starr'd, a boat
steals by me laden with singing and young laughter,
and, higher, a wide-flung casement casts afloat
pulses of waltz the which white robes sway after;
vowed Priest of Beauty, these thy shrines among,
though kneelst with old folk, thou that dancest with young.

C.S. Sherrington

'Now in the cloister few the feet that roam'

Now in the cloister few the feet that roam,
ours that must stay, who little can than wait,
exchange our tidings, good, ill, early, late,
and send our 'god-speed' to them past the foam,
the young folk, splashed with death in the trenched loam.
Ay, oil the hinges of the ancient gate,
keep burnished bright the goblet's silvern state
against the hour shall hail the soldier home.
You stately tower, from high you saw them go,
and have full many doughty scenes and fair
watched and swung bells above, shattering the air
to honour heroes, you too wait as though
of our poor hearth-bound presence scarcely ware,
you heard from far the filial bugles blow.

C.S. Sherrington, 1916

structure of the body's various tissues. When he came to write the chapter on the nervous system there was practically nothing to write, for very little was known of its microscopic structure. So Cajal set about examining it, just at the time that Sherrington was beginning to do likewise in England. Cajal sent reports of his work to "the greats" of medicine in Europe who, knowing no Spanish, threw them in the wastebasket. But Sherrington instead learned Spanish in order to read this amazing work that was coming from behind the Pyrennes. In 1894, as foreign secretary of The Royal Society of London, Sherrington invited Cajal to come to England to give the Croonian lectures. Cajal came and converted his bedroom at Sherrington's home into a miniature laboratory, anxiously producing last–minute microscopic slides for exhibition before the most critical scientists of the world.

As Cajal cleared up many of the mysteries of the structure of the nervous system, so did Sherrington the functional problems. (They were each Nobel laureates in later years.) Students flocked to Sherrington's laboratory, wherever he was working. Harvey Cushing studied with him at Liverpool, and gained an insight there into the possibility of localizing various acts and movements of the body to finite portions of the brain by the use of electrical stimulation. After 1913 the trek was to Oxford, and not a few of Sherrington's disciples were to be found at the top of the ladder in the medical and surgical world thereafter.

Hugh Cairns has recounted the story of an experimental operation in which he and an American fellow researcher were engaged, when they heard a gentle tap on the operating–room door. The door opened just sufficiently to allow them to hear a whisper, "How is it going?" Then, after a few words, the door was opened a little further, and the professor's pince–nez could be seen through the crack. Then the greying head and the merry eyes were visible, and finally Sherrington, still anxious lest he disturb the operation, came up like a jack–in–the–box between the two surgeons and the table, peeped in, whispered "Good work," and disappeared on tiptoe.

Once a chimpanzee was sent to Sir Charles so that he might further study localization in the brain. The ubiquitous laboratory major domo, George Cox, was assigned to get it into a cage in the animal sick bay. Cox poured an enormous quantity of ether into the crate and managed, in the end, to lasso the chimp and take it to the basement. The animal hospital had two doors to it, supposedly to frighten infections away. One day when the professor went below to see if the chimpanzee was watching the cricket game outside, he had a curi-

The League as a whole has done very well in regard to Abyssinia.

Earl Stanhope in the House of Lords,
reported in *The Times*,April 1936

Grosvenor House (Park Lane) Directors have decided, in view of the death of the King, not to distribute annual divd. on Ord. shs. They state that business of the Company has been, and is continuing to be, satisfactory.

Financial Times, March 1936

5,000 books wanted by gentleman, for recently purchased country house, to fill library. Subject immaterial, but must be clean. No dealers.

South Bucks Free Press, August 1936

Sir Thomas Cook (Con., Norfolk, N.), who runs a fire brigade of his own, said that, at a village fire shortly before Easter, only two old men answered the call and it was found that the other 12 on the brigade roll had been dead for several years.

News Chronicle

Pierre Laval in the days when he was a revolutionary socialist, uttered words which sound like a prophetic description of his own subsequent career. "The bourgeoisie" he said, "no longer has any men. It is obliged to go and find them in the garbage heap where the proletariat throws its refuse."

The Nation, September 12, 1936

ous experience. He opened the outer door noiselessly and looked through the key-hole of the inner. To his dismay he found everything dark inside, and was about to withdraw when he saw the darkness had a white circle around it. The chimp too, was a keen observer!

The laboratory boys, with the English love of pantomime, used to stage mock operations for my benefit. The shortest one present would play the part of Sir Charles, and the "operation" would begin, in thin air. The chap playing Cox would roar, "Ay there, Meadows, go an' get the doin's." Whereupon Meadows would shout downstairs, "Bring up the doin's" (which meant anything but the right thing). Then Sir Charles would sputter: "Throw in, boy, throw in! Don't you know the size of a pea?" The sponges would then be cut down to the size of a pea, and the operation would go on silently, until the size-of-a-pea admonition had to be given again. The laboratory boys were paid 15 shillings a week, for the most part, so they had to supplement their earnings by playing in a swing band. They practised after work in the machine shop: worse jive was never heard anywhere this side of perdition. It was probably to keep up their spirits after anaesthetizing cats all day, but the harmony was awful.

Still revered at Oxford is the late Sir William Osler, who left Canada and the United States to become Regius professor of medicine in 1905. He had been a hard worker and a practical joker all his life, so that Oxford offered, or perhaps forced, an abrupt change in his activities. The Englishman's well-known ability to see a joke was too much for Osler at first, so that he sought out the almshouse at Ewelme and proceeded to befriend the 13 old pensioners there. They were under his charge because of a statute passed by King James I, to the effect that the professor of medicine at Oxford should be master of this ancient and beautiful almshouse, using the 13 pensioners, when necessary, as clinical subjects for the medical students, miles away at Oxford.

The brick quadrangular almshouse was built in the 15th century by Alice, the Duchess of Suffolk, as a memorial to her first husband, Geoffrey de la Pole, killed at Agincourt. In return for her beneficence, the old almsmen were to pray for Alice daily — something that they promptly forgot about until Osler reminded them five centuries later. Alice's second husband, William, Duke of Suffolk, was a regular scoundrel. Edward Martin, the editor of the original *Life* magazine, states that William "went into politics and his body was never recovered." Actually, William was impeached in parliament and on trying to flee the country was intercepted off the east coast.

There, according to an early chronicler, "They cut off his head with a rusty sword."

Typically, Osler's first anxiety was to learn the history of Ewelme at first hand, and to this end he sent a note asking the rector of the attached church to meet him at an appointed time with the keys to the large almshouse safe. The rector absented himself on two occasions, so that when Osler set out with Sherrington on a third trial he had fire in his eye. On finding no rector at home, he phoned at once to Chubb's in London for a safe–cracker, who came by the first train to Wallingford nearby. The expert asked Osler, "Have you tried it, sir?" and on being told "No" in a loud voice, took his mallet and rapped around the edges of the safe door, only to have it swing open before him. It had never been locked!

We used to have clinics on tuberculosis at the Osler Pavilion, a memorial hospital built some years ago on Headington Hill. A cup of tea was always provided by Osler's former pupil, the redoubtable Dr. Stobie, before ward rounds began in the late afternoon. It served to take the chill off many an abominable afternoon, with rain often coming down in torrents, and one's poor old bicycle groaning up Headington Hill. On a fine day, the view to the north from the spacious grounds was magnificent.

Five and six members of the same family would be in bed with the disease or in attendance at the hospital at one time. Oxfordshire's record in tuberculosis was not enviable, despite the untiring efforts of Osler and a county association intent on preventive measures. For that matter, the record for the whole of the British Isles was appalling. The enlightened policy of the London County Council was responsible for compulsory pasteurization of milk in and around London. For the rest of England, the slowly emerging milk monopoly called the tune, with the result that demonstrable tubercle bacilli were still said to be common in the milk in many cities. This was especially alleged in the kingdom's renowned steel city.

The problem of adequate medical care had long perplexed England. In 1911 Lloyd George decided upon a programme of national health insurance, which helped to win his election. Organized medicine in England at first refused to advise on the details of any such heretical system, and as a result it has taken years to eliminate many of the medically unsound features in it. No one will suggest for a moment that the people would willingly revert to the old haphazard system, but many improvements are still necessary.

Oxford had not escaped the symptoms of a struggle going on in the hospital world in England. The Acland Home had been rebuilt on the Banbury Road, the busiest thoroughfare in the city — much as St. Georges was rebuilt on Hyde Park Corner, the busiest traffic point in Europe. The tussle revolved about the matter of so-called voluntary hospitals, which, according to their critics, perpetuated a feudal hobby for a few at the expense of good medicine. As Don Marquis' inimitable cockroach, Archie, used to say, there were still a lot of people loose in the world whose chief mission consisted in "being gracious to their inferiors." There were exceptions, as at the Radcliffe Infirmary in Oxford.

With the Nuffield benefactions, which were truly staggering in size, Oxford bid fair to become a great centre for clinical medical research in England. Osler's Oxford home, the Open Arms, 13 Norham Gardens, had a history of hospitality unmatched in Europe. During the Great War Sir William and Lady Osler entertained every doctor who could find his way from America to the Open Arms, with no more than his M.D. as his introduction. Osler's death in 1919 left vacant a place in the medical world that may never be filled. Oxford, which at first had been cool to this jocular Canadian, came to revere him as a clinician, a public health dynamo, a benefactor of libraries, a scholar and her greatest Regius professor. As one of the old almsmen at Ewelme said when Osler died: "He was a good man. If I go to Heaven after I die, and he is there, he'll pick me out among a thousand."

CHAPTER SEVEN

The Oxford Group, 1935

For several years the world had been afflicted by a group of trained performers brandishing the fair name of Oxford as their password, while their leader chanted Hitler's praises and assured us that "God is a millionaire." In the mid–twenties, the smooth–tongued Dr. Buchman hit Oxford: for its name. Ten years later he had the Oxford Group incorporated, ostensibly in order to cash in on a bequest of money. As the honourable member for Punch and Oxford University, A.P. Herbert, shrieked at the time, that was the ultimate disgrace, capping one slimy trail of misuse of Oxford's name.

One hundred years previously, the theological Oxford Movement had flourished and had contributed a great deal to English life. The Oxford Group movement of the 1930s flourished, fattened and contributed a great deal to Brown's Hotel in London, to resort towns like Stockbridge, Mass., and to first–class passenger lists à la Cunard. Some thought they contributed Austria to Hitler. Quien sabe? They bemused rich old dowagers from coast to coast in Canada and the United States with their trick words of "sharing," "surrender," "God–control" and "moral rearmament." They wore blisters on their buttocks sitting in the world's swank hotels, waiting for the gravy train.

After observing their antics at Oxford, I was not surprised to read of Bud Firestone's statement before a group meeting of businessmen at Akron, Ohio: "A man with Christ in his heart can outsmart all others." Nor surprised by Frank Buchman's smarmy talk as he arrived in America to save us all from bolshevism. Nor by his highly spiritualized interview with Mae West in Hollywood, where she said: "It is a wonderful work. I owe all my success to the kind of thinking moral re–armament is." Dr. Buchman replied: "You are a splendid character, Miss West. You have done wonderful work too."

My first English connection with the group in Oxford dates from the first week after taking up residence. A Rhodes scholar who had been so "groupy" in America that he had missed getting his degree called on me, as an old friend, etc., of a globe-trotting relative of mine. He invited me out for something to eat at Fuller's in the Corn. I arrived there to find on the top floor the same old talkative troupe of unemployed "share" croppers that had played to audiences from one end of America to the other three years previously. There were some fresh new faces interspersed, as though a few students had joined the ranks.

The "sharing" began with good old General Winser, dressed to the hilt, thumping on his cork leg in praise of jungle hunting, and maligning the beleaguered Ethiopians as "a rum lot—not a damn bit of good." Then some drawler from "Noo Yawk" was guided to turn on the heat, and he set out to give us "the cold dope on religion" in five minutes. His breezy streamlining of the world's difficulties was calculated to keep the undergraduates in hysterics, but I saw a couple of hard-boiled Yanks wringing their hands. The slick-haired insurance salesman pattered on, likening the group to the radio dial that could "tune in God in a jiffy."

Then the old "cricket blues" were stuck up for an inning, as they turned on the record and ground out the good old "true stories." Austin Reed, not a bit ashamed of the price he had charged me for a suit in London, got up and gave us a haberdasher's view of heaven, after which the group's chronicler brought the good news of the "settlement," through the group's machinations, of the dock strike that had tied up the west coast of America all summer. When I protested to my friends that the strike had broken out afresh, I was reverently advised to have "a quiet" time to get a little (safe) guidance!

Then came a sumptuous "little bite" where we undergraduates were plied with endless delicacies and cocoa. I still have a picture of three students wrapping their long woollen mufflers about their throats, and stepping out into the brisk air of the Corn, one saying, "There you are Freddeh, I told you there was nothing to this bloody silly war talk of yours."

I resolved, after this experience, to spend any spare time I could with the Hitlers and Napoleons at the neighbouring mental hospital. However, "the chain gang," complete with peg leg and all, hounded our college to death. Finally, to see what undiluted undergraduates thought and said about the group, I went to a posh luncheon at 65, the High. These attractive quarters were furnished beautifully and the meal was excellent. Over coffee I was introduced to a prize catch (a Springbok rugger, etc.) with a toothpaste smile. I most distressingly stumbled on the fact that he was not a student at Ox-

Dr. Frank N.D. Buchman, streamlined revivalist who prefers to hold his "house parties" in high-toned summer resorts and is prepared to herd the richest camels through the needle's eye, provided they join the Oxford Group, arrived in Philadelphia last week to help the Democrats. He and his associates came straight from "helping" the Republicans in Cleveland. Dr. Buchman did not state what success he met with in the attempt to push the elephant through the needle's eye, but he was full of advice for the Democrats. He said his hypothetical answer to any hypothetical question from any hypothetical delegate about the platform would be, "I'd let God write your platform." The thing can be arranged by "getting in touch" with God, for whom Dr. Buchman seems to be the public-relations counsel in a nice way. So far the writing of the Democratic platform has been conducted on a strictly mundane basis, and the donkey has not applied for admission to Dr. Buchman's heavenly circus. Meanwhile, the good doctor, who would rather hear about a fellowman's more cardinal sins than be President, has presented his credentials in the form of a telegram from the Stockbridge group of his society. It reads, in part, as follows: "Shoe leather wearing out from activity and progress. Life-changing becoming epidemic."

Nation, June 27, 1936

Barriers between age and youth disappear in this spiritual army. Brig. Gen. P. Winser, D.S.O., trainer of racehorses and Great War veteran, describes himself as a "recruit in this new enlistment." "I have tried pig-sticking, war and racing", he says, "but this Oxford Group game of changing the world is the most thrilling thing I have ever met."

Daily Record. April 3, 1937

I have now worked with the Oxford Group over the whole of Norway, Denmark, Sweden, Holland, and England... I have taken part in hundreds of meetings, attended by hundreds of thousands of people, and I have never heard of anything confessed in public which could not have been said in Piccadilly Circus.

Mr. Frederik Ramm, "a distinguished Norwegian Editor," in *The Church of England*

At present I am reading a book which gives some of the facts with regard to unemployment and malnutrition in this country. If I had not found the answer in God-control I should be appalled at the picture presented.

The Oxford Group News Column of the *British Weekly*

ford at all; whereupon I was hastily introduced to someone who was! I had had enough of this colossal ramp, but thought it better to see it out gracefully. Then the squeeze–play began, and bewildered freshmen wondered how their hosts could have done all the naughty things of which they now shared a sweeping account. The speedboat hit a reef, however, in the person of the scion of one of England's famed political families. This inconsiderate realist did not quarrel with their tall stories, or their religion, but with their infantile analogies of physics and electricity! His persistence was most upsetting, and in Chicago he would have been taken for a ride for a lot less. The circus being about over, I apologized that I had a cat waiting for a little brain operation and really had to leave.

Realizing that I had heard most of their silly stories, and did not want them even when served up for the hundredth time by Bunny Austin and Daphne du Maurier, the group finally gave up on me. But I had seen so much of their simpering propaganda and pro–fascist leanings that I could not forget them. If ever another War Guilt trial should be held, the Geneva lobby of the group should be first on the list over the Austrian or the Czech disasters.

Oxford has suffered too many indignities to forget them. Queens College was subjected to an unhappy siege by the soft raiment boys who tried to hitch their chariot to Canon Streeter's liberal theology. They peddled a type of prattle that was a travesty on the religion of Jesus. They eulogized Hitler and toasted his barbarian legions. Typical of these draft–dodging, tea–sipping prigs was the Christmas manoeuvre devised by one of their number in a neighbouring college. In place of the usual pound note traditionally given to the scout for Christmas cheer, this soul–straightener tendered a copy of the group's bible, *For Sinners Only*. In no time the scout appeared before the dean and said indignantly: "Wot's this 'ere? I haint no sinner. I wants m' quid, hat's wot I wants."

There is too much sloppy talk about the oppressor and the oppressed, for in this case the oppressor is clearly Abyssinia, which has again and again in the past defied Italy's desire to impose decent Government upon it.

Saturday Review, February 1936

We can say without exaggeration that an attack by poisonous gas is another form of the effect of environment to secure the survival of the fittest and the elimination of decadent and unworthy persons and races.

First Aid, September 1935

"The public", said the General, "probably judged the inhumanity of mustard gas by recollections of Sargent's picture of men blinded at Ypres, but this was a masterpiece of sloppy sentimentalism."

Star, February 1936

The League of Nations union, it is scarcely necessary to add, is a war-mongering institution dominated by war-mongering politicians and prelates.

Daily Mail, November 1935

Reports about the insolent and provoking behaviour of some accused produced a different effect on the broad masses of working people than we had originally in view. It has been noticed that in several factories these reports caused considerable excitement and numerous discussions. Reports written in order to arouse public opinion against the criminal awake feelings in favor of them.
Therefore I order that henceforth reports about political trials shall be suppressed. Only the sentences may be published in less than two phrases, but only on special command.

Order issued by Dr. Goebbels,Minister of Propaganda,
The Nation, January 15, 1936

The more countries fight, the better for the British Empire. We shall then be able to develop our trade with whatever countries are not fighting.

Mr. C.G. Grey in *The Aeroplane*, August 1936

Surely everyone knows that the most remarkable thing about this great Empire is the fact that nearly all of our overseas possessions literally fell into our lap, and in many cases were acquired with the greatest reluctance.

Major-General L.C. Dunsterville, in a letter to
Royal Central Asian Society Journal, 1936

The Foreign Secretary Sir Edward Grey... will go down in history as a man who was the foremost in keeping the bond of this country when he thought that the interests of the country required it.

Sir Arnold Wilson, M.P. in the House of Commons, February 24, 1936

Whether a democracy based on a universal vote is possible in any country except it be an island, is open to doubt.

Letter from Prof. E.W. MacBride in *The Times*, 1936

CHAPTER EIGHT

Oxford Second Term, 1936

The first term passed all too quickly. For many of us the London season opened with the Goldsmiths' ball. Over–seas students were invited in great numbers to these annual affairs put on by the wealthy merchant companies whose history and plate date back several centuries. The fairy godmother of these students was Lady Frances Ryder, and no one worked harder to let over–seas students see England and the English than she. At one of the parties given before the ball I met a very trim Australian girl who was studying home economics at Kings College, London. One of the English debutantes present asked her what course she was taking, and on being told remarked, "Oh, cooking, and all that," in a typically insular way. It is indeed surprising how little some English women know anything about nutrition. In fact, it would seem to be in inverse proportion to the contributions made to the chemistry of vitamins by such English scientists as Gowland Hopkins.

I went to stay with friends in Dorset, and had an insight into the theory and practice of fox hunting. It seemed to be all that made life in the country bearable for a certain class. Agriculture was pursued on a conservative scale, and no query of mine as to possible methods of increasing the productivity of the farms met with any success. "Not another blade of grass can be forced out of these fields," I was told repeatedly. The hedges and fences took up a great deal of land it seemed to me, and I must have appeared a very mercenary type of farmer to my host.

Then I went down to the farthest part of Cornwall, with its palms and beautiful hydrangeas. There I visited one of the country's best–known historians, who lived in a house that had been owned by pirates for centuries. Except for the occasional visits by the Japanese and German ambassadors to St. Ives, there were few signs of pirates abroad. The comings and goings of these two jackals, and their fortuitous meetings, provided conversation aplenty for the "little athenaeum" that gathered at Par. One day the guests would include Julian Huxley, down to seek out a property where he might grow eucalyptus leaves for his Australian koala bears in the London Zoo. Another day it would be some famous geographer or economist. Pirate's Point was literally the "Open Arms" for a very distinguished section of Britain's intelligentsia.

I had never seen better walking country, with high reddish cliffs looking out to the blue Atlantic. The lanes were so narrow that one had to climb up on the walls when a large bus or lorry passed. These walls were really fences, grown wide with centuries of stones thrown out of the fields by farmers, with grass and moss knitting them together. One could walk for miles on them, surveying the countryside. Besides farming, a little fishing was carried on, while shipping and ship–building occupied a few men. On the harbour quay at Fowey there seemed to be endless consulates (to judge by the crests over their doors). Actually, a little steamer still ran from this ancient port to Spain! Centuries ago the good people of the town had a chain across the narrow mouth of the harbour, which they secured each night. When I was in Fowey the chief frequenter of the quay was the redoubtable Quiller Couch, known affectionately to the world of letters as "Q." He used to sit in the sun thinking up new and finer ways of baiting the young vicars of Cornwall in the local newspaper. To them, every word that Q wrote was cunning propaganda, and they fought hard to keep up with his pungent pen. Having taught generations of bright young men at Cambridge how to think and write, he could not help it if at times he had to set right the "frocked cyclists" of Cornwall.

My host was a commissioner of the ancient tin mines of Cornwall, and took his mining and archaeology very seriously. Two buried Roman camps had just been sighted from an airplane, and while I was there all hands were pressed into service to determine what yield could be expected of a thorough excavation. One thing seemed clear to an amateur: there was a suggestive pile of crockery and china fragments at the sites of the blockhouses of the camps, as if a bibulous time had been had by all prior to the decline and fall.

Just before leaving to spend Christmas at Bristol, I, (as chaperon of the children of the house) was sent to a tremendous party at a neighbouring pirate house. No lights had been allowed by the ancestors and the present generation had never gone in for electricity. In this eerie atmosphere the party decided to play the ancient game of murder. No sooner were the candles extinguished than I was playfully pushed down a set of stone stairs by some boisterous lads just home from England's fashionable schools. They were full of vitamins and vinegar, and in the ensuing days set their parents a merry pace. My host's son would ride down the steep hill into Fowey on his bicycle with his arms folded on his chest, his feet dangling from the pedals. He was a wild, but talented, lad, aged fourteen, and would periodically startle the greybeards sitting around the fire in the library at home as they listened to the B.B.C. news. Using a microphone hidden in his bedroom and connected to the wireless, he would suddenly cut into the news and in a "hot potato" voice announce that Hitler had just invaded France and that England was about to experience an air–raid, by kind permission of Mr. Baldwin. He and his schoolmates subscribed to all the latest books concerning the continental debacle, and in a sense knew far more about it than did their Micawber elders.

After a marvellous English Christmas at Bristol I went up to the potteries in Staffordshire. Some Oxford friends were in charge of university extension and social service work there, and took me over the Five Towns very thoroughly. Many of the mines had been closed, so unemployment and hopelessness hung over the countryside. The Pilgrim Trust had financed some recreation centres for men out of work, and the Kidsgrove Club that I visited was certainly a good one. It had 200 members who played games, learned cobbling and enjoyed a bath at a cost of a penny a time. Wooden soles were worn exclusively, and these could be obtained for four pence half–penny in the club. Each man learned to tack his leather uppers to the wooden soles.

It was hard to tell whether it was night or day because there was so much smoke in the air from the potteries. A resident told me that some of the districts saw the sun only one day in three, and to judge by the rickets that were evident everywhere, he was not far wrong. It was utterly depressing to see so many young people with crutches and metal braces clambering in and out of the buses.

With the damp chill of January evenings, a sooty mist settled down over everything, so that the gas lamps at the street corners looked like mere candles. Children would clatter along the cobbles with their wooden clogs and press their faces to shop windows to see the cheap gew–gaws inside. Their language was the queerest mixture of "thee" and "ye" that I have heard. Going into a club one day an old miner called out to me, "Mind ye's 'ead, lad."

I naturally was interested in the health situation, and found that while the local authorities and the government at London provided a half pint of milk daily for babies and for school children, none was available for those between the ages of three and six—just the time when teething and bone growth demanded calcium and sunlight. We stopped to see one anaemic woman who was burdened with five children, none of them old enough yet to do up their shoelaces. I shall never forget the pitiful sight of this woman coming to the door to say good–bye, surrounded by her ill–clad children and a sixth on the way. My mind went back to all the eye–wash I had read in America on "England, a garden" and to all the prattle I had heard in chapel about the sanctity of human life. I could only hope that these poor suffering shells of humanity would be spared any such "life everlasting."

Before leaving I visited the Copeland works to see the beautiful Spode ware made. The delicate hand painting still done was a treat to watch. But the "clean whiteness" of their finest china, alluded to by the guide, was forgotten as I looked out of the window at the dirty blackness of the smoke belching out of the pots over the scarred and grimy countryside. I went back to Oxford feeling I had seen some preview of hell, populated with stunted, crippled people, housed in dreary miles of unvarying tenements, devoid of flowers, of light and of any reason for existence. Somehow I had missed reading about all this in the old school paper, the *Times*, and somehow the guide books said nothing about this side of things. Only one word could describe it: **disgraceful**.

Term opened with a big dance at Rhodes House in aid of the Fairbridge Farm schools. These schools were begun in West Australia by a South African Rhodes scholar who, after seeing the slums of England, decided to work for the emigration of orphaned and poor children from England's worst areas to the open spaces of the British Empire. Largely financed by English benefactors, these schools became model institutions and opened up a new hope in life to several thousand children. They received in the Dominions not only a better formal education than would have been their lot in England, but also a most practical training in agriculture. On leaving school they apprenticed, in a sense, to acceptable farmers who had to pay them decently. Half the student's pay was put in the bank for him (or her) until the age of 21, at which time it could be withdrawn to enable the person to marry or to buy a farm.

Kingsley Fairbridge died at an early age, just as his first school was beginning to flourish in Australia, but he gave a practical demonstration of the fact that slum children, given a chance, could become useful, educated and productive citizens. He did his share to dispel the myths often repeated by a few feudal Englishmen that "the poor love the slums" and "the poor make the slums." I never could see how even a wretchedly poor man could be so depraved as to design and build mile after mile of tenement cells for subhuman habitation. There is no record of the poor collecting the rents off the slums. In fact, their life was a scramble to pay the rent for those slums.

The chief controversy of the day centred around the Italian invasion of Abyssinia. The press showed the turncoat nature of many "paper democrats" and there was a sickening amount of fence-sitting by supposedly responsible men.

There was, however, one real bulwark within England: a peace ballot signed by ten million people. No other extra-parliamentary expression of the public will has, in modern times, rivalled this in importance. Smooth Stanley Baldwin knew this, and his facile tongue, lisping peaceful nothings to a tired England, got him into office as a champion of the League of Nations. When the people discovered that his Samuel Hoare had ventured to carve up Abyssinia with that arch fascist Pierre Laval in Paris, they were properly outraged.

England's historic faculty for throwing up a group of intelligent world citizens in times of crisis had come into play only two years previously, when some of her citizens stood courageously with the common people of Vienna against the prelude of fascism involving Dolfuss, Stahremburg and Schussnig. Now, once again, people sprang to the defence of Abyssinia. Men like Dr. John Melly took ambulances out to Addis Ababa for the Red Cross, only to be killed by cynically aimed bombs. But for the most part the papers (with a daily circulation of over a million each) either said nothing, or brazenly championed Mussolini. It could hardly be otherwise, when the largest single block of advertising in Britain's newspapers was controlled by patent medicine makers, whose eye for gain and sneer for truth had been proverbial. The League of Nations was paralysed by such devotees of peace as the Canadian Prime Minister MacKenzie King, who hastily recalled Canada's representative at Geneva when this experienced man dared to suggest that oil must come first on the sanctions list if Italy were to be stopped.

On January 20th King George V died, and the university went into mourning. The bell in Tom Tower at Christ Church tolled long into the night, and everything became still. Stanley Baldwin came to the fore once again and began to brace himself for a final showdown with Edward Windsor.

A strange thing happened in the laboratory at that time. We had

Lest We Forget

I wonder whether, for the League's sake and our own, we ought not to give formal notice now that we propose to leave it.

A. P. Herbert, *Standard*, October 5, 1936

We submit ourselves whole-heartedly, nay gladly, to the Covenant of the League of Nations.

Winston Churchill, September 24, 1936

Ways of our fathers known of yore,
Who bagged the earth by right divine,
And beaconed lesser breeds before
The League arose to our design,
Self-interest plus self-righteousness
No longer seems a great success.

The Island Race, the Nelson touch,
The word-more-binding-than-the-bond-
Do not appear to count for much,
The lesser breeds do not respond,
And none our services engage
In tasks of honest brokerage.

The lesser breeds, not in our care,
Who hailed the League with hope renewed
Imply that we their evils bear,
With far too noble fortitude,
While at Geneva nothing's heard
But Eden breaking Baldwin's word.

Now while we still equivocate,
And neither lead nor leave alone,
Should we not quit the doomed debate
Lest the League's cause become our own?
And with our Fascist friends depart
Lest we might make a fairer start?

Lest we reverse the role antique
We inauspiciously prolong
Of always pleading with the weak
While always siding with the strong,
Lest we forget, lest we forget,
And make good Europeans yet?

Sagittarius, in the *New Statesman and Nation*, 1936

sent a Leitz microscope to London for repairs months previously. No results were forthcoming, so we told the company that we would be forced to speak to Dr. Goebbels about it! A few days later it arrived back by Lufthansa Air Express from Germany. It recalls the story often told in the laboratory of Sherrington sending some valuable microtome blades to the Sartorius factory in Gottengen for refinishing in July 1914. When the war came, and while it lasted, the professor wrung his hands daily and muttered to himself, "They are using that steel to kill our boys, why did I send it?" Early in 1919 the blades came back with a letter from the company that read, "Due to unforeseen circumstances your order has been regrettably delayed."

Towards the end of term I was notified that the Osler Trustees would assist me in going to Madrid during the Easter vacation to work with the Spanish microscopic anatomists. Thereupon I started on typhoid inoculations and conversational Spanish. The former was a joke, for, as I later learned, there was so little typhoid in Madrid that it was difficult to find cases to demonstrate to the medical students there. The grammar, however (studied under an Oxford woman born in Valencia), was the best investment I ever made. It proved to be the "open sesame" to a vast new world of little-known scientific research over which the Spaniards held a virtual monopoly.

The last weekend before the term closed saw the Canadians at a conference on the problems of social betterment in Canada. Very enlightened papers were given on economics, public health and related subjects. Thereupon the dancing mania seized all the overseas students, as it did with great chronicity, and work was forgotten while all cavorted on the three-inch oak planks supported by 18 inches of cement at Rhodes House. A mad gallop to the tune of "John Peel" brought term and the winter to a close, and we all set out for a six-week sojourn in every conceivable part of Europe.

CHAPTER NINE

Spanish Adventure

On March 15th I set out for Madrid, travelling through Paris and to the south by rail. The electrification of the railways in France was very striking and the speed at which trains roared through the countryside rather amazed me. Paris had a charm to it, even in the chilliest weather. There was no time to lose in boarding the train for Hendaye, so I had to leave my exploration of Paris until later visits. On reaching the Spanish frontier, another student and I transferred to one of the greatest menageries on earth: a third-class Spanish coach. The seats were like the slatted park benches in New York, hard and not a bit "simpático."

Well in advance of the departure time, whole families began to climb aboard, each with some cackling chickens in big straw baskets. The people were thick-set Basques, the women wearing bright shawls over their heads, and the men little black berets. The farewells were tumultuous and although the men did not kiss each other as in France, they pounded each other on the back as they embraced fondly. With the arrival of a pair of Guardia Civil wearing three-cornered hats, the train started and soon we were climbing up into the Pyrennes.

As soon as the children and chickens had been stored away, out came the accordion. The songs resembled French Canadian folk tunes, with the cantor carrying the verse itself, and the crowd joining in the chorus. As it became dark we passed hydroelectric plants blazing into the night, and everyone set about finding a bed, either on the "park bench" or in the baggage racks with the chickens.

My friend, Dr. Webb Haymaker, had an old Spanish grammar text that his mother had used at college in America. He kept practising the first sentence in it all night long: "Hablo español." First he would try it as if he were in New York, and next as if in Virginia. Then he would throw the book across the car and swear at everything Spanish. After a while he would say, "We might need that, you know," and soon would be back at it: "Hablo español." A moose of a man sitting across from us was highly amused at this, and while his wife and children slept, he began to talk to us in a low voice. He asked me if I knew Uzcudun, the wrestler. When I said I had heard of him in America, he jumped up and started slapping me on the back. It turned out that this was no other than one of Uzcudun's cousins. In a flash, he took down a basket and offered us bread and cheese, which we washed down with some of his excellent wine. As the sun came up over the boulder-strewn plains of Madrid, the accordion began again and the chickens stirred in their baskets.

We arrived in Madrid and were met by our Castillian doctor, Sanchez Perez, with whom we had studied in Montreal. He told us, "is a hell of the train, these one," and took us off for coffee. The café that he frequented was closed, though it was eight in the morning. The employees were washing the floors and cleaning up from the night before. Sanchez roared at them to open up, that he had two doctors from America who had come to study at the Institute of the late Don Santiago Ramón y Cajal, etc., etc. On being told that a new wages and hours law had just been introduced, our host turned to us and said, "You see, is a revolution." He then admitted that this was the earliest he had been up in Madrid for many years, and we all laughed and went off to the University City.

There we stopped at the Fondación del Amo, a beautiful student residence built rather recently by a doctor of Spanish birth now living in California. The building housed several hundred boys who were studying for one of the professions. The congenial head told us he had very pleasant memories of his student days at St. John's College, Oxford. He was very proud of his Residencia, as well he might be. It had a large outdoor swimming pool and tennis courts, while it shared the university's playing fields and track on one side, and the extensive Western Park on the other.

We walked across to the neighbouring Cancer Institute, where the renowned Pio del Río-Hortega had his laboratory—in the morning! In the afternoon he worked in another laboratory across the city. With flowery speeches on both sides, we were introduced to this vivacious little man, whose embarrassment at not being able to speak English was extreme. Like most North Americans, we felt no sense of shame at being unable to speak the tongue of so distinguished a man as this. How patronizing we are to "these foreigners!"

There was not a moment lost in assigning us to a bench for our work, and it soon became clear that our place in the laboratory depended on stern application to the problems we had brought with us. Our host became involved in conversation with Don Pio, in the course of which we must have heard the word "claro" a hundred times. Every time one would say it was all "clear," the other would start off again. The speed with which they talked was phenomenal, like machine guns chattering. The director apologized for his father's death, which meant we would have no instruction that afternoon. We eagerly jumped at the chance to see Madrid while we might, for by that point we had realized that we were studying with a man who worked at a breakneck pace all day and half the night. His laboratory was a marvel of organization. It was clean, up–to–date, well stocked and hospitable.

In the afternoon we went across the playing fields to visit the University City, still under construction. The campus covered 1,000 acres. The buildings were of light brown brick, with white stone trim. Neither before nor since have I seen anything to rival their modern interiors. At that time, 100 of the 250 million pesetas set aside for construction had been spent. A national lottery brought in an annual eight million pesetas for upkeep. The main block of buildings consisted of the schools of medicine, pharmacy and dentistry. Eventually, 5,000 students were to have studied in these faculties alone. The entire University City was planned for an eventual 25,000 students. Beyond the clay expanse that was being turned into a "formal English garden" was the modernistic reddish brick building, the Faculty of Philosophy and Letters. The auditorium there boasted the latest methods for visual education, one of which was a device whereby a professor traced out a diagram on a page on his lectern and the students saw it on a large screen behind him. All the buildings were air–conditioned. The Faculty of Architecture on the north side completed the sector of new buildings. The School of Rural Economy had long existed at Moncloa, as had the Casa Velásquez, of French origin.

We were taken through the white–tiled laboratory of Dr. Juan Negrín, professor of physiology in the medical school, and later to be Spain's fighting premier and head of her government in exile. Our guide was a biochemist who had studied in London and spoke excellent English. He was a well–read scholar, and in the course of our visit reminded us that the first description of pellagra came from Casal, a Spanish physician, in 1755.

From the framework of the 3,000–bed hospital under construction, we had an unobstructed view of the snow–capped Guadarrama mountains, only a few miles distant. Students from the residence used to ski in the Guadarramas on their free weekends.

The University City idea formally took shape in 1928, but it was comparatively slow in coming to fruition until the Republican government began pumping money and men into it. In a country where illiteracy flourished and education was once considered dangerous, it was heartening to see such a great project coming to life. "The Española Invertebrata" of Ortega y Gasset was passing, and a new national university was developing under the guidance of Juan Negrín.

It was interesting to learn how practical the studies to be pursued in the laboratories of this new colossus were. One aim was to bring about a revival of agriculture and rural community life on a national scale. The engineers were concerned with the harnessing of Spain's wealth of hydroelectric power, and the provision of modern machinery and lighting throughout their country. The physiologists were working on methods of improving nutrition in the wretchedly fed populace. In short, the university was one bright beacon in a land long dark. And for some, this was dangerous.

One day, I set out to find the Instituto Cajal, which the people had built to recognize their greatest scientist, who had won the Nobel Prize for medicine in 1906. I asked my way of a tram conductor. At the mention of Cajal's name, he pointed to his head, for had Cajal not studied the brain all his life? No, the conductor was not sure of the location, but he called out to the entire car, telling them an English doctor wanted to find Don Santiago's institute. One man pointed to his head and said sadly that Cajal was dead. This I had known for two years, but where was the laboratory? Finally, the newsboy riding on the couplings on the back of the tram said that the easiest way to find it was to go through the Retiro Park, find his statue, and then take a path to the right!

Fortunately, I took his advice, and after a long walk under beautiful eucalyptus trees and Spanish chestnuts in full bloom, I found Cajal's statue. The great stone figure looked into a pool labelled "the pool of life." Two streams of water were feeding it, "the font of life" and "the font of death." As I stood admiring it, two little children climbed up to the font of death to get a drink. How little did I know then that this was soon to be more than symbolic in Madrid.

I came upon a guard toasting his feet on a basket-like charcoal burner. He set me on the path to the Instituto Cajal, and after another long walk through veritable banks of rhododendrons, I came to the institute. It was set on a hill overlooking the southern part of the city, facing out towards Toledo. After a set of muscular and voluble introductions, I was shown the laboratory where Cajal had worked.

Actually, he did most of his work at home, since he found the institute too grand and noisy for his simple tastes. The history of this prodigious worker is one of the world's finest stories, embodied in his *Recollections of My Life*, translated by Professor E. Horne Craigie of the University of Toronto. The son of a barber–surgeon, Cajal suffered the torments of the damned at the various Jesuit schools in which he was enrolled unwillingly. He was starved for failing to prepare his Latin, and was imprisoned for inventing a large wooden cannon that caused considerable damage.

It is little wonder that collecting bones in the moonlight from cemeteries with his surgeon father appealed to this youth. He became an outstanding student and graduated in medicine at Zaragoza. On a visit to Madrid to write for a higher qualification, he saw a microscope for the first time in his life, and after observing the magic of blood corpuscles coursing through the vessels in the web of a frog's foot, he set out to explore the world unearthed by the microscope.

Within a few years, Cajal was invited to London by the Royal Society to give the Croonian Lectures. By 1906 he was in Stockholm, receiving the Nobel Prize. His career is one unending story of hardship. He was so poor as a young professor that he had to work on insects and mice because he could not afford the glass for microscopic slides large enough to mount sections of the brains of the usual laboratory animals. He was ridiculed by his compatriots, who believed implicitly that nothing of importance could ever come out of Spain. Today, there is not a textbook published on the basic medical sciences that does not draw upon Cajal's discoveries in the minute and complicated structure of the nervous system. The impetus that his pupils have given to the study of brain tumours has been immense, and such men as Río–Hortega and Wilder Penfield carried on the tradition in research that Cajal established. I had the good fortune to work each afternoon there with Fernando de Castro, a master scientist who unravelled the microscopic structure of the blood pressure regulator known as the carotid sinus.

I was shown over the Instituto Cajal by the famous Adolfo Sebastian Carnoy y Mora, a prematurely aged dwarf with a fez cap, a braided coat and an armful of keys. After seeing the valuable library and the operating rooms, I was taken to the ground floor, which had been intended as a hospital. The walls of several rooms were covered with the most bizarre and yet delicate modernist paintings I have seen. Adolfo had his studio in one corner, and when there were no visitors to be shown about, he turned out these amazing creations as a man inspired. He was obviously running short of crayons, so I gave him a set that I had for my laboratory notebook. In a short time, he turned out something that resembled the mouth of a frog, but that he labelled "Meridional fish in ether." Then, with the flourishing handwriting of the true Spaniard, he inscribed his name, and as his address wrote "four square kilometres from the moon." It was worth many packages of crayons.

On my first Saturday night in the Residencia there was a motion picture show. The beautiful new theatre, furnished with steel tubular chairs and indirect lighting, was filled to capacity by cheering students. They called incessantly for "Señor Mickeeee," and when Miguel Ratoncito appeared on the screen the uproar was deafening. Mickey Mouse never had more friends through all his sorrows and narrow squeaks. In fact, American pictures had a great influence in Spain. The most popular while I was in Madrid was *Sombrero de Copa (Top Hat)* with "Hinhair Rohairays" and "El Claque" as they called Fred Astaire. The attempts to imitate American blondes were usually distressing. The daring damsels (very realistically) were called "oxidos."

Sunday was luckily a day of rest in the laboratory and, by common consent, was a day for visiting the art galleries. Madrid might well be proud of her Prado; it had so many paintings that warmed the heart. From the overly healthy cherubs of Murillo one could turn to the shocking, haunting black works of Goya. He loved to lampoon the royal coterie and painted the awful truth about wars, conquerors and buzzards. Velásquez was well represented, and he too painted Spanish royalty with his tongue in cheek.

I played truant from the laboratory long enough to see an operation on a man suffering from a brain tumour. I was asked to assist my famous friend J.M. Sanchez–Perez—a pupil of Nobelist Egaz Moniz, of frontal lobotomy fame. No sooner had we begun what was to be Spain's first arteriogram than the patient's relatives burst into the darkened X–ray room and snatched him off the table!

The San Marcos Hospital was seething with excitement, and I had to be searched, since there had been a real brawl in which a medical student was stabbed. It began when several fascist–minded students tried to prevent a professor from lecturing to his class. Spain had a lot of self–appointed young vigilantes in the universities, who felt themselves called upon to keep those of different views from "poisoning the air," as they called it. I recall my amazement at reading a high–temperature editorial in one newspaper prophesying the end of Christianity itself if the monster of co–education was allowed to raise its head in "pure Spain." This line of reasoning ran all through the group of "over-privileged children" that I met in Madrid. I endured one long afternoon tea while three very demure young women told me how "magnifico" the American *Good Housekeeping* was!

Early one morning our host, Sanchez, took us to the market, where we wished to find three donkeys on which we could sit for a photograph together. We found a leather-faced mule driver who would oblige us. As we dismounted from his aged, white mules, he asked if we were "americanos." We said we were, whereupon he asked if we were from Buenos Aires. We told him we were from much further north. He said, "Ah, from Montevideo?"

On a bright Sunday afternoon I went to see a bullfight. The star turn of the performance was provided by a female matador. She gave a remarkable exhibition, though once she had a narrow escape. Not to be outdone, a "voluntaria," a girl of about 20, leapt over the barricade and, with a large red blanket, sought to compete with the official female bullfighter. The police caught her in time to save a catastrophe and hastily took her away. As the seventh bull entered the ring, the crowd was electrified to see a mad young man in a grey suit running out into the circle, brandishing an old piece of canvas on a stick. The bull swung his course and roared down upon this gypsy. The tip of the bull's horn caught the chap's leg and threw him into the air. The crowd went wild, and two toreadors rushed in with their cloaks to deflect the pawing animal. The bull rushed them, and just in time they vaulted over the barricade, below the block of seats in which I was sitting. The bull hit the wooden wall like an express train, and then, really angered, tried to climb it. Meantime, the young voluntario, bound that he would break into the game somehow, ran over towards the bull again, daring it to come on. In a second, police and toreadors were streaming over the boards to avert a sure murder of this crazed lad, and the first to lay hold of him received a clip across the face with his canvas-covered stick. The crowd screamed and roared imprecations that made me shiver. They certainly liked their sport raw, and this day they surely had it.

The matador of the day was a gold-suited, strutting little warrior who annoyed the hissing crowd to no end. However, when a lithe Mexican Indian clad in silver clothes finished his bull, he was given a great ovation. It was a wild scene, as the team of three mules on a whiffle-tree hooked on to the deceased bull's horns and pulled the carcass three times around the ring, then out to the howling mob of poor people waiting to buy the warm beef!

I have often wondered who would win if the bull had half a chance! In the first place, he enters the ring and charges at one of the picadors mounted on a cadaverous old horse, which, thanks to Alfonso's English wife, was protected somewhat by an old mattress slung over its ribs! As the bull hit the horse, the picador thrust a great lance into the shoulder region of the bull, thus slowing him down and also infuriating him. After two or three such encounters, a banderillero appeared. Sidestepping the lunging bull, he would implant three–foot fire crackers with hooks right into its shoulder wounds. The more the bull tried to shake off these infernal affairs, the more would they crackle and sparkle. Then the six or eight toreadors would brandish their purplish–red yellow–lined cloaks in various parts of the ring, and the bull would charge like something possessed from one to the other.

Finally, when the bull was well winded, the perfectly groomed matador would trip out to thrill the crowd with his masterful strokes and his bright red cloak and sword. Then, when the bull was in a state of collapse from whirling, bolting and butting, the matador would take his short sword and perform a perfect cisternal puncture just as the bull lowered his head to charge. The cries of "Olé!" and "Hombre!" that greet the bull's last breath are echoes from another age.

My next Sunday was not to be spent in such lurid surroundings. I went to Toledo, the storied city famous for its steel blades, and for the number of times since history began that it has changed hands. The chief attraction, however, lay in its El Greco paintings. This legendary genius had emigrated from Greece with a long name meaning "Bird of God," but had been dubbed El Greco by the rather sceptical citizens of Toledo. Even without his paintings, Toledo would be one of Spain's most picturesque cities, with its great walls, Moorish bridge and portcullis. Beggars thronged the gates of the town as they had for centuries. Cervantes' birthplace, and the home of El Greco, were very well preserved.

For lunch there was Toledo's famous "Las Perdices," where the roast partridge and wine were the kind one dreams about. After lunch I began the round of the El Grecos. The painting *The Death of the Duke of Orgaz* fills a whole wall and contains probably the finest study in human fingers and hands in existence. One could not help being struck, even at first glance, by the mastery of the painter, especially in his canvases of the saints. It is little wonder that my teacher in Madrid, Don Pio, frequently would forsake his laboratory and go off to Toledo to commune with El Greco's strong characters.

One evening I went to the theatre in Madrid to see a series of tableaux of Romero de Torres' paintings, in which the characters sang the haunting "Cante Hondo," the music of the south of Spain.

The plaintive, half–Moorish songs (accompanied by a guitar) were poured out as if the world's heart were breaking. At the end of each verse there would be cries of "Hombre" from fat, jovial men in the audience who quivered like jelly, as they imagined themselves in the hero's role in each tableau.

Life in the Residencia was full to the brim, with mock bullfights by young bucks with inverted wicker laundry baskets over their heads. A troupe of musicians came from the Sorbonne to entertain us, first with 16th–century music and then with a very amusing parody on it.

Finally, it came time to return to Oxford for another term, and regretfully I left Madrid. It was a city of great contrasts, and one with a great future. Nowhere had I seen such a renaissance in culture and science, and such an insistence on the importance of establishing good schools and universities. It was still a city in which a flock of sheep could be seen trotting down the Gran Via tended by a rustic shepherd, while great double–decker buses, built in Middlesex, thundered along amid the trams and donkeys.

Before returning north, I spent a day at the Escorial, one of the wonders of the world. This vast palace of the arthritic Phillip II had just been converted into a college, and thus the wheel had come full circle. Phillip II had sentenced millions of Protestants in the low countries to death as he sat in his mountain "silla" looking out over the desert–like plains of Castille. The vast tapestries, the paintings and the royal tombs reminded one of Spain's former pomp and feudalism. The Republic had let the air in upon this great treasure house, opening the library and the galleries to scholars and visitors. To have seen the Escorial was to have asked oneself a hundred times, "Why and how was the power that could build such a mighty palace and fortress squandered?"

In Paris there was only time to visit the Faculté de Médicine. Emerging from Odéon metro station, I was confronted by statues of Danton and Paul Broca, the famous anatomist and phrenologist. "Broca's Area" in the human brain was for years thought to be the speech centre, an assumption based on the fact that a medical orderly in Broca's laboratory literally had been struck dumb by an injury to his skull in the region of the temple. When this "Adolf" died, it was held that the rather circumscribed lesion found in the brain was the cause of the speechlessness. Before long, we were all to be wishing that Adolf's namesake in Germany would be similarly affected, but to no avail.

Third term fairly shot by at Oxford, with days filled to overflowing by laboratories, games, dances and the river. Once again, the

Empress of Britain afforded a four-day period of recuperation for the North American contingent returning home. Most of them struggled aboard in evening dress (minus shirt studs) at about mid-day. Their Oxford years were over.

I set out for Spain again, sailing from Southampton on a German ship. The harbour was crowded; coming out we passed the Queen Mary and the Bremen, the latter just off for New York, with the inevitable ship's band playing, "Wenn Ich Komm." After two blistering days, we put in at the north Spanish port of Santander. Sitting out on a promontory was the glistening palace, the Magdalena, once the summer home of Alfonso, but now a summer university for foreign students like myself. It proved to be a very enjoyable home for several hundred of us, coming as we did from all parts of the world, the foreigners to study Spanish language and culture, and the Spaniards to study English, German and various sciences.

Meals were served in the royal style, and at hours that stretched the stomach to a shadow. Dinner at about 10 p.m. usually consisted of beef steak and fried potatoes, which, agitated by a couple of hours' dancing, paved the way for a wakeful night. I could never understand why German students came so late to meals until I overheard one of them boasting to the other about what he had picked up at the head table by coming so late that there was nowhere else to sit. As the civil war got under way, the Germans pressed harder and harder towards the tables frequented by Spanish Republican dignitaries to pick up crumbs of communiques and cables. They were not beginners at the Spanish language, much as they tried to appear so.

One German professor and his wife who came to give lectures were both accomplished musicians and democrats. They could no more abide Hitler than could a rotund little German doctor who had lived in the Residencia in Madrid with us. This poor man had spent 30 years studying the life and voyages of Columbus for some institution in Berlin, and had now come to the conclusion—sadly for his future—that Columbus was a Catalan Jew! The professor already mentioned at Santander liked to talk English with me. One day, while walking back from swimming at the Sardinero, he told me that he was one of the German professors who had been invited to study at Cambridge University at the end of the Great War. His voice quavered as he said, "That was an act of great humanity by Cambridge." Then he stopped and held his head in his hands and said in a most forlorn way, "And now, and now." He was a courageous man, and stood out till the last against returning to Germany on a ship sent to Spain to evacuate German nationals when the misnamed civil war

I look across the purple bay
And see the steel mills hulking grey.
Behind the distant Picos fades
A sunset quiet in its salmon shades.

The fishing boats are scudding home
From arduous toil in tide and foam.
The noisy market now is still
The struggling mass have bought their fill.

And this is Spain, mañana land,
So hard for us to understand,
Because the changes are so great
Within this fairy-storied state.

And now the sky has changed to blue.
I can but think what Spain will do
To show the world how men may live,
What fruits the tree of life may give,
With justice and security,
With happiness no luxury.

W.C.G., Santander, July 12, 1936
(Within a week, Italian bombers arrive in Spain.)

began. He may have paid for his devotion to democracy and its champions. He was a real man.

I moved into Río–Hortega's laboratory at the Casa de Salud de Valdecilla, and awaited his arrival from Madrid. He had seemed uncertain about this when he called over the long distance telephone: soon the reason became clear. The uneasiness grew in the town and it was hard to push through the crowds on the streets by afternoon. Between the balloonist Professor Piccard's lectures, we gathered snatches of news, all very disquieting. The day before we had had an uproarious time swimming with him: he had shown us his remarkable spectacles, which had one set of lenses that flipped up and down with a little side wheel. But now all attention was gone at lectures, and students began to look for mail that never came, or to place long distance phone calls that were never completed.

Out of the confusion that settled down over the north, it gradually became clear that a long–considered plot to overthrow the Republican government had been set off prematurely with the murder of the Falangist leader Calvo Sotelo.

The German representatives in Barcelona were planning for a rising about July 10th, as their captured files have subsequently shown. The Italians were behind time, and their troop–carrying planes failed to arrive in Morocco at the appointed hour. One of them failed for a very good reason—it was forced down in French territory, and the crew interned. The plane had but a few days previously been in service by the Italian army, who very hastily and crudely tried to paint over the wing markings.

So much was clear, but it was some time before it became clear that "an English firearms expert" had flown from England to Tenerife, in the Canary Islands, to pick up the exiled General Franco, who, disguised as an Arab, was then flown to Tetuan, Spanish Morocco, where the insurrection was launched formally. Franco was in the Canary Islands for a very good reason: in 1934 he had brought over 40,000 black troops from the Spanish foreign legion to smash the Asturian miners' revolt against the hated rule of Gil Robles. No one in the north ever forgave Franco for his brutality and his burning of the University of Oviedo. The *Daily Telegraph* of London had a reporter in Asturias at that time, but sportingly refused to print the truth about the black mercenaries of Spanish feudalists. As Gil Robles admitted: "The only argument against the use of African troops is that they are utterly lawless and unrestrained in war, and are therefore liable to offend against the laws of common humanity."

Rather than witness such offenses as he had planned against com-

The Dress Rehearsal

The Spaniard's blood is fiery, the Spaniard's head is hot,
The Spaniards' quarrels are their own, the Spanish war is not;
As amateurs they flew to arms, not even knowing how,
And, lacking expert aid, the scrap would be all over now.

But war-trained Powers took the field with small hope of reward,
To save the modern world the shame of fighting with the sword,
They lavished field equipment and the necessary men,
For just a little looting and some plunder now and then.

They shelled, and they bombarded, and they mechanized the ranks
With armoured-cars, machine guns, and artillery and tanks,
They filled the sky with bombers and they strewed the seas with mines
And mowed militia down with guns of delicate designs.

So when all volunteers were by non-intervention banned,
They had to send out armies and assume the high command,
And the hundred-thousand Fascists who now animate the scene
Are naturally hostile when the Spaniards intervene.

While sharing full expenses in the observation posts
To make all neutral ships "move on" around the Spanish coasts,
Their expeditionary force involves a double cost,
But they know the opportunity too precious to be lost.

The seven-and-twenty nations who agree to stand apart
From this striking demonstration of the military art,
Combine to make these critical manoeuvres a success,
Whatever other sentiments their citizens profess.

In Spain the newest theories of the Staffs can be applied,
In Spain they test inventions, never previously tried,
For Spain's the dress-rehearsal, with effects not seen before,
For the final presentation on a world-wide scene of war.

Sagittarius, 1937

mon humanity, Gil Robles cut short his holiday near San Sebastian and drove madly through the night in order to cross the French border to Biarritz. Though unable to serve with his protégé Franco in Spain, he nevertheless regaled the British ambassador to Spain with delightful little titbits about the war, as this senile old man sat safely in the sun at Hendaye representing "the mother of parliaments." Doubtless Gil Robles told the ambassador what he thought of parliaments. In 1933 he had said the Republic was like smallpox, something to be suffered temporarily. When asked in July 1936 if he did not think the February (1936) elections represented the will of the people, he said, "elections never do." This choice law professor and political racketeer was finally shown up when the former conservative prime minister, Portela, stood up in the Cortes (by then moved to Valencia) and told of how Franco and Robles had come to him with a proposal at 4 a.m. on the day following the February elections. The proposal, as one might guess, was that Portela should refuse to hand over the government to the legally elected majority, and instead set up a dictatorship with the help of Franco's army backers and Robles' church politicians. Portela refused to have any dealings with them, and publicly called upon the president of Spain to transfer the state power to the Popular Front, which had won a majority in the house on a Rooseveltian platform.

While in Madrid in the spring, I learned of the lengths to which Robles' henchmen would go, even to attempts on the lives of men like Río–Hortega. Thus, I decided it would be useless to remain at the summer university and wiser to get out of Spain while there was a chance. This came rather unexpectedly, when an American teacher studying at the university told me that the American Consul at Bilbao had sent a message saying that there would be an American warship in Santander about noon to take off U.S. citizens. Shortly after lunch a great bluish–grey "battle wagon" came over the horizon, and soon students shouted, "Hurray for the Swiss navy." How surprised they were when the U.S.S. Oklahoma, 29,000 tons, dropped anchor out in the bay, and began lowering fast motorboats over the side!

We rushed to the quay with our belongings and were met by a corps of dock workers wearing "Popular Front" badges on their overalls. They stowed our bags on the tender and refused to take a cent for their trouble. I think they were waiting to get their hands on any German bags they could find! Soon we were wallowing in the Bay of Biscay, trying to pull alongside the Oklahoma long enough to embark. With each wave we rose high enough to shove one more stout

I have never been able to see a fire, although I have often chased fire-engines.... Perhaps because someone had heard of this gap in my education a machine from the 17th Squadron was ordered to bomb the Adi-Abo zone exclusively with incendiary bombs... We had to set fire to the wooded hills, to the fields and to the little villages... It was all most diverting... After the bomb racks were emptied I began throwing bombs by hand.... It was most amusing. Surrounded by a circle of fire about five thousand Abyssinians came to a sticky end.

Bruno Mussolini's book, *Voli Sulle Ambe*, pg. 639

"The great tragedy of Spain was that in the nineteenth century the working classes apostasized from the church... It was poverty, destitution and injustice which made them apostasize. They got to hate the church because they hated the friends of the church, who exploited them and whom the church did nothing to rebuke or correct".

Father Wilfred Parsons, S.J., former editor of the Jesuit Weekly *America*, writing in the September 1936 issue of *Columbia*

I personally own a bull terrier, and would say here and now that I have far more in common with my dog and any horse than I have with 99 3/4 per cent of the people I meet.

Letter in *Daily Express* 1936

Whoever serves Adolf Hitler, the Fuhrer, serves Germany, and whoever serves Germany serves God.

Baldur von Schirach, Reich Youth Leader, July 29, 1936

Sir James Irvine, the Principal of St. Andrew's University, in his address at the June graduation ceremony said: "Surely it is not in vain to hope that some day the machinery of government will include, as a matter of course, a Ministry of Knowledge, whose function to put it in the briefest possible way, is to look ahead". We may add the hope that when such a Ministry is constituted only qualified astrologers will be regarded as eligible to fill the post.

Modern Astrology, September 1936

woman on deck, with the help of some struggling midshipmen. One of them held a baby up with one hand, which caused the mother to shock the U.S. Navy with a few cuss words.

We set out for France on the following morning, which, being Sunday, called for a church service. Only the so-called refugees attended, with the exception of two officers whose duty it was to read the lessons. The padre was a young milk-fed lad who warned us about the decay of the home in America! (He had reported so many midshipmen for profanity that none cared what he preached about: they would not turn out.) When the band was required to play a hymn, they opened the engine room door and blasted forth the tune. When the hymn was over, they closed the door and went on with their crap game. Sitting at church beside the guns, while domestic troubles in the Midwest were set right, the great ship plunged ahead towards France. The change from 10 p.m. dinner with tough beefsteak on shore, to 5 p.m. American meals with hotcakes and maple syrup was rather a relief! As a farewell offering we were given a chicken dinner with ice cream, of course, and then we were lowered over the side into a small fishing sloop to be taken into Bayonne in France. The chief engineer gave me a six-pence that he said kept turning up in his pocket ever since he had been in England a year before. It was later to prove valuable.

Our little craft stood on end as we made for shore. The motor sputtered and wheezed as each wave broke over us. Many of the women were ill, but the red-faced old skipper in a black beret just sat smoking his pipe and holding the tiller. As we reached the dock a crowd gathered, and a lot of mustachioed little gauleiters fussed around in a maddening sort of way. Every confounded little French customs official I had met in my travels had insisted on taking my microscope out of its case and screwing the lenses around, and this one was no exception. As if examining some infernal machine, this one gingerly looked into the draw-tube. I told him he ought to know better than look down a gun barrel. He jumped back and slammed the door on the cabinet!

I phoned the British Consul for help in converting some American travellers' cheques, but he drawled that it was, after all, Sunday and he was too busy resting to drive in from the country on such petty affairs. So I took a room in the station hotel, prepared to spend the night, waiting for Britain's emissary to attend to his legitimate business. I heard an express train roll in, and dashed down to ask the Wagon-Lits official on it if he would cash an American money order so that I might take this train. The "commission" he wanted

Major Harding de Fonblanque Cox, known to intimates as "Cookie", appointed at the age of eighty-one by Lord Tyrrell, film censor, to act as assistant reader of scripts, raised a warning finger. He said: "I shall preserve a perfectly open mind, but I will not countenance vulgarity. No, my boy, let us show clean films in the old country". His enthusiasm grew as he continued, "I shall judge film stories as I would horseflesh or a dog. I shall look for clean lines. The same critical faculties with which I think I am gifted in the show ring will be brought to bear in my new task." Major Harding Cox, educated at Harrow and Cambridge, a former M.F.H., life member of the Garrick and Leander Clubs, authority on fishing in Bosnia and Herzegovina, spoke of Mae West. He also spoke of the survival of the soul, his conviction that the aura lives on after death, and his grave doubts whether the ego survives. His book *Fringes of Philosophy* is now in the hands of publishers. But Mae West came first. He said: "I am a man of the world, a broad-minded fellow, and they used to say I was a good judge of women. Personally, I think Mae is interesting as a curiosity, but, as I say, I shall judge her as I would a horse, er...er...or, say, a fox terrier. You know I founded the Fox Terrier Club. I shall Look for good clean lines". The Major is a keen cinema-goer. He never pays more than half a crown for a seat, and rarely attends evening performances. This reminded him of a problem that confronts him in his new work. He said: "I fall fast asleep if I try to work during the day, but can tackle any mortal thing at 4 a.m. I suffer from lethargy inherited from my father. Lord Tyrrell understands my disability."

Sunday Express, May, 1936

With regard to Lord Strabolgi's suggestion (that there should be R.A.F. women pilots) he (Lord Swinton) said he could not agree that a fighting formation, such as the reserve would be, should recruit women pilots. War was a beastly enough thing, and he did not want to add to it.

Daily Herald, August, 1936

Whatever part the great barons of the Ruhr and the Rhine played in the early days of the National Socialist movement, there is no doubt that as they saw approaching the crisis of their regime they threw their millions behind Hitler and saved their system. Always a dangerous policy - for a dictator is not fond of acknowledging his debts to his financial benefactors - fascism is entered upon only as a last recourse. Usually the dominant economic group will prefer to manipulate democracy, leaving intact the camouflage of civil freedom. But it is essential to note that the final test for modern democracy does not appear as a clear issue, and the demoralization of public thinking tends to become so chronic that faith in democracy has vanished before the death blow to democracy is struck.

Prof. J King Gordon, McGill University. *Towards the Christian Revolution*, 1936
(He won the federal seat for Victoria, B.C. but lost on a recount.)

would have so reduced the value of the cheque that I would not have enough for the fare. This did not matter to this swaggering "servant," so I had to get off the train again. Next morning, the hotel proprietor tried a similar stunt, designed to endear France to all travellers. Strange that in 24 hours I met three such public benefactors.

On reaching Paris, I rushed to the Canadian Pacific offices and tumbled a pile of now-worthless pesetas on the counter before the manager, an amazed Scot. I asked if he would, on this security, give me a pass to London whence I could at once mail him good sterling notes. He stared at me wide eyed, and when I told him I had 15 minutes to catch the train across at St. Lazare, his hair stood on end. As he opened his mouth to tell me I was *touché*, I reminded him that Sir George McLaren Brown had once told my look-alike brother, one of the Rhodes scholars, that if ever he was stuck in Europe just to mention his name, etc., etc. So here I was, no more a Rhodes scholar than my astonished friend across the counter, mentioning the versatile Sir George. I took out my pen and asked him if there would be anything to sign. The poor man was so taken by surprise that he called forth an assistant to run six blocks with me to get a pass. The assistant could not figure it out either, but did his work well. I arrived at the Gare St. Lazare several minutes late, and my heart sank. I ran past the barrier and found that the train was having trouble getting its hilarious passengers on board. They consisted of a large contingent of Canadian veterans returning from the unveiling of the Vimy Memorial. They kept pulling each other off the train and raising hell generally with the guards. I wearily dragged my bags and microscope through a dozen cars before I saw even 12 square inches to sit on. I asked two girls in the compartment, in the best French I could muster, if the seat was occupée. They looked at each other and giggled, one finally saying, in English, "We wouldn't know, we're from Winnipeg." I shouted "Hallelujah, I'm going to Vancouver, move over!"

By evening I was standing in Paddington Station, counting out enough money to buy a ticket to Oxford. I was six-pence short, and in a quandary until I remembered the tanner given to me by the chief engineer of the U.S.S. Oklahoma. I found it in my coat, and planked the money down at the booking office with quite an air of finality, making the old boy with half-moon glasses and black moustache look out at me, as much as to say, "Another fresh Yankee, oih?"

Next morning I cycled out to Boars Hill to see my guarantor, Sir Reginald Coupland, one of Oxford's most renowned tutors in the

We are facing a conspiracy of the entire sub-human world of a degenerate continent against.... Germanism.

Deutsche Freiheit

Nazi culture burning bright
With its nordic-Grecian light,
What sub-human dare defy
Its full totemic majesty?

Greek to species who are not
Aryan to the final clot,
Its ethnic-ethnic-technic dwells
In nordic livestock's sacred cells.

Stainless Aryan youth-bands now
Teach the tourist Herr and Frau,
That all folk-stems may in turn
Kraft durch Schadenfreude learn.

Arts of blood by bloodbaths purged,
In pan-Germanic sunburst merged,
Will their rays as they aspire
Come to set the Thames on fire?

Nazi! Nazi! burning bright
In Europe's deep degenerate night,
Who but Nazis can descry
Thy primitive sublimity?

Sagittarius, 1936

The reason why the little sons of the rich in England are, as a rule, humble fellows is that most of them go to Eton, which, though you may not believe it, is one of the few democratic institutions left.

Lord Castlerosse in *Sunday Express*

The public school spirit is Christianity in action.

The Symbol

Mr. R.J.R. Kerruish (Magdalen) opened his speech by quoting Lord Redesdale's remark that to abolish the House of Lords would be to strike at the very foundations of Christianity.

The Isis, 1936

realm of foreign relations and government. Trans-Atlantic students were required to have a guarantor against any damage caused. He was interested in what I had to tell him, but he was uneasy about the way in which the English press was rocking the people to sleep with flowery assurances that this was either an internal family brawl in Spain, or a settling of accounts between Germany and Russia—in either event, none of our concern. He knew better, and I shall never forget his lined, anxious face as he looked out over the hills and said: "If it comes to a showdown between Germany and Russia I must choose Russia. This won't be popular, I assure you, but what have the Barbarians to offer the world?" I could hardly believe my ears. Here was a man whose life and friendships had been rooted in imperialism, whose comfortable status and cloistered life were dovetailed intimately with the old school tie up. I was beginning to believe that Abyssinia was coming home to at least some Englishmen, and that eventually there was hope that Spain would too.

I reclaimed my pesetas from Paris and sent them to Madrid for the milk fund. I found out later that another student descended on the C.P.R. offices in Paris about a week following my visit, with the story that he had left his purse in Geneva, but that his father was a C.P.R. man in Calgary, Alberta, etc., etc., and that a pass across the channel would make it all lovely. The manager dryly asked him how many more lads he should expect during the summer with similar stories, so that he might have the tickets ready and thus save their all-too-precious time!

In a day or so I sailed for Canada on a ship jammed with the still-hilarious Vimy veterans and a number of German explorers (read spies). In Montreal I had the good fortune to find a Chinese train in need of a guard, so I landed on the Pacific coast in short order. My duties as guard consisted mainly in keeping order at stations where Chinese restaurant owners and laundrymen came to the train to kiss their twenty-seventh cousin on his way to ancestral China. As most of the Chinese passengers were ex-cooks returning from Boston or New York, I lived on the fat of the land for four days. On arriving on the Pacific coast I forgot the war long enough to go fishing—a very welcome change.

CHAPTER TEN

Second Year at Oxford, 1936–1937

I spent the month of September at home on Vancouver Island. The return journey through the Canadian Rockies was very delightful, as the leaves were just turning red and sufficient snow to trim the mountain tops and ledges had fallen already.

In Montreal I collected a Master's degree at James McGill's institution of learning. Returning to England via the Empress of Britain, we ran into very heavy seas. The only person to be seen on deck continuously was Sir Frederick Gowland Hopkins, discoverer of most of our early knowledge of vitamins. He paced the deck as though he had the whole problem of sea–sickness entirely under control.

I arrived back in Oxford to find most of the people sharing a crisis mentality. This next year was to be, for England, the most depraved in her political history. Already the group who had backed Mussolini in Abyssinia was growing cocky and was openly backing Japan in her iniquitous invasion of China. Now they were training their guns on Republican Spain. Soon they were openly to be the mouthpieces of Hitler, in England and throughout the English–speaking world.

In America President Roosevelt had already said that so far as he could see, Europe had divided itself into two camps: the respectable and the non–respectable. He added that the non–respectable had all the courage and the respectable none. The British government was determined, in so far as it could, to prevent this analysis from gaining a foothold in Europe. Chamberlain's and Sir John Simon's method of dealing with the continental crisis was an entirely new one. Their stock in trade was one word: "Peace." At all costs peace, or passivity, was to be maintained. In other words, every democratic country in Europe that was weaker than Germany and Italy combined did not have a chance. To defend itself would have been to bring war, and war was to be avoided under the Chamberlain–Simon formula. Therefore, the smaller countries must be sacrificed. No indication was given as to what we should do after we had raffled off all our smaller democratic friends in Europe.

The treatment that the British upper crust meted out to the democratically elected government of Spain was typical. They chose to forget that during the First World War it was only the Spanish Liberals and Trade Unionists who, with Alfonso, kept Spain neutral, while Germany connived, in every possible way, to bring Spain in on the side of the central powers. It was England's duty in 1936, under international law, to allow the legal Spanish government to purchase such arms as she needed for her own protection against German and Italian invasion, but England chose to disregard international law when it suited her. Then the British government resorted to a real farce: the Committee of Non–Intervention. This committee was set up in the summer of 1936 to hear submissions placed before it (by all members), which would lead to a cessation of external intervention in Spain. As was later found out, the British government made its last submission of evidence on October 16, 1936—a bare two months after the committee had been set up—yet for the next two years, Great Britain continued to take credit before the world for the "success" of this committee. Its success may be judged by the fact that the Italian newspapers gloated over "their" victories on a daily basis. They were even so indiscreet as to argue whether or not certain successes in the north of Spain were German or Italian victories. The British government was unconcerned that German Junker Bomber squadrons were sent directly from Germany by Hermann Goering on long–range expeditions to bomb the very daylights out of the Spanish people. Ambulance planes flew injured German Condor Legion soldiers back to Berlin in eight–hour, high altitude flights. It was of still less concern to the British government that the Germans secured the world's greatest mercury mine at Almaden, and one of the world's largest copper mines at Río Tinto. Nancy Astor was later to boast that Germany had these things and that, therefore, we must make friends with Hitler.

A group of impudent Japanese backers, including Sir Nairn Stuart Sandeman, chorused to the world that General Franco was a great Christian statesman. In the next breath they demanded that the thousands of Basque refugee children who had been brought to England be returned at once to Spain, where they would get a fine Christian education, with the permission of Mussolini and Hitler, no doubt. They wished to place them under the protection of a general who had to resort to 40,000 Moors for his conquest of his native country.

The Army is the only neutral power today in Spain.

Observer, November 14, 1936

They Saved France: Major Hugh Pollard, firearms expert to the "Sporting and Dramatic", is here seen with his daughter Diana (black habit) and Miss Dorothy Watson. "Disguised" as tourists they took an aeroplane from England to Teneriffe, rescued General Franco, and sent him to Tetuan where the anti-red standard was set up. It takes good fox hunters to do jobs like this.

Caption beneath photographs in *Sporting and Dramatic News*, November 21, 1936

Mussolini offered the world an "olive branch" in a speech at Bologna on Saturday, October 24, 1936, on the 14th anniversary of the Fascist "march on Rome". "It is an olive branch", he said, "springing from a forest of 8,000,000 well-sharpened bayonets held by courageous youths. I wish this message of peace to go beyond the mountains and the seas".

Daily Herald, October 26, 1936

Duff-Cooper speaking at a dinner of the English Twenty Club October 25, 1936: "It is not a beautiful thing or a desirable thing—indeed it is a hateful and a damnable thing—to think we should have to shoot fellow man, but, as it has to be done, it had better be done well." "In this country there is a charming little animal called the fox which does some good and a great deal of harm. He has to be kept down, and in order to keep him down, the English people have developed the great art of fox hunting. Abolish it tomorrow and the fox would be shot and finally exterminated." Duff Cooper said that in fox hunting they had exemplified the human characteristic of being able to do unpleasant things in such a way that they became an art.

News Chronicle, October 26, 1936

Hans Johst, President of the Reich Chamber of Literature, speaking at Book Week. "The buying public is our public and our people want to be and shall be convinced and led; that is the essential principle of our age. Christian art was likewise forced on its age with loving force, and National Socialist books are the only books that will go to the people. Our state needs a revelation of our spirit. Resistance will be broken with dynamite."

Montreal Gazette, October 26, 1936

It took centuries and several crusades to rid Spain of the Moors, but it did not take Franco long to bring them back. Each Moor, strangely enough, was given a little medallion with Franco's leering countenance on one side, and on the other the Virgin of the Pillar.

Two small points ought perhaps to be made. The Franco story was that the Spanish government supporters were armed and ready to massacre their opponents. However, the *Sunday Times* of London pointed out, in its November 8, 1936 issue, that the Republican government could only muster 1,400 rifles for the defence of the front lines of Madrid. Regarding "volunteers" on Franco's side, i.e., Spanish volunteers, we have the words of Queipo de Llano, Franco's declamatory radio general, to the effect that after two years he gave up all recruiting efforts in Andalusia because in that time he had been unable to raise even one battalion.

All in all, it looked very much as if the British government's policy was to keep Europe "safe from democracy." Not content to stand quietly on the sidelines, Britain's Tories obligingly undertook to run interference and carry the ball for a Fascist aggressor, wherever he might be found.

This was far from being the general attitude of the British public. By now the man in the street was getting used to this betrayal of democracy's champions abroad. He had seen Austria, Abyssinia and now Spain deserted when they most needed help. The stoutest champions of the Spanish republic came from those great amorphous, anonymous 40 million Britishers who earned pitifully small wages. Poverty–stricken coal–mining valleys gave till it hurt; children and invalids offered their small contributions wherever an aid–for–Spain meeting was held. The necessity of providing food and milk became obvious at the first of the war, so much of the voluntary British effort was directed towards this end. The champion of the Spanish democrats, both inside parliament and outside, was the Duchess of Athol. I shall never forget the scene at the great "Spain and Culture" meeting at Albert Hall when, after listening to many distinguished speakers from all parts of Europe, the audience was suddenly electrified as Paul Robeson, the great Negro bass, walked on the stage having just arrived by airplane from Moscow where he had been singing. Until then I thought that an English crowd was conservative and sedate. But these people, thousands upon thousands of them, cast off all inhibitions and simply roared for five minutes on end. The poor little duchess would stand up and shake her finger at them, even to the point of scowling over her glasses, but still they continued to shout. Finally Paul Robeson called for silence and said that

Japan has a very powerful case based on fundamental realities... (invading China) with the object of creating peace and order in Manchuria and defending herself against the continual aggression of vigorous Chinese nationalism. Our whole policy in India, our whole policy in Egypt, stand condemned if we condemn Japan.

L.C.S. Amery, 1937

The hypocritical sob-stuff of the Archbishop of Canterbury and his co-meddlers who supported the Albert Hall meeting in their pursuance of a most war-provoking piece of interference with Japan is, to say the least of it, disgusting. Why should civilians not be slaughtered? To pretend that civilians are a lot of innocent victims who look on while the murderous soldiery do the slaughtering is utter bunkum.

Letter in *Western Morning News*, October 16, 1937

Speaking as a total abstainer, Lady Montgomery-Massingberd said it would help a great deal if people who did not care for alcohol would "take the pledge". "Those of you who go to sherry parties and cocktail parties," she added, "finish what is in your glasses. Do not let it go away to be drunk in the pantry by somebody who, perhaps, has not taken it before, or who has not acquired the taste."

Lincolnshire Echo, July 31, 1937

Mr. Walter Elliot (Secretary for Scotland) caused some surprise when discussing the suggestion that surplus herrings should be made available to the poor at prices lower than those charged in the shops by saying: There was nothing the unemployed would resent more than being used as a dumping ground for food products.

News Chronicle, July 1937

before he sang for them he wished to speak. His speech was a masterpiece of clarity and brevity. His message was "Artists Must Choose." He rapped his words out with the force of a sledge hammer; when he finished, the audience was trembling. He then sang the Georgia chain-gang song, "All I Want's Them Cold Iron Shackles Off My Leg," followed by "Shortnin' Bread" and "Old Man River." The "unemotional English" certainly wept as he finished "Old Man River." It was impossible to restore order until Robeson left the platform, waving them a cheery good-bye.

One story of how the Spanish refugee children were loved by all England is worth recounting. Several hundred Basque children arrived in Southampton on a small ship from the north of Spain. As they marched from the docks over to the railway station, merchants came out of their stores and loaded them down with fruit and cookies and toys. One little English boy was not to be outdone. He waited anxiously at the kerb, and then suddenly darted out to hand something to one of the Spanish boys who had nothing in his hand. He gave him this something and then rushed back to the kerb sobbing. The little Spanish boy was dumbfounded: he could not understand it, but when he opened his hand he found that he had been given 12 cigarette cards. Though he did not know, of course, what they were, he did realize that parting with them had been a great wrench for the English boy.

But all this was to no avail. No action could be forced from an unwilling government. No general strike was possible. That had been seen to in 1926 by the astute reactionary Stanley Baldwin and his dedicated casuist, Sir John Simon. I once heard Sir John say in the Oxford Union how proud he was that he had always taken the part of the workman. An American sitting beside me who knew better was not long in calling out "liar."

The debates in the Union improved considerably as the political tempo of the nation quickened. In November, Christopher Mayhew, the President, gave Lord Londonderry the worst dressing down in public that I have ever heard. Londonderry, of course, used his reply to try to refute the accusations, but every time he opened his mouth he got himself in deeper and deeper. The question was whether or not he had said at the World's Disarmament Conference that bombing must be preserved so that Britain could keep certain Indian frontier tribes in order. Though never saying it in so many words, Britain's social cyanotics really hoped to temporize with Germany and finally offer her a free hand in the East. This was the Amery and Lothian formula. To top off the evening's debate, Archibald Sinclair gave a brilliant exposition of why Greta Garbo wanted to join the Liberal party: to be alone.

In the middle of all this political chaos, which was fast giving Stanley Baldwin hypertension, came a little white dove: Mrs. Simpson. For some weeks the Americans at Oxford had been getting advance information by having copies of *Time Magazine* wrapped in the New York *Times* and sent over. In this way, they were not censored, and we would compare their contents with that of the censored English copies. It was here that we found not only the material on Mrs. Simpson, which had been censored, but also the story of the Right Hon. J.H. Thomas and his conversion of Newfoundland bonds, while he was colonial secretary, at a handsome profit. The Simpson affair was a godsend to the government. Mr. Baldwin took a much firmer grip on the reins of state as he led Edward VIII off the field. The Spanish war was pushed into the background as all the old denizens of the all–male clubs of London got their heads together about "this Baltimore queen." The Archbishop of Canterbury saw it as a chance to bring his hammer down on the anvil, and with Mrs. Simpson as his text, he set out upon a "Recall to Religion." Once again, the British Empire was most theatrically saved. Not everyone, however, was bamboozled. Many recalled Edward's words as he visited the wretched colliery town of Dowlais in Wales, when he said: "This is a damn shame. Something must be done about it."

Christmas vacation afforded an opportunity to go to Paris to visit several laboratories and libraries. The University City there was one of John D. Rockefeller's projects for international education. Central features such as a dining hall and auditorium had been provided by the foundation, while over a score of nations had their Houses bordering the campus. Unfortunately, the University City was some distance from the centre of Paris, where most studies were still pursued. This was particularly so in medicine. Naturally I enquired if there might be a vacancy in the Maison Canadienne, but when I found it full to over–flowing with students over from England for the holidays, I turned to the Spanish College where I was very hospitably received and where I enjoyed the company very much. I was not sorry to be relieved of the duties of discussing the current political situation with the head of the Maison Canadienne, who was a contributor to the notoriously pro–fascist *Gringoire*, and whose ambitious wife was more interested in throwing champagne parties for her friends in Paris than in the students' welfare at the Maison. The director very sternly viewed the news one morning in his paper and remarked that Roosevelt's victory over Landon in the

United States was, "the firm 'NO' to Marxism!"

I spent several days visiting laboratories in the Sorbonne and was met everywhere with the warmest hospitality. The size of the large city hospitals staggered me. The seemingly endless public wards at La Pitié, many of them filled with neurological cases, were rather depressing. Still, from these wards came much of our knowledge of clinical neurology. No one seeing them could forget the famous teacher Charcot. I visited Claude Bernard's old laboratory and found that his successor, Professor Lapique, was the proud possessor of a Canadian honorary degree. The work going on in his laboratory was generally related to ours in Oxford, but always with a slightly different approach.

I had the good fortune one evening to hear André Phillipe speak on the religious basis for social change. He was one of the really rare spirits in European politics.

I spent my Sundays either at the Louvre or at Versailles. Imagine my astonishment when, one Sunday afternoon at the Louvre, I looked up to see the Sitwells sweeping by in all their glory! There was something very sad about Versailles, in spite of the millions that John D. Rockefeller put into its restoration. The exhibition of the table on which the Treaty of Versailles was signed seemed to me in very bad taste, as was everything in France connected with that ethereal word "Gloire." There was more "Gloire" than democracy in many high places in those fateful years of Laval's reign.

Life and conversation at the Spanish college revolved about the war in Spain, of course. The chief centre of attraction in any such discussion was the well-known Spanish writer Pio Baroja. This very old man with his pointed beard and black beret set jauntily on the side of his head made a real picture. When the war broke out, poor old Don Pio immediately was arrested by the Requetes, or Carlists, a fanatical group of Catholics who thought that the succession of the Spanish throne was derailed about a century ago. Don Pio's gaoler knew that though the old man had, on occasion, written a few things derogatory to the church, he was still the best loved son of the Basque land. Fearing what would happen when the people of Irun found out about his arrest, the gaoler came to him at midnight and begged him to escape. So with pleasure Don Pio obligingly escaped and came to Paris. He had since found, of course, that his books were being burned in Spain and his bust was thrown unceremoniously down the stairs in front of the city hall in San Sebastian. He loved to sit in the sunshine and tell us about the origin of "La Cucaracha" and other famous Spanish songs. When he found that I came from Canada, he

Mussolini's censorship orders to the Italian press from January 1937 have been published abroad:
"January 18. Don't publish any news of bombardments of inhabited centers by the Nationalists in Spain, and, above all, refrain from mentioning Italian or German aviators."
"February 9. Don't picture the military situation of the Spanish reds as disastrous. Be less optimistic."
"March 5. Absolutely suppress any news of the arrival in Naples of wounded volunteers from Spain".
"The popular front government in Spain was a liberal, bourgeois government.... Juan March and the Royal Dutch Company financed the uprising.... This government was not well liked by the small minority of large landed proprietors because of the division of their land.... Nor was it liked by that part of the clergy which possessed large agrarian wealth.... One should not permit oneself to be deceived by the excesses of an unchanged populace in the large cities...the Spanish employer is characterized in a manner unique in Europe by his lack of social sense. Today he still misses the good old days of the military dictatorship of Prímo de Rivera, who once too often shot down workers out on strike."

Austrian Catholic Weekly *Christliche Standestatt*, March 14, 1937 was always asking for "los esquimales," and he wanted to know how they built their igloos and what they ate all winter. He once wanted to go to visit a friend in Whitechapel but he could not gather up courage enough to say "Whitechapel" on the back of the horse-drawn street car. He waited until three or four passengers had got on and paid their fare, each one saying in turn "Whitechapel." Then he stepped up and attempted to say the same word, but the conductor could not understand him at all, though Don Pio thought his pronunciation perfect—every bit as good as those who had just preceded him.

We were all maddened by the December 23rd news that the Instituto Cajal in Madrid had been bombed. As in the case of the Prado Art Gallery, not far away, the bombs used were incendiary, evidently well chosen for the destruction of such things as paintings and books. In both cases the fires were soon extinguished.

On Christmas Eve I joined some other Canadians and we attended Mass at one of the large central Paris churches. The outstanding feature of the service was the playing of a beautiful harp, accompanied by the organ. We left the church after a rather long service and walked through the Quartier Latin where we heard several men standing under a lamp post singing the "Internationale." Then, at about six in the morning, we came upon a Salvation Army man distributing Bibles outside a dive called the Tango du Chat club. The Boulevard San Michele was full of well-dressed Americans making asses of themselves, doing drunken dances on top of café tables.

I arrived back in England to find Sir Oswald Mosley's "British Union of Fascists" paying Oxford an official call. These annual visits by the great gauleiter had in the past been associated with a number of serious injuries, and this was to be no exception. The local organization had been housed in the Broad in a very innocuous manner, except that one of the town's volunteer fire inspectors had disapproved of a large pile of egg-sized stones in their premises and ordered them taken away as a "fire menace!"

However, when Mosley's black-shirted, leather-legginged thugs arrived in town, the little pipsqueak local members began to walk around as if "the day" were at hand. It was reported that there would not be enough lamp posts to go around. On a memorable Friday night, both floors of the Carfax Assembly Rooms were packed. Upstairs you paid a little extra to see the superman, while downstairs a loudspeaker carried the good tidings. At the appointed hour, the lights went out, trumpets sounded and Americans began to shout, "Bring on the bogeyman." Then a single spotlight picked out Mosley

The philosopher in the Parks was certainly right in speaking of Oxford as a changed place, and in connecting this change with the influx of foreigners. The university, which in the eighties of last century was aristocratic and national, has now become democratic, imperialistic and cosmopolitan.

That the university has benefited greatly by this larger hospitality seems to me to be incontestable. The Rhodes scholars have been, and continue to be, a helpful and stimulating element in our society. Let us hope that, as they are good for Oxford, Oxford may be good for them, and that they may take home something more valuable even than blues or firsts: a rich store of English friendships and a true appreciation of the peculiar people of dreamers, poets, explorers, landowners, tradesmen, soldiers, sailors and statesmen, who have converted a small island hardly known to antiquity into one of the greatest powers in the world.

H. A. L. Fisher, "The Flow of Time," in *Oxford*, Summer 1934.

on the stage, giving a frozen Fascist salute. A piercing Cockney voice shouted: "Yes, Oswald, you may leave the room." The laughter was terrific, so they turned on the lights and Mosley began to speak. Then most of the audience began to turn their newspapers over, and to fold and unfold them. It was barely possible to hear the barking Oswald, now well on his way to defend the Japanese in Manchuria.

One of Professor Gilbert Murray's relatives caused much laughter as he walked up near the front and took a seat right under Mosley's nose. He was sporting a fantastic beard. Mosley eyed him as the head of the rumpus, but went on blasting away at the Labour Party, which, much to its credit, had expelled him years ago. There was a bus strike on in Oxford, and dozens of men had come in their uniforms. One of them, a spirited little Cockney, objected to being called "a silly little schoolboy" by Mosley, and as he stood up to object, Mosley gave the signal to the imported thugs who were gradually moving up the aisles looking for victims to be thrown out.

The melee broke out in a dozen places at once, and two dons who tried to get to the platform to call for order were knocked flat: one of them, the Honourable Frank Pakenham was "out" for a week. The sound of tea–room chairs being smashed as one partisan swung at his enemy was like fire going through a dry forest. The one police officer who idly had watched the thugs creeping up the aisles now made straight for the students who were trying to defend themselves against the over–powering blackshirts. A number of these students were hailed into court, but only "bearded Murray" was fined—I can only suppose for not coming clean–shaven to a thug's meeting. Toynbee Junior nursed a slashed face for some time.

CHAPTER ELEVEN

The Rhodes Scholars

The Rhodes scholars and the Rhodes Scholarships make up one of the important ingredients in Oxford life today, though their purpose is little enough understood beyond the shores of England. It fell to a Canadian professor, himself an unsuccessful candidate for a Rhodes Scholarship, to define a Rhodes scholar as "a man with a brilliant future behind him." A well–known American weekly cryptically wrote: "It's fun, and it's free." Some critics, when pressed as to the value of an Oxford education for men from over–seas, fall back on an ex–chancellor of Oxford's famous pearl that the only visible contribution of higher education has been to enable younger and younger people to write more and more obscene things higher and higher on the walls of public conveniences.

Such world–shaking concepts were far from the mind of that tuberculous diamond seeker of 24, who sat down in South Africa in 1877 to write his first will on an upturned barrel! He knew what he wanted to do, and he set up a trust fund of 2,000,000 pounds to do it. He wrote: "I consider the education of young Colonists at one of the universities in the United Kingdom is of great advantage to them for giving breadth to their views, for their instruction in life and manners, and for instilling into their minds the advantage to the Colonies as well as to the United Kingdom of the retention of the unity of the Empire. I also desire to encourage and foster an appreciation of the advantages which I implicitly believe will result from the union of the English–speaking peoples throughout the world, and to encourage in the students from the United States of America an attachment to the country from which they have sprung, without, I hope, withdrawing them or their sympathies from the land of their adoption or birth."

By the time he wrote his sixth will, Rhodes had polished his scholarship idea to one of great lustre and exactness. In a codicil dated

October 11, 1901, he emphatically stated that he wanted scholars who were "not merely bookworms." He hoped that those selected for the then ample 350 pounds per year scholarships would combine the following attributes in the proportions noted: "literary and scholastic attainments," 3/10; "fondness for and success in manly outdoor sports such as cricket, football and the like," 2/10; "qualities of manhood, truth, courage, devotion to duty, sympathy for and protection of the weak, kindliness, unselfishness and fellowship," 3/10; "attributes likely in after life to guide him to esteem the performance of public duty his highest aim," 2/10. He added, significantly, "No student shall be qualified or disqualified for election to a scholarship on account of his race or religious opinions."

If one tried to draw up a balance sheet after nearly a century of scholarships, one would indeed be surprised at the global and occupational distribution of this fraternity of several thousand men, and more recently women. The professions have by far the greatest number with law and medicine pre–ponderating. A few have remained in England, but most have returned to their native lands. It is strange that in every large community one can find a self–appointed critic of the Rhodes Scholarship experiment. Often it is no more than a disappointed aspirant, working off the complexes that he may have developed and coddled over a number of years. Little public attention is paid to such spleen, however.

Wherever brain surgery, medicine, astronomy, international law or history are mentioned, a former Rhodes scholar will be quoted as one of the authorities. Most of the foreign offices of the English–speaking world have been invaded by these "rash young men from Oxford." Again, few of the major universities in the English–speaking world are without a Rhodes man or woman, and already dozens have been chosen to be university presidents. It is doubtful if Rhodes, in all his dreaming, could have imagined how successful his scheme was to be in bringing to Oxford a few dozen young women and men each year who would return to their homes at the four corners of the earth to put science, culture and government on a higher plane.

Some have decried the reluctance of Rhodes men to enter into political life, where the benefit of their training is sorely needed. Except for conspicuous exceptions, it is true that the bulk of the scholars have not, on their return, entered into public political activity. A few lawyers have aspired to parliament, and a flood of economists have poured into the manifold new agencies of government that, in every quarter, have been set up to find out where the country is going, at what speed and why, and how to stop it. Lester Pearson and John Turner in Canada and Bob Hawke in Australia have been prime ministers. President Bill Clinton now leads the U.S.A.

As to the quality of the scholars sent to Oxford, much could be said. Here again, the type of person chosen may depend on the selection committee's idea of what a Rhodes Scholarship means. In some American institutions the scholarship was once regarded as a reward for some campus politician. All too often an athlete riding the crest of the wave may be sent, and he in turn will have his searchings of heart at Oxford when he finds no band to meet him and hardly a dozen people watching him play his particular game. Long ago the English realized the value of sports for all, rather than for a few bulldozers. As Thorstein Veblen once remarked concerning American college athletics, "They are related to the physical well–being of the student body as bullfighting is to agriculture."

Far from being a reward, a Rhodes Scholarship should be considered the opportunity it truly is. Only the student who regards it in this light will come to appreciate the truth of the saying that "the more one puts into Oxford the more one gets out of it."

While most Rhodes men and women have fitted in well at Oxford and have returned home greatly enriched by their experience in Britain and in Europe, a few have failed notoriously to contribute or receive anything useful during their time there. Only one had stomach enough to go home when he saw that he was not cut out for the Oxford atmosphere. The adjustments that even a healthy personality must make at Oxford are difficult enough without carrying forward pre–existing problems.

The tutorial system has been developed to a high degree at Oxford; at first it presents a problem to incoming Rhodes scholars who, for the most part, have been lectured to in classes numbering up in the hundreds. Usually each student has a moral tutor and an academic tutor: the former to keep him out of debt and trouble if possible, the latter to criticize papers read to him twice a week in his study at a fixed hour. In the final year this ordeal may be reduced to once a week.

Naturally, to the tutors this all seems very simple, but to a newcomer it can be very exasperating: groping around trying to find how to write the required essays, where the most accessible library is located and where the most audible lectures on the right subjects are given. With time, the student learns to rely less on cut and dried material, and branches out into his own lines of thinking and research. His days are his own, and he pursues his studies as he pleases. It may seem to a few that they have been blessed with the most miserable, gouty old tutor ever born, who fails to appreciate the time-honoured Fourth of July phrases. These students usually cease blaming their tutor early in the game and get down to hard work. Otherwise they will awake after their examinations are over to find that they have captured only a third class. Competition is stiff at Oxford. Only a very limited number of firsts are given.

All problems of plumbing, heating and eating aside, there is a sense in which Oxford may not appeal, at once, to trans-Atlantic students. In the first place, each college tends to be a cross-section, more or less, of contemporary society. There is none of that protection from the world that is so often afforded by fraternities on the American or Canadian campuses. Every viewpoint is represented at Oxford, and sheer blustering and prejudice against an idea will not silence it. The good old house debates of the "frats" in America are replaced by sharply contested debates in Oxford, with no holds barred and the flesh and bones of the real issues served up uncompromisingly. The Rhodes scholar who is either a mouse or a "mutton-minded" gladiator most certainly will be unhappy in such surroundings. The case comes to mind of a Canadian Rhodes man home on vacation, being telephoned by an over-bearing brewer who wanted to know "how to go about getting my eldest boy a Rhodes Scholarship!" Such people make the lives of Rhodes selection committee members miserable.

Before leaving the much-maligned selection committees, a few words should be said about those that have shown real courage and insight in the selection of scholars, year after year. Even the best committee is likely to be faced by an unpromising group of applicants on occasion. In such a case, I know of one committee that, under the guidance of a crusty old Scot, refused to elect a scholar and held the award over until the following year. In another case the chairman, who was head of a great railway system, asked an applicant if he had any political ambitions. The student replied, "Yes, sir, I aim to be the first socialist prime minister of this country," whereupon the railway president asked, "What will you do then?" The applicant replied, "I will immediately proceed to nationalize your railroad, sir." It was this chairman's deciding vote that sent this student to Oxford, there to become president of the Oxford Union—no mean accomplishment in itself!

Selection committees could be more useful to the scholar-elect than they have been if they would refrain from plying the poor, bewildered winner with offers to get him into their former colleges. Great unhappiness settles down over some scholars when they ar-

Almost Without a Murmur

It is a singular circumstance in Bonaparte's political conduct that, so far from concealing his designs, he purposely publishes even the most violent of his projected innovations, some time before they are put in execution: and the consequence has uniformly been that, instead of being alarmed and prepared to resist, the world has, by anticipating conquests and changes, become by degrees reconciled to them, and submitted almost without a murmur to the mandates of a tyrant.

Lord Palmerston, age 23

You stiffen your backbone and listen to the night. There is a sense of danger. It is not the people. They don't seem dangerous. Out of the very air comes a sense of danger, a queer **bristling** feeling of uncanny danger. Something has happened. Something has happened which has not yet eventuated. The old spell of the old world has broken, and the old bristling savage spirit has set in... and it is a happening of far more profound import than any actual **event**. It is the father of the next phase of events.

Lawrence of Arabia on a visit to Germany, 1923

rive at Oxford to find themselves enrolled in a college that has no tutor in their particular line of study. In such cases the student is farmed out to a tutor at another college, who may or may not give him inspiring guidance in his work.

Guidance as to what course to follow at Oxford should be more readily available to prospective applicants, and especially to those elected to a scholarship. There is no reason why a student graduating from a first–class law faculty in his own country should then go to Oxford to plod through a course that may have little connection with the type of law to be practiced later. If Oxford offers anything, it offers a real opportunity to get a liberal education. The Great War forced the university to offer an alternative to the course in classics or "greats." "Modern Greats" (philosophy, politics and economics), which then came into being, has certainly been one of the finest courses offered in the English–speaking world.

With post graduate studies (in the sciences particularly) developing rapidly at Oxford, more thought must be given to the age of the candidates. Although a Rhodes scholar can be 25 at the time of taking up his residence, preference is often given to younger candidates. In the case of those with medical degrees, this age factor might be interpreted liberally because of the prolonged training now required in medicine. With Lord Nuffield's benefactions, it is to be hoped that more medically qualified scholars will be sent to Oxford, and fewer medical students who are only half way through their course. Such medical students have usually repeated most of their pre–clinical training at Oxford. In the past Oxford offered a medical degree only after 33 clinical months in a recognized London hospital, but today boasts a fine clinical school, as well as its basic sciences. It has been said that Cecil Rhodes originally wanted medical scholars to go to Edinburgh, but the lack of residential colleges there prevented this development.

The Rhodes Trustees decided that the Oxford secretary of the trust should have an office and residence commensurate with his rapidly increasing responsibilities. They built a beautiful brown stone structure on ground purchased from Wadham College. The building houses a fine library on the Dominions and Colonies, and is open to all students. The large, central Milner Hall has served Oxford well as the scene of going–down dinners, or for the once–a–term dances for Rhodes men "by kind permission of the proctors." Other rooms have been designed for use by Oxford's innumerable clubs, such as the Raleigh and Bryce Clubs. It should be stated definitely that Rhodes House is not a residence for Rhodes scholars, as was widely proclaimed at one time by some misinformed old colonels, who were afraid that Rhodes men were trying to evade the feudal quarters in the colleges. The Rhodes Trust insisted, and quite rightly, that scholars shall live in college for part of their time, the better to be shaken up and mixed into the Oxford stream of things.

So much, then, for the Rhodes Scholarships. The world has been enriched immensely through their institution by a "dreamer," who little realized to what extent his plan would bring young poets, musicians, doctors, engineers, lawyers, linguists, historians, architects and philosophers to Oxford.

CHAPTER TWELVE

Nazi Germany

My first introduction to Germany was through the remilitarized Rhineland. Early in 1937 I went to visit laboratories at the University of Bonn, situated high on the banks of the Rhine, a few miles south of Cologne. The town itself was interesting, and the university especially so. Like most German universities, this one had had a chequered career. A century earlier Karl Marx had spent a year there studying Greek and Roman mythology, Roman law and modern art. He spent a day in gaol for drunkenness. By 1937 the Nazis had already dismissed all women studying for the professions there.

The medical school had long been famous for men like Sobotta, whose anatomical atlases were used the world over. I was therefore amazed to find that he was no longer director of the large Anatomical Institute, but I said nothing. I later learned, from a former student at Bonn, that a plot had been cooked up by those who wanted to depose the old man. The rumour was circulated that his wife was of faintly Jewish extraction. To scotch it, the professor offered a large cash prize to anyone who could prove it. He might as well have saved his breath, for soon the Nazis had him out of his chair, and his career was at an end. He had to rent part of his home for a beer garden, and he looked completely broken by the change. In a small office in the institute he still kept up his dissections and paintings. He installed me in the library where I worked while waiting for the new director to come from Wurzburg.

A strange thing happened in the library. I was reading up on the new director's various papers and came to a violent criticism of his work, written by a Spaniard in New York. I left the journal open at this article and went for lunch. On my return, I could not find the journal anywhere, and then discovered, on going to the shelves, that the entire set of this anatomical publication had been removed from

On a point of honour, Old Harrovians will rally round the Government in the House of Commons today, writes our Political Correspondent. It is the Fourth of June at Eton, and the Government, anticipating a general exodus of old Etonian members, numbering over 100, have included in their Whip a reminder to this effect, and earnestly requested non-Etonians to fill the breach.

Morning Post, June 1937

Germany today is the nearest approach to Utopia, with a single political creed, wholehearted worship of the Fatherland.

Motor, July 3, 1937

The cinema...serves the proletariat as well as the middle classes. So long as we have the cinema and commercialized football, the proletariat will give no trouble to their masters in England.

Rev. J.C. Hardwick at the Conference of Modern Churchmen,
report in *Morning Post*, September 11, 1937

We reject international science. We reject the international republic of learning. We reject research for its own sake. We teach and learn medicine, not to increase the number of known germs, but to keep the German people strong and healthy. We teach and learn history, not to say how things happened, but to instruct the German people from the past. We teach and learn science not to discover abstract laws, but to sharpen the instrument of the German people in competition with other peoples. If the German universities make and keep this vow, then they will naturally be the first to be consulted in all cultural and spiritual questions.

Dr. Kahrstedt, Prof. of Ancient History, Gottingen, at the bicentenary. 1937 the library! I took the hint and spent the weekend walking along the Rhine, not in reading verboten passages.

I had no sooner started for the Bad Godesberg ferry to cross over than I was set upon by a brown-shirted fanatic shaking a can in front of my face for the "Winterhilf." He looked so much like Adolf himself that I could not keep a straight face. I kept on walking while he began to fume. At every block these heel-clickers rushed up, trying to pin a little japanned tag on my sweater to show I had contributed. But knowing that the Osthilf had gone to the squires in East Prussia, I thought to myself that the Winterhilf must be going to the moon. (As things transpired, most of it went into the Air Force buildings in Berlin.) I finally became annoyed at one persistent beggar and stormed at him. A little boy of six rushed up to the uniformed demi-fuhrer and yelled, "Dass ist sehr musicalische" and ran off.

The paths along the banks of the Rhine seemed covered with young Nazis swaggering by with Alsatian dogs and long whips. Their soft green-grey uniforms seemed much too pretty for warfare. On the river a marine branch of the Hitler jugend was learning to man the longboats. The swastika floated over Siebenbergen and a group of future gauleiters wearing tyrolean hats paced about the grounds. At night they roared through the countryside in long Mercedes Benz cars.

The path to the Drachenfels was crowded with every sort of uniform. To some it was just another Sunday's walk, but to the rather large number of tourists it was awe-inspiring to get to the topmost part of the Drachenfels from which one could see the Rhine's furthest expanses. The grape terraces were visible in every direction. I had an inside picture of the wine-making from a Spaniard who was describing it to his little child at the top.

In the evening the lights came on in hamlets pocketed in the mountainside. Far below each tug-boat had its string of heavy-laden barges dotted with lights behind it. The monastery bell tolled for evensong. The old people greeted each other with the civilized "Gruss Gott," and the old Germany was not far away. By morning it would be gone again, with the brownshirts out on the pavement in force, and Julius Streicher's hideous, red-bordered glass cases in every square displaying Der Stürmer, his violent, anti-Semitic rag. The drawings and slogans in it were of the crude sadistic type found in mental hospital wards.

Beethoven's house was a shrine in Bonn to which a steady flow of people came. His pictures and music, which are excellently preserved, made up most of the exhibits. The programme of Beethoven's

The German people found themselves in an atmosphere of freedom. The forces of liberty and democracy had triumphed over the prevailing oppression and tyranny. The conforming mind was replaced by the free mind as intellectual activity once again flowered...

But then with the suddenness of a thunderclap and all of its terror, reaction struck back. The liberal constitution was summarily abrogated. The universities and their leaders were the first to suffer. Professors and scholars were expelled; in disgrace many went into exile. The structure of tyranny was being re-erected and intolerance was once again its cornerstone....

This was the Germany of 1837 — this is the Germany of 1937. It was the University of Gottingen that suffered so disastrously one hundred years ago. For protesting against the revocation by King Ernst Augustus of Hanover of the liberal constitution which he had sworn to accept... seven of its most illustrious professors — Die Gottinger Sieben — among whom were the brothers Grimm (of fairy tale fame) ...Thomas Mann...we hear confess his love for the "true Germany"...in the words of Heine: "the real Germany, the great, mysterious, anonymous Germany of the German people, the sleeping sovereign with whose sceptre and crown the apes are playing."

Letter by E.J. Lasky, *Nation*, July 17, 1937, pg. 84

Germany certainly does not want to attack England, and if ever she did it would only be through the stupid, arrogant, interfering folly of British politicians. If Germany were forced into an attack she would try to teach a salutary lesson swiftly and heavily, but in such a way as not to arouse too keenly British national spirit. She would broadcast her reasons for attack, and her conditions for peace. As her demands would be few and simple - non-interference, some territory outside Great Britain, and a few strategic places for temporary occupation - our General Public would probably see to it that her conditions were accepted.

Aeroplane, March 6, 1937

first appearance, at the age of six in Cologne, is headed "Klavierkonzert." Beethoven's last piano can be seen: a large instrument specially strung because of his tragic deafness. The modest garden in back of the house was well kept up. It was a musical phrase I heard in Bonn that made me believe that the problems of a musical education are the same the world over. Every morning on my way to the laboratory, I passed a house where a child could be heard practising a Bach selection in D major. Without fail, the poor, beleaguered student would be in trouble with a C–sharp, the one that used to annoy me as a child, playing the same piece thousands of miles away.

I returned from my weekend, ready for whatever was in store for me at the Anatomical Institute. When the director came, I just let him talk. It was not long until he began mopping the floor with the British physiologists, from which he went on to the Spanish histologists, and finally to those indescribable fellows in the Soviet Union. He plainly wanted to wash his mouth out for even mentioning them. This was very amusing, but not science, so I took my life in my hands and asked to be shown some microscopic preparations by the good doctor.

Thus act two began. I pretended not to understand the most violent parts of the monologue, and blandly asked the most obtuse questions that I could, in an innocent sort of way. The director's eyes went the size of saucers when I asked him for proof of his "nerve net" theory. Finally we got down to microscope slides, which we studied until lunch time. After lunch I asked him to interpret his slides for me, and I still have the pencil drawings he made to support his theory. The Zeiss equipment was of the highest quality, but I could not help remembering that Professor Abbe, in a memorable charter, had given the Zeiss works at Jena to the workmen when he died. Now the Nazis had gone in and thrown out the more liberal clauses of the charter.

As the afternoon was slipping away, I pressed my questions on experimental work a little too far, and was met by a long tirade on English experimenters being able to do things, "even on humans, elephants and frogs!" It was not until some time later that I heard that Goering was one of the anti–vivisectionist influences in Germany, and that laboratory work was under very definite strictures. I saw that the game was up and I had better leave before I was given a picture of Hitler for my laboratory in Oxford. There seemed to be one over every wash basin and desk in this laboratory.

I took the train to Holland determined to get to the bottom of this nerve net theory, which had been superimposed by the German work-

The only new attraction at Numberg this year was the presence of the diplomats of the principal democratic countries. They were displayed in a private car which had been graciously provided by the Fuhrer; and seventeen military scouting planes welcomed them by flying over in the form of a swastika. As a prelude to their appearance, which was limited to one day, propaganda Minister Goebbels made an unrestrained attack on democracy, and Otto Dietrich, Nazi press chief, carried on with taunts at "the powerless governments of democracy". Dr. Dietrich also paid his respects to the gentlemen of the press, particularly those representing New York papers, whose duty he said it was to "tell lies and bow down in the temple of Mammon". For the rest there were parades and more parades, in which a nation of slaves walked past their master, cheering wildly his threats of war abroad and of hunger at home. That any diplomat of a democratic country should have been allowed, let alone instructed, to witness such a spectacle and thereby passively condone it almost merits the sneer of Dr. Alfred Rosenberg, who also spoke. Democracies, he said, are "piteously shortsighted and terrified as a rabbit before a rattlesnake", which reminds us that of all the name-calling that went on at Nurnberg, Dr. Rosenberg's designation of his leader as a rattlesnake strikes us as the neatest.

Nation, September 18, 1937

ers on a less virulent form of hypothesis arising in Utrecht. Utrecht I found to be a delightful canal city, trim and clean. The Laboratory of Histology and Embryology was the compact and well-stocked abode of an international figure, Jan Boeke. He was very hospitable, and once I explained my mission, he set out two microscopes and we started over his preparations. He lamented the fact that his middle-of-the-road theory of nerve transmission had been streamlined "across the border." This phrase was to mean something by the time I finished my travels in Europe. The Russians used it exclusively in referring to Germany. After a day in Utrecht, I crossed over to Amsterdam, a roaring metropolis with quaint canals and trams that blew a little whistle when about to stop. The profusion of American cars was remarkable, though I could well understand how useful it was to have a long wheelbase when it came to covering long distances on the cobblestones in the Netherlands.

From Amsterdam I took a train to Antwerp, and in typical fashion spent 20 minutes at the border while the officials converted Dutch to Belgian time. This gave me an opportunity to see Netherlands train men shunting freight cars about. Each man was equipped with a little brass horn, slung around his neck, with which he signalled to the engineer of the shunting locomotive. A fellow passenger had just returned from Japan, where he had been sent by his employers in response to persistent complaints that a large automatic telephone system that they had installed was defective. He had been able to save his company a pretty penny by demonstrating that the telephone system had ceased functioning simply because a particularly hungry little Japanese beetle had eaten the insulation off the wires in numerous vital parts. The chief cinema attraction in Antwerp at the time was *Mr. Smith Goes to Washington*. Even with Flemish subtitles on each scene, the audience grasped the significance of the key word "picsillated" and laughed uproariously.

A few miles outside Antwerp, I went to see Colonie Gheel, one of the most remarkable mental institutions in the world. A legend runs that an Irish princess fled from her oppressive father and took refuge in this little Belgian town. She undertook works of mercy for the insane at a small church near the village square. Eventually she was pursued by her father and killed in Gheel. The town has remained the centre for this most humanitarian work. Several thousand non-violent mental cases are placed, by the large state hospital nearby, in the homes of the townspeople, there to live in normal happy surroundings, coming and going to their trades or to their work in the fields daily. The success of this experiment is to be seen in the size

Ignace Jan Paderewski, ex-premier of Poland, caused a sensation in Poland today by issuing a manifesto in grave, admonitory language, warning his countrymen against the introduction of totalitarianism in Poland, which in his opinion would lead to civil war. The manifesto was confiscated immediately by the police. A Warsaw paper publishing it today was seized and not even allowed to explain the reason for its confiscation...

He called for immediate elections, abolition of concentration camps, and permission for the return from exile of Wincenty Witos, ex-Premier. Mr. Paderewski warned his compatriots against believing too much in Germany, which, he said, has "aggressive plans toward Poland."

New York Times, September 3, 1937

The conservative paper *CZAS* was confiscated today for printing Ignace Paderewski's reply to the Government's confiscations of his recent manifesto urging the Poles to resist fascism.

The statement which was reprinted from the *Lille Narodowiec*, the most important Polish newspaper in France, follows: "Having withdrawn from active life in Poland, where further work was made impossible for me, I left with all loyalty a free hand to those who came into power after me. I did not point out their errors. I did not rejoice at news of their failure. On the contrary I waited patiently for positive results of the work of my successors... Alas, however, I waited in vain. In Poland things are constantly getting worse... The Government has declared my proclamation a legal offence. The newspapers which published it were confiscated. There is however, no doubt that it was read by the members of the Government and by all those who will have some day to render account of the present state of affairs."

New York Times, September 22, 1937

Paderewski wrote from Switzerland to the newly formed Labor Party in Poland: "Poland needs a strong government, but only through the people and by the people. The Pole never will be a slave of his ruler. Poland wants no dictatorship." The letter severely criticized the idea of "government by an elite."

New York Times, October 12, 1937

of the outpatient population, and the high standard of the farms maintained by them. Patients are required to keep in touch with the hospital and the psychiatrists in charge, but otherwise they pursue, in this quiet town, as normal an existence as many in New York City — and perhaps even more so!

As I crossed the town square, a youth of about 20 rushed up to me muttering something I could not understand. He held out an oak leaf and put it in my hand. I did not know what this meant, but I gave him a small coin for it. He smiled and bowed profusely. I began to wonder what kind of a town this was, as I continued across the cobblestones. By chance I held the oak leaf up to the light and was amazed to see that an intricate and beautiful design had been worked into the leaf by puncture holes of a fine needle. I felt ashamed of the little I had given for this work of art, and went back in the direction of the incomprehensible youth. But he was gone probably to find another oak leaf and, doubtless, some relief from the cares that beset his mind.

The hospital itself was a large rambling institution, with many modern units, trim barns and gardens. The waiting rooms were filled with remarkable posters, in French and Flemish. One in particular impressed me. It pictured the brain and spinal cord in the body being freed of devils by a large hand coming from a doctor's white coat. Visual education of this sort, concerning the most misunderstood of all diseases, spoke more than words could to the perplexed relatives of many inmates, as they sat waiting to pay a visit. The head of the institution was a modest, well–educated doctor who spoke English well and who knew many of America's leading psychiatrists.

As I boarded the train to return to Antwerp, a burly man got on and asked if I was a doctor. He said he had seen me at the hospital, where he had just taken a patient. He turned out to be a special state policeman, whose duty it was to convey cases to and from the hospital when an escort was definitely indicated. As we passed a monastery with high stone walls, he said: "You see that, monsieur? That is where I used to take them. Yes, with handcuffs. When I took them away, they still needed handcuffs. But now, it is different. I take them quietly to Gheel. And as you see, they don't need me on the return journey. They are able to go home by themselves." Never have I seen a policeman with such conviction in his work. The fact that his heart was in his rather unenviable job was proof enough, if proof were needed, of the success of the Gheel Colony method of treating many of the mentally distressed.

After a busy trinity term with my cats and students, I set out again

Insanity was the order of the day at Heidelberg, with representatives, official or unofficial, of 20 American colleges and universities participating at least passively. Before these witnesses and those of 30 other countries, the 550th birthday of Germany's greatest university was made the occasion for an orgiastic celebration over the dead body of German culture. One touch in the preparations set the tone of the whole procedure. Where Pallas Athene had stood over the doorway of the building presented to the University in 1931 by a group of American graduates and friends... a swastika had been placed, surmounted by an eagle; and in the inscription, "To The Eternal Spirit", the word "German" had been substituted for "eternal". In the third Reich the German spirit means the Nazi spirit, and the Heidelberg orators made it clear that the Nazi spirit in the "higher learning" is the spirit of fascist propaganda. We note with a certain chagrin that the British Universities did themselves the honor of abstaining. We hope the Americans present got their money's worth out of the show - particularly the elevation of the Rector of the University to a captaincy in Hitler's private army.

Nation, July 11, 1936

Liberty remains an essential characteristic of science, and spiritual and intellectual freedom is a necessity for scientists.

Dr. Ferdinand Sauerbruch, Germany's leading surgeon, speaking at Dresden (later involved in the bomb plot vs Hitler)

The epoch of "pure reason", of "objective" and "free" science is ended. Absolute academic freedom is absolute nonsense.

Dr. Ernst Krieck, Professor of Philosophy at Heidelberg, *Nation*, October 3, 1936 for the continent, with a fellow Canadian. We crossed to Ostend in Belgium by ferry, and then started for Stockholm in one of the little half-pint Fiat cars that resembled beetles on the road. The gas tank held only two gallons, so we had to wean the little black chariot. Over the cobbled roads in Belgium and Holland we had to hold on to our teeth, but after dusk we would slip up on to the cycle track parallel to the road and roll along in comfort. At 40 miles per hour, we averaged 52 miles to the gallon, which made for inexpensive travel.

One of the most interesting towns was Delft in Holland. It was famous not only because Antony van Leeuwenhoek invented the microscope there, but also for its famous student corporation, the Phoenix Club. We were invited to a dinner at this palatial club, on the occasion of one of the engineering teachers of the university leaving for the Dutch East Indies. After a very long and very spirited meal, toasts were called for. The guest of honour sought to mystify his audience with an exhortation in Portuguese, a language he had learned during some engineering operations in Lisbon. They really were mystified when I spoke in Spanish.

About midnight we adjourned to the elaborate common room, where an expert accordionist entertained the party until dawn. The Hollanders loved to sing and perform. We eventually lodged in one of Delft's famous student boarding houses, which we entered by climbing in after crossing several courtyards barefoot in order to deaden the sound at such an unorthodox hour. When I awoke I was astounded at the large drawings of all phases of college life on the walls. Evidently an artist with a sense of humour once lodged here, and did a lot to educate generations who were more keen on lying in bed than on formal lectures.

We crossed the frontier into Germany at a rural border post in the north–east corner of Holland. As we rolled up to the simple wooden pole across the road, an elderly German customs official strode out of his hut and beamed down on us through the opened roof of our little car. He must have thought us part of a musical comedy, for he looked under the hood to see if this little road insect had an engine at all. We talked to him but found out nothing about the Nazis. That was something. We wanted none of their "guides" who were assigned to enquiring English–speaking tourists. I had heard sufficient of their function from an Oxford friend to know that they were a pest. This student had been secretary to one of the British delegates at the world's penal congress held in Germany. He had no sooner settled into his hotel in Berlin than two young men dressed in Oxford bags and Harris tweed jackets called on him and offered to drive him around the city in their ancient Austin motor car! They performed the Gestapo assignment to perfection, and only once did their English charge elude them. This was when he ingeniously managed to see the dissident Thaelmann, gaunt and wasted, in a penal institution, which, strangely enough, was not on the list of those to be visited by the congress!

Just at dusk we pulled into a provincial German town and put up at a little inn. The host allowed us to put our car in the stables, but his cows looked annoyed about it. After dinner we talked with the farmers who had gathered for their pipe and beer. The first thing that impressed me was the fact that they were all old men. One man who spoke good English was greedy for news of the outside world. We offered him a newspaper that we had in the car, but he said he would rather have it verbally. It became evident during the conversation that he had been a prosperous cotton trader before Hitler's time. The fact that he was now in this provincial town, miles away from any seaport or industrial town, made us wonder. As often as we would approach that question, he would begin to talk about the soccer matches he had seen at the Arsenal in London, or some lovely scene on the Thames.

The next day we learned what military highways really were. The *autobahnen* running to Hamburg and Bremen were tremendous undertakings. The width of concrete, and the cleared right-of-way, were reminiscent of aerodromes in America. The gasoline stations, which all seemed part of the highway system, carried gasoline made from coal. Our nine-and-one-half-inch motor objected to this, but there was no alternative. As we pottered along at 40 miles per hour, the big open Mercedes-Benz chariots of the Nazi gauleiters whizzed by us with a roar. One big fat devil turned around in the back seat of one of these and gave us a fiendish grin. My mate called him some choice things. When we arrived in Hamburg and pulled up at a restaurant on the main street, we were astounded to find this over-stuffed clown just stepping into his car, and all the people in the restaurant standing to attention. It made us sick, but we sat down and had the specialité de la maison—Hitler's gift to Germany—beans and goat meat!

While I went off to buy some goggles, my friend toured the waterfront in the car. He was almost annihilated by an American woman driving her big car furiously across an intersection. She stopped to apologize, and in the course of the conversation it developed that her husband was employed by the same company as was my friend. With a rather devil-may-care attitude, she pointed out the docks from which the oil had been sent to Italy during the Abyssinian campaign!

Unable to reach the Danish frontier by midnight, we stopped on the outskirts of Kiel. A kindly frau gave us beds on the third floor of her house. There seemed to be a peculiar odour about the place, and a lot of snoring somewhere, but we were dog–tired and were soon asleep. At about daybreak we were awakened by the sound of the frau letting a couple of pigs out of the attic and driving them downstairs and out into the yard!

In Kiel we saw the smooth, gleaming sides of submarines and torpedo boats on the ways in the shipyards. The rivetters filled the air with their din. The town was enjoying a rearmament boom, following the signing of the naval parity agreement with the British government in 1935. Once across into Denmark, we stepped off the highway to commune with nature for a moment. It was not long before the rata–tat–tat of a machine gun cut the air. We retreated to the highway and drove off in a hurry. As we were to find out later, army manoeuvres had been in progress on the border for several months! And little wonder, when the Nazi press in Copenhagen, with its large circulation, openly trumpeted Hitler's claim to Schleswig and Holstein.

Even in 1937, Denmark was facing the same infiltration tactics by the Nazis that I had seen a year earlier in Spain. The German travel agency was the chromium–plated front for the whole show. The press was subsidized heavily by German industries, and, in return, the party line was poured insidiously into every corner of the paper. To refuse was to lose advertising contracts. Then a "German School Committee" was instituted and convened in every important centre, either by a paid Nazi agent, or involuntarily by some poor soul who had holdings or relatives to protect in Germany. Everyone with the faintest connection to Germany was coerced into contributing to the School Committee, where all the money went into the Nazi party funds.

Despite these ominous shadows, Copenhagen was one of the world's happiest cities in 1937. Under starry blue skies crowds danced the nights away at Tivoli, the great amusement park in the centre of the city. At midnight the beautiful tower of the city hall stood out against the summer sky as in a movie set. By day the Vimmelskaftet was thronged with tourists all looking for Scandinavian table sets, Georg Jensen's silver and Royal Copenhagen china. The book shops were of the best, and I wished for a few extra dollars so that I might bring home the wonderful old works of Bartholin on the flow of the lymph in the body. I spent some time at the physiological laboratory attached to the Army Gymnastic Institute, of all places. There, Fritz

The last few days have brought several contributions to the question of Germany's colonial claims. M. Spaak, the Belgian Foreign Minister, last Thursday in the Senate declared the integrity of the Congo to be a fundamental principle of Belgian policy... Portugal in its press, took the same view of Angola. There as in Belgium, German statements were noted that colonies are not demanded from countries which have taken none from Germany. It will be gathered that, in spite of the discreet official record of the talk between Lord Halifax and Herr Hitler, unfounded rumours are rife in Europe that the two statesmen played a game of bargain with other people's possessions as counters.

Times Weekly, December 9, 1937

The semi-official commentator expresses satisfaction that Lord Halifax's report served to set aside certain misunderstandings as to German aims and methods, but suggests dryly that the Fuhrer's speeches should already have created all the clarity necessary.

Times' Berlin correspondent, December 1937

Lord Halifax's visit to Berlin - for the purpose, as he said amid laughter, of seeing the great Hunting Exhibition - was a topic for congratulation at the second annual dinner in London of the Anglo-German Fellowship. The Duke of Saxe-Coburg and Gotha, who is president of the sister society in Germany, was the chief guest, and in reply to the complimentary toast, spoke of the exchange of views by the Lord President and the Fuhrer as of great importance for the relations of the two countries. Lord Halifax, in turn, expressed warm appreciation of the courtesy, frankness, and friendliness with which he was received in Berlin.

Times Weekly, December 9, 1937

Nurses' Hours. The House rejected the Bill by 122 to 111, and gave a second reading to the Quail Protection Bill.

Evening Standard, December 1937

Buchtal was working on the transmission of the nerve impulse to muscle fibres. We talked over the electrical theory versus the chemical theory, and the new Danish contributions to this rather vexed question. I was very impressed by the highly efficient and ingenious approach that this laboratory was taking to the problems of muscle physiology. I was introduced to Professor August Krogh, whose research on the capillaries had won him the Nobel Prize.

I was no less impressed by Copenhagen's art gallery. The sculpture was satisfying and simple, though often on a massive scale. The statue of Hans Andersen's Little Mermaid, sitting on a great rock in front of the Copenhagen Yacht Club, was to me the nicest single thing in Denmark.

In many ways Denmark was a far more enlightened country than any in the western hemisphere. The very complete coverage of social services was but one example. There was a system of public medicine no less extensive than their system of public education. There was something nearer to equality of opportunity in Denmark than in North America, or in class-stratified England. For all the rural nature of the country, with its dearth of high incomes, Denmark took in and sheltered four times as many Spanish refugee children as did any part of the English-speaking world. They were not a powerful country, but they had a heart.

We spent some time at Elsinore, admiring the moated castle where Hamlet is supposed to have walked. The swans swam gracefully below the great drawbridge. The views out towards Sweden from the towers were superb. Yachts skipped lightly over the water, as the gulls dipped gracefully in their wake. The guard at the castle was a droll old man who told us of the flood of Oxford Group visitors he had had. When I asked what impressed him most about these visitors, he pointed to a large statue of Shakespeare in the courtyard and said, "They didn't make much impression on him, they didn't!"

After crossing to Malmo, Sweden, on a ferry, we started up the Baltic coast road, and from then until we reached Stockholm the sea got the better of us. Every little while we would say, "Why are we wasting our time on the road—there's the sea, let's go for a swim." The water was warm and surprisingly unsalty. The cement highways, the evergreens, the little farms cut out of the bush, all brought back memories of British Columbia.

Stockholm may have been dubbed "The Venice of the North," but it is a whole lot better than that. It has all the bustle of a tough new American city. But essentially it has the culture and beauty of the world's great centres. New housing developments had given a real

General Franco is no reactionary. He is about as different as possible from the Fascist with horns and hoofs denounced by our Left-lungers. He is a great gentleman.

J.L. Garvin in *Observer*

Give me your tired, your poor,
Your huddled masses yearning to breathe free,
The wretched refuse of your teeming shore.
Send these, the homeless, tempest-tost to me,
I lift my lamp beside the golden door.

Inscription in the Statue of Liberty, New York Harbor

The conception of a universal community of mankind is in itself an enormous revolution in human thought. But for Jesus this is more than a bare possibility. It is the expression of the true nature of man himself and, therefore, it is grounded in the nature of reality. The creation of the universal family is the meaning of the religious impulse. Therefore it becomes at once the conscious end of all human effort and at the same time the purpose of God for human life.

John Macmurray, *Creative Society*, 1935

community appearance to many large sections of the city. Some very fine modern architecture had been applied to factories, schools and retail stores. And above all, the famed Rathuset gives Stockholm a city hall to compare with any in the world.

The islands and inlets of the sea about which Stockholm is built make for an infinite variety of sea-side terraces, landing stages and bridges. In summer many people sail little craft from their apartment blocks to their work in town. To gain a view of the city, we went up in an observation tower elevator located at a busy corner. The operator was a chubby-faced Swede who wore a bow tie and his cap on the side of his head. I thought to myself, "a telegraph boy for Hollywood." In the course of conversation, it developed that this chap actually had worked for seven years for Western Union in Chicago. I can picture him as he must have been then, pumping his bicycle around the Loop, draped over the handle bars, whistling his teeth out.

In the evening we crossed the harbour on a small ferry to Tivoli where Lawrence Tibbet was singing. Beyond Tivoli we visited Skansen, which had an amazing zoo that covered the rocky side of a ridge. Bear, reindeer and elk lived in their nearly natural habitat. Not officially part of the zoo, but not far off, was a large jitney dance pavilion. The crowd entered the dance floor through turnstiles into which each dropped a small coin. After three vigorous dances, they filed off the floor again while the orchestra regained its wind. The leader of the jazz band announced that he was about to play America's latest hit: "Miss Annabel Lee!" Most of the singing was in English, as were the eructations of a group of tough hombres who had drunk too much schnapps and wanted to tear out the turnstiles. This reversion to the language of the movies when carrying out the acts characteristic of some movies was very interesting.

Finally we climbed up to the tea garden on top of the Skansen area and sat down to eat in one of the lovely cubicles surrounded entirely by honeysuckle hedges. The view out over the harbour, with its twinkling lights and moving ships, was unforgettable. In the distance we could see a great splash of light—the Luma Factory—that had upset the world's electric light bulb monopoly. The music at the tea garden was supplied by a brassy band, which was driven hard by a typical music professor.

I spent several pleasant days at the fine Serafimerlasarretet Hospital, where Professor Olivecrona performed as many as three brain operations in one day. He still had the hustle and bustle of his Baltimore days and had every conceivable time-saving device in his operating room. One morning I joined a group of neurosurgeons from London and watched the professor go in from the scalp to the brain in eight minutes! He was fortunate to work in a country where steel specialties were manufactured—in this case, surgical instruments by Stille. We all bought a supply of this beautifully designed equipment. The hospital had an excellent X–ray department and in every detail the place reflected quiet efficiency and good medicine.

I spent a day at the university in Uppsala and wandered through the gardens of Linnaeus, the father of botanical classification. The university numbered among its members such eminent men of science as Professor Svedberg, a long–haired hypertensive genius with a family of ultracentrifuges in his laboratory. Only those capable of revolving at least 100,000 times a minute are admitted to the galaxy. With the corruption and destruction of true science in Germany, more and more Swedish investigators were turning to Britain and America for postgraduate training. This is not to suggest, however, that Sweden itself had not produced great scientists. In my own specialty of neurology, the names Holmgren and Retzius stand out as first–class contributors.

Finally it came time to take the ship to Finland. Sailing through the archipelago from Stockholm to Abo was reminiscent of the inside passage to Alaska. Many of the islands had summer homes of great beauty; sailboats dipped and swooped everywhere in the clean white spray. The train journey through Finland was like a trip in Washington or Oregon. The farms had been hewn out of the evergreen forests, against which the golden grain waved in pleasant contrast.

The train was crowded with Americans bound for Helsinki and Leningrad. I had crossed with them on the boat from Stockholm and had heard all the news, which they insisted on exchanging in loud voices. One ubiquitous little bantam, wearing a pince–nez and Esquire clothes, struck up a conversation with a tall grey–haired man who was absorbed in the patterns made by our wake. The fussy little gadfly said, "I think we've had enough of that man John L. Lewis back home. I'd like to see him locked up. All these steel strikes! Wouldn't you?" The tall mid–westerner said dryly, "I wouldn't have any opinion, mister. I'm just one of Lewis' organizers!"

Once on the train I thought I was rid of the pest, but we had not travelled many miles before two men and their wives began the barrage all over again. One of the men, as though addressing his Rotary lub in Oshkosh, Wisconsin, proceeded to read from Marquis Child's book, *Sweden: The Middle Way*, while the other heckled him: "You can't do this trip as cheaply as he says. We should have thought of that before we left America." Then suddenly the train came to a stop. The first man jumped out and ran ahead, to see if we were about to be hijacked, I supposed. He soon returned with the news that it was a complete breakdown on the engine's part. "It may take hours to fix. Never mind, though, we're stuck in the biggest farm in Finland!"

Then this extrovert's wife came to life and demanded that he take the camera and get some pictures of the fair-haired Finnish children who had come running to see the train. "Poor Henry" dutifully rounded them up as best he could, but he was annoyed when they laughed at his language. He might as well have been talking Dutch to them. Here he was, probably some respected small town attorney or lodge president in America, running around in a Finnish wheat field at 100 degrees in the shade, to get some pictures that he didn't want anyway! The breaking point came when he returned sweating and mad, only to have his dear wife say: "Oh Henry, take this notebook and get their names. Tell them we'll send them each a snapshot for Christmas." Poor Henry took the book and sadly went out and lay down beside a haystack. The Finnish kids thought he must be crazy and laughed their heads off. Henry lay there against the stack, wishing he were back home at the Elks Club, where no woman could make his life so miserable!

Eventually we reached Helsinki and toured its fine new buildings. The parliament boasted two things: over a dozen female members and electric push buttons on each desk for voting. The mechanical wizards had so arranged it that he who voted twice lost his vote! There was, of course, no mention of the members of parliament serving long gaol sentences for belonging to the wrong party.

Finnish food was wholesome and inexpensive. Modern architecture characterized the enormous central station, as did such Americanized department stores as Stockman's. English was very widely spoken, as was German. As I took the train to Leningrad, I bought a Finnish newspaper. Next to the Basque language, this seemed to me the strangest I had seen. By afternoon we arrived at the Russian border station of Belo Ostrov, and there one stepped into a different world.

Despotism is the essence of my government and it suits the genius of the land.

Czar Nicholas I

Employers will give time to eat. They will give time to sleep, but what they dread giving to their employees is time to think.

G.K. Chesterton

But one day the conscience of society will awaken, and we shall realize that... man has the same claim to mental treatment that he now has to surgical aid. And we shall also come to see that the neuroses menace the health of the people no less than does tuberculosis, and that, like tuberculosis, the neuroses cannot be left to the ineffectual care of the individual himself. When that time comes, institutes and consultation centers will be established and staffed with... trained physicians, so that men who would otherwise give way to drink, women who might break down as a result of overwhelming deprivations, children whose choice would be limited to delinquency or neurosis, may be strengthened... to resist such unhealthy tendencies, and... become capable of social achievements...

Sigmund Freud, an address given in 1918 at the International Psychoanalytic Congress in Budapest, *The Psychoanalytical Quarterly*, 9:164 (1940)

CHAPTER THIRTEEN

Soviet Russia, August 1937

I entered the Soviet Union at Belo Ostrov, on the border of Finland, near Leningrad. The Customs house was a recently completed stone structure with interesting statues and a cut frieze. After buying some roubles and kopecks, I clambered into one of the highboard third–class carriages with the broad gauge tracks. It looked more like a dark restaurant than anything else. Four others got in, and after half an hour we began to roll towards Leningrad. The first thing that struck me was the prevalence of log farm houses and buildings. We began to see women with the usual shawl head–dress, old men driving buggies, horses with queer high yokes, dusty road, and general confusion at the approach of the train. A woman entered the back door of the car and locked it. She began to sweep it out, and we began to think that perhaps this was the children's car on the train. How they piled in: young mothers with two or three hanging on, all extremely polite to each other and to us, no one demonstrative, all minding their own business and trying to figure out the giraffes on the wall. Then in came a school teacher, surrounded by pupils, who stood at the window with him all the way to Leningrad, asking questions about what they were seeing. The train rattled on with its old oil lamps shaking on the walls. All trains in Russia were not to be as picturesque as this, with these ponderous lights, each with a chimney out the roof. We saw two black sheep butting their heads together over a right of way and this delighted the children.

Entering Leningrad we passed over the Niva River, crossed and re–crossed by little bridges. The canals and gold spires stamped this as the city of old Russia. The streets were busy with people who moved briskly, especially before the marauding motors. The 25th of October Street was a fine, wide thoroughfare traversing the city. There were endless squares and some excellent statues from the old regime. Beside the station stood a large statue of Lenin in a characteristic pose, with his thumbs stuck in the armpits of his vest, as though talking to farmers about the price of grain. The great red brick Winter Palace covered an enormous area. A few Ford V–8s whistled by and beautiful trolley buses were constantly on the move.

We were driven in a bus to the Europa Hotel. We had an excellent dinner of wood hen, consommé of chicken, strawberries and cream and some vodka washed down with beer provided by one of the Swedes in our party. The vodka tasted just the way ether smells.

Then on to a sightseeing drive of Leningrad in a big Lincoln touring car. Nearly all the cars on the street in 1937 were four–door sedan Ford V–8s of about the 1935–36 model. They were beginning to manufacture a long Lincoln eight cylinder limousine used for conveying visitors and Red Army generals. It had a radio, heaters, clock, beautiful upholstery, a streamlined body and a noiseless motor.

Four Scandinavian travellers were with me, and the guide talked either Danish or Swedish, while they told me what I could not get from it. We saw the Peter and Paul fortress. This had been difficult to construct because of the water all around the city. We saw the Smolny Institute, which had been the girls' school for the aristocracy, and now served as the home of local government. There was a children's parade going along, with a profusion of freckles and hair–ribbons. Their songs were extremely simple and vital. We passed a palace and yard that had served as an orphanage. We saw a very large and sad Communist funeral. Then to Lenin's small house and the porch from which he made his speeches.

There were a great many women driving trams and practically all the ticket collectors were women. Many others were sweeping the streets. They had a deft way of using the end of the handle in difficult cases. I saw some stalwart women in bare feet shovelling sand in a place where a new road was being made. The people all looked washed and had bronzed faces. We passed the new Communist University, which was said to be the main centre of the humanities. In the downtown area there were annoying loudspeakers blasting out something that was doing no more than keeping the babies awake.

Then to the train for Moscow. There were crosswise sleeping compartments for four. In mine was a lad who had just graduated in law from the University of Michigan; an old man from Estonia who had been in Philadelphia for 30 years; and a woman from New York who was sure the doctors were the cause of this world's troubles, and that sniffing pine cones would cure everything, even Russia.

We arrived in Moscow in the morning to see a city swarming with people, and motor cars with bugle horns blaring chasing the life out of them. Moscow had an elaborate system of first–aid stations and trauma hospitals. There were no motor cars for sale to the general public. The roaring Fords belonged to government offices, factories, hospitals or co–operative farms. A few had been given to individuals by the government.

We were taken to the New Moscow Hotel, on an excellent site on the Moscow River. It looked across the water to the Kremlin, with its high stone walls, terraces and palaces. They are not individually impressive, but the whole walled "city within a city" covering many acres,surely is an historic spot. The Kremlin tower at the entrance from Red Square had chimes that at midnight used to play "God Save the Tsar," but now, oddly enough, played that well–known French tune, "The Internationale." Red Square had its name long before 1917. At the river–end stood the cathedral of St. Basil, like an eastern mosque with bulbous turrets and spires. The high walls of the Kremlin seemed to dwarf the Lenin mausoleum. I had seen this in black and white pictures, but had entertained a complete misconception of it. It was reddish brown marble, with black blocks making the base. The only marks on the whole structure, inside or out, are the Russian characters spelling out the name LENIN, in a brown type of stone set deep in the black marble. One afternoon I heard it was to be open, so I hurried up there and took some medical reprints with me to read, luckily, for I stood in line for an hour before getting in. The crowds who waited after work were simply astounding. They were there in over–alls, shirt sleeves, best clothes, some Chinese in native dress, children and old men and women with white hair. The entrance was into a large marbled hall, then down steps on the left, and through a passage to the very cool main room with indirect lighting. In an east–west direction there was a large glass case with the embalmed body of Lenin resting very naturally in a dark blue suit, looking impressively diminutive. His bald head and little red beard were his chief characteristics. His death while still such a young man must have shaken the new country. As a figure in social history, I can imagine few others in his unique situation. One readily can imagine this blunt little man telling the cheering mobs in 1917: "We shall now proceed to construct the Socialist order."

The other two sides of the square were made up by older buildings, one of which served as a museum of the revolution. The other was to be demolished in time, to make the square twice its present size. Beyond the square, there were a few buildings of the new city of Moscow. These buildings were of white stone, with rather conservative lines. The old surroundings towards the river were of the cheapest junk imaginable. Machines were knocking down great sections of this trash where one of the 19 new bridges crossed the river.

I was having a good time in Red Square with my ciné camera, taking pictures of the different types of people who passed—the Chinese, the Cossacks and so on—when a police officer indicated to me that pictures in the square were forbidden. The same went for the Kremlin and the bridges. I smiled and went on taking them. Ninety–eight percent of the people were wearing European clothes, but now and then one saw Cossack coats and Russian winter hats. Nearly all the little boys had their heads shaved for the summer. In the square preparations were going on for a big Physical Culture parade, with girls making thousands of paper flowers and pinning them to big boards that were then hoisted up on the buildings opposite the Kremlin. I watched a chap hewing a piece of plank to fit the kerb for some sort of temporary platform. He tried driving a spike with a hatchet; when he bent it he just tossed it away woefully.

The people always seemed to be eating. Cafés had very long hours, open until 3 a.m. in our hotel. There were actually shoeshines on the street, as in New York. Food seemed to be distributed from a varying array of stores. Some were beautiful new groceterias into which you could hardly wedge your way, and if you pulled out your money at the cheese counter you might end up down with the crackers, the crush was so vigorous. There were other dark looking places that could not have been turning over much of their stock. Yet all the food selling had to be licensed by the government, and all food sellers given a health examination. In one of the new groceterias, I saw a National Cash Register of the latest American type, while at the butter counter there was a boy working out things on an abacus. The night after the big display I saw an old lady, not a tooth in her head, gathering up broken pieces of wood from the scaffoldings in Red Square, tucking them into her apron to take home for firewood.

I was surprised to see two beggars operating together. One was a woman sitting on a rubbish can. The other was a man who was trying to get money from a crowd of about 200 that had lined up to buy newspapers. I have never seen any phenomenon quite like this line–up for papers as soon as they were thrown off a truck to a newsboy, who sat handing them out leisurely. That and the motor horns needed attention! The traffic lights were regulated at wide corners by policeman in grey uniforms who had control switches. I saw a sturdy red–haired woman doing this one day.

I was delighted to learn that there had been a Basque soccer team playing at Leningrad; it seems they licked the USSR. The Metropole

Hotel seemed to be the place for much dancing and evening dress. "Russia as I saw it through a glass case!" Bill Wells, a Rhodes scholar from Virginia, told me of a visit he made to the Young Pioneers Camp. It was for Moscow children who needed a camp holiday and was financed by Pravda, the newspaper. They were taught singing and dancing, and were playing basketball when he saw them. It seems that a man who raises seven children gets an annual bonus of 4000 roubles! Another friend I met was from the University of Oklahoma. He was the commissioner of education in the Yukon some years ago and now was working on records in Moscow libraries on the history of the Alaska purchase.

Passenger traffic presented a problem in Moscow, even with trams, trolley buses, motor buses and the Metro. I found that women with children invariably were given seats first. Pregnant women merely had to show a card issued by pre-natal clinics to be allowed to enter the tram by the front door. The Metro, very elaborate, had just been completed in record time. The lighting and ventilation were extremely good, while the stairways and wall facings were of beautiful materials. No two stations were alike, some in brown marble, others in pink. And above all, there was no advertising to mar the place. The street-level entrances to these stations were often beautiful, with figures of workers, or industrial or agricultural motifs in stone. Leyland buses like those at the University of British Columbia were still running in Moscow!

I was interested to learn from what small beginnings the large Russian medical research programme had grown. In 1890 the Institute for Experimental Medicine was organized in Leningrad. In 1932 Maxim Gorki called an important meeting of the government representatives and professors in Moscow. They resolved to set up an All-Union Institute for Medical Research, which has since been called the A.M. Gorki Institute. In 1934 the All-Union Institute was transferred from Leningrad to Moscow, and the Leningrad branch was maintained as a special section. A station for the study of primates was opened on the Black Sea coast at Sukhumi.

In 1937 the work in Moscow was being carried on in a six-storey, 500-room building that the government made available. Each department had access to clinical material. The library contained half a million books, and there was even provision for research in medical history. The problems occupying the researchers included: the physiology of "the higher nervous activities," the growth factors in nerves, the physiology of the sense organs, the problem of exercise, metabolism, old age and cancer, the chemistry of protoplasm, the biological effects of radiant energy, infection and immunity, air pollution, standards of medical service and equipment, and experimental cinematography in clinics and laboratories. There were several expeditions at work, such as those on parasitology in central Asia, one on the micro–organisms in the medicinal mud and waters of the Caucasus, and surveillance of the climatic environment study stations in the Arctic and on the southern Crimean coast.

In an effort to unite all the laboratories in all parts of Moscow that were supported by the institute, and to bring all clinical material together under one roof, it was decided to proceed with the building of VIEM, a new medical city on the outskirts of Moscow. One thousand acres of land in the beautiful Silver Birch Forest, on the banks of the Moscow River, were set aside for the purpose.

The laboratory in Leningrad that I visited was that of the academy of sciences. The director, Professor Orbeli, was attempting to re–unite the field of conditioned reflex study with the parent field of general physiology. He had studied at Cambridge, and he and his wife spoke excellent English. About 20 miles outside Leningrad was the village of Pavlova, where Pavlov began his experimental work on animals. The government had provided 200 acres for the development of the work there on conditioned reflexes and genetic factors in the development of the nervous system.

The most important "man" on the farm was the chimpanzee. He had just lost his wife and was said to be studying the New Constitution to see what he could do about it. He had a full–sized bungalow, with great glass walls, or, in the summer, he could run in his large park. He had a playroom and a gymnasium with a rope for swinging. His food was prepared in a kitchen, and he sat up to a little white table on a doll's chair. He had a bedroom with his bed slung on springs that recorded his movements while sleeping. But he was not the only one with good quarters. The dogs had a house with tiled floors that were heated in winter. There was good ventilation and the pens could easily be washed down. Each dog had his little porch in the open air and access to a large running pen. There was even a she–wolf there. Sir Frederick Banting was impressed with the care of the dogs when he visited Pavlov's farm.

There was a large obstetrical unit to ensure that there were no accidents at delivery; for these were valuable animals, some of them having been studied for years. There were "family rooms" from which well–behaved dogs could graduate to "community rooms!"

Duplex houses were being built for 35 researchers, and apartments were being constructed for the technicians. The central dining halls could be converted for cinema use. All the food was grown on the farm. I saw neatly hilled potatoes, and we had honey from Pavlov's bees for lunch. The buildings face west, over–looking a little river around which the old and minute village is built among silver birches. One could easily imagine oneself in the gently rolling hills of Idaho.

In Moscow's VIEM, in a special theatre for about 20 spectators, I saw a film of the action of the muscle fibres in the beating heart of a frog. The magnification was immense: the black. spider–like pigment cells of the heart muscle looked as large as a man's head. We could see the bouton terminal endings of the nerves on the nerve cells of the auricle. When various drugs were applied to the heart, we could see the minute changes in the individual strands that, in the mass, made a great difference. The researchers had been making other films of regeneration of nerves, and of tissue culture growth. How flat the pages of a textbook seem after such a real picture of what is going on in the body. They were very proud of their films, and had good reason to be.

Professor Lawrentjew had just heard from my friend Tello, the director of the Instituto Cajal in Madrid, that he was still working there though the place had been war damaged. We talked in French long and vigorously about our work, and the things we had found in Oxford which had been independently corroborated in Moscow. These were modest fellows compared with the Germans whom I visited the previous Christmas. These men had far better microscopic preparations than their drawings had shown, and I hoped they would use more photomicrographs in their publications.

I had Professor George B. Hassin from the University of Illinois Medical School with me the first day, and he chatted in Russian with the chauffeur all the way out to VIEM. In every laboratory Hassin would snap out some comment that would make the workers roar with laughter. Many of the girls who were just beginning research there spoke good English.

It was a useful thing to have Professor Hassin with me, for he could not only translate everything said by all we met, but he could tell me from his own experience in medical practice in Russia years ago of the great strides that had been made since. I met him in a queer way. I was in a party visiting a collective farm outside Moscow. We were questioning the manager as to facts about the place, and the three language translators were each making such a racket that no one could hear anything. Along the bench from me I heard some awful moaning: "Gash, verdad. This is no use. I was at a better one in Gorki yesterday." A woman next to this fellow told him to keep quiet and listen to what the translators were trying to say. He said he did not need the translators, he could speak Russian. So I thought I would see what he did know. When we went out to look over this farm, I asked him some things about the Gorki farm. He told me a lot and then added something about being an American, and a doctor. So I said I was a medical student and asked where he was from. "From Chicago!" I asked if there were many Russian doctors in Chicago. "Not many!" "Did he know Dr. Hassin?" He stood back and put a queer angle on his cap and said, "I'm Dr. Hassin!" I had only seen him once, at a distance, in Montreal when he staged the best scrap with Archambault, the French pathologist, that the American Neurological Society had ever seen. They had stood on their chairs to shout at each other.

I arranged to meet him again in Leningrad. We went to Pavlova together and had lunch with the Orbelis, where he excelled himself in Russian, greatly to the delight of the other guests. They had just been reading a Russian book that was very popular. Hassin said it was "full of lies." His best crack was "So and so, he's a bold fellow. I like bold fellahs." He met one down in Gorki who would not let him look at something he said he had come all the way from Chicago to see. So Hassin spent an hour giving him a dressing–down, and ended by calling him a "chequista," which is the worst thing you can call a man, for it identifies him with the Star Chamber and its arbitrary powers of old.

Hassin also had some hot names for a fat chap who could not squeeze into a jammed street car far enough to let Hassin on the running board out of the rain. That cost him $2.50 to have his suit pressed. He was sure three pairs of glasses had been stolen from him, but they all turned up in the end, which annoyed him still more! He gave a dinner for his former classmates in Kazan's medical school, including the professor who embalmed Lenin's body. After the dinner, he found his expensive American hat gone!

A very interesting place I visited was the mother and child room at a large railway station in Moscow. It was for the convenience of mothers from the north who had to wait a day, or part of a day, for their train to the south. Children could be left here while their mothers went into the city to shop or to attend meetings. A considerable number of children could be kept over–night if necessary. The travellers who had only a short wait rarely came because of fear of missing a seat in the crowded trains.

The first event for the children seemed to be a shower bath, and the nurses certainly gave them lots of bathing. One easily could tell which child was sad at going away after an enjoyable day, and which child was just bustling to get inside where the music was playing. From the showers and dressing room, the children passed upstairs to the club rooms. They seemed to accept children from three to 12 years of age. Most of the 50 I saw would be from four to eight. There was a very picturesque teacher in a white smock teaching them music, and he was entering into it so vigorously that his face was covered with perspiration. A little girl of about eight was doing a dance in the centre of a large ring, while all the others were clapping out the time with their hands. Not to be outdone, there was one white-haired lad of about three years clapping his hands above his head, then his knees, and then a couple of times with his feet. In one window was a very large goldfish case. The walls had many children's posters, and a large selection of children's books was available. There was a large doll's house, a model railway and a model ship; also a cupboard full of very intriguing toys, with the latch well out of reach (as were the electric light switches).

The cost for the day was one rouble five kopecks. A small tree had been placed in one window, and in a large cage around it there were very beautiful singing birds. On one side of the room there was an excellent painting of children swimming and playing in the surf. The music teacher came for one hour a day. I should think he would need to recuperate for a long time after the energy he put into it.

There was a model house with pictures of Pushkin the poet on the walls. The music hour finished while we were watching, and the children set to work to pull the tables out for lunch. Such a racket as they sensed lunch in the offing!

There was a similar room in each of Moscow's nine railway stations. Right after lunch, the children were all put to rest, and we saw a large room filled with cots. There was, in addition, a room for infants, with various kinds of cradles and cots in it. Most of these had a rod across, from which hung coloured rings that the kids could bite or use to pull themselves up. There were some sets of minute furniture for the braver ones who could barely push around under their own power.

The sleeping room for the infants was separate from the other cot room, and a number of mothers were feeding their children there. The mothers could have a meal on the premises also. Most of them meant business too. I saw one changing an infant right on the receiving clerk's desk! I believe the railway was free to children under six, and a quarter fare until 10 years of age.

Returning at mid-day to the hotel, we saw the usual crush on the trams. There was a man sitting next to the window trying to read with his book half outside the car, but he wasn't perturbed in the least. In that sense the people were very much like those in Madrid: clothes covered with clay, and so deeply immersed in a newspaper or book that nothing else mattered.

We passed some new six–storey office buildings stuck up on cement stilts so that the ground under them was used for parking the cars of the people who worked inside. Men were constantly hosing the streets or sweeping the cobblestones, which made up for the shabby look of many of the old and derelict buildings. The parting shot of the day was to hear an American girl on the bus whine out to another, "Oh, just to be able to buy some good cheap clothes in New York, again." They had the impression that the government owned a lot of the things in Russia!

The next place I visited was the One Day Rest House in the Silver Birch Forest just outside Moscow. It is a section of the Central Park of Culture and Rest. In former times the area was the rubbish dump of the city, but was cleaned up for a large agricultural fair in 1923, and in 1929 was turned into the park. It had a parachute–jumping tower and elevator. In one day, 75,000 people might visit the park, but on the busiest days they have had over 3,000,000. Each of the 23 districts of Moscow had its own park, but this was the Central Park of Culture and Rest. The rest camp here was five years old. It had been taken over from some civil physical training organization. The camp owned 150 boats and had five swimming instructors and playground supervisors. There was a sunny library along one side of the main lounge.

I returned to the centre of the city in a brand new Intourist sedan, which, as I have already mentioned, was like the big Lincolns in America. It appeared that the word "Lincoln" had come to mean a limousine, because of the number of them in use in Russia.

One afternoon we went to see the Thaelmann Collective Farm, about 50 kilometres from Moscow. The place was alive with sunburned children who clamoured for American coppers when Dr. Hassin began to talk Russian to them. I gave a few some Swedish change, and I did not think the rest were going to let me away alive. Dr. Hassin said that it was all very reminiscent of his boyhood in the south, but the difference was that the children now had shoes, each family had a few animals and a garden, and they took the cows in during the winter instead of trusting that they would not freeze to death outside by spring time. He was deeply moved as he thought back over the hardships he had known as a child.

In some ways scientific research and teaching in Russia owed as much to Maxim Gorki as to Lenin. It is no accident that there was a fine bust of Gorki in the main building at VIEM, for it was largely on Gorki's initiative in 1932 that medical research in the Soviet Union was put on a secure footing. This famous writer assembled a conference of eminent medical men, and plans were formulated for the development of something akin to an Institute for the Study of Man. The three basic principles for the medical aspects of the study were just those that many enlightened men in British and American medicine have advocated for years. The first concern was to reunite "in the service of medicine" the many ancillary sciences that medicine had mothered. Second, these men wished to have the very latest developments in physics and chemistry taught to, and used by, medical students wherever they could be applied to the theory and practice of medicine. Finally, and most important of all, the experimenter was to consider the hospital ward as nature's laboratory. The Russians had contrived to teach living anatomy, histology and physiology, and thus had narrowed the gap between the basic laboratory and the university clinic.

What shall one say by way of summing up this unusual country? After a brief visit one is no more qualified to speak than if one had spent a short time in New York or Chicago in an attempt to understand America. But in whatever country, it does not take long to find out the truth, or otherwise, of much that he has heard or read about it. This was my first reaction to Russia. I found that such Hearst–press bogeys as "the nationalization of women" were just brazen lies. Actually, women had more rights—in practice and not merely on paper—than in many of our self–confident English–speaking democracies. These rights were not of the "kuch und kinder" variety enforced in Germany. In Bonn I had found women in the medical college to be absolute rarities, but in Moscow they made up a good half of some schools.

As I wandered around Moscow and Leningrad at night, I came to believe that the Russian people had the same problems to face and to solve as human beings anywhere else in the world. All was not sweetness and light. Over–crowding in Moscow was the rule, not the exception. Passing through narrow alleys, filled with the music of the balalaika, reminded me of some of the cobbled little streets in Madrid. I wondered what it would be like to deliver babies in some of these homes in winter time. My mind went back to the slums I knew in Montreal. The medical care there would be adequate, but would be charity. In Moscow, it would also be adequate, but would be a mother's right.

In summary, I came away convinced that these "once ignorant" people had no need to hide their light under a bushel, for they really had accomplished something. This was no experiment any longer, it was a going concern. Instead of sniping at it, I thought I and others would do well to study it. For one thing was sure: no one was going to take it away from the millions of people of Russia!

1. John Wesley Gibson, 1874–1954.

2. Belle Crawford Gibson, Ottawa, 1912.

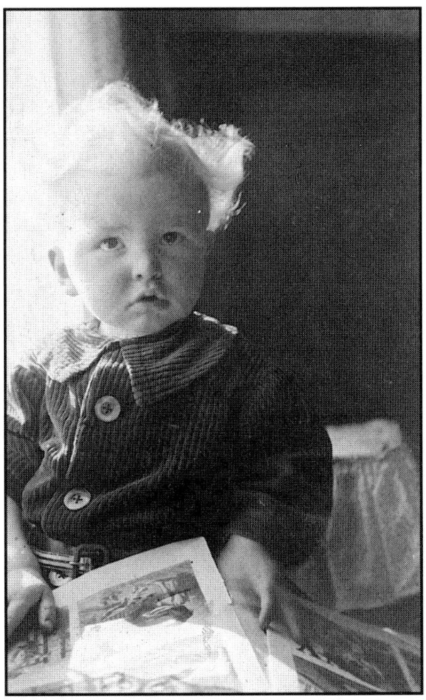

3. William Carleton Gibson, 1½ years, Victoria, 1915.

4. With brother James at Butchart Gardens, Victoria, 1926.

5. Victoria High School, 1929..

6. Four Gibsons, 1931.

7. Four Gibsons, 1942.

8. McGill Master of Science graduate, 1936.

9. New College Garden, Oxford, after Doctor of Philosophy graduation ceremony.

10. Oxford, Doctor of Philosophy, 1938.

11. Wing Commander William Carleton Gibson, Senior Medical Officer, 19 Wing, R.C.A.F., Vancouver, 1959.

12. With Dr. Wilder Penfield, York Lecturer, U.B.C., 1960.

13. Retirement dinner from Kinsmen Laboratory, 1959.

14. Professor of the History of Medicine, U.B.C., 1960.

15. With President Truman Blocker, University of Texas. Medical Branch, Galveston, revisited.

16. With Governor General Vanier and President Dr. James A. Gibson at the opening of Brock University, St. Catherines, Ontario, 19??.

17. W.C.G. in the Sherrington Room, Woodward Library, U.B.C., in front of the Eves portrait of Sir Charles.

18. 1977, World Conference on Mental Health, U.B.C.. W.C.G. with Lloyd Detwiller, D.F.C. Kent Kallberg photo.

19. With student in the Memorial Room, Woodward Library, showing bust of Dr. William Harvey, and in the background, the sculpture by Edward Apt, "The Nurse."

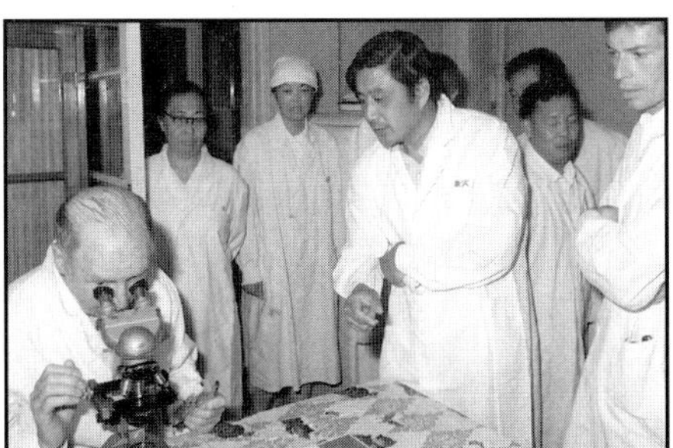

20. At the microscope studying cancer of the liver. Beijing, China, 1980.

21. In the Memorial Room, Woodward Library, U.B.C., 1980.

22. W.C.G. in California (Portola Valley).

23. The Chancellor of the University of Victoria, 1987.

24. Normal School (Camosun College), Victoria, B.C. at Dogwood Tree Ceremony, memorializing J.W. Gibson. September 17, 1986.

25. Accompanying Rt. Hon. Denis Healy at Rockerfeller Study Center, Bellagia, 1988.

26. Chancellor, University of Victoria, 1988.

27. Awarding a prize at Royal Roads Military College, Victoria, 1988.

28.

29. With Cecil Green (r) and Lord Walton, Oxford, 1990.

30. Ian, Kate and David Gibson, U.B.C., 1993.

31. Dr. William Gibson and his wife Clotilde in Victoria.

32. W.C.G. looking to the future in Mystic Vale at the University of Victoria.

CHAPTER FOURTEEN

Third Year Oxford, 1937–1938

I returned to England through Norway and by way of the North Sea. Oslo impressed me as a city with great civic pride. The harbour was large and dotted with yachts, cruise liners and five-masters. Norwegian sailing ships have long been the envy of every boy living on the south coast of England, as he has watched the great winged galleons come up the channel in the grain race from Australia. I crossed the harbour in a cutter to see Amundsen's last ship, which was exhibited in a large hangar. I noticed the early morning ferries filled with office workers on their way into the centre of Oslo. The bright sun and the soft air combined to make Oslo a memorable spot in my travels.

The train south into Sweden was filled with Norwegian families bound for their summer vacations. The flaxen-haired children hung out the windows and cheered as the train set out. I was surprised to hear them saying "Mr. Eden" over and over again. It finally dawned on me that they were watching billboards as we passed, and the first one to spot Anthony's smiling countenance won a point, much as Americans would play "beaver." The signs said, "Get your 'Edens' at so-and-so's haberdashery," Edens being very swish dark suits with the inevitable Homburg hat!

As we rolled south, we passed a station called Ski, and on the hills nearby one could see many large ski-jumps. The sea and the evergreens reminded me of the Washington State coastline. In the fields hay was being put up over wires strung between poles, in order to guarantee a high protein content. Small fields of golden grain were pocketed among the hills. Truly Norway was a placid land, with easy-going, gracious people. It was no accident that Nobel's will stipulated that the Norwegian parliament should award his peace prize annually. In some ways Norway was the most "other-worldly" country he could have chosen, but it was by no means an "isolationist" or backward country. In fact Norway showed more spunk at Geneva than did countries with many times her population. In public education and public medical care, Norway had done wonders. Not that the test of her educational policy should be the number of people who could speak English, but it was remarkable with what perfection the majority of Norwegians with whom I had contact could speak English.

At the old Swedish seaport of Gotenburg, I took a ship for London. The sun was setting as we passed out of this old city of canals and quays into the North Sea. The wind on deck was warm and the passengers, mostly students, danced half the night away under the stars. By daylight everyone on board was sea-sick. Our ship was set upon by a violent storm that lasted until we reached the Thames estuary. Passing up the Thames again was to be reminded of the passing show of the port of London. Ships from every imaginable corner of the globe rubbed noses here. It was hard to realize that the harmless little stream that wandered through Oxford was the parent of this bustling inland sea.

As the passengers left the ship at Tilbury, they were bluntly separated by two burly constables into "Them as been to Russia, and 'em wot's not." So I was with "'em as 'ad" and was ushered into an office where the pride of the British civil service sat as if made of wax. This ambitious young Whitehaller, to judge by his manner, was practising to be a B.B.C. announcer. Immaculate in his "Edens," he looked at me as through his eyelids, and with a bored "Good afternoon" began thumbing through my passport. Then he began to write down details in a little book, as if to teach me a lesson. Then with a faked air of enthusiasm he asked, "How did you like Russia?" I looked as bored as possible and concentrated on the ceiling as I replied, "It was very interesting indeed." This "brought him to" in a hurry and he looked as if he would have liked to knock my block off. Then he said, "Precisely why did you go to Russia?" "Precisely because I was sent there," I replied. This was too much for one of His Majesty's servants, fresh off the assembly line at Oxford. He handed me my passport and showed me the door with icy respect. I climbed into the train and had a good laugh.

After a visit to my cats in the laboratory at Oxford, I went off to the New Forest for a week. I had expected it to be a mesa full of wild ponies, kicking up their heels. But actually it was a peaceful, park-like expanse with Scotch pines and oak trees and a lovely river flowing by. Salisbury Cathedral was not far away, and a visit there was well worthwhile. There were several camps of gypsies in the forest, but their campfires were rather tame in comparison with one I visited, where dozens of otherwise sedate university people chanted the song that is the delight of all English children: "There's a hole in my bucket."

I spent a day at the Basque children's camp near Southampton. The supervisor of the camp was an old soldier whose chief claim to fame was that he was named T. E. Lawrence. After looking at blonde Norwegian children, it was certainly a change to see these dark, saucer-eyed Spanish youngsters. They were shy and secretive until they found that I could speak Spanish. Then they were on to me like a pack of wolves, pulling my shirt out and being very exuberant. The busiest man in camp was the barber, and though he worked as one inspired, he saw little hope of shearing from this mob of children enough of their thick black hair to make any real difference.

I crept up behind one little girl of about six years old, and took movies of her washing some clothes in a bucket with a big red bar of soap. When she saw me she only smiled, and went right on washing, as much as to say, "I'm busy!" The absolute naturalness of these young children, as of all children in Spain, has never ceased to amaze me. It recalled a conversation I had during the Spanish war with a five-year-old in Santander. This sunburned little lad was sitting on the beach near La Magdalena cracking shellfish with two stones. I asked him if there would be bread that day in the city. There had been rumours that the bakers were off to the war. He began: "Well now, sir, I wouldn't know. I'm not much of these affairs. But you could ask my oldest brother, because my oldest brother, he's 'un gran político.'"

Just before Oxford term opened I went off to Scotland, up the west coast and down the east. Loch Lomond was one of the most peaceful and satisfying things in the whole of Europe. The mist rising from Ben Lomond in the early morning and the friendly tinkle of the cowbells on the farms at the water's edge were things to remember. I stopped to talk to farmers about their cattle, but I could hardly understand some of their dialects. When I came to Glencoe, I could well understand why William Osler had described the view as one of the greatest prospects on earth. This was the home of Donald Smith, who emigrated to Canada and became Lord Strathcona, a builder of the Canadian Pacific Railway and chief benefactor of McGill University.

The Scottish moors were purple with heather. The spring water tasted of heather. The air was full of heather. Even the honey sold in the tea rooms tasted of it. And truly, how could one forget such a sea

Advice to Agressors

Meine Herren and Signori,
Clients of the British Tory,
Kindly note that Number 10
Requests your patronage again,
Opening, as from today,
As Chamberlain et Daladier,
Messrs, Hoare, Laval, successors,
For doing business with aggressors.

Frontiers promptly liquidated,
Coups d'etat consolidated,
Pledges taken and exchanged,
Acquisitions rearranged,
Loans on Fascist risks advanced,
Nazi enterprise financed,
European intervention
Given personal attention.
Have you problems of partition?
Let us send a British Mission.

Breaking with Geneva's firms,
We offer Nazis favoured terms;
Let us lend to back your claim,
England's honourable name;
For dirty deals both great and small
Our representative will call.
Orders carried out with speed,
Satisfaction guaranteed.
We obsequiously remain,
Daladier et Chamberlain.

1938

Humanitarian

As Franco's high explosives rain
From Barcelona's falling skies,
The Premier, recklessly humane,
Expostulates with his allies.

The world his pious horror hears,
But for that overflowing grave
It falls unheard on murdered ears
And mocks the dead he feared to save.

Saggitarius, 1938

of colour, stretching off to the horizon, in places broken by the clear blue of a loch? I visited friends at Dornoch who instructed me in Gaelic, which seemed to have some words in common with the Scandinavian tongue I had recently heard. More important still, they saw to it that I ate enormous quantities of the real oatmeal ground in the Carnegie's mill at Skibo Castle. They gleefully reminded me of Dr. Johnson's definition of oats as something fed to men in Scotland and horses in England. The rejoinder: "That's why Scotland has such good men, and England such good horses." These were true Scots, with a fierce pride in their countryside and its natural beauties.

The father, therefore, sent the sons out every morning on bicycles to tear down all the Daily Mail posters they could find on trees and rocks along the highway. Even Lord Rothermere and his airplane that brought the post daily were not welcome. I began to believe that these Highlanders were determined folk when I saw the ruins of the early stone factories that their forefathers had torn down at the beginning of the Industrial Revolution. They were hard-bitten men, bound that no devil-inspired machines and factories would pollute the Scottish countryside. This was one of the factors contributing to the gradual depopulation of Scotland. The reason usually advanced, however, is that Scots were needed to run London—and run it they do!

I returned from this vacation to the country that was more familiar to me via the Great North road. The scarred face of the mining regions and the over-crowded tenement areas were as depressing as ever. Towns like Rugby were a madhouse in which to drive, so full of cycles were the streets. In Oxford the same old scene was repeating itself: parents depositing their heirs at college gates, freshmen looking lost and forlorn, and the knowing old scouts saying as of yore: "You remind me of your father, sir. Many's the time I put him to bed, the worse for wear, sir. Roll call at eight in the morning. Good night, sir."

The atmosphere in Oxford was quite different from that of the previous year. By 1938 people were beginning to feel that something was slipping through someone's hands somewhere. Prophets were being proven correct in international affairs so constantly that they had little left to prophesy about. Except for one thing—the inevitable. The more "the undertaker from Birmingham" said, the more it was borne in upon our minds that the old gang in power had no guts.

While the five men who controlled London's 10 million morning newspaper circulation prattled away about the Anti-Comintern pact,

From the Japanese note to America–February 12, 1938: The Japanese Government always were prompted by a spirit of non–menace and non–aggression and have no intention whatever of possessing armament which would menace other countries.

New Yorker, March 5, 1938

Remarkable scenes were witnessed at Linz, where great mass meetings awaited Hitler's arrival. Armoured cars rattled over the cobbled streets as 300 war planes zoomed overhead. When it was announced at one of the meetings that Mr. Ward Price of the *Daily Mail* had arrived, cheering went on for nearly a minute. In broken German, Mr. Price congratulated Austria on her "hour of happiness.

Reynold's News, March 19, 1938

Miss Unity Mitford.... Since her return to England she has had tonsillitis and loss of voice due to the strain she put on her vocal cords shouting "Heil Hitler" during the Fuhrer's entry in Vienna.

Evening Standard, March 26, 1938

We reject illusions and Utopias and for this reason we have left the shop that sells them at Geneva. That which always has counted and still counts among peoples is their war-making potentiality. We place spiritual power in the first line of our potentials. It never was so deep in Italy, so widespread, so ardent and so willing as today.

Mussolini's speech to the Senate, Rome, March 30, 1938

Hitler moved ever closer to his oft–declared objectives. It became harder to sit through the debates at the Union, where the chief appeasers in the Conservative ranks sought to persuade us that Britain was awash with Jonahs, and that in truth all was well and order was being maintained. In fact the antics of the cabinet reminded me of the way in which "the respectable" in Germany 10 years previously had tried unsuccessfully to placate their then–domestic gunman and racketeers. The Nazis gouged unwilling German donors for large and repeated donations to party funds. To refuse was to be branded as a Communist supporter, since by definition the Nazis were divinely charged with a great cleansing mission. By 1938 neighbourhood blackmail and racketeering had become international, and any move to kerb the wanton ambitions of the Axis was heralded as "bloody revolution."

In Spain the struggle was coming to a sad impasse, later to end with the surrender of the exhausted elected government. Mussolini was quick on the trigger and began compiling Franco's bill for services rendered. According to the Italian press, it covered: 763 planes, 1,930 cannons, 10,135 automatic guns, 240,747 small arms, 7,514,537 rounds of artillery ammunition, 324,900,000 rounds of small arms ammunition, 7,668 motor vehicles, 2 submarines, 4 destroyers and 4 armed motor boats. Germany was more subtle. She just took over the copper and mercury production of Spain, set up a few submarine bases and prepared to ruminate over what her forces and engineers had learned in their Spanish dress rehearsal.

One highly diverting pastime that fell to me was that of digging out material from the Public Records Office in Chancery Lane for my historian brother in Canada. I fear I was their most unorthodox customer, breaking into the place before the opening hour of 10 a.m. and then proceeding to take notes with a fountain pen—the forbidden instrument! Such an array of bookworms it would be hard to duplicate. Several old ladies with pince–nez and poker faces were bent double from 10 till 4 every day, searching out titles, documents and historical miscellany. Then there was a large group of Indian students who kept unwinding long scrolls and complaining about the lighting. At noon there was a frightful rustling of lunch papers, and the bread and cheese of all the students from Bloomsbury was spread on H.M. Records. I thought my fountain pen an innocent corrupter of the king's parchments compared to the food. By noon I would become so tired of the smell of old books that I would go across to Mr. Lyon's establishment for lunch. One had to squeeze into a sea of bowler hats for a bite to eat. There was no need to look at

As a result of rather exhaustive investigation on the spot, I came to the conclusion that the magnificent principles of the American Bill of Rights will be religiously respected by General Franco and his advisers.

Rev. Joseph Thorning, Baltimore *Sun*, April 18, 1938

As far as we are concerned we do not believe in a democratic liberal regime.

General Franco, April 20, 1938

Spain has shown once again that at the moment when the masses in any country are within grasp of real emancipation and freedom, the army and the church and royalists and aristocrats and white–collar classes will turn on them with cannon, and if necessary call in foreigners of even black troops to help suppress them.

For some reason Franco is popular in England. Madrid is an execrably bad propagandist and the word "red" is coming to have such hypnotic force that it blinds people to all reason, and produces such oddities as the letter written to an English newspaper by a rabbit-trapping reader who said, "All this talk about the inhumanity of spring–traps is nonsense and in my opinion Bolshevik money is behind it."

Douglas Reed in *Insanity Fair*, 1938

Carl Von Ossietzky Dies in a Berlin Hospital. Nobel Peace Winner of 1935 Was Imprisoned by the Nazis as 'Enemy of State'" So ran the headlines on May 5, 1938. They should have read: Carl Von Ossietzky murdered by slow torture lasting more than five years; his teeth knocked out with a Hitler pistol; his liver smashed by a Hitler boot; his lungs destroyed by tuberculosis.

the menu; it was the same from Land's End to John O'Groats.

I learned a lot at the Records Office despite the work I was supposed to be doing there. The porters talked football with such enthusiasm that I decided the Arsenal was the place for me. So I went out there on the tube one Saturday to the best soccer match against West Bromwich Albion that I ever expect to see. The crowds were enormous, and the alternations between rabid cheering and well-known hymn tunes was something that must be heard to be believed.

Most of the long-hand copies of letters from the famous Bulwer-Lytton to his henchmen out in the wilds of Canada were just polite business transactions, but now and then I came on one that made my eyes pop. One day, while reading along as innocently as I knew how, I came upon a letter from Sir George Cornwall Lewis, editor of the *Edinburgh Review*, to Sir Edmund Walker Head, later to become Canada's Governor-General. It was written from Malta, October 8, 1837, and said, in part: "The scum of England is poured into the Colonies: briefless barristers, broken-down merchants, ruined debauchees; the offal of every calling and profession are crammed into colonial places." I began to think Chancery Lane a dangerous place.

In the laboratory in Oxford I was packing my specimens one morning, preparing to return to McGill to complete my medical degree, when Professor Howard Florey came into the laboratory. He told me that I was staying in Oxford for another year! Because we often talked hilariously about our experiences at the Instituto Cajal, I laughed at his jesting, then he said: "You see, we need eight students if we are to offer six months of clinics here at the Radcliffe Infirmary. I have seven, and you are number eight."

Thus, with the seven other guinea pigs, I took the clinical course for credit at Oxford. Clinics were given out of term at the Radcliffe Infirmary, and lectures in pathology and pharmacology were given in term. A more informal course never existed. The clinics were excellent, quite the best I have attended in some subjects. Others were like radio talks from another world—but none the less humorous. Old Papa Malam used to twiddle his big gold watch chain while he chided us for not knowing how many teeth a baby should have at a certain age. His son, a great rower, cursed us for knowing so little about oarsmanship. F. G. Hobson gave us first-class lectures and bedside clinics, while the inimitable Abernethy told us of his Mrs. Jones, who was always having seizures while crossing the main thoroughfares of Oxford. One evening after the lamps had gone on in Holywell, the traffic was stopped by one of Mrs. Jones' bad spells,

Dealing as we clinicians do — from our several lines of approach — psychiatric, neurological and neurosurgical — with the most important subject in medicine, how can we expect to make unimpeded progress and meanwhile rid ourselves of the subtleties and futilities that beset us unless we advance together as a common group along some new path? What each of us has to contribute we must generously share, and at the same time, being members of the same family, it may be permitted to discuss our separate origin and trends without misunderstanding or giving offence.

Harvey Cushing, M.D.

The characteristic activity of this closing medical epoch is its emphasis on the treatment of existing disease. We wait and watch for diseases to appear, ready to devote ever increasing knowledge and skill to its cure. The idea of health as a form of beauty and necessary for physical, moral and even spiritual exhilaration, scarcely enters into our thoughts. We do not yet regard the large mass of illness with a sense of social shame as we look on material ugliness. Complacently we see ill-health and sub-health around us as a necessary evil but a new consciousness of the scandal of preventable disease would turn our energies into the direction of prophylaxis and the final eradication of the fundamental causes of ill-health, whether they be social or individual.

Medicine must first proclaim the futility of employing most of its energies in treating end-results, and put forth a new enthusiasm for prevention, by an attack on all the many fundamental social evils out of which so much disease arises. It must teach the ideal beauty of health and the ugly cruelty of disease. Concentration on the paramount necessity of prevention must be the characteristic of the new world which is coming. The new emphasis on positive health will afford medicine a place of dignity and opportunity for service in the state second to none. Let us see to it that we shall be ready.

Aleck Bourne, M.D. in *The Lancet*

smack in the middle of the street. "Abers," who was passing at the time, ran up to see if he could do anything and recognized his hysterical patient. He shouted, "Mrs. Jones get up off this street and go home," whereupon the crestfallen Mrs. Jones did just that.

There was one lecture I shall never forget. The much–beloved Rose–Innes gave us a good solid hour on tuberculosis, showing us numerous X–ray films and detailing the history of the case minutely. Then, he said quietly: "I'll not be lecturing to you again. The films I have just shown you were taken of me yesterday. The history I have just recited was my own history. Good luck and good–bye." Everyone closed their eyes as he walked out of the lecture room, and we trooped home that night in silence.

The outpatient clinic was an ever–changing show. Dr. Alec Cooke impressed courtesy and cleanliness on us from the beginning. Sometimes we had to restrain our spirits when some particularly fantastic story was told by the patient. The most interesting case I remember was that of a destitute old lady who was cared for by a religious order in the city. She had an umbilical hernia that would fill a laundry basket. The professor asked how long she had suffered from this affliction. She said it occurred on the day of King Edward's coronation! We reminded her that Edward VIII had never been crowned. She said, with a little sigh, "Ooh man, I mean Edward VII!" At that time she had been a housemaid in London and had watched the coronation procession from the top of a kitchen table placed near a window. When the parade was over she gaily jumped down, and most of the large and small intestine burst through the abdominal muscles at the umbilicus. Only a thin layer of skin covered them from that time until 1938! This was a rare opportunity to study the peristaltic waves passing down from the stomach. The surgeons cured her hernia 28 years late! There were other less spectacular, but equally instructive, cases on the wards. At the Osler Pavilion on Headington Hill, we saw the ravages of tuberculosis. England's lack of pasteurization laws came home to me then with a jolt.

In the autumn of 1937, my teacher, Río–Hortega, had been brought to Oxford by the Nuffield group of professors. Hugh Cairns, the Nuffield professor of neurosurgery, built him a superb laboratory and furnished it exactly as his former laboratory in Madrid had been. What a headache it was to translate Don Pio's plans from centimetres to inches for the English carpenters! But when it was all finished we had a fine laboratory. One of my functions was to teach the great professor English, but there was no opportunity. Don Pio spoke a very beautiful and persistent Castillian, and I was afraid to talk

There can be no doubt that practically the whole of the free exchange available to Germany for the purchase of raw material was supplied directly or indirectly by Great Britain. If the day of reckoning ever comes the liberal attitude of the British Government in this matter may well be responsible for the lives of British soldiers and civilians.

World Finance, 1938–39

Last week the *Saturday Review*, the 'blood and culture' paper had a review about my book (*Das Kapital*) in a review of recent German books. I have come off pretty well, as you will see from the following passage: 'The author's views may be as pernicious as we conceive them to be, but there can be no question as to the plausibility of his logic, the vigour of his rhetoric, and the charm with which he invests the driest problems of political economy.' Ouff.'

Karl Marx to Dr. Kugelmann, January 30, 1868

The somewhat socially conscious nephew of a solid Boston lady last week met her at one of the North River piers upon her return from Europe, and on the way back through the West Side tenement district took occasion to remark, more in the spirit of discussing an interesting phenomenon than anything else, that some of the people who lived there lacked hot water, central heating, and in extreme cases even baths. "No baths?", said the lady from Boston, eyebrows lifting. "You'd think that they'd make inquiries before they moved in."

New Yorker, April 23, 1938

back to him in English. His experiences with our language were not always happy. He believed in observing Spanish customs on the Oxford streets, and when passing acquaintances would wave his hand and call out "Good–bye," the literal translation of the casual greeting one gives in Spain! Consequently, everyone was moved to laughter as they encountered him in the Banbury Road or in the Cornmarket.

Don Pio's "bodyguard" was the dashing Nicolas Gomez, a sort of Spanish Douglas Fairbanks. No knowledge of Spanish was necessary in order to understand this swashbuckling hombre with a black beret and a black moustache. In Madrid he really had been a character, appearing at the theatre or at the cafés in his cloak. He could smile a smile that would break one's heart. When he talked about Chamberlain you could tell he was swearing. When he was buying vegetables in the market and cakes in Little Clarendon Street, he was the idol of the toothless old ladies.

One Saturday afternoon Nicolas was paying a visit to the second floor of Woolworth's store in the Cornmarket. He called this "the Promised Land," for he loved to look over the gadgets for sale, most of which he had never seen before. He was buying seedling plants, as he later told me, and as usual the moist earth ate through the bottom of the large paper bag in which the plants were carried. He cursed so vehemently in Spanish that an amused Scot and his wife came up to help him. The man bought him a heavy shopping bag and helped to pick up the plants. The bon vivant Nicolas was full of smiles as he told the lady in Spanish that he "kissed her feet." He says the pair invited him to tea with them, but he, the great bullfighter, had no use for such pastimes—he must go forth to till the soil! Actually, he knew he had still to buy the vegetables for the household, and was guilty of having dawdled away the afternoon inspecting gew–gaws and sixpenny wonders.

The political news became so depressing as the spring turned to summer that I felt the need for some diversion from cats, patients, B.B.C. announcers and school papers. So I set about making a garden behind the Schola Rustica. (Ernie Weeks and John Cripps looked on with amusement from their statistics offices.) After digging up endless tiles and bricks from some former college pathway, I had the ground ready for the seeds. The great Nicolas had come to show me how an artist planted lettuce "como no!" My flat garden was all wrong. There was no culture to it. So Nicolas divided it into four plots, which he banked up with earth, leaving neat little paths between. After we had planted the lettuce, and some of his beloved garbanzos (chick peas), Nicolas stood back and proudly surveyed "his" garden. The moon was coming up and the sky was clear blue. He said, "It reminds me of a cemetery," and writing with his finger in the earth, he labelled the four "graves" Hitler, Mussolini, Franco and Chamberlain!

Third term whistled by as I sent in my doctorate thesis to the examiners, half praying that they would turn it down and save me the large graduation fee. Clinics mercifully stopped, so that I could concentrate on my cats and on the students in the laboratory. During the day the latter moved as in a trance, having spent half the night on the river drifting in punts, dreaming and loafing, trying to get up courage for the finals. On Sundays the shrill little gramophones outdid the bees in the lovely meadows along the Isis.

The American Rhodes men took a bus to Lady Astor's estate at Cliveden and came back more determined to fight Hitler than ever! The medical students among them were rubbed the wrong way by various cultist remarks. The friends of Spain were angered by the charmed view taken of Hitler's conquest of Europe's greatest store of copper and mercury. The mid–westerners fumed over the "waste of good land" at Cliveden. The historians were revolted by the Lindbergh isolationism. The climax was reached when a younger member of the family asked a visiting lord why Americans played jazz on the family piano and behaved so queerly. The reply was, "You must realize, they are from all classes!"

One afternoon, as I was finishing an operation in the laboratory, some Canadian friends dropped in on their way to Scotland. They had been studying in London all year and wanted one whirlwind trip around the island before going back home. I signed on without much persuasion, and off we went, stopping the first night in Birkenhead. Then on to Loch Lomond, dear old Glencoe again, spending the night at Ballachulich! The charming old grandmother with whom we stayed spoke Gaelic. Before we left next morning we lined up by the hearth and she read us, in the most beautiful tongue imaginable, the Twenty–Third Psalm. I really admired the dour, independent Scottish people. Life might be hard in Scotland, but there was an equality of opportunity, especially in education, that possibly was greater than their southern cousins enjoyed.

We stopped in the glen near Killiekrankie to make some tea, and in pulling some bracken to kindle the fire, I got a splinter or a thorn in the pulp of my right thumb. In Edinburgh I went to the outpatient clinic to have it taken out, but the girl who was in charge of surgery could not find it because of the blood and swelling. While she probed around an American student came into the surgery and said, "Whuz wrong kid?" He came from Indianapolis and sounded like a Yankee newscaster.

I arrived in Cambridge in time to hear Chamberlain's long–awaited, but pitiful, pronouncement on foreign policy. He was continuing the old line: "solid for fluidity." I had lost all respect for this arteriosclerotic old man since he tried to pooh–pooh Henry Stimson's book, *The Far Eastern Crisis*, in parliament. It did not mince matters, and held the mirror up so that the world might see the results of crass opportunism in foreign politics. There was little to be done now, but most of us hoped in our hearts that the Simons, the Londonderrys, the Hoares, the Amerys and the Chamberlains would get it when it came. We knew in our hearts that many of our generation would get it first.

Graduation was the usual circus. The public orator filled the Sheldonian with Latin patter as the students whistled and stamped. There was the usual tying of undergraduate gowns together, the inevitable stiff collar off its trolley, and the age–old horseplay when it was all over. I graduated with a learned–looking bunch of fellows, and felt distinctly out of place when I read the titles of some of their doctoral theses. My brother's thesis in history I knew well through assisting in its final production. He also received his D.Phil. degree in 1938.

Term came to a close with the "finest dance ever given at Rhodes House." The weather was perfect, the stars were out in myriads, and the band played on! Three years rushed past in our minds as we took leave of the friends who made Oxford so good and so enjoyable. As the homeward bound trans–Atlantic gang trooped aboard the Empress of Britain, all felt an awful sag in the rope. One of life's great adventures was over—all save the memories.

CHAPTER FIFTEEN

Farewell to Europe

A peaceful Atlantic crossing to Quebec gave me leisure time—the first in three years—in which to think back over my European adventure. I gave up reading the ship's news, for it was heavy with the results of blundering in British foreign policy. I tried to forget the immediate present in order to cast my mind back over the period that had passed since I gave up my fishing in 1935 and went off to England.

Naturally, most of my thoughts revolved about the British Isles, since I had spent most of my time there and my forefathers had come from these shores. For the rest of Europe, there seemed to me to be one common denominator, one underlying factor that gave meaning to what I had seen: the German octopus. Spain was by way of becoming a German pawn. France and the Netherlands were pathetically hamstrung in politics, but were still great storehouses of culture and of the free spirit. The Scandinavian countries were having trouble with a few noisy Nazi mosquitoes, but for the most part lived tranquil lives. The Soviet Union was different: it knew it was fighting for its life. Treated as a leper in Western Europe and hailed as an easy victim by the Nazis, Russia set to work to brace herself for the inevitable thrust from across the border. The scientists with whom I had most contact in Russia made no bones about it. They simply said: "How can we ask for more new laboratories? What we need is an army. That now seems to be the only way to stop Hitler." And this had been their view in 1937! As I was later to discover, these very men were soon to be engaged in aviation medical research. By January 1939, 30 of them had published a textbook on the physiology of flight that was to become a classic. (It was translated for the Royal Canadian Air Force by Flight Lieutenant Iser Steiman.)

First, about England. I was thankful for the opportunity of studying at Oxford. In that atmosphere, despite many outward signs to the contrary, serious work was going on in every branch of science and learning that comes to mind. True, isolation from the world of hard fact was evident, but, on the whole, life was simple and devoid of the dull routine of London traffic, tubes, tenements and fog. To be able to go up to London in an hour's journey suited me. The day–return fare was cheap enough and the only disadvantage was that one was sure of meeting the dean of the medical school on the 4:30 train.

To have access to the library of the Royal College of Surgeons, the British Museum and Oxford's Bodleian was to be spoiled for the rest of one's life. Not to mention the English booksellers in the Broad at Oxford and around Great Russel Street in London! Blackwells in Oxford and Heffer's in Cambridge have long been institutions in the reading world, and thanks to their generosity to undergraduates they reap large accounts, mostly collectible in time.

Many an over–seas student has sighed after a few weeks at Oxford that what the place needed was a few executives to organize it and make it more efficient! How many young campus bucks have cracked their heads against the stone wall of tradition trying to bring the good news up the Thames!

But of the larger, more real England, what? I could only feel sad at the way things were going. And this sadness was merely because there was an alternative—things could have gone very differently since about 1931. Though Russia or Mars or Utopia might be painted as the bugbear, the real nightmare of the governing class was the great mass of 40 million Englishmen who lived on a mere pittance. The chronic and settled state of malnutrition that Sir John Orr showed to exist in the bulk of the working population was no mere accident.

The British attitude to public health puzzled me greatly. Despite the works of Jeremy Bentham, Southwood Smith and Sir John Simon, the public conscience had been little disturbed over the scandalous prevalence and transmission of tuberculosis in England. Men such as Patrick Manson and Ronald Ross, who were among the best–known British medical scientists, elucidated the nature and cause of malaria and thus made great areas of the colonial empire habitable. The great men in public health in England still remained relatively unknown and unheeded among the populace.

Just before leaving England, I visited the home of Dr. Charles Singer, the medical historian in Cornwall. One evening we had a chance to see the disparity between military and useful history. His daughter was mumbling some dates by the fireplace as she tried to prepare for school examinations. The events she was trying to commit to memory were:

1662	Act of Uniformity
1665	War with the Dutch – The Plague
1667	War with France
1670	Secret Treaty of Dover
1685	Battle of Sedgemore
1688	Flight of James II

Her father took up his pen and wrote down the dates which he would consider important in that period in history. These were:

1662	Founding of the Royal Society ("The only wise act of Charles II")
1664	Willis and Wren's book on the blood's circulation to the brain
1665	Hooke's *Micrographia*
1671	Draft of Newton's *Method of Fluxions*
1673	Leeuwenhoek's work on the red blood corpuscles
1674	Morland's Water Pump (The self–registering barometer)
1676	Newton's work on prisms
1687	Newton's *Principia*

It was indeed an instructive lesson in what we expect children to study in their tender years.

The British Broadcasting Corporation is one of the useful enigmas that has grown up on a parallel line to parliament's, but been little influenced by it. The services rendered the nation, day in and day out, are of a very high quality. At first it is amusing to an American to hear a British announcer say profoundly, "There will now be a delay of two minutes." But soon it becomes a relief to him to know that as soon as Brahms or "In Town Tonight" is finished, there will be no gush of words about soup, soap, kidney pills or floor wax!

This is as well, for the English take their wireless very seriously. I read a letter in *John Bull* by a man in Streatham who complained bitterly of the German propaganda against England and her dominions, which was cluttering up the ether. He said that he had tuned in at 10 p.m. on a certain night and heard a high–ranking Nazi haranguing a crowd of obviously hysterical supporters about Germany's right to colonies. The listener said he knew no German to speak of, but he could catch the repeated references to England and Canada, and was convinced that either Hitler or Goebbels was inciting the Germans to violence against us. As usual the letter said all this was monstrous and must stop. The editor of "John Bull" appended a little footnote to say that what his correspondent had been hearing, with such disgust, was a German re–broadcast of the European hockey finals between Canada and England being played a few blocks from his home in London at Streatham Arena.

While the B.B.C. did perform a great service, the severity of its censorship of material was challenged frequently. John Macmurray, the well–known London professor of philosophy, was asked to give another of his annual series of broadcast talks over the B.B.C. and chose as his subject "The Christian Process in History." His manuscript was scrutinized by some great mind who simply scribbled "Communism" across the front page and returned it. Mr. Baldwin and Mr. Chamberlain made good use of the B.B.C., but no varying views were welcomed. However, J.B. Priestly did manage to sandwich in a little realistic material as the world got started on the toboggan, and as a result he was one of the most hated of all broadcasters among the Tory blimps.

The National Trust was developing rapidly when I left England. It was a body to which citizens could leave their property for the enjoyment of the public under specific conditions of taxation and tenure. It had given the people of England one means of preventing large estates, which had been closed due to taxation, from falling into the hands of jerry–builders and racketeers. In addition many public–spirited people, who came by their wealth in all innocence, have bought large stretches of coastline and river valleys and have donated them to the trust. Therefore, the country gradually was being given back to the people.

The newspapers, journals, books and radio programmes in 1938 reflected the endless panaceas of pathics of every shade. While the rest of Europe wallowed in plans, offers, threats and non–intervention, Hitler consolidated his domestic position. He had little difficulty in trimming his plans to suit German heavy industry. With the Strassers long since out of the party, he streamlined the programme in a way that brought new cheer to Dusseldorf. His maniacal leanings guaranteed at least a good fat war, and his border–crossing zeal led his backers to hope for new worlds to conquer and a new colonial empire to exploit. All the destructive and sadistic forces in a land of inferiority complexes were added to the Nazi bandwagon, and Hitler's "peace" pipe began to sound ominously throughout Europe.

The democracies were caught in a sort of schizoid position: the mass of the people earnestly believing in a man's right to choose his way of living, yet with the governing class in most countries determined that the encroachments and demands of the democratic spirit be stopped somewhere. When these rulers belatedly asked for armaments, the populace naturally was incredulous. There was much sentiment wasted over the fact that it was potentially dangerous to vote arms to governments who had given Hitler carte blanche in countries "of which we had scarcely heard." In Germany the presses flayed the corrupt, "semitic" democracies, and everyone brought up fuel for a big bonfire. Hitler was ready, but the democracies were still scratching their heads.

It seemed to me that the root cause of the trouble was that since the Great War, "there had been a new spirit abroad." It had shown itself before, but now it was becoming disturbingly prevalent. A steadily developing mass consciousness held that things as they were in the twenties and thirties were not bound to continue forever; they could be changed, and the people themselves could change them. Gradually it was dawning on Europe's peoples that the feudal remnants still hovering over them could be replaced with a better, workable order. Perhaps because of German thoroughness, this realization struck the German masses first, and startling changes began in that country. It was logical to suppose that resistance to change in any form would be offered by the palace guard in any country. In Germany Hitler came to represent this resistance to social change, and, as a result, he was looked upon by the old gang everywhere as their saviour.

With the devil's logic Hitler opened his attack by stamping out one of the most dangerous of the Christian tenets: that of universalism. Then he flew at the equalitarianism that had been preached for 2,000 years. Next he put women back into "their sub–human place," and finally summoned up enough audacity to smash free thought in churches, universities and in the press.

By this time Hitler had religious circles agog in Europe, the more feudal bishops saying, "Amen! This man will stop the red hordes." They went on preaching an other–worldly religion about Jesus. In the other wing, the bishops and their men who had spent their lives with the disinherited and the poor struck out against Hitler as the devil's advocate, and more vigorously than ever they taught the religion of Jesus. It was not long before England had 14,000 members of various religious book clubs. Controversies developed over patrons of cathedrals demanding that organists play "Deutschland

Uber Alles" and the "Horst Wessel Song" when von Ribbentrop attended service as the German ambassador. Britain's clergy were shocked into activity. People who had heard since childhood that all men were brothers were not going to swallow any paperhanger's dream of a caveman's world and a master race.

While the old and the young men of England argued about what a "nuisance" Hitler was becoming, the smart set at Westminster played out their game. The rules were simple and there was but one end in view: the solution of two problems, which was to be achieved by turning Hitler eastward into the Ukraine. Some knew in their hearts that this was less than a solution, but they stayed in the game. Others, many others, looked on "almost without a murmur," if one may quote Lord Palmerston's description of a Europe paralysed by Napoleon—another little corporal who trumpeted his plans well in advance and marked out his next victim.

PART TWO

CHAPTER SIXTEEN

1938–1945

In September of 1938 I re–entered the McGill Medical Faculty in Montreal in the class that was to graduate in 1940. Actually, Dean J. C. Simpson thought he might give me one year's credit for my work at Oxford, which was certainly very generous. But when he heard that I had studied pharmacology with the famous J.H. Burn and pathology with Howard Florey (who later shared the Nobel Prize for his work on penicillin), the dean was in no doubt as to the year I should enter. Of course the original class at McGill with which I began in 1933 graduated in 1938, the last of the five–year courses that McGill was cutting down to the American four–year style.

I was very fortunate to get a room at Douglas Hall, which was an excellent stone residence built by the Honourable Lewis Douglas, who had been the American Ambassador to Canada. He came from the Douglas copper family of Arizona and his grandfather had been the first head of mental health in the province of Quebec. During the terrible cholera years that accompanied the influx of settlers from over–seas, he had superintended the hospital on the Isle of Orleans. The hall was newly opened and beautifully thought out architecturally.

Douglas Hall boasted a very fine dining room with a full–time dietician, a very large drawing room, a library and many essential services. For anyone studying at McGill or at the Royal Victoria Hospital next door it was a great boon. In my first term back at McGill I was assigned to medicine at the Montreal General Hospital in lower town near the St. Lawrence River. It had been built a century before by the Molson family and by now had the second largest outpatient department in North America, the first being at Bellevue Hospital in New York. The patients came in huge numbers and only a few real emergencies could be assigned hospital beds. My first patient was an old gentleman who, as he said, had his head squeezed when he was caught between the couplings of two freight cars. He certainly did, and one of the carotid arteries to his brain became transferred to one of the venous sinuses in the skull, so that he had a constant bruit of which he complained day and night.

As the late autumn and winter developed, I began to have more and more trouble with pains in all my joints, and even greater difficulty in climbing the hill up University Street to Douglas Hall. The chest pain became so bad that I went to see Dr. J. Wendell Macleod, the well-known internist at the Royal Victoria Hospital next door. He put me in hospital in the Ross Memorial Pavilion, where McGill students had insurance protection that was covered by their tuition fees. It was not long before Dr. Macleod asked the professor of medicine, Dr. Jonathan Meakins, to see me. Then began a series of short admissions to the Ross, followed by more trouble in trying to cope with the cold weather. The professor of surgery at the Royal Victoria Hospital was good enough to say that I could take my clinics there to avoid the cold and to avoid the long hill up from the General Hospital.

However, none of this worked out very well, and Dr. Maude Abbott, the world-renowned cardiac expert, began to talk of the necessity of my going to bed for a year. Professor Meakins heartily agreed with this and the question was then where to go. Dr. Paul White's cases of rheumatic heart disease from New England had been sent frequently to Puerto Rico. However, I consulted the meteorologists and found that the rainfall there was very heavy. My former classmate George Degnan, the great football player from California, had been to Acapulco on the Pacific coast of Mexico and highly recommended it to me on his visits to the Ross Pavilion.

Dr. Penfield came to see me often in hospital and agreed that a year in bed would be a very wise investment. The history of rheumatic heart disease in Montreal, as in New England, was one of extremely poor prognosis if the disease had been acquired in childhood. However, having acquired it at Oxford (so I assumed) with the foul winter weather and the limited nutrition that I could afford there, the prospect for survival was much brighter.

Therefore, as I prepared to leave for my home in Victoria, B.C., Dr. Penfield provided me with wonderful books to take to read, including the excellent biography of El Greco, the Greek immigrant to Spain who made Toledo such a mecca for artists. The book was entitled *Bird of God*, a literal translation of El Greco's original name.

After a few months in my parent's home in Victoria, I learned that the S.S. Washington was about to sail from Los Angeles to New York, stopping at Acapulco. I was able to get a berth on this large ship and after a few days off the coast of Mexico arrived at that most perfect harbour, which is the remains of a crater several miles wide.

In Acapulco, then a town of possibly 20,000 people, mostly Mexican Indians, I had the luck to find a small hotel on the Playa Langosta, a little–frequented area with a very simple type of accommodation built by a retired American navy officer. He had drilled his own well and had an absolutely spotless and inviting small establishment. The cooking was done by a Chinese woman called Ming, who visited the markets for fresh vegetables and meat early in the morning. In fact, some of the fowl that we enjoyed was undoubtedly from Canada geese that had been shot in their winter habitat nearby.

Next door was a beautiful residence on the waterfront owned by Portes Gil, who had become the President of Mexico at a very young age, when the incumbent president, Obregón, had been assassinated. Portes Gil enjoyed talking about the world at large and when he was having a party, usually at Lunada when the moon was full, he would invite me over to listen to the Mariachi Band and to watch the dancing. I was not able to do anything of course but observe things in Acapulco, most days lying on the beach covered with raw coconut oil. It was not long after I took my little grass mat down to the beach that a lanky English–speaking youth walked by, stopped and said, "Aren't you Bill Gibson from Victoria?" I could not believe that Juan MacDonald, with whom I had gone to school so many years ago, would recognize me in Acapulco of all places.

I began to find out some interesting things about the history of Acapulco. I learned about the lives and exploits of the early Spanish explorers who came in quite small ships to what is now British Columbia, and had their headquarters at Nootka on the west coast of Vancouver Island. It was there in 1792 that Admiral Francisco Bodega y Quadra handed over Spain's North Pacific Empire to Captain George Vancouver of the Royal Navy, who had been sent out to accept this land following peace treaties in Europe.

Not only did the explorers use Acapulco: the Spanish galleons, laden with pearls and precious metals that they were bringing to Mexico from the Philippines, depended upon the little port. It seems that five of Spain's emissaries in the government of Mexico were actually sent home in disgrace for operating a small port north of Acapulco where they had goods landed privately and not taxed.

I had no idea until I began to read Mexican history how the original territory of Mexico had been whittled down by American invasions, sheltered always by President Polk.

Originally Mexico was more than twice its present size and it is said that the United States took 900,000 square miles away from it in the early part of the 19th century. As I have said, President Polk sent an army south of the original boundary, to the Rio Grande and then announced that he was fighting a war of defense against the Mexicans. It is alleged, therefore, that he stole California, Nevada, Utah, New Mexico and Arizona from Mexico and paid only 15 million dollars in all.

Mexico City, built by the Aztecs in 1325, was a remarkable place that had advanced calendars, mathematics and religious orders. However, in 1519 Cortes destroyed the city. He did this by using Indians he recruited down at the eastern or Gulf coast of Mexico and then pressed into service. Unfortunately, the succeeding Spanish rule destroyed the Aztec culture. In 1810, after three centuries of plundering and murder, Spanish rule was seriously challenged for the first time by a parish priest called Hidalgo. His insurrection, however, was unsuccessful and he was killed. Father Morelos and others eventually liberated the country from Spain and today, out on Lake Patzcuaro, you can see a monument to Morelos that is so large that 12 men can stand around the cuff of his upraised hand.

There was a French intervention during the reign of Napoleon III, when Maximillian and Carlotta set up court in Mexico. Finally, beginning in 1876, Porfirio Díaz ruled Mexico with an iron hand for a 45–year period. The concessions that he gave out to his friends amounted to national burglary. However, in 1917 a revolution took place that changed this completely. One of the problems in Mexico was that there were about 150 dialects spoken; a fair proportion of the population did not even speak Spanish. The way that Spanish became the official language of Mexico was a little like English becoming the lingua franca of India. In 1939 one of the major problems that President Cárdenas had to address was the reservation and protection of all subsoil rights, such as oil and minerals, for the state. He inherited a tremendous problem of illiteracy. I saw some of this at the little hotel where I lived in Acapulco. One of the teenage boys employed at the hotel used to bring me long pages of handwriting, which turned out to be love letters to his long distance girlfriend. He did not want her to realize that he did not know how to create separate words in his sentences and asked me to go through each letter with a pencil, cutting up these long phrases into actual words. Due to the fact that Spanish is a perfectly phonetic and musical language, this young swain needed a lot of help. After I had divided his scribbling into words, he then re–wrote his letters as if he had complete knowledge of the grammar.

Visitors to the hotel included a staff writer for the *New Yorker* magazine, as well as a Yale novelist. He had the misfortune of spending most of the day in the sun without realizing that he had split his bathing trunks at the crotch. By evening his vital parts were severely burned.

Not far from our little beach was the beautiful Caleta, where people gathered in the mornings when the sun had warmed the clear blue water. In the afternoon they went to another beach called Hornos. As the waves came crashing in, people surfed on small mahogany boards.

I was preparing to leave after three cloudless months in Acapulco when Professor Angel Costero, one of my Spanish friends from the summer of 1936 at Santander, arrived. He was probably the most senior pupil of the Spanish pathologist Río–Hortega, with whom we had both worked in Madrid. At the end of the Spanish civil war, Río–Hortega had appealed to Dr. Wilder Penfield, director of the Montreal Neurological Institute, to take Costero as a research fellow. All was agreed until Costero went into Thomas Cook and Sons' office in Paris and asked for passage on a ship for himself and his family to Montreal. The travel agent made all the arrangements and suggested to Costero that he come back in three months, by which time the ice would have melted in the St. Lawrence River. Costero had never heard of such winters and quickly backed off and sought a new life in Mexico. This he achieved with great distinction and he became very well known at the Heart Institute in Mexico City, which was developed by Professor Chavez, one of Dr. Paul Dudley White's pupils.

Costero and his pupil Villaseñor were kind enough to take me to Morelia, which I still consider the orchid capital of the world. You could buy beautiful "chocolate orchid" plants for five American cents. The Morelians claimed that their university was the oldest in the Americas and that they actually were inoculating cases against smallpox 20 years before Jenner developed his vaccine in England.

On my way home to Victoria for the remainder of my 12–month sojourn, I passed through Galveston on the Gulf coast of Texas where the University of Texas Medical School was based. I was very impressed with the one hospital they then had, and especially with their excellent medical library. I told the dean that I would like to complete my medical degree there to avoid the Montreal winters. He explained to me that that was impossible for me as an undergraduate, because only those born and living in Texas could be taken in as medical students. However, he suggested that after I graduated

I should get in touch with his office regarding a possible internship. This turned out to be wise advice.

I returned to lovely spring and summer weather in Victoria. The Second World War broke out in early September of 1939 while I was living at a beach cottage with my parents. The war was well under way when I had a request from my old teaching mate, Dr. Humphrey Leach, in Sherrington's Laboratory at Oxford, to let him know if I might be available to return to teach microscopic anatomy if their demonstrators were called up in the services. I had to explain that my health made that very unlikely, but if it were urgent I could go. A week later the professor of anatomy at Oxford, the distinguished LeGros Clark, wrote to ask if there was any way in which my family could look after his two children for the duration of the war. Almost simultaneously, however, a cable came to say they would be accommodated in Toronto by well–known neuropathologist Professor Eric Linnell, of the Banting Institute.

On my way back to McGill in December of 1939, at the suggestion of Dr. Maude Abbot I went to see Dr. Paul Dudley White in Boston. He placed me in the Baker Memorial Institute for study and we became great friends. Years later, when he was retiring fully from practice and was disposing of his wonderful library, he asked me, during a Boston visit, to take anything from the shelves that I wished. He gave me the scrap book he had kept in 1913 when he was a postgraduate student in London. He had been, along with Jonathan Meakins and John Parkinson, a pupil of Sir Thomas Lewis, the pioneer in heart disease at University College Hospital in Gower Street. Dr. White loved to tell the story of the frightful weather in March 1913, a month in which there were only two hours of sunshine. He had the misfortune to be developing films in the dark room during those two hours. His scrapbook is now one of the prized possessions of the Woodward Biomedical Library at the University of British Columbia. He apologized that there were certain early tracings missing from the scrapbook because he had to use those in his classic *Heart Disease*, published in 1925. He had the good sense to leave Boston for six months and to go with his wife to the island of Capri, off Naples, to write the definitive book on the subject. The tracings in this scrapbook are very interesting; first a tracing from Meakins, then one from a dog. Then it was White's turn, then Parkinson's, and so on.

After reviewing my electrocardiograms done in Montreal in 1938 and comparing them with those done at the Harvard Medical School, Dr. White felt that it was safe to go back to McGill, provided I was not exposed to the inclement winter weather.

I therefore returned to Montreal and was given a room on the ground floor at Douglas Hall. My friend from Dartmouth, Dan McEndy, was kind enough to give me his room in exchange for one on the third floor. McEndy was a most amusing fellow and had a trick whereby he shuffled cards and put them one by one on the ceiling. The cards were held there by electrostatic attraction, but the secret of course was that he first rubbed his corked–soled bedroom slippers on the deep pile carpet before this marvellous display took place.

Luckily there was a tunnel system joining the Neurological Institute with the Royal Victoria Hospital and my only venture into the cold weather was between Douglas Hall and the Neurological Institute about a hundred yards away. However, I was invited to Dr. and Mrs. Penfield's home frequently, and if I could not drive with him I would go there and back in a taxi. I had inherited a long, large otter coat from my medical uncle who had sent me to McGill, and this protected me from the worst of the cold. However, I returned several times to the Ross Pavilion as a patient of Professor Meakins with more joint pains and strange capillary changes in the skin. This fascinated him because he had not seen this phenomenon before though he had been a professor of medicine at Edinburgh and at McGill for years.

As spring and summer came I was able to go out to the Verdun Mental Hospital where I must say I was introduced to some of the most amazing chronic patients who were clearly going to spend their lives there. The first patient assigned to me was a 19–year–old blonde girl whose father was a prominent Canadian businessman. She had run away with a sleeping–car porter and continually got herself in deep trouble. She was admitted to the mental hospital for several suicide attempts, and she exhibited many scars from when she had tried to cut the arteries in her wrists in the past. One interesting aspect of the work at Verdun was to see the application of malaria, a strain of which was kept alive there for patients with syphilis of the brain. Syphilis produced what was called GPI, General Paresis of the Insane, with tell–tale delusions of grandeur. I later had a patient in the Montreal Neurological Institute who had been hospitalized because while her husband was at his office she would get on the telephone and order grand pianos and $100 canaries and so on. She did well on malaria and went out cured. Howard Florey was amazed when he found that the penicillin which he had worked so hard to produce was actually going to help these infected people and probably enabled hospitals to empty 10 percent of mental patients' beds. In the same way Banting used to say that he had no idea that his insulin would be of use to schizophrenics in the early insulin shock therapy.

The summer of 1940 was to have been spent at Harvard University with Professor Stanley Cobb on his neurological wards in Boston, but as more and more interns left the Montreal hospitals for over–seas, Dr. Penfield asked me if I would stay at the Montreal Neurological Institute and work on the wards there where they were dreadfully short–handed. A neurological hospital under Colonel Russel and Lieut. Colonel William Cone had already left for work at Basingstoke. I therefore called Dr. Cobb by telephone and have rarely had such a slow reply to my request to be released from our earlier understanding. I had not recalled that Professor Cobb suffered from a serious stammer and as the seconds ticked by on the telephone I was conscious of the cost of waiting for the eventual words, "Alright, I understand."

On occasional summer weekends it was possible to get away with Dr. Penfield and his family for a respite at Lake Memphremagog in the eastern townships about 90 miles away. There, at Mansonville, he had a farm that had belonged to Ezra Ball, one of the pioneers of that area. I had known some of his distant relatives at McGill and was later to find that Lady Banting was also one of the Ball clan. Sometimes I drove the Buick and sometimes Dr. Penfield did. We exchanged many stories on the way, but none so amazing as the one he told of his former colleague in New York, Dr. Charles Elsberg, a well–known neurosurgeon. Elsberg was operating on the wife of a wealthy stock broker in New York. The husband in some way had been able to get into the outer reaches of the operating suite and paced back and forth there waiting for his wife to come out from her ordeal. Imagine the look on the husband's face when who should come out on a stretcher but the neurosurgeon himself, Dr. Elsberg. He had suffered a collapse during the operation and his assistants had taken over. Wilder Penfield remarked dryly, "Billy, I don't believe he collected any fee for that operation."

One Sunday morning at the farm the telephone rang, and of course the Penfield line was but one of 19 sharing the thin copper filament. As the farming community wives knew the doctor's ring, they would pick up the receiver just to find out what was going on in the world. In this case, it was the well–known philanthropist William Donner calling from Montreal. He had become rather deaf but retained a great interest in medical research. As he kept saying to Dr. Penfield,

"How much was it you needed for that brain chemistry laboratory?" Dr. Penfield would shout into the phone, "$30,000." Donner said that he could not hear the figure so the words "$30,000" were repeated.

As more people lifted their receivers the voice level went down and Mr. Donner again said he could not catch the amount that was required. Dr. Penfield shouted again, "$30,000 Mr. Donner." Mr. Donner then said "Good, you will have a cheque on Monday." When the cheque arrived at the Neurological Institute it was for $90,000.

Once, when Dr. Penfield was preparing to give a lecture in Washington, D.C., and had just arrived by plane there, his hotel telephone rang and a woman doctor introduced herself as one of the two women in his physiology class of 1915 at Oxford. He carefully asked which of the two women was speaking and was quickly told, "I was the one who had her hair done every day." A very neutral conversation ensued because The Chief was still not sure with whom he was speaking.

Once, when we were driving back from the farm and I was coping with the traffic, The Chief called out, "Billy, I think we are getting a flat tire." We jumped out and saw that it was all too true. He had long boasted to me that while dressed in his white tie and tails in New York, he had changed a tire on the way to a dinner without getting dirty. Now was the time to test that talent. We produced a spare rim and tire, though not an entire wheel, from the boot of the Buick and proceeded to try to get it to fit on the hub of the wheel. We pushed and prodded, cursed the designers at General Motors, and wondered how automobiles could be sold with spares that did not fit. However, we stopped cursing and put our wits to work for a moment and realized that we were trying to put the wheel on backwards. After much laughter we congratulated General Motors, bolted the wheel in place and took off again for Montreal.

Weekends on the farm were always a pleasurable event. Sometimes there was sailing. Other times tennis. Soon after acquiring the farm in the early 1930s, Mrs. Penfield and the children spent a late autumn weekend at Memphremagog, only to awake one morning to find that they were snowed in. Unfortunately, she developed pneumonia, despite the fact that the children tried to keep the house warm by burning wood. Never to be put down by such a calamity, Dr. Bill Cone flew down in a plane and landed on the snowy meadow, carrying a container of the precious pneumococcal anti-serum. This was given to Mrs. Penfield intravenously and later in the week she began to recover. When the roads opened and Dr. Penfield was able to come he brought something very special for the family: a record of the then–popular song "Who's Afraid of the Big Bad Wolf." This was played repeatedly and the spirits of the party rose. They were all safely evacuated to Montreal.

A similar medical emergency arose when I was on the wards in 1940 and was summoned to the operating room. There Dr. Penfield spoke to me through the gauze–covered porthole that we used for communication in the glass–enclosed operating room. I was asked to take an ambulance down to the farm to rescue Dr. Marshall Fulton of Harvard. He had been spending his honeymoon there when he had a spontaneous pneumothorax and turned blue as one lung shut down. There was no time to be lost and I was asked to guide the driver of the big Cadillac ambulance from the Montreal General Western Division over the short cut across a large glaciated area to get to the farm quickly. As we passed through the little town of Sweetsburg, I noticed a sign that pointed to their small hospital. We turned immediately and asked the matron in charge if she had an oxygen cylinder and mask, which she quickly produced. To her amazement we took this into the ambulance and went off at great speed. The patient down at the farm was placed in the ambulance, the oxygen turned on full, and off we went again. He was so recovered by the time we passed through Sweetsburg that I returned the cylinder and mask to a slightly confused matron. The patient did well in Montreal and took up his work again at Harvard with no recurrence for the rest of his life.

When it was too cold to go to the farm for a breather, the interns and their wives used to gather for Sunday tea at what we christened "the Open Arms" at 4302 Montrose Avenue, in Westmount. At Christmas members of the large group read in rotation the various parts of Dickens' *A Christmas Carol*. On one such occasion John Gordon, a blind patient of The Chief, read his part from the Braille edition he had been studying for the great event.

The Penfields had a wonderful grand piano that I enjoyed playing and we sang endless songs. Some of them came from a very rowdy "theatre night," which the original fellows had staged in the library in the Neurological Institute in 1935. To the tune of "John Brown's Body," the neurosurgeons castigated the neurologists and psychiatrists who kept patients under investigation instead of sending them straight to the neurosurgeons. This deep vein of musical interest kept cropping up over the years with the neurological personnel. To run ahead of the story, at the end of the Second World War, Mrs. Penfield produced a piano for the so–called ninth floor of the Neurological Institute where a refrigerator and some chairs had been installed to meet the lunch–time needs of a growing battery of interns and researchers. When Dr. Garfield Kelly's wife produced a baby, we celebrated late at night, the beer being provided by Professor Russel's brother–in–law John Molson. Of the 24 on the intern and resident staff at that time, all of whom gathered for the celebration, 18 could play the piano! The professor of neurology, Dr. Donald McEachern, had a novel way of addressing the keyboard. He would sit down on the piano stool with his back to the instrument and reaching around would play "The Old Folks at Home," bringing down the house. It was for sessions like this that I later wrote "The Old Dilantin Pill." This was set to the tune of "My Darling Nellie Gray," and there was one of our number, Dr. Francis L. McNaughton, who would have to sit down because he laughed so hard at the words. He was known throughout the institute as St. Francis, and while talking with people he would put the three remaining strands of hair across his rapidly balding head into place. He used to convulse with laughter when hearing stories and especially the wild songs I wrote.

"Gub" Kelly was a great raconteur and Dr. Penfield used to ask him to repeat for his friends the story of Dr. Walter Alvarez, a one–time consultant at the Mayo Clinic. Despite his Spanish name, Walter, who began his career as a physician in San Francisco, could not speak Spanish. Nevertheless, he had all the Spanish–speaking patients that a general practitioner could wish for. At 2:30 one morning he was called on the telephone by an exasperated mother who said her daughter was dying. Poor Alvarez put on his clothes and went down to this large home, which had been built, he said, on profits made by this Mexican family by selling mules to the U.S. Army in the first war.

As he entered the living room he found the 22–year–old daughter screaming and squirming on the floor. As he took his coat off and opened his black bag, the daughter shrieked "Get that doctor out of here, I won't have that doctor." As he bent over to listen with his stethoscope, she screamed the same phrases even louder. He looked to the mother and wondered what he could do with such a case at 2:30 in the morning. The daughter gave one final scream, "I won't have that doctor, get him out of here." At this point the mother struck the daughter across the face very sharply and shouted, "At a time like this you'll take any damn fool we can find." Alvarez always used this story in introducing himself to a medical audience when he made one of his thousand–and–one speeches in North America.

Back to the musical strain for a moment, I was amused to learn of

Dr. Penfield's request to the manager of the theatre in New York in which *My Fair Lady* was breaking all records on Broadway. The Chief had written begging for two tickets so that while he was giving an address in New York (accompanied by his wife), they might be able to see a performance of the great new musical. The secretary to the manager wrote back that her boss had "laughed not a little" at the request. However, he sent two tickets and we had glowing reports of the musical for weeks.

One of the things that annoyed Dr. Penfield mightily was an offending buzz that came out of the very fine radiogramophone combination that he had in his home. On two occasions the instrument had been taken back for investigation to the company who supplied it. The buzz persisted. One Sunday afternoon, when I was visiting the Penfields for tea, I went to shut off the whining machine and my hand touched the metal nameplate of the company that had manufactured it. Suddenly the buzz stopped. I tucked some Kleenex behind this metal label and from then on there was no more trouble; however, I must say that for months Dr. Penfield slandered the manufacturer and the sales people of this particular instrument.

The discussions I had with Dr. Penfield and his family ranged over a vast number of subjects. Once, when we were driving, he told me that his first craniotomy had been performed with an axe on a bear swimming in a lake in Northern Idaho. He was at a boy's camp when very young, not far from his birthplace in Spokane, Washington. Evidently several boys paddled a canoe up to inspect the bear and it fell to Wilder to open the cranium of the hapless animal. He would always say "Billy, I was not very proud of that." He then told about the father of one of the boys of the camp who came up to visit for the weekend, overly dressed with hunter's clothes and with a fantastic new double–barrelled shotgun. As he was paddled by the boys in a very large canoe, some ducks flew over–head. Without a moment's thought the man stood up in the canoe and fired this musket at the disappearing birds. Of course the recoil was so great that the canoe immediately turned over and all the passengers were soaked, including the would–be hunter. The Chief remarked dryly, "Out of loyalty to the son who was our good friend, we all kept straight faces."

He was a great conversationalist and made many of the over–powered young people who came to work in the institute very much at home as they chatted. His opening gambit was usually to say "I suppose that," which would open up conversation in an easy way. He always had interesting comments on unusual phenomena. We would be scrubbing at the neurosurgical sink on operation days at 8:00 a.m. with the timer set for exactly 10 minutes. One day The Chief thought the timer must be a bit slow and giving his hands a final rinse before the alcohol bath, dropped his scrub brush into the stainless steel sink. At the very second that the scrub brush hit the bottom of the sink, the timer went off, and Dr. Penfield said "You see there, Billy: a good example of cause and effect." He had many trenchant observations to make and "at the worst of times" he would shake his head and say, "Billy you will learn during your lifetime that it is hard to help some people." He roared with laughter when I told him that my 99–year–old grandmother in Ottawa used to say "Willyum, you will learn that some people serve the Lord by being miserable."

Dr. Penfield greatly enjoyed his grandchildren and I can remember an 11–year–old granddaughter coming to dinner one night. She could hardly contain herself because she wanted to tell us about a new discovery made at school that day. It turned out that her discovery was the field of "Spoonerisms." The Chief asked naively, "What in the world are those?" The granddaughter then regaled us with a list of the most amusing Spoonerisms I had heard, and since Spooner had been the Warden at New College where I was a member at Oxford, I was amazed at the number of new ones unveiled. After these were exhausted Dr. Penfield said: "Let me tell you about Spooner, not really a Spoonerism. Evidently one of the dons at New College had taken ill in the first term and a young substitute had been brought over from Wales. On the day of his hasty arrival Mrs. Spooner had said to her husband, 'Now William, we must welcome Mr. Davies who has come all this way to help us. You go out and get all the fellows of the College and tell them to come for sherry before Hall this evening. Now William don't procrastinate.' So the beleaguered William, who was an albino and had serious visual problems, set out to find fellows who might be airing themselves in the spacious grounds of New College. In the main quad he encountered two fellows and told them to come for sherry before Hall to meet the new fellow Davies. Then in the garden quad, surrounded by the old City Wall of Oxford and a gorgeous perennial border, he encountered more fellows and said that they must come for sherry. Finally, in the cloisters, he encountered a young man and said 'I say, we're having sherry before Hall this evening to welcome our new fellow, Davies. Won't you come?' The young scholar in his black gown replied, 'But sir, I am Davies.' Spooner replied 'Good, come anyway.'"

When Penfield was fatigued at the end of the day he dragged his once shattered leg, a reminder of his survival from torpedoing in the English Channel during the First World War. He was very athletic, however, and played a tremendous game of squash, usually on Saturday afternoons against his surgical and pathological rival, Dr. William Vernon Cone.

The year 1940 brought many changes in my family also. My father was appointed to direct the correspondence courses, or the "high school by mail," for the Canadian Legion Educational Services, which provided high school education for any member of the armed forces who wished to complete matriculation. My parents, therefore, came to Ottawa during 1940, returning to scenes of their childhood and early adult years. One of the saving graces of Ottawa was of course the Gatineau Valley, where a little Toonerville trolley climbed up the valley into the province of Quebec as far as Wakefield every night just after 5:00 p.m. and came down with a full load of passengers in the morning for work in Ottawa. While it might be 100 degrees Fahrenheit at midnight in Ottawa, it would be much cooler up in the Gatineau and we enjoyed, for the succeeding five years, a summer cottage for relaxation and for providing temperatures low enough to sleep at night. My brother was one of the prime minister's secretaries at Laurier House in the Sandy Hill area in Ottawa. One sister, who was a dietician at the University Hospital in Iowa City, joined the 129 dieticians that the Royal Canadian Air Force employed both in Canada and over–seas. After orientation training she was sent across to the Canadian Bomber Group in Yorkshire where she spent the rest of the war. My other sister joined up with the Canadian Army as a bacteriologist and went over–seas with a hospital from Victoria, British Columbia. My brother was invited to join the intelligence section of the Air Force but every move that he made in that direction was soon trumped by the Prime Minister, MacKenzie King.

The final year of my medical course began in September of 1940, and I had not proceeded very far with my lectures before the dean of medicine, Dr. Jonathan Meakins, called me to his office in the Royal Victoria Hospital. He said that since I had a doctorate from Oxford, people were not concerned with the fact that I might not have completed a medical degree. This was an attempt on his part to get me to the Ross Pavilion to help look after his private patients. In the rest of the McGill hospitals, residents and assistant residents were being lost to the armed forces almost weekly. I protested to the dean that I had to attend medical school in order to graduate, but he very quickly made it clear that he was the dean and decided such matters. I therefore put on my "whites" and under the supervision of his senior staff started to look after private patients in the Ross Pavilion. I must say that I never learned so much medicine so quickly as I did in that year. There were some extremely ill patients, and a few who had been "parked" in the private pavilion by their relatives who went off on skiing holidays. The senior staff men who had taught me in third year medicine were not alarmed, but rather seemed grateful that I was caring for their patients. I made it a rule to telephone them before anything was done to study their patients, and they seemed grateful for this practice. They were known to huff and puff about junior personnel deciding on courses of treatment for their well–heeled patients. At the end of the year, when I left the service in order to write my final examinations at McGill, the senior men told the dean that they wished they had more interns who listened!

However, Dean Meakins knew the thinness of the dividing line between my being healthy and my being back on his hands again as a patient with recurrences of rheumatic fever. Those were providentially short because I lived inside the hospital and was not exposed to the tough Montreal winter. In fact, he allowed me to arrange an internship at the University of Texas in Galveston rather than remain in Montreal over the ensuing winter.

During all this time I was carrying on experimental work for Dr. Donald MacEachern at the Neurological Institute on the relationship between vitamin B–6 and epilepsy in vitamin–deficient rats. I was assisted in a very limited way by a patient of Dr. Penfield's who became famous at the Neurological Institute because of his unusual personality. I think he found that watering and feeding my rats on a regular basis was both time consuming and boring. This chap had a very interesting history. At the age of five he was struck down by a taxi in Chicago and thereafter was unconscious for 43 days, which seems to have been a record then. At age 17 he developed epileptic seizures and was, I understand, left quite large sums of money by his doting grandparents as they passed on. Soon he was part–owner of an amazing ranch in southern California, his partners being well–known movie stars. I think he may have run this ranch into the ground. At all events his seizures became more frequent and he was referred to Dr. Penfield for possible surgery to clean up the scarred frontal lobes injured in the accident when he was a child.

During the operation both frontal lobes were found to be very seriously involved and considerable scar tissue had to be removed. He made an excellent recovery and became the institute's mascot in a remarkable way. He was on hand at 8:00 a.m. every morning to welcome Dr. Penfield to his institute and to advise him that it had been a very quiet night and that all the patients had slept. He did this with great suavity and self-assurance. Dr. Penfield would bow seriously and thank him.

While I was spending Easter weekend with my parents in Ottawa, The Chief called to ask if I could come down to see him with a view to taking this 23-year-old patient on a cruise through the Panama Canal and out to the west coast on one of the fleet ships belonging to his father. I agreed to do this and arranged with the University of Texas medical authorities to turn up late to start my internship in Galveston.

We travelled to Baltimore in order to take the ship, with several heavy cases bulging with correspondence courses that my father had happily provided. It was Dr. Penfield's feeling that soon after frontal lobe surgery was the best possible time to teach a patient the mathematical skills that would see him through his life, as well as other standard school material. While waiting to board ship in Baltimore, I thought we should go to visit Johns Hopkins Hospital where Sir William Osler had done great things for medicine as a teacher and patron of research, and where modern neurology and neurosurgery as well as psychiatry had been pioneered. The resident in neurosurgery, Dr. Charles Troland, had been a summer student with us in Montreal and agreed to take us on rounds. We had no sooner met him in the rotunda than the famous Dr. Walter Dandy, the father of pneumo-encephalography, swept in and took us on his rapid ward rounds. Troland only had time to introduce us as coming from the Neurological Institute in Montreal. After the obligatory visits to all his patients, Professor Dandy took us into a side room where there was a cot bearing a small child with a very large head. It was not a straightforward case of hydrocephalus. Dr. Dandy leaned over one end of the baby's crib and my frontally lobotomized friend leaned with great confidence over the other end. After Dr. Dandy had described the unusual features of the case he looked forward and said to my patient, "What do you think of this case doctor?" With the greatest assurance in the world my friend looked straight at him and said, "Dr. Dandy, I am frankly puzzled." Dr. Dandy then made the rash remark, "I am glad to see somebody from Penfield's outfit is puzzled."

Professor Dandy never learned the facts about my friend or he would have been reminded of a former patient whom he had operated on at Johns Hopkins Hospital in the early days of frontal lobotomy. The Baltimore case was a man in his late forties who could not settle down in business because of obsessive-compulsive neuroses. These were so disabling that the psychiatrist recommended a frontal lobotomy. After Dr. Dandy had removed part of each front lobe, the man went on to become a very successful businessman and actually a millionaire. Each year there was an exchange, for a week, of Hopkins students who went up to Harvard and vice versa. Dandy thought it would be a great joke to play on the famous neurosurgeon, Professor Harvey Cushing, in Boston. So he dressed his recovered patient in the clothes of an intern and sent him with the students to Harvard. During the whole week that the students were visiting Boston, Dr. Cushing never tumbled to the fact that this was a bilaterally lobectomized patient rather than a trained physician. So it is possible that we had the last laugh on the hard–driving Dandy.

One interesting thing that I learned from Professor Dandy was that, after five years of headaches, it was found that George Gershwin in Hollywood actually had a brain tumour. He was sinking rapidly and his physicians and surgeons in California telegraphed for Professor Dandy to come. Unfortunately, Dandy was on a yacht cruising in Chesapeake Bay and it took some time to find him. However, he rushed to the first airplane that would carry him to California, but before the plane could take off he was handed a second telegram saying that Gershwin had just died.

The second chapter of my safari with my patient from Baltimore to Victoria, B.C., was incredible. After several days at sea on the way down to Savannah, where the freighter stopped briefly, the lessons in mathematics and in fact all subjects bored my patient so much that he collected all the materials sent by my father and threw them over–board. He felt that was terribly amusing, so we forgot about it. The captain of the freighter taught me elementary navigation and I plotted the course of the ship down to the Panama Canal and then up to the port of Los Angeles in California. There, my patient suddenly went missing and I wondered if he had jumped ship and taken off. Not at all. He came down the wharf after half an hour with a huge tub of ice cream for the crew under each arm. I remonstrated with him that I was the only one of us that had money and asked how he was able to purchase this large volume of ice cream. He said that he had found an old cheque and just made it out for the right amount. I said that his father had told me in New York that all chequing accounts had been closed. I told my patient, therefore, that this would be a very delicate matter for his father who would be called in by the head of the bank and given a lecture. The reply was that there was no danger of that because his father was the head of the bank.

We spent a day at Hollywood with my patient's distinguished relative and saw Betty Grable making a film. We then went by train to Seattle and crossed by ship to Victoria, B.C., where we took rooms in a delightful, seaside, natural park known as Grouse Nest. Among the much travelled immigrants who spent the summer at this spa was a grande dame from Vienna who complained of her arthritis. Before I knew it my patient was giving her a hot water foot massage, and before long had her convinced that he was the doctor and that I was his apprentice learning the trade.

For some reason there was a strike in the ice plant near Victoria and the restaurant that fed us was in great trouble. I therefore went to see my friends at the B. Wilson cold storage facility and wrote them a prescription for 50 pounds of ice for my patient. This saw the restaurant through the next few days. Years later, my friend Richard B. Wilson, who preceded me as the chancellor of the University of Victoria, explained to me that he had divested himself of all the family businesses except that of the ice plant, because they had not changed the formula and he could keep up with any technological advances there.

As September approached (the date when I was due to report at the John Sealy Hospital at the University of Texas in Galveston), I said good–bye to my patient who went off to California, and eventually was hospitalized for years with recurrent epileptic seizures. He certainly was a backslapping extrovert who could have sold coconuts to the Inuit and was a most plausible and friendly fellow.

On arrival at Galveston, which then had a train service for the 65 miles of track south of Houston, I was assigned to Dr. Luther Terry, later well known to the American public as the U.S. Surgeon General. However, in 1941 he was the professor of public health at the university and among other duties was in charge of the health of the whole hospital's employees and nursing students. I must say that I had never seen such varied diseases as I encountered then. We had an excellent diabetic clinic under Professor Gregory and in the chest clinic we were giving pneumothorax (the injection of sterilized air through the chest wall) in the considerable number of tuberculosis cases still existing. It was a safe way to collapse a lung and to rest it, there being no chemical treatment available in those years. The clinic was run in three shifts: one for whites, who usually were dreadfully poor; one for patients of Mexican descent; and one for black patients of whom there were a great many.

In dermatology it was common to see cases of "creeping eruption" usually limited to the side of the body touching the ground when someone had been working under his house on foundations and drains. Because I was one of the few single interns, I was assigned to the emergency room almost every night of the week. I welcomed this because of the experience involved but I must say that sleeping on hard x-ray tables is unrewarding. The "cuttin' fights" among the wilder elements of the Negro population meant that one might spend the night putting as many as 100 stitches into the brown skins of each of these people. Luckily there were Negro police who kept the combatants apart in the emergency room or we would have had bedlam. Occasionally I was able to scrub with the professor of surgery, the enormous Dr. Truman Blocker. He was well named for his powers on the football field as an undergraduate. He was one of the world's finest plastic surgeons, and because of his presence the Shriners built their internationally acclaimed burns unit in Galveston. Today it is a hive of industry in plastic surgery and research. We became good friends and started collecting rare medical books and immersing ourselves in medical history at about the same time.

It was a relatively small band of interns who lived in a wing of the psychiatric hospital. The lower floor was our common room and it was not long after I arrived that I found a disused piano in the main attic of the hospital. Four blacks of enormous strength simply picked the thing up, put it on the elevator, and brought it through to us, where it found good use at noon every day. As I played the piano, more and more instruments arrived from the homes or under the beds of interns and residents. By the time Pearl Harbour occurred we were getting quite good at playing ragtime tunes and, of course, we always had to have "The Yellow Rose of Texas" and "The Eyes of Texas Are Upon You." The devotion of some of the busiest of the surgical residents to their musical instruments was really amazing and they became regular participants in our new jam sessions.

One assistant professor at Galveston was of great interest to me. This chap with a highly affected English accent had arrived at Galveston some years before, professing a great interest in the history of medicine. He cleaned out all the duplicates in this field from the medical school library and sported a Trinity College, Cambridge, crest on his blazer. It was said that he encountered the unfortunate dean of medicine at meetings in Chicago, and sold him a "Bill of Goods" for sure. His proposal was that he would teach physiology to the students in internal medicine, and medicine to the undergraduates in physiology. He certainly was fluent in his delivery but in actual fact neither side could understand what he was talking about. An intern in one of the medical clinics caught him using an ophthalmoscope with the light penetrating his own eye instead of the patient's and thereafter rumours began to spread and the poor dean of medicine suffered greatly. However, all this was brought to a sudden end when emissaries from the Draft Board in New Jersey took our man off to a Houston gaol. There our famous "Doctor Fell" gave a fatuous interview to the press, ending with the momentous words "C'est la vie," and added "For your information gentlemen, that's life."

CHAPTER SEVENTEEN

The Air Force

My career in the Royal Canadian Air Force began in an unusual way at Randolph Field in Texas. Because of my running battle throughout medical school with rheumatic fever and its well-known effects on the heart, McGill allowed me to intern at the University of Texas Hospital in Galveston on the Gulf coast. A group of us were sitting on the floor of the house of Dr. Arthur Ruskin, the distinguished cardiologist and pianist, on that fateful day in early December 1941 when the symphony concert on the radio was interrupted by the announcement that Japan had bombed Pearl Harbor.

As soon as I could get away I took the train over to San Antonio to see if I could join the U.S. Air Force at its large research base. I was shown to the imposing office of General Reinartz, a permanent force medical officer of commanding presence who had a chest covered with medals. In keeping with his rank he had silver hair and a waxed mustache patterned (so it seemed to me) after Texas longhorns. I could see that time was of the essence so I told him very quickly that I would like to join his medical research group. He very quickly told me that since I was not an American citizen, under the present law I could not be an officer, which meant I could only be a stretcher bearer!

He roared with laughter at the absurdity of the situation and said: "Now look, you Canadian. You have come a long way by train to help us. Now how can I help you?" So I explained that it was very unlikely that I would be accepted by the armed forces in Canada because of my medical history. That was the bell that summoned the old firehorse to duty!

In a moment he was on the telephone to Ottawa and after a few cordialities dropped the brick on the commander there. It was quickly agreed that with a D.Phil. in Physiology from Oxford and an M.D. from McGill, I should be taken into the medical research group of the Royal Canadian Air Force.

The general winked at me and whispered, "Where do you want to go?" I whispered "Vancouver." So it was settled: I was to proceed to Canada's west coast as quickly as the trains would take me. Then the general asked the person on the phone: "We're going to have lunch together. Could you send me an immediate signal to say what my friend Gibson is to do?" After a fine lunch in the Officers' Club we returned to his headquarters where, wonder of wonders, a telegram signed by the chief of the Air Staff was waiting. General Reinartz smiled and I was gone.

After five days on the disrupted trains, which traversed through unheard of parts of Wyoming, I reached Vancouver and went straight to the old granite building that had once been a post office. My entrance was treated with merriment by my former classmates, now in uniform, who said: "You can't get into the Air Force, we know your history." I rejoined, "Can you read?" and showed them the telegram from the chief of the Air Staff. I was "in" in 15 minutes, and stayed 15 years in various active and reserve capacities.

My duties for the next three months in Vancouver were entirely devoted to the examination of recruits. There I saw what the endless Great Depression had done to the health of many young Canadians. The dental work and minor surgery required was a revelation, and I traded words with a few standoffish medical officers every time I took these deprived lads into the service with clearly correctable shortcomings. My clinical colleagues in military hospitals were only too pleased to have such work to do.

It was not only "lads" that we took into the force, but women recruits too. The recently formed Women's Division was very popular. One evening the corporal in charge of the recruiting documentation took me aside to explain that in civilian life he had been a policeman, and had just noticed two women "with a past" in the waiting room. He cautioned me that they "were not ladies." He sought permission to tell them that there were no openings in their category.

On the final day for the reception of American citizens into the Royal Canadian Air Force, we were inundated with hopeful young men from the south. Twelve came from Warner Brothers studio in Hollywood and were very impressive recruits. Each in turn made sure that I knew that Jack Warner had sent him. All but one passed the medical examination with flying colours; this short, stocky chap had blood pressure too high to be considered. He was keen to join his friends on the 7 p.m. train for the Edmonton manning depot.

I told this worried man to go for a walk to Stanley Park and then to come back. He became lost and evidently ran most of the way back to the recruiting centre. By then his heart was pounding and he was highly upset as his "buddies," as he called them, sat waiting for the verdict. He was on the verge of tears so I thought I would divert him from the blood pressure problem. On asking him what his role in Hollywood was, he replied that he was Betty Grable's physical trainer and had to keep her weight at 115 pounds. He and his friends made the train.

After three months of this interesting but repetitive duty, I was sent to the school of aviation medicine at a run–down former normal school in Toronto. Eventually my fellow scholars were allowed to see the Institute of Aviation Medical Research, which had taken over the Toronto Hunt Club. This fascinating place boasted a remarkable human centrifuge that had been built with the assistance of David Cass–Beggs, with whose family I had lived for part of my three years at Oxford.

Perhaps I should retrace my steps to note that his family was on the ill–fated Athenia, which was torpedoed by German submarines in the North Atlantic in 1939, days after the outbreak of war. The ship had sunk so fast that the call went out to pass all infants over the heads of the adults crowding the deck. As a result, Cass–Beggs' 2–year–old daughter, clad only in the top of her pyjamas, finally landed on Axel Wenner–Gren's yacht, the Southern Cross, and eventually on the City of Flint, which brought her to Halifax. Her parents, in another lifeboat, were picked up by a British destroyer and taken back to England. Only six weeks later were they able to sail for Canada, where David was eagerly awaited by the scientists at the department of electrical engineering at the University of Toronto. There he was able to apply the very sound training he had received at Metro–Vic's large electrical engineering works to the problem of the much–needed human centrifuge.

To return for a moment to the two–year–old daughter, Rosemary, she was headed for Halifax under the care of a fine woman passenger from Winnipeg. It was first necessary to try to identify her from the passenger list published in Britain and in Canada simultaneously. My brother in the prime minister's office at Ottawa first spotted her name: Rosemary followed by a phonetic rendering of what the little girl said her family's name was. She had been frightfully seasick and suffered from exposure until sailors on the rescue ships made her canvas clothes.

Hearing of the child's safety, I gave up the bed rest in Victoria to which I had been condemned by the cardiologists, and enlisted the help of my local friends in the Canadian National Railways. The wires were alive with telegrams to Surgeon Commander Wendell Macleod in Halifax asking him to examine the child, and to Dr. George Haythorne of the Economic Council of Nova Scotia who was asked to provide a teddy bear and clothes for Rosemary. By the recently established air mail service, I sent my photograph, which she could recognize as being that of the student at her home in Oxford who had taught her such Negro spirituals as "No Hiding Place Down There." (This and other songs she had sung in the lifeboat to cheer the chilled survivors.)

Finally she reached Montreal where my brother's wife met her and took her by train to their home in Ottawa. Her shrill voice and English accent convulsed the passengers, especially when she announced: "You people say 'toilet' but I say 'lavat'ry.'" So much for this diversion.

After a one–month course in aviation medicine in Toronto, I was sent to the recruiting centre in Montreal because I was able to speak French. During that interval I took my Medical Council of Canada examinations, which were standard across the country both for practice and, in some schools, for graduation examinations. They were very thorough and highly regarded national examinations.

The oral examinations in surgery were remarkable. With many of my classmates, I turned up at the Royal Victoria Hospital, Montreal, where Professor of Surgery Dr. John Armour was handing out the assignments for the surgical ward. He was already dressed in his operating clothes and was clearly in a hurry. No sooner had I found my surgical patient than Dr. Armour went the rounds of the ward collecting up our reporting papers. There had been no time to write anything down so he shouted at me as he hurried to the bedside, "Bill, what happened to this patient?" I replied that a wall had fallen down on him and I was about to examine him. "That's fine, that's the diagnosis: a wall fell down on him, good–bye." John Armour's stock saying was "See a lump, take it out," and this has been a very good guide to a lot of practising physicians ever since they studied with him.

I was next posted to No. 2 Clinical Investigation Clinic in Regina—the middle of the Canadian Prairies. The Saskatchewan weather was not something that I looked forward to, since it could be fearfully cold in winter and extremely hot in summer. However, it was a pleasure to get back to medical research with the excellent group of physiologists that I found at Regina. For a brief time only, squadron leader Chester B. Stewart was in charge, but soon he was sent to command the large "Y" Depot with its 12 decompression chambers in Halifax.

He was aided by two medically qualified Rhodes scholars, squadron leader O.H. Warwick and flight lieutenant Donald Lloyd–Smith. The object of that establishment was to test the high altitude susceptibility of the air crew going over–seas, something that could be done in Canada, where decompression chambers and the accompanying high altitude equipment were easily available, as compared with the situation in Britain.

Chester Stewart was succeeded by the gregarious Squadron Leader George Manning, another of Sir Frederick Banting's close associates in Toronto from the time he was a medical student. George recounted his first meeting with Banting to me. He sat in a corridor awaiting his appointed time to meet the great man, when suddenly a newspaper reporter was bodily ejected from Banting's office. A nervous George found, however, that he was given a very quiet interview and before long he began working with Banting on the coronary circulation of the heart, a subject that occupied Manning as a consultant cardiologist for the rest of his life.

The term "medical research laboratory" could not be used because of the busy–bodies who, giving comfort to the enemy, went about shouting that their sons were being treated as guinea pigs. The strange thing was that the number of volunteers who applied for high altitude work far surpassed our capacity.

The Clinical Investigation Unit was accommodated on a large college campus in the centre of Regina, where most of the activity concerned the six weeks of initial training for potential air crew. At first its duration had been only three weeks! At one time the station was commanded by the great World War I flyer Scott Williams, who had learned to fly after 20 minutes of instruction. He was the best commanding officer I ever saw in the 15 years I was associated with the Air Force. Alas, he was dying of cancer when he came to us, but his great spirit and belief in young people shone through. His role in creating a separate airforce in Canada after the Armistice of 1918 is too little known. He was a professional engineer between the wars.

Regina from 1942 to 1944 was a most hospitable home. The civilians could not do enough for us, and I came to know many of them when I was hospitalized with recurrences of rheumatic fever. The station itself was an ever–changing cross–section of society: all in the war effort together, but with just as many views on that effort as there could be in peacetime on non–military matters. We had windbags, hustlers, chisellers, poker players, musicians, theologians, messing officers and other women officers, civilian batmen from the First War, service police, nurses and medical officers.

The Officers' Mess, like everything else, was administered with close attention to King's regulations. It was stated therein that "politics and religion would not be discussed and ladies' names would not be mentioned." As many junior officers observed, "What is left to talk about?" Because I could not venture out in the fierce winter weather with its numbing winds, I spent a great deal of time in the laboratory at night, or in reading and writing in the mess or in quarters. In the laboratory I was safe, but in quarters there were always some homesick officers who wanted the piano played. Even the Sergeants' Mess would track me down and end the day with bad singing and worse songs.

One interruption of which I never tired would begin with a little rap on my door on Saturday nights about 11 p.m. It was always the scholarly Father Downes, an Irish priest who had lived in Quebec so long that he spoke English with a French accent. He always led into the subject of his call by saying quietly: "Doctor, I'm not sure about the wine for communion tomorrow. I wonder if you could advise me on it? I just have a sample of it here with me." So out would come the glasses and we would sample the brew while the winds whistled outside and the over–worked radiators hissed and banged. He did not seem to worry that I would be playing the little pump organ at the Protestant service on the morrow. He was a classical scholar who lived for things of the mind and of the spirit. How he put up with the noise and clamour of a building full of extroverts I could never fathom.

The research which we did in our little unit of four officers was interesting and useful. The equipment consisted largely of a decompression chamber, a good chemical laboratory and skilled technicians. Our personnel came from Banting's group at the University of Toronto, Penfield's at McGill or from the University of Western Ontario.

I was fortunate in the problem assigned to me immediately after I arrived. Sherrington's pupil, Cuthbert Bazett, who had been professor of physiology at the University of Pennsylvania, had come to the Banting Institute, along with Major Harry Armstrong of the U.S. Air Force, after Sir Frederick's tragic death in a lost Hudson bomber in Newfoundland. Bazett was in search of a method of removing nitrogen from the joints so that its action in causing the bends (severe joint pain) could be prevented. He toyed with the idea of having subjects sitting in a box while oxygen flowed around their body, thus ridding the corpus of nitrogen by diffusion through the skin. He gave up this impractical idea in favour of an eminently practical one in which subjects proven susceptible to the bends would breathe 100 percent oxygen for eight hours over–night. So we slept on issue double decker beds in the large decompression chamber room, wearing custom–made transparent plastic face masks with a peak cap, in which the hollow peak contained enough pure oxygen to fill our lungs every time we inhaled. This worked very well, and after a sound sleep and breakfast we could carry on any activity for up to five hours—baseball for the air crew candidates—before "ascending" in the decompression chamber to 42,000 feet simulated altitude for a one–hour period.

The theory was that the body would be de–nitrogenated by the eight hours of over–night oxygen, and would slowly re–nitrogenate in the following five hours, while leaving a margin of freedom from joint pains of about three hours. With this technique we were able to stay up without symptoms for one hour at 42,000 feet and occasionally we would make a brief excursion to 45,000 feet. These runs were to simulate the problems encountered by photographic reconnaissance units where it was essential to fly above the range of anti–aircraft guns. My joints were so susceptible to pain that I was a good test subject on these runs.

Where did we get the human guinea pigs, as our detractors called them? It was my job to select from air crew candidates at the large manning depot in Edmonton, Alberta, those who had developed the bends on a test run to 35,000 feet. For that purpose we ran a decompression chamber in the basement of the Edmonton normal school all day and half the night, seeking out trainees who suffered the bends. Those who had to descend because of pain were put on a confidential list. Imagine their surprise when they found they were to join us for four to six weeks of clinical investigation in Regina. All had to be volunteers. Our policy was that no enlisted men would be put through an exercise unless one of our officers had experienced it first!

One remarkably keen airman asked at the decompression chamber in Edmonton if he was eligible because he had been blown off an oil refinery installation three years previously and had only recently been given a clean bill by the orthopaedic surgeons who had put him back together again. Evidently, as he peered down into an "empty" gasoline storage tank, his co–worker had struck a match for better vision. Our man flew some distance through the air and landed with almost every bone in his body broken.

In run after run in the Regina chamber he suffered no bends in his damaged joints, but only in his uninjured joints! He is now in the medical literature. Post–war he became one of the pioneers in what was for a time the world's largest helicopter operating company. Like other research subjects, he periodically returned from distant battle zones to the laboratory to tell us how his experience in the decompression chamber had been of great value to him in operations.

Motivation played a large role in the air crew boys that we came to know during their sojourn with us. We learned that one candidate had left high school before the war, without his matriculation, in order to become a mink farmer. With the war under way he came down from the north to Victoria, B.C., and convinced my father at the parliament buildings that he could complete his matriculation in six weeks if allowed to take all the high school correspondence courses for the four years of high school over to the Empress Hotel. He did just that, and was one of the first volunteers at the Regina laboratory. In a year he was back with the Distinguished Flying Cross. After a second tour of duty over–seas he returned with the Distinguished Service Order.

Another research project at Regina was sparked by the Russian claim that physical training with a major component of rotation of the head and body could prevent motion sickness. For this purpose we set up swings that had 19–foot–long ropes connected to either side of a wooden seat, attached to the ceiling of our research building at the Air Observer School in Edmonton. Again, test subjects were selected from the seemingly endless supply of air crew volunteers at the manning depot in Edmonton.

There, in a former parachute section of a large hangar, a battery of such self–propelled swings was set up, and the time taken to produce nausea or vomiting recorded. Again the most susceptible were taken to Regina for conditioning. Edmonton's manning depot housed hundreds of Australian trainees, who came by ship to Vancouver, usually accompanied by Dr. Richard Bligh, a distant descendant of the famous intrepid navigator, Captain Bligh. (I was later to meet the doctor in Australia, with his father Erasmus, a distinguished surgeon married to a relative of Dr. John McCrae of "Flanders Fields.")

These Aussie airmen were great pranksters with a picturesque language. One never mentioned the hub of Sydney's traffic, King's Cross, without being corrected to "King's Bloody Cross." Everything was wild in concept and in execution. A contest developed among these "mytes" to see who could rip the insulating chip–board off the hangar wall as the arc of the swing reached its limit. At first, feet were used for this destruction. Finally, the Aussies would crane their necks forward and rip it off with their teeth. The civilian head of the flying station where all this went on was "Wop" May, the legendary one-eyed bush pilot. He tolerated this wild behaviour until he learned that the Inspector General was on his way from Ottawa. With that stimulus he told me we would have to clean up the mess created by these "bushmen," so all the insulation was removed quickly, leaving a spic-and-span hangar.

Meantime, across the city, the Aussies at the manning depot were harassing the commanding officer. It was alleged that at the outbreak of the war he had been a lowly stores clerk in a Permanent Force station. At all events, late one night the Aussies chopped the base of the flagpole in the parade square almost all the way through, and covered it with earth. The next morning the C.O. gave the usual orders from his stand in front of the pole: "Trumpeter sound the still," followed by "General Salute." The Air Force flag was pulled up with such vigour that the enormous pole wavered, and with a splitting sound crashed down a few feet from the unpopular commanding officer.

The Aussies were a law unto themselves and sported beautiful, dark blue, pure wool coats in winter—in marked contrast to the less-than-wool clothing of the RAF trainees from Britain. Those poor chaps, lost in the most godforsaken prairie flying schools, were the salt of the earth. They never complained, though they had much to complain about. When a dozen of them came into Regina to assemble a Spitfire plane in the town square in order to spur on a drive to popularize the sale of war bonds, their clothing came to the notice of the most considerate stores officer in the RCAF, Squadron Leader Harry Williams. In the 1914–18 war he had served with the RAF in Russia. By 1942 he had forgotten most of the language, but at mess parties he specialized in the Cossack dance with his legs flying. He told the RAF mechanics to come into his clothing stores, pick out an entirely new set of battle dress, and to keep accounts even on his books, leave their old clothing behind. He was not surprised a week later when a different dozen arrived in Regina to disassemble the Spitfire and to exchange their battle dress as well.

One of the prices I paid for repeatedly going to Edmonton to collect the guinea pigs was that the commanding officer of the Air Observer School, where we did our preliminary selection, heard that I played the piano. The Officers' Mess had a very fine instrument that was unused. No matter where I hid on the camp, in the evenings the commanding officer would have the orderly officer and his crew run me down and bring me to the mess to play until midnight for his fellow officers and guests. This became very time consuming, so I spent some of my evenings over at the Medical Faculty of the University of Alberta dissecting at the Anatomy Department.

In an effort to relate the amount of "G" (gravity) developed in the swings and its relation to flying, I spent several days at the classified station at Suffield, Alberta, where there was a single runway. We were loaned a Mitchell Bomber (B–25) for these tests and with a gravity recording machine borrowed from physiology at the University of Alberta, I was able to make tracings of the changing gravitational forces as the B–25 was put through its paces. I was in the plexiglass–enclosed nose position, which seemed to me to be about two feet off the tarmac, so that on landing the nose wheel and the ground seemed to go by in a flash. The commanding officer at that station insisted on serving us antelope for dinner.

One of the welcome visitors at the Clinical Investigation Unit in Regina was Flight Lieutenant Iser Steiman, from a nearby bomber and gunnery school. He had been born in one of the Russian satellites and was bilingual in English and Russian. While visiting New York on one occasion he found a copy of the *Russian Aviation Medicine Textbook*. He brought that back to Canada and translated it for us. Though you could buy it on the open shelves in New York, it immediately was classified by the Canadian authorities. However, it turned out to be a most instructive volume, telling about the efforts in the First World War of the Russians to use pressurized suits for high altitude work. There was much also on the gravitational forces to which pilots were subjected in dog fights. This was put in final shape for publishing at Yale University, where Steiman had been made welcome by Dr. John Fulton, the Sterling professor of physiology. Fulton's laboratory and his home became the crossroads for much of the Allied aviation physiology during World War II. He and his wife were great hosts.

The commanding officer of the Air Observer School in Edmonton told the touring Coca–Cola Concert party that went across Canada that I had written a piece of music and words called "Flying Home." Before long I was drafted into playing this while one of the singers belted it out at a bond drive concert. There were many such drives during the war.

The boredom in the isolated hamlets that played host to RAF stations was terrible. A "large" population centre—Moose Jaw—had hotels, dance halls and bars, to which many RAF officers repaired on 48–hour weekend passes. From one of these hotels our Clinical Investigation Unit in Regina received an unlikely package containing a shoe riddled with buckshot. As the drama unfolded it became clear that it should have been directed to the local Criminal Investigation Unit, under R.C.M.P. Surgeon Maurice Powers, of ice hockey fame in his McGill days. Soon an RAF officer who was totally "bushed" was charged with bringing a double–barrelled shot–gun into a Moose Jaw hotel and discharging it at 2 a.m. True to British custom, the officers placed their shoes outside their hotel room doors at night, and the "wacky" officer had discharged his gun close to the floor, on one side of the hotel corridor and then on the other, blowing all the shoes into a lead–injected heap at the top of the stairs.

Moose Jaw had a famous RAF court marshall in which an officer was charged with pursuing a retreating female down a hotel corridor—neither party arrayed in any clothing whatsoever. The officer's defence when hailed before the court was that, under King's regulations, he was entitled to wear "sports dress suitable to the sport in which he was engaged."

As the war moved into the Pacific the need for high altitude, night vision and survival training became obvious, and No. 2 Flying Personnel Section was promulgated for the Sea Island RCAF base in the estuary of the Fraser River near Vancouver. With my crew from Regina we converted a small building beside the Boeing factory with our own (concealed) hammers and saws. It was to become a way point for RAF officers who were able to hitch a ride over the pole as far as Vancouver. Their destination—by whatever means—was Hollywood, Los Angeles. I had no sooner made a pot of tea one afternoon than Squadron Leader William Goldie, of night vision fame at Farnborough, walked in with a big smile. On another occasion a Wing Commander medical dropped in. Since he was also a qualified pilot, he had navigated for a trans–polar flight, sharing the duties as pilot. He told me of his surgical internship years before at the Montreal General Hospital. He held his white uniform trousers up with an old school tie, a practice common in English rugby players. Sometimes a frisky nurse would quietly enter the operating room and with her bandage scissors cut his necktie from behind while he was intently holding two retractors.

Immersion trials in the nearby Gulf of Georgia (40°F water in January) were hard on the nerves, though the pilots who volunteered took it in stride. The value of quick–donning protective devices was certainly proven, for the problem of downed flyers was more that of hypothermia than of drowning. One of the subjects, fair haired and ruddy, had to come out of his inflated life–raft, not because of hypothermia or sea–sickness but because he was violently allergic to the woollen long underwear he had donned for the trials.

The night vision training was done using a silhouette of a village, at very low levels of illumination. For some reason the subjects tested late in the day had unusually high scores. The reason was soon discovered: the Boeing plant next door shut its heavy electric motors down for the day at 4:30 p.m.

The Sea Island base was home to many sorts of formations, from fighter squadrons to weather flights, some of which ranged far into the Pacific. The pilot of the Hudson bomber who undertook the weather reconnaissance was a skilled American named Ritzel. He had worked in mines and oil fields before coming to Canada as a volunteer. He swore only in Spanish, but I doubt if he knew what he was saying, the phrases were so purple. He had the reputation of being able to "fly" a Link trainer—a flight simulator bolted to the ground—with such precision that the recording "crab" would trace out his name while he operated "blind" inside the contraption.

He had nerves of steel, as we saw on one spectacular occasion. He had just taken off in his two-motored Hudson, fully fuelled for his long flight out over the Pacific, when a pheasant (of which there were many) flew right into the air-intake of one motor. The plane staggered but Ritzel managed to gain enough altitude with the surviving engine to glide over the chimneys in Marpole village. As he approached the runway to set down his heavily-laden plane, a farm tractor appeared on the airstrip. With much cursing the pilot made another circle above the chimney pots and came safely in on his single motor. The fellow was fearless—even of higher authority. One morning he entered the hangar late for the Alaska flight he was to take. The commanding officer of the squadron sent for him and asked why he was not ready for the 8 a.m. take-off. Ritzel cocked his battered cap on the side of his head and, while sitting on the edge of the wing commander's desk, said: "Sir, I want to make it clear. I am never here at 8 a.m., not just this morning."

As a bachelor I was usually assigned weekend duty as station medical officer. This was a great opportunity to scour the very large Sea Island base while driving an innocent-looking four-by-four ambulance. With the stretchers folded out of the way, it was remarkable what useful things could be taken on board. These liberated items greatly enhanced our little laboratory and survival training building. A judicious calling up of obstructionists for their inoculations went a long way to solving our outstanding equipment problems, without resorting to filling in any forms.

In September 1944 two seriously burned Air Force girls, with multiple fractures from a plane crash on northern Vancouver Island, had to be flown to Christie Street Hospital in Toronto for plastic surgery. Because of my interest in oxygen and air ambulances I was asked to accompany these two once–beautiful patients. A Lockheed Lodestar was selected as the air ambulance, and for several days it was put in first class shape. A sign appeared on the door of the plane after it had been steam–cleaned saying "Do not enter this plane unless you are sterilized!" A nurse proceeding to Montreal was selected to accompany the patients and we had a most helpful crew man in Corporal Clare.

We laboured up over the Rocky Mountains and landed at Lethbridge, Alberta, to refuel. We were presented with a signal from the Prairie Air Command asking by whose permission we were proceeding into their territory. We tore that up and went off to Rivers, Manitoba, to a large Air Force installation. Due to the time changes, we were facing a night landing in Toronto as we pushed ahead east from Rivers. At each stop the pilots and the radio operator had to pass through the plane from the forward cabin in order to check the fuel and the weather. They could hardly abide the smell of the infected fractures of the two girls. The nurse had become air–sick and was useless. The corporal filled in wonderfully and kept the girls comfortable.

As we proceeded into Ontario we ran into a furious electrical storm with winds so high that we were driven north along the Albany River. We all recognized that it emptied into Hudson Bay, not in the direction that we were headed. Swinging south, therefore, the pilots kept in touch with Duluth in the United States as we continued to be buffeted by the storm. The flashes of lightning were incredibly bright, despite the heavy downpour. The captain wisely decided to put down at Port Arthur in Northern Ontario.

Suddenly I heard the radio operator on board telling someone on the ground "you know what you can do with your unlit grass airport." I went forward to find that he was off his oxygen altogether and was shouting obscenities at the ground. I got him back on his oxygen and told him to shut up, that we simply had to get down. Suddenly the storm ceased and by a full moon we were able to land on the grass airport. The fuel we were offered was not of a very high octane rating, but we had to take it anyway. Once more we proceeded towards Toronto and once more the skies declared themselves. It was a very rough ride. However, to save time we landed at the Island Airport in Lake Ontario, just in front of the city of Toronto. In taxiing to the appointed hangar, the lights on the aircraft failed entirely, but we were able to deliver the patients to the waiting ambulance. Once again our corporal distinguished himself in the careful way he attended the severely injured girls.

As we taxied in, I computed that in the 13 hours that had elapsed since leaving Vancouver, we could have been only as far as Revelstoke, British Columbia, had we travelled by train. So the air ambulance, with its problems, was still the best way to come.

I was not impressed by the aging physician in tennis shoes and an old lab coat that met us at Christie Street Hospital, so the next day I began to shake things up. By great good luck Squadron Leader Tom Watters, one of our high altitude physiologists, who had been severely injured in a crash in Alaska, was by now in a wheel chair with his fractured legs in casts protruding in front of him. He was the first to see the injured girls the next day and during their entire stay he was their pater familias. He would never admit that he had been even more seriously injured, but the fact was that while in a large Stranraer flying boat in the Alaskan Panhandle, the plane suffered a powerful downdraught and dropped several hundred feet into the cold ocean. When Tom was picked up, though he had two fractured legs and a rent in his liver, he was nevertheless attempting to inflate one of the dinghies that had failed to open following the crash.

I am happy to say that the two badly injured and burned girls, thanks to Squadron Leader Farmer, the Air Force plastic surgeon, were restored to health and have returned to live on the west coast of Canada.

We were so tired after this unusual flight that we stayed over–night at an Air Force station nearby. The next evening Mart Kenny's Orchestra was playing on the station, so all of our crew remained an extra day. In the middle of the night an earthquake occurred that really jarred the Air Force huts in which we slept. The first thing I knew, Wing Commander Marshall Foss, the commanding officer, was shouting up and down the quarters for the service police, saying that some rascals had entered his room and had been under the bed shaking it to pieces. We soon quieted him down and explained that an earthquake had taken place. He was one of those fliers who was always ready for a fracas. He reminded me of what Squadron Leader Claude St. Onge, at the Montreal Recruiting Centre, had said about the fighter pilots. On one of the high floors in the recruiting centre in Montreal, he pointed out the open window and said: "If I say to a fellow jump out that window, and on the way down he says 'Why am I doing this?' then I know that he is a good fighter pilot recruit."

As the war ground on our unit in Regina was closed and we were assigned to the Clinical Investigation Unit in Toronto. At the Toronto unit I encountered my former physiology teacher from my University of British Columbia days, Dr. Edgar C. Black. His flaming red hair was covered with a beaten–up old hat; he walked very slowly, having suffered for a long time with an unusual heart ailment. He always had this hat on in the laboratory so it was easy to spot where he was working. He also sported a magnificent train conductor's gold watch with a heavy chain so that he was constantly reminding the staff where they were to be at a particular time. Dr. Penfield told me that he had come to regard Black as the most useful man in all the subcommittees of the National Research Council that he attended. His high blood pressure, his Baptist background from Brandon College and his inflammatory language, became proverbial in the research group in Toronto. Often he would resign at committee meetings and walk out, taking all his papers with him. It was the job of Group Captain Hall to mollify him the next day and get him back to the committee table. Black's work on oxygen masks was superb; with the Japanese in possession of most of the rubber of the world, there was much to do to find adequate substitutes. Black was actually a fish biologist who had taken his Ph.D. degree at Swarthmore, where he had met his wife. She was part of the team and one of the best cooks I have known. Their home in Toronto became the meeting place of many of the researchers.

To run ahead of the story slightly, Edgar Black went back to physiology after the war, teaching first at Dalhousie University at Halifax and then at the University of British Columbia. While chasing trout fingerlings up and down a large trough during his summer's research in the Okanagan Valley, he felt something snap in his head and quickly ran to tell his wife. He was taken immediately to Vancouver, where with a needle biopsy he was diagnosed with the most malignant of all brain tumours. He was dead in a few weeks.

Eventually I was promoted to the rank of squadron leader and posted to Air Force Headquarters in Ottawa to take over the physiological training of air crew. This entailed flying to stations as separated as Yarmouth, Nova Scotia, and the RCAF Station on the Queen Charlotte Islands in the northwest Pacific area. Sometimes we were "socked in" by bad weather—as at Greenwood, N.S., where it was reported that in January of 1944 they had only one day of flying weather that whole month.

Occasionally I was driven from St. John, New Brunswick, to the RCAF station at Pennfield Ridge. The driver always blew his horn steadily as we approached an isolated house on the highway. Suddenly a little hand would appear at the window and it would wave as we passed. The drivers knew that there was a sick child in bed at that house, but had never seen more than the little hand waving. (The same phenomenon occurred at a river mouth in 1941 when our ship was going up to Savannah, Georgia. A captain's widow appeared high up on a little walkway to wave to the passing ships that whistled in sympathy.)

Early in 1945 I was made deputy director of medical research. Sometimes the air at headquarters was blue with curses. On one occasion I heard Dr. Gilbert Adamson, the psychiatrist for the service, shouting at an emissary from the personnel branch: "listen to me you — — —, ask that — — upstairs if he wants my opinion or my resignation." Then there was the Okinawa committee—short lived I am glad to say—to which I was briefly attached as secretary. The official minutes were circulated but I added a mock set, in which the first agenda item "purpose of meeting" carried a note: "To be decided at the conclusion of the meeting." This produced much merriment but, as always, some stiff–necked disapproval.

A pleasant interlude was supplied by the Reverend Father Danis, from the University of Ottawa, who in some way managed to invade RCAF headquarters. He wanted to talk to me about his dream of starting a medical school at the university. He had spent much of his life in South America and spoke excellent Spanish. He had been given three small houses on the edge of the campus and wanted to know if he could, in some way, offer the pre–clinical years of the medical curriculum in them. I described the plan developed by Professor Chauncey Leake at the University of Wisconsin, whereby teams of four students each would carry out their entire two–year curriculum in one room specially fitted out with every laboratory facility required. Tutors would circulate between the units. One day a sad Father Danis appeared, to say that he could have only two, not three, houses. I encouraged him to stay with his project and told him that his vision could still come to fruition, which it did. He inspired people to give help.

My reputation as a deflator (derived from a "prayer meeting," as Dr. Edgar Black always characterized high level discussions with endless participants) had preceded me to headquarters. The one that blew all the fuses took place at the Institute of Aviation Medicine in Toronto. The subject of the meeting was "Lack of Moral Fibre": the serious charge, close to treason, that many flyers were compelled to face if they could not complete several tours of duty over–seas. Broken in spirit and physiologically unsafe to fly, nevertheless they were publicly stripped of their wings and degraded. The bemedalled discussants at the Toronto meeting were pounding on the table to the effect that all this air–sickness over–seas was criminal nonsense and had to be stopped. Each speaker vied with the last in the punishment recommended.

I innocently asked if the experts castigating our graduate pilots so volubly could state at what season of the year the pilots and navigators had been trained. Eyebrows bristled and silence descended until I said that our work at the Clinical Investigation Unit at Regina, Saskatchewan, had shown clearly that air crew trained in the cool dense air of the Canadian winter had met with very little rough air. Consequently, when they entered upon their flying duties in the cloud–infested skies of Britain—especially on Coastal Command—the true selection began, and for some, motion sickness soon developed. In contradiction to this unhappy group, it was found that those who had survived the rough air of the hot Canadian summer in training were unaffected by the rough air over England. In other words, the selection had already taken place.

Consternation reigned at once: the chairman could find no one who wanted the floor, so he adjourned the meeting and the advocates of the "Lack of Moral Fibre" charge were silenced temporarily in Canada. Over–seas there seems to have been a witch hunt for air crew who broke under stress. One of the chief hunters in this shameful business was left wondering shortly after the war whether his domineering personality caused his son's suicide. Possibly there is no blindness equal to that of the divinely guided.

One of the very pleasant features of a posting to Ottawa was the ability to take a Toonerville Trolley of a steam train up to the Gatineau Valley after a hot and hurried day in town. For five summers my parents had a cottage at Kirk's Ferry, over–looking the river with its purses of wood bolts heading for paper mills downstream. My father had been brought east early in the war to be, in effect, the schoolmaster to the Armed Forces. With him he brought all the courses that had been developed in the Great Depression for North America's first full high– school correspondence school in Victoria, B.C. By the end of the war there had been approximately 250,000 service personnel enrolled for courses through the Canadian Legion Educational Services in Ottawa.

Another enjoyable by–product of the Ottawa sojourn was the ability to go over from Air Force Headquarters to the East Block of the Parliament Buildings for tea with the legendary Leonard Brockington, Q.C. Early in the war he had been hired by Prime

Minister MacKenzie King to travel across Canada making patriotic speeches. As an orator Brockington had no equal. Audiences could scarcely believe that they could be charmed, swayed and energized by this little man who was bent nearly double with Marie–Strümpell arthritis. But from the moment he spoke he had them in the palm of his hand. Whether from a Welsh heritage or from years in courtrooms I do not know, but his imagination lifted even the most jaded listeners to new heights.

Over tea he would tell me of his labours on behalf of the prime minister who was invariably called Willie. Brock said that after a gruelling speaking tour through western Canada, he arrived in Vancouver to speak to a large gathering of service club members. After his oration was over, old friends came up to greet him. One of them asked: "What is your real job at the Prime Minister's Office?" Brock, not realizing that the microphone was still on, replied gaily: "I'm the oratorical midwife to an old maid." This led to a suspension of his contract by Willie, but that didn't last for long.

One day, over tea, Brock said: "Well my boy, it's a sad day at Laurier House. All days are sad, I suppose, for your brother James and those other chaps working up in the attic for Willie. He once wrote a book for the Rockefellers, *Industry with Humanity*. Your brother should write one now, *Industry without Humanity*." Then Brock went on: "Willie is very sad today. Pat died." I asked who Pat was. Brock replied: "Oh, that's Willie's smelly old dog. But I'll say one thing for Pat. He was the only member of the Cabinet that would admit he was a S.O.B."

Brockington bore his medical problems well, as did many in Ottawa. He knew and respected Sir Frederick Banting, the source of his insulin. They flew over much of the Arctic together. There they met Archbishop Fleming, who, to Brock's amusement, signed all pastoral letters, "Archibald The Arctic." Just as insulin had changed Brockington's life, so had penicillin changed that of Tommy Douglas, M.P., the father of Medicare in Canada. He had suffered with osteomyelitis since boyhood. Alas, there was no such remedy for the multiple sclerosis from which Stanley Knowles, M.P., the dean of House of Commons procedure, suffered for much of his life.

In the spring of 1945 Dr. J.B. Collip, who was chairman of the National Research Council's Aviation Medical Research Committee, sent me to the Marines' Camp Pendleton in southern California for field trials of a barbiturate that Canadian researchers had produced in an attempt to reduce or limit motion sickness, both on the sea and in the air. These were very interesting trials, which entailed, among other things, marching for five days without sleep. We stopped for meals of course, but no sleep was permitted. I found that by the fifth day the marines assigned to the experiment were becoming very scatty. At night we would have large campfires where everyone was encouraged to sing until one of the distraught members of the party would throw an ammunition belt into the fire and we would all have to take cover. The urine from the experimental subjects to be tested was daily taken down to the California Institute of Technology at Pasadena for analysis. I was sure that by the end of the marching the young marines would fall into bed. However, within an hour of the end of the trials, our experimental subjects had changed into their dress uniforms and were lined up along the highway heading for Hollywood.

The immensity of the Marine base at Camp Pendleton, which covered the original Santa Margarita Ranch, was for me an amazing discovery. I was particularly interested in the clothing for the enlisted ranks. All seams in the clothing were turned outward to prevent skin friction. This was especially useful in the shoes, which were actually boots with the rough side of the leather out and the polished side in, also making good sense. Clearly none of the officers or men there had ever seen a Canadian Air Force Medical Officer with the Caduceus on either lapel. I was introduced to this problem when one of the men saluted as he passed me at the camp and addressed me as "Father," assuming that I was a padre.

My final posting in the war was in September 1945, to the demobilization centre at Lachine, Quebec. While I waited for my discharge, I returned to the Montreal Neurological Institute as resident in neurology and to fulfil the requirements for the diploma in neurology offered by McGill University. On my return to Canada from the University of Sydney in Australia in 1949, I was approached to return to the RCAF full-time, as I had been accredited to the RAAF while away at the University of Sydney. With the opening of the medical faculty at the University of British Columbia in 1950, however, I was asked to take on the duties of the Wing Commander in charge of medical units in the RCAF auxiliary force in Vancouver.

With time the Reserve Air Force was disbanded. Unfortunately, the scheme for the summer training of university students who sought eventually to join the permanent force was likewise abandoned, so that a superb asset in manpower was lost.

CHAPTER EIGHTEEN

Post–War Training at McGill, 1945–1948

With the breakup of the Air Force headquarters medical staff well under way, I was assigned to the discharge depot at Lachine, Quebec, to await my release. The commanding officer there told me that he had so many physicians on his staff by now that he did not really need me. I therefore went to the Montreal Neurological Institute and put on my white togs again and started working on the neurological service. For the first month I was supposed to act as registrar of the institute, but I found that utterly boring and asked to be released to do clinical work only. Dr. Penfield asked me why I wore my Air Force uniform occasionally. I had to explain to him that those were pay days at Lachine and I had to attend for that very good reason. Colonel McEachern had just returned from a distinguished army career that covered everything from clinical neurology to night vision and nutrition. His M.N.I. Wards had been carried by "St. Francis" McNaughton during the war years. The only intern I had on the service with me was Dr. James Chen from China. Whenever I could not find him on the wards, I would go to the interns' residence where, sure enough, he would be reading a textbook on neurology. I explained to him that we had to make the patients our textbooks.

Unfortunately, in 1946 a serious polio epidemic occurred, with diagnosed cases and suspected cases raining down upon us. The head of the Royal Victoria Hospital, Dr. George Stephens, was not in very good health and called to ask if I could occupy the suite in the intern's residence set aside for him, but never used, so that telephone calls could be channelled there instead of to his office. I found that it was a very fine suite, with adequate room for two interns, a private bath and, of course, the all important telephone. For many years thereafter the Neurological Institute hung on to that excellent accommodation. By 1946 Theodore Rose had joined me on the wards and took his full share of polio patients across University Street in the Royal Victoria Hospital outpatient department. He did this despite the fact that he had a wife and four children at home. The load became extremely heavy and ambulances were bringing people from great distances. It was tragic to see the bulbar polio cases in which breathing and swallowing became next to impossible. I recall one wild ride in an ambulance down to the St. Lawrence River and through the tunnel under it to the Royal Alexandra Infectious Diseases Hospital, with a motorized suction apparatus in use all the way. I found the physician there over–worked in an understaffed hospital. He was wringing out hot towels and applying them to the crippled or affected limbs of the children involved. I spent considerable time with him doing just that and studying the unfortunately terminal cases, which seemed to me to be legion.

People with strokes were brought from great distances by ambulance simply because they had a paralysed limb. Thus, the sorting out of the true polio cases from other cases of weakness of one or more limbs became a major problem. After the epidemic was over I wrote a paper on "The Diagnostic Problem in Polio Myelitis." In submitting this to the Montreal Medico–Chirurgical Society, I was fortunate to receive a prize of $100, which to an unpaid intern meant a great deal.

At the end of the war McGill University decided to provide postgraduate diploma courses and I took the one in neurology. In addition to much clinical neurology, this diploma required six months in neurosurgery and six months in psychiatry. Dr. Penfield asked me with whom I wanted to do my neurosurgery. I suggested that I would like to do it with him because he did surgical neurology; whereas his counterpart Dr. William Cone, I said, was more interested in neurological surgery. The Chief had never heard this distinction before and proceeded to use it frequently! I never saw a man so ready to accept a new idea. Neurological cases flooded in from the Arctic to Latin America. One memorable trapper from the northern shores of Hudson's Bay, Damasse Gagnon, arrived with a bizarre form of respiratory paralysis. I found it easy to understand his French, except for some words I had never encountered before. I took all the French–speaking patients on the neurology service, and found that the French I had learned in Victoria, B.C., was perfectly adequate. At no time, except in Damasse Gagnon's case, did I find difficulty in understanding Quebecois—contrary to all the guff talked about the lack of Parisian French in Montreal. I asked the senior resident in the institute, Dr. Claude Bertrand, to help me with the strange words used by my patient Damasse. Try as he might, Bertrand could not understand some of the language, which turned out to be expressions used by native people in the north. A neurological examination, however, is the same no matter what land a human being comes from. Alas, the tumour invading the spinal cord high up into the neck region could not be removed entirely by Dr. Theodore Rasmussen and my northern friend eventually died.

As I translated for Dr. Penfield the anxieties of the Spanish–speaking relatives of patients being operated upon, I used to reflect on the role of language—developed for communication—as a barrier to understanding what geographically dispersed humans of all colours were saying, let alone meaning. One of my patients echoed these thoughts when she said that if all the pigment in the skin of a non–white person were scraped off the surface of the body it would not fill one teaspoon! I have yet to see a difference in the opened abdomen or the exposed brain of members of allegedly different races, despite all the anti–scientific garbage talked by the people I met in Bonn University in 1936–37.

I had the same feeling many years later, when Lester Pearson said, in effect, "How can there be peace in the world if we cannot grasp what other people are saying?" This is the cardinal tenet of the faculty and students at Pearson College near Victoria, B.C., the history of which will be detailed in a later chapter.

The work with the neurosurgical patients was very interesting, though I must say that the long standing at the operating table became a problem. We would scrub at 8:00 in the morning and might complete the first case by 3:00 or 3:30 in the afternoon. The Chief would drop out about 1:00 p.m. and the resident would finish up the operation, closing the cranium and scalp. Eventually I was given a counter–weighted seat with a revolving top, which certainly solved the physical problem for me. After a while, I am glad to say, many of the neurosurgeons and their assistants procured such seats. There was no way of eating during these long operations, of course, so a glass tube was inserted behind one's sterile mask through which orange juice and glucose could be sucked up.

Dr. Penfield's patients came from many parts of the world, including many from Latin America. While The Chief remembered some of his Spanish from his time in Spain, he would ask me to explain to the Spanish–speaking parents of a child exactly what the procedure was and why a temporary swelling of the tissues might cause a loss of speech for three to five days after a brain operation. This was a standard precaution taken so that no one became excited about the aphasia that sometimes supervened.

The clinical neurology and neurosurgery practised in the institute were of a high order. The objective was to do the best for the patient, at whatever cost in time or effort by the staff. The Chief carried a back-breaking load of administration within the institute, heavy responsibility vis-à-vis McGill and the constant worry of financing the hospital and the research endeavour. He had his clinical acumen severely tested one day at the scene of an accident on the country road running from his farm at Memphremagog up to the St. Lawrence River, where he and his wife were to take a ship up the beautiful Saguenay River to see the autumn leaves. A car had overturned on a curve in the road and the driver had been thrown free into the grass.

Dr. Penfield rushed to help the unconscious patient and found a total loss of reflexes in a middle-aged man whose breathing was slow and noisy. As the minutes ticked by the doctor's wife reminded him of the ferry schedule. In getting to his feet he slipped on the grass and fell on the patient's chest, which produced a great exhalation of alcoholic mist. The diagnosis was then all too clear and the Penfields caught their ferry.

At the end of my neurosurgical stint I proceeded to Vancouver, where I was married over the Christmas holidays. On my return I was assigned, for my psychiatry, to the excellent Allan Memorial Institute, which adjoined the Royal Victoria Hospital grounds and had been the residence of the Allan steamship line family. The staff was extremely well conducted and I came to have great respect for the nurses on the psychiatric wards, who in actual fact did much of the prescribed ward therapy. One of the difficult situations I encountered was a pair of married sisters who were twins. The husband of one was a very successful businessman and the husband of the other was clearly a plodder. I explained this to the wife of the plodder, who was losing out year after year in a vain attempt to keep up with her sister. I finally convinced her and her husband that they should live in another city where the competition was not so keen nor so obvious.

A star patient was an out-and-out schizophrenic whose mother was a manic depressive. This combination has been known for generations but remains unexplained. However, while in the manic phase the mother arranged with her powerful local friends to have her son put in charge of all messages going out from the naval station in

Montreal at the beginning of the war. The son, even then, was approaching a full-blown schizophrenic profile. Enquiries began to be made and it was found that instead of sending out signals, as required, he was depositing these signals one after another in the bottom drawer of his desk. It is little wonder that there was confusion. By the time I saw him after the end of the war, he was, of course, a very deteriorated schizophrenic case with few teeth left and in very parlous condition. His henpecked father would do anything to satisfy the mother and prevent the son from being released on a weekend pass. The father would always come armed with a bottle of whisky, which he would deposit in various places in my office. There was little we could do at that time for such an advanced case of schizophrenia.

Insulin shock therapy was still in vogue and for a few depressed cases limited amounts of electroshock were used. The aversion treatment for chronic alcoholics, in which a colourless and tasteless solution of an emetic was introduced into the favourite drink of the patient concerned, was carried out successfully. After a few minutes intense vomiting took place. This treatment was repeated on successive days for up to two weeks. The effect that this had on some of the otherwise hopeless cases was remarkable. It was life saving to a lawyer's wife who would lock herself in a closet at home until she had consumed a full bottle.

A bizarre incident briefly panicked the service: an important-looking man admitted himself to the Ross Private Pavilion as the self-declared patient of a psychiatrist in the city. I was asked to see this patient and objected that the physician allegedly admitting him was not on the hospital staff. The criticism I underwent mounted alarmingly until suddenly a phone call revealed that the important patient was actually a well-known impersonator in Montreal who had, of course, engaged the most expensive suite in the entire hospital system. He was discharged with no further questions asked.

In summing up my years in Montreal, I would say that some of the most interesting patients and interesting personalities came to the Montreal Neurological Institute for help. One of the most charming women seen at the institute was Mrs. M.J. Coldwell, who had a long history of multiple sclerosis. Her husband, as a veteran member of the House of Commons and Leader of the Cooperative Commonwealth Federation, became a firm friend of the institute and paid an annual visit on our behalf to Prime Minister St. Laurent who succeeded MacKenzie King.

Their annual consultation in Ottawa on the federal grant to the institute took about 60 seconds. The prime minister would always assure Mr. Coldwell that he shared his great respect for Dr. Penfield. Nothing more had to be said. It is interesting, but also sad, that the dean of the house of parliament in Ottawa, the Reverend Stanley Knowles, was also struck down with multiple sclerosis. We outlined a rehabilitation agenda for him and he kept his part of the bargain throughout, emerging from a wheelchair to crutches, to canes, to walking without canes and finally to driving a motor car. A vicious termite in the House of Commons snarlingly said, when Stanley took his place on the floor again, "It proves that the whole thing was hysterical." I wish there were a special hell to which we could assign such mendacious donkeys.

A tragic case from which we learned a lot was a huge, very well muscled man who had been a milk handler able to lift large milk cans on and off trains in Vermont singlehandedly. He arrived almost totally paralysed and even with artificial respiration was not able to make it. He was, on admission, fully conscious but one after another his limbs became totally paralysed. It had been thought in his home town that he might have poliomyelitis but the rapid advance of his symptoms caused his physicians to send him by ambulance to Montreal.

His family was devastated but co–operative and asked us to do a complete autopsy. To our surprise *every* intervertebral disc in his body had been ruptured, extending presumably over a period of several years. The autopsy showed that Dr. William Cone, as usual, had made the right diagnosis: total obstruction of the anterior spinal artery by one or more protruded invertebral discs. This patient is now in the medical literature; his x–rays, and the pathological discs studied under the microscope, appear in the excellent book on intervertebral discs by Dr. Reuben Rabinovich, who was one of the research fellows at the institute. Parenthetically, I should remind readers that Rabinovich received a very high French decoration for his part in the underground during World War II. Born in La Macaza, Quebec, he had trained in neurosurgery in Paris with the famous Professor Clovis Vincent. When he was transported to Poland to serve in the prison camps as a neurosurgeon, he arranged to ship alleged patients, solidly supported in plaster casts, to Paris for further treatment, where they served the underground well.

In 1947, with my Air Force gratuity, I purchased a small English motor car. Taking it for a spin on Sherbrooke Street one evening, I noticed a man limping on the sidewalk and carrying a very heavy briefcase. I slowed down and recognized that it was Wilder Penfield.

I stopped and offered him a ride; he congratulated me on the new car but I saw that he was very fatigued and very depressed. As I drove him home he said, "Billy, come in for a chat. I must talk to you." So we sat down at the Open Arms and he explained to me that the research programme at the institute was having very great financial difficulties and that the authorities in Quebec City were being very tough on the hospital itself. I enquired as to the amount necessary to keep the institute as a whole in the black. This turned out to be about $40,000 annually. Later that evening I talked to my brother on the telephone in Ottawa and explained this situation. The Chief had said to me "perhaps I should have gone to Philadelphia after all." This set off a train of thought in my brother's mind and he said, "Send me all the information you have and I will talk to the prime minister tomorrow." I quickly expressed the papers to Ottawa and my brother formulated a brief for Mr. King.

After 10 years with the prime minister my brother knew what could excite his righteous indignation and produce swift action. Suffice it to say that two days later, at a farewell dinner given me by the institute and my McGill colleagues, an urgent call came to Dr. Penfield who took with him to the telephone Dr. William Cone. Clearly it was the call from Ottawa we had been waiting for. The two athletes wriggled into the phone box at the Faculty Club at McGill and had a considerable conversation with the prime minister. He made it clear that whatever was required was going to be found on grounds of patriotism. He found the $40,000 in one of his Privy Council funds, "and the show went on."

I finished up my clinical work and was granted McGill's first Diploma in Neurology. En route west I took the examinations in Chicago to qualify for the American specialist status known as the National Board in Neurology. The examination was entirely oral, beginning at 8 a.m. and finishing at 6 p.m. The section on neuropathology was rigorous. I was shown two dozen microscopic slides and these had to be discussed with experts who had been assembled from many American medical schools. There I met the Canadian Dr. Earl Walker, trained at the University of Alberta and now professor of neurosurgery at the University of Chicago. I had last seen him at Oxford where he was lecturing on his classic work on the thalamic nuclei of the human brain.

The clinical examination was conducted by outstanding neurologists from across the continent. I had the good fortunate to draw, as my examiner, the distinguished Professor Ben Bosches of Northwestern Medical School. He assigned me a female patient whose

English was very limited so I spoke to her in German. Before examining her neurologically I walked across the ward and closed the window to shut out a chilling wind. After all, this was Chicago.

My patient clearly had multiple sclerosis. When I went over my findings and my diagnosis with Professor Bosches, he said: "You get the highest marks I have ever given. I saw you close that window and I heard you speaking to that patient in her native tongue. Good luck to you."

At 6 p.m. each of the hundred or more physicians was handed a telegram. There was rejoicing and there were tears. I had never seen so many middle-aged men weeping. They had come as refugees from Europe and had little training outside of mental hospitals in the U.S.A. They would have to try again a year later.

Then on to Winnipeg where the dean of medicine examined the candidates for specialist qualification in neurology and psychiatry in Canada. He asked many questions about the work in those fields at McGill. With my wife and 6-week-old son, I arrived home in Vancouver in time for Christmas, 1947.

CHAPTER NINETEEN

Australia, 1948–1949

My Australian connection began about 1937 when Jack Eccles, my supervisor in the doctor of philosophy programme at Oxford, left England to become the director of the Kanematsu Institute in Sydney. (The search committee set up by Oxford University to find a successor to Sir Charles Sherrington foolishly passed over Jack because at age 37 he was, in their view, "too young.")

For years Dr. Oliver Latham, exactly Hollywood's idea of an absent-minded professor, had filled two roles in Sydney: lecturer in neuropathology in the university, and at the same time director of research for the mental hospitals in New South Wales. He was anything but absent-minded in his youth and had invested in Peters ice cream company with fabulous results.

Just before World War II began Oliver thought he should retire and Eccles was consulted with regard to a successor. Thus, the professor of pathology, Keith Inglis, wrote to me at McGill asking if this post held any interest for me. Then the war burst upon us all and no appointment was made. Oliver carried on, despite his age, and turned his laboratory into a blood transfusion centre.

After the war Keith Inglis once again contacted me to know if I could be persuaded to go out to Australia. I telephoned him to say that I was considering it but would be occupied with the postgraduate diploma in neurology that McGill had just launched, involving work in neurology, neurosurgery and psychiatry. The Australians were willing to wait, and in the meantime I found that one of the interns in the Royal Victoria Hospital in Montreal would trade his house in Vaucluse, a beautiful area of Sydney, for a year, in exchange for my new English motor car.

So off to Australia it was in March of 1948 with my wife and four month-old son—all this on a slow freighter on which I was to be ship's doctor. As there were 40 passengers, one was required. The ship called at Honolulu, which had not yet sprouted skyscraper hotels. The dignified Royal Hawaiian was still the centre of things and its drinking fountains produced pineapple juice instead of water.

With the assistance of Dr. Tom Bennett, who had trained in neurosurgery at McGill, we saw a great deal of Honolulu in a few hours. He gave me some stainless steel wire, of threadlike diameter, to sew up the scalp of one of the crew who, because of his great strength, was called Samisone. He, poor fellow, came up under the keel of a lifeboat on deck and split his scalp, though not his skull, from front to back. By the time we arrived in Melbourne he had recovered fully.

As the ship ploughed on in a south–westerly direction towards Fiji, more and more flying fish and seabirds came in sight. The unusual feature of Suva was the apparel of the huge native policemen, who wore colourful skirts with decalled edges.

We touched down briefly at Fiji and New Zealand. One of the incredible sights was to pass Canton Island with its single tree and to see a large American liner high and dry on this low, lonely island. The official story was, of course, that the Japanese navy had been in hot pursuit, causing this bizarre dry–docking.

A fleeting stop was made in Botany Bay in order to let off a Czech refugee diplomat whose wife had suffered a stroke. Dr. W. Lister Reid, another of Wilder Penfield's pupils, came on board for a consultation; the patient and her family were transferred to a waiting tender. Though we could see the Vaucluse house we were to enjoy for a year, the captain would not permit my wife and child to get off. Instead we were all taken to Melbourne, then they flew back to Sydney. I had to stay an extra day in Melbourne transferring the pharmacy to the right authorities and finding our trunks on the wharf. A stevedore and drayman, en route to the train, took me to see a typical Australian pub. The interesting thing was that there were no seats whatsoever in it, so that if you could not stand you literally would be swept out. As the law held then, there was a nightly closing of all pubs at 6 p.m. and the kerbside might be littered with non–standees.

Finally we installed ourselves in the large, one floor, rather spread out rented stone house. The view of the Sydney bridge and harbour was marvellous. My friend at New College, Bill Bradfield, was the son of the designer of this great bridge, who incidentally designed other great engineering projects in Australia, such as redirecting rivers that ran uselessly into the Pacific so that they ran into the parched heartland of Australia. Bill's D.Phil. gown kept me warm at ceremonies in the unheated great hall of the university. The Royal Prince Alfred Hospital of approximately 1,400 beds shared the campus with the medical faculty of the university. The peninsulas and bays all the way from the towering heads where the Pacific rolled, to the end of navigation for large ships to the west, was said to offer 100 miles of shoreline. Before long we found our way straight down the slope to Neilson's Bay, where safely placed behind steel nets one could look out at the sharks anxious to come in! On the outer shore, on the open Pacific, was the magnificent Bondi Beach with its sun–tanned, muscular sea rescue teams always practising with their unsinkable boats.

Life at the university, seven or so miles away, began every morning after a hair–raising (for me) drive on the left side of the road, particularly through Bondi Junction. The trick there was to calculate how close one could go to the tram tracks without coming out pleated. The department of pathology was a large one in a building built on the campus years before with help from the Rockefeller Foundation, on land adjoining the Royal Prince Alfred Hospital. Across the road was an excellent hospital for mothers and babies. It was doubly excellent in the view of the medical students and interns because it boasted a pub on the street corner that had never been acquired—because of price—when the hospital was built. Conveniently, a door had been cut through from the hospital and the telephone in the pub seemed to be a local of the hospital switchboard.

Many of the patients in Royal Prince Alfred Hospital were actually out on balconies for 12 months of the year. In the impressive entrance to the hospital was a very large bronze memorial to American physicians who had come to Australia for the war and had camped on the site. One day, as I passed this memorial or celebratory plaque, I mentioned to Professor Inglis that Captain A.M. Harvey, noted therein, at age 34 had just been made professor of medicine at Johns Hopkins University in Baltimore. The professor stopped short, shook his head and said, "I am sure they would never do a thing like that." We visited Sir Herbert Schlinck, the medical director of the hospital whose power seemed to be that of an emperor. I got on very well with "Berti" and his wife, whom we visited out at Careel Bay on several weekends. He was a hard–driving medical man who used to quiz me about new things that he could do for his hospital.

A dozen of us in pathology used to have our lunch around a large table in the departmental library, with the professor "in the chair." His eyebrows would go up at some of the many stories told. The political life of Australia had never been dull: I heard many times of the scene at Versailles, at the end of the first world war, when Billy Hughes, the prime minister of Australia (a country that lost legions of men in the fighting at Gallipoli and in Europe), stood up to the erudite President Woodrow Wilson of the United States. One of my colleagues told of riding in an airplane years later when a white-haired gentleman kept throwing letters into the centre aisle. On picking up a handful of these and handing them back to the former, but still feisty, prime minister, he was told: "Leave them down there. Any fool that can't address what he has to say to me on the back of a business card doesn't get read."

I was ushered into my alleged laboratory with suitable fanfare and preparation only to find it empty! The blood transfusion centre had long since gone and there was no sign of furniture or apparatus of any sort. All hands offered to help, but Australia in those days was not on the world's trade routes for specialized equipment and chemicals. Nevertheless, the ever-hospitable Australians ransacked their own laboratories for apparatus and eventually I could start work.

Of the many visitors to my laboratory, none was more interesting than Dr. Robert Morison of the Rockefeller Foundation. He had the same wanderlust that characterized his uncle, Admiral Samuel Eliot Morison, who re-sailed Columbus' first voyage to the New World. Robert had come to Sydney to survey the medical school buildings to which his foundation had contributed. He could not believe the width of the corridors in the excellent structure, but it was said to serve for "air conditioning." In the evenings, at our house at Vaucluse, he would say, "Have you any real coffee in the house?" He had heard the local children's rhyme "coffee boiled is coffee spoiled" and he swore that as soon as steam rose from a coffee pot in Australia the brew was dashed with milk, producing a dilute product, little more than warm. With a gas strike in Sydney we were limited to a very small flame, but that applied to the edge of a topless old coffee pot did wonders for Morison. It paid off handsomely years later in New York.

I soon met the health authorities of the state of New South Wales, who were the source of the funds for the research laboratory. I asked if I might be taken to see the mental hospitals and not long after was driven to a number of them. The state has a great variety of terrain: with its rivers plunging through mountains to the coast there is an ever-changing environment to be seen. There was no such variety, however, in the mental hospitals. One near Sydney had been built by convicts who had quarried the stone on site. In fact, the airing yard for the patients was the former quarry. In another, the postmortem equipment was so primitive and the autopsy room's single electric light bulb of such low wattage that I could scarcely imagine that many examinations of the brain after death had ever been made.

In marked contrast was the high standard of the interns and residents in these hospitals. As I taught the future colleagues of these doctors, in the fourth year of the six–year undergraduate course in medicine, I was very impressed with the abundant supply of grey matter that Australia possessed. I felt sorry for the psychiatric residents whose clinical work as postgraduates would have to be spent in that mental hospital system. Those who could hope for a posting in or near Sydney had the advantage of lectures by a very dedicated but disillusioned professor of psychiatry. He told me that as his ship docked at Singapore, en route from England, he chanced to meet the psychiatrist who was vacating the chair in Sydney, en route home to London. The recently appointed man was shocked to learn the real facts, but went on to Sydney anyway. Again, it was his students' talents in class that sustained him.

Christmas was spent in Canberra at the home of Canada's High Commissioner. The heat was stifling, but the company wonderful. At a garden party our one–year–old son divested himself of all apparel and went around the lawns and fish pools on all fours at a remarkable pace. The Chinese ambassador shouted, "He is the spirit of Christmas." Canada was well represented by the Hon. Kenneth Greene, not a career diplomat, but a pillar of the ruling party in Ottawa. His business partner was pater familias for H.M. loyal opposition.

Our white–haired host was the son of one of the rulers of the Ottawa Valley, where J.R. Booth was king and his logging empire made the rules. So he had seen a great deal of political life and specialized in deflating the pompous, often by giving caricatures of their worst speeches. As a young man he had attended a reception at Rideau Hall—the house of the representative of the Crown in Ottawa—at which he warned a newly appointed senator from the prairies that the liquid he was ladling out of a punch bowl was champagne. The senator blew a cloud of it over him and shouted, "Mind your business, young man. I know ginger ale when I see it!" He was carried out on a door.

Ken Greene's stories of Canadian politicians were legion. When the Hon. Charles Dunning visited London as Canada's finance minister, it was the return of a native, for he was born in England. He left as a young boy to work in the harvest on the Canadian prairies. Gradually he rose to become a leader in the Winnipeg grain exchange.

After visiting Canada House on Trafalgar Square, his first desire was to drive out to Hyde Park to see if all the stories about unfettered free speech there were true. Proceeding slowly through the park in his car he saw a group of a dozen people listening to an inoffensive little man on a soapbox shouting: "The police of London are the most pusillanimous in the world." Dunning could not believe it, as a helmeted policeman was standing right there listening to every word. Suddenly the policeman made a move, and Dunning said to himself: "There it comes. He's going to arrest the speaker for blasphemy or worse." Instead, the constable walked over to Dunning's car and said: "Sir, would you either shut your engine off or move along. The crowd cannot hear what the orator is saying."

Greene had been cited by a member of the raucous House of Representatives in Canberra as a foreign agent attempting to glean state secrets by "poisoning" parliamentarians somewhere along the ambassadorial row with drinks made of equal parts maple syrup and rye whisky. The stream of callers increased.

I first met Greene in person at a hospital bedside. From Canberra he called me at the medical school in Sydney to say that his very beautiful blonde daughter had broken her leg while skiing in the Australian Alps and was on her way by ambulance to Sydney, 202 miles away! Would I get the best surgeon on the faculty to look after her at the Royal Prince Alfred Hospital? So I called up my New College, confederate, the orthopod Hugh Barrie, and he was to stand by. The only bed available was in a side room off his ward. (Side rooms are used for dying patients, and are often located beside the desk of the ward sister.)

When the poor girl arrived, pale as a sheet, she was placed carefully in the bed and Barrie was about to examine her when the ceiling fell down! Plaster and dust and confusion reigned. However, he did such a fine job on the spiral fracture of the femur that the girl was dancing at Harvard six months later. Whenever my family was returning from a visit to Canberra thereafter, I was charged to deliver the makings of the maple syrup restorative to Barrie's apartment. Soon the telephone would ring and a booming Australian voice would erupt: "I say, someone has been tampering with my milk supply."

These interludes added spice to an otherwise quiet pace of life. The neighbours and faculty friends were very hospitable and helped us to cope with the rationing of food such as sugar, tea and meat. The dean of medicine was a very cultivated man who spent many evenings with me discussing a neurological institute for Sydney. For years there had been an excellent Saturday morning seminar to which all the clinicians, teachers and researchers interested in diseases of the nervous system would come. The dean had heard of attempts around the world to house these types of people together and wanted details of the arrangements at McGill in Montreal.

Eventually, with the ready help of the machine shop next door to my laboratory, I constructed a clear-plastic model of what such an institute might look like in the Sydney context. Years later it was built and its first director was one of my former Australian students.

The machinist was a man of many skills and I ran the gamut of them. I had asked Sir William Osler's nephew at McGill, Dr. W.W. Francis, if any wood had survived the fire that had destroyed the home in which Osler had been raised. One day the Australian customs office called to say they had intercepted a contraband parcel and would I come to see them. The forbidden object was a charred verandah post from the Osler homestead. The customs people enquired about a crime, foul play, the scene of the incendiarism, etc. I told them it had all happened a century ago, but then they complained that the wood probably contained insects and could not be admitted to the country. I asked what they were going to do with it. Dead silence. Then one of them uttered some mild Australian obscenities and told me to get it out of their sight. Soon the medical school's mechanic had made from it a beautiful gavel, which I presented to the dean of medicine. He wondered if the gavel alone would keep order at his meetings. He then relayed to me the Australian definition of a dean: The dean is to his faculty as a hydrant is to the dogs of the neighbourhood.

Strangely, the Neurological Institute was eventually built near the veterans' hospital in the Concord area of Sydney. That is precisely where 100 Canadian prisoners were confined when they were transported from Canada after their uprising against the British government failed in 1837. Their crime was that they sought responsible and representative government in both Quebec and Ontario. When their effort collapsed, some fled to the United States, while others were sent to Van Diemen's Land (Tasmania). Those sent to Bermuda were sent back by that colony's governor. The imprisoned Canadians (known in Quebec as Les Patriotes) were allowed out of the Concord stockade by day, each on a "ticket of good behaviour," which meant working gratis for one of the civil servants of the settlement. By night the vaulting Canadians combed the beaches for shells, which they eventually sold to farmers for the soil's enrichment. Their tribulations at Concord are to be found in the Toronto Public Library, in diaries written by Ducharme and Prieur. The Australian historian Dr. George Mackanness, of the faculty of education in Sydney, gave me many of his publications on this sad situation. My brother, Dr. James Gibson, is now expanding this story. Five years later they were able to board a ship for England where a parliamentarian, Mr. Rowbottom, M. P. for the city of London, helped them to get passage back to Canada. One of the Canadians, Joseph Marceau, stayed in Australia, where there are now descendants of his numbering in the hundreds. One of them attended the University of Chicago and ended up as the psychologist at a maximum security prison in British Columbia.

There is an interesting connection between Brockville, Ontario, and the Murray Valley in Australia where superb wines are grown. Over a century ago the prime minister of Australia visited an area outside Los Angeles still known as Ontario. It was in this area that the early irrigation of fruit crops began in California. Since the pumps for the irrigation came from Ontario, the area was so christened. Two Canadians who had much to do with that early irrigation, the Chaffee brothers, were taken to Australia by the prime minster to help him with the early irrigation in the Murray Valley. One stayed in Australia and the other returned to California. The names have been perpetuated in the Ontario area of southern California by the Chaffee School of Aviation at the Ontario airport.

I suppose I had been in Sydney six months when I was asked to meet the minister of health, a very jovial Irishman who had too much on his plate. Shortly thereafter I was sent for by a commanding figure in the civil service who enquired about my work and then presented me with a document to sign. It was a rosy review I was supposed to have made of the mental hospitals of New South Wales and, most importantly, it stated that I found them equal to the world's best! I am afraid my opinion of the official, who spoke as "the admirable Crichton," went through the floor. I said I could not sign such a statement for it was patently untrue. I walked out realizing that when my year's contract was up I would have to leave. It tore my guts out to see such a charade being practised not only on the tax payers but on the patients and, most of all, on the unsuspecting medical students who would soon be their doctors.

I wrote to Professor Robert Burns Aird, the professor of neurology at the University of California in San Francisco, to say that if the visiting professorship that had been offered a year before were still open I could begin in March 1949. It was necessary to arrange passage for that date either to California or to Vancouver. My wife was pregnant and it would be a race against time to get home safely to Vancouver. Luckily the Canadian–Australian line's M.V. Aorangi was to make its last voyage to Vancouver in March, and the friendly Canadian in charge in Sydney accepted my motor car in exchange for our passage (cars were still rationed).

Gradually the news leaked out and the press began to enquire. Vincent Fairfax of the *Sydney Morning Herald* had been a kind host and took an interest in my work. However, it was the publisher of the *Sun* who was quick to offer to take up the fight. I had to tell him that I would say nothing until I was safely on board the Aorangi and moving out of the great harbour towards the Heads. As good as his word he had a reporter come out to the departing ship in a tender and I was able to tell my story in such detail that it could not be denied. The reporter got it right (or as he said "roight") and enabled me to tell the citizens of New South Wales what their government was trying to conceal.

Predictably, there was a cable waiting for me in Auckland from the minister, and another in Honolulu, to which I never replied. I gather from some of my students that the fireworks increased daily, until the government announced a Royal Commission under a distinguished British psychiatrist. In the end he was able to lever the financing for an improved system and my students found something better for their work and their patients well into the future.

In retrospect, I found the fun–loving Australians among the most hospitable people in the world. They have come into their own since those tough post–war days. World medicine owes Australia a very great debt, starting with Howard Florey and his wife Ethel: the penicillin pioneers and man's benefactors. I will discuss him in another chapter. There was a succession of Australian Rhodes scholars who brought great credit to their homeland; men such as Sir Hugh Cairns, the Nuffield professor of surgery at Oxford, and Brian Maegraith in tropical medicine, to name but two in medicine. The internationally known physiologist Sir John Eccles was a Nobel laureate, as was Sir Macfarlane Burnet of the Walter and Eliza Hall Institute in Melbourne. Never to be forgotten was "Pansy" Wright, who was invited to join Florey's group at Oxford in 1936. (His first name was short for chimpanzee.) He was a tough customer, eventually to become chancellor of the University of Melbourne, where he had served as professor of physiology since 1939.

Decades removed from these giants was A.W. Campbell, born on a sheep station, who graduated in medicine at Edinburgh in 1889 and thereafter spent 13 years as neuropathologist to the Rainhill Mental Hospital near Liverpool. With the encouragement of Sir Charles Sherrington, then the professor of physiology at Liverpool, Campbell produced what is probably the best, and least contentious, map of the surface of the human brain. His contribution in 1905 put Australian neurological science in the vanguard.

Since Campbell's time, Australians have made very significant contributions to the neurological sciences. Sir John Eccles, F.R.S., shared the Nobel Prize for his discoveries on the internal working of nerve cells, after monitoring them with microelectrodes. As a Rhodes scholar from Melbourne, he worked with Sir Charles Sherrington, O.M., at Oxford, as did Howard Florey, a Rhodes scholar from Adelaide. Florey's persistence produced penicillin for the world. Another Rhodes man from Adelaide, Sir Hugh Cairns, the distinguished neurosurgeon, was the moving spirit behind Lord Nuffield's princely endowments, which brought Oxford its clinical medical school, which today is at the top of the tree.

A truly unique and grassroots medical development in Australia was the flying doctor service. The Rev. John Flynn spent his long life at the Inland Mission of the Presbyterian church in providing, through small cottage hospitals in the vast outback, mobile medical and nursing services. By 1920 Flynn was convinced that the light airplanes developed in World War I were the solution to his problem of rapid response to emergencies in rural Australia. A pedal-powered radio transmitter provided the nervous system for his purely voluntary organization. Flynn's ingenuity gave the outback a ready means of flying medical and nursing help to isolated areas, or of bringing patients to first-class metropolitan facilities. It was a pleasant surprise to him to be awarded the Order of the British Empire, as well as an honorary doctorate from McGill University in Montreal. The Australian model has been copied, especially in Canada and in parts of Africa.

The fauna and flora of Australia are so different from other parts of the world, as Darwin was to discover, that even the casual visitor is conscious of the muted tones of grey, green and brown, as compared with the darker colours in Canada. The bird life is incredibly varied, as we found from early morning kookaburra recitals on our chimney top in Sydney. Fishing in the rapidly flowing rivers of the central massif is a pleasure, especially at Talpingo, near Camberra. There one can sit on the back stoop of a forest pub and fish in a chuckling stream all day.

In all, Australia was a wonderful experience. One can only echo, on leaving, their patriot cry, "Advance Australia fair!"

CHAPTER TWENTY

University of California at San Francisco, 1949

Having arrived home in Vancouver with my family on the Aorangi, a ship I had long admired in the waters of the Strait of Juan de Fuca, I flew to San Francisco where, for three months, I was the visiting professor in neurology under the friendly aegis of Dr. Robert Burns Aird. While he was not related to Sir John Aird, the Canadian banker, he had the same profile and could have passed for him at any bankers' meeting.

Professor Aird had a very active diagnostic outpatient service at the University of California Hospital on the slopes of Mount Parnassus. While his beds were largely at the University of California in San Francisco, his responsibilities included the endless wards of neurological patients at County Hospital. He was labouring uphill to prepare a major address to the World Neurological Congress in Paris concerning his electroencephalographic studies of many diseases. I told him that if he would stay at home and write his paper and prepare his illustrations, I would take the wards for him for three months. This was agreed upon, and I must say the three months went by far too quickly. Aird was a Boston–trained neurologist: there have been few better than those trained there by Stanley Cobb and Derek Denny–Brown, a New Zealand Rhodes scholar who had studied with Sherrington and at Queen Square in London.

I was amazed at the great distances travelled by people to visit the epileptic clinic that we ran. They came from as far south as San Luis Obispo. The University of California at Los Angeles was just being organized and eventually would take over that distant group of patients. The neurosurgical side of the house under Professor Howard Naffziger was largely made up of Americans who had trained at the Montreal Neurological Institute. They and their classmates in

Pasadena, hoped that I had come to the "sunshine state" to stay. However, I was more interested in helping to build a new medical school in Vancouver.

One of the residents at Parnassus was a remarkably gifted Swiss, Dr. Rudi Schmid. He later became one of the world's experts on what to do about people in the armed forces and Turkey, etc., who had been served drinks into which methyl alcohol or fluid from duplicating machines or anti–freeze of various kinds had been mixed. He was a superb skier. He became professor of medicine and eventually dean at California. An intern who was cubical in his dimensions, and a terribly hard worker, was Dr. Edward Shev. He developed a life interest in myasthenia gravis. Patients with this disease have a profound weakness due to the fact that the transmitter, supplied by the nerves to the muscle, does not have adequate time to act before it is swept away and muscle function becomes dangerously reduced. The first case I saw of this remarkable disease was in a young woman in Montreal who complained that it began after eating "gefillete fish." However that might have been, she was unable to raise her head from the bed or engage in any muscular activity on waking in the morning until she had swallowed a pill containing prostigmin. This enabled the electrical and chemical activity, which proceeded down the nerves to the muscles, to move a limb. Without this pill first thing in the morning, she was helpless.

One day I received a phone call from the preclinical part of the U.C. Medical School, across the bay in Berkeley, from the Canadian–born professor of physiology, Dr. Olmsted. He had been an excellent physiologist all his life and was very interested in the history of French physiologists such as the great Claude Bernard. He called to ask if on a Saturday morning he might bring his class across the bay to Parnassus to be shown some neurophysiological problem. I replied that I had a woman who lived at Richmond, up the bay, who was severely disabled with myasthenia gravis and I would ask her if she would agree to a demonstration in front of his large class of medical students. She was only too willing to do this, so I sent a taxi for her early in the morning and her family co–operated fully in lifting her, without any medication having been taken, into the taxi. When it arrived at Parnassus I recruited four athletic students to carry her up to the lecture hall. Every seat was taken and there was an air of great expectancy. The patient was totally incapacitated in so far as any muscular activity was concerned.

I asked Dr. Shev to give her some prostigmin intravenously. Within a minute her eyelids began to flicker, then she smiled, then she was able to raise her head, to grasp his hand and to sit up, and finally to stand up. Thereupon Shev did a dance on top of this long counter to the cheers of the amazed students. The patient had been so co–operative that after asking her a few questions, I had her return by taxi to her home in distant Richmond. That all cost me a pretty penny but it was worth it to see the enthusiasm displayed by the students.

Then on the blackboard I outlined exactly what the problem had been and what the temporary solution to it was, i.e., medication that the patient always had with her. Professor Olmsted, bless him, came forward and said that though he understood the theory of this he had never seen it in practice before. He had thought that it might take two or three hours for the synaptic medicine to function, so he was astounded that within two to three minutes full muscle function had been restored. He was a very honest man and carried his students with him. They all went home after much chatter, and I suppose most of them decided that morning to become neurologists.

To run ahead of the story a bit, I should add that the faithful Dr. Shev, through his outpatient clinic activity, provided a number of myasthenic patients to Dr. Peter Dau, the pioneer who later tried a form of dialysis on such patients. Dau became one of the star researchers supported by the Muscular Dystrophy Association in New York and I was always happy to vote for his grant application. In lay terms, he had been washing the blood in such a way that an offending immunological chemical within the blood was excluded, to the great relief of the patient. Each year in the Jerry Lewis Telethon, one or more of the myasthenic patients in the country who had benefitted from Shev's early interest and Dau's daring were exhibited. One most impressive case was a concert pianist in her thirties who had had to give up performances entirely. After this treatment she resumed her concert appearances very successfully. So one never knows where a single demonstration to a large class may lead.

Part way through my visiting professorship I flew home to Vancouver where my second son was born. He was a "blue baby" for sure, with what was thought to be an imperfect closure at the point of the over–lapping flaps making up the inter–ventricular wall in the heart. I am happy to say that at age eight the opening closed spontaneously and he became a giant of 6'4" who can play three games of hockey a day.

During this brief visit to Vancouver, I was called upon by the director of the Mental Hospitals of British Columbia, Dr. Arthur Crease, a rotund man with a red face and white, white hair, who looked exactly like Santa Claus. He had a wonderful grasp of the need for research into the biochemistry of mental illness, and as a young man in 1913 had tried to build such a laboratory in British Columbia. He was now about to retire from the provincial service, and the crowning glory of his years was the development of the Crease Clinic at Essondale (a large mental hospital complex named after Henry Esson Young, Osler's pupil who had been the most successful minister of health in the province). Dr. Crease proposed that I should return to British Columbia after my time in California and set up a research laboratory for the Crease Clinic. The laboratory would have to be on the university campus in order to keep in touch with the scientific developments in the field of biochemistry and neurophysiology. I agreed to this and within a short time arrangements were made on the university campus for just such a laboratory, thanks in large part to the highly enlightened president of the university, Dr. Norman A.M. MacKenzie. After the first war he had, on his veterans' credit, entered the medical school at Dalhousie University in Halifax, Nova Scotia. That had been a compromise arranged with his parents. They wished him to follow his father's footsteps in the Presbyterian ministry, but Larry MacKenzie wished to do law. They "sawed it off" in such a fashion that he was able to study medicine. After his distinguished first year the parents relented, and said that he had done so well (being one of the few to get a first class in anatomy) that he was encouraged then to go on to study law and he became a celebrated international lawyer.

President MacKenzie was devoted to mental health education and research, and had been one of the early backers of Dr. Clarence Hincks in the Canadian Mental Health Association in Toronto. Dr. Crease helped me to acquire a small corridor that had once been used, literally, as a radio shack in which RCAF wireless personnel had been trained on the UBC campus. This corridor was about 20 feet long and four feet wide. I engaged a technician to help me with analyzing the brains that kept pouring in from the mental hospital. We had glass jars piled high in this corridor, and though the chemical engineers next door would look in occasionally, they did not stay very long.

Then came the deluge: UBC's long awaited medical school began.

CHAPTER TWENTY-ONE

University of British Columbia, Vancouver, 1950

When the medical school opened for its first class in September of 1950, I was promoted to a small part of an army hut. There after my activities grew out of all recognition. During the first year of the school I taught histology, neurophysiology and neuroanatomy for Professor Sydney Friedman and Professor Harold Copp. I had the help of a wonderful group of demonstrators from city neurologists and those in the mental health system. I was asked to help design the histology or microscopic anatomy laboratory and produce something similar to what we had had at Oxford. We left no level surfaces on which students could lean or put drying microscopic slides covered with balsam. I had seen too many of these slides firmly attached to the seats of trousers of the medical students at Oxford. So we sharpened all the edges in the laboratory to prevent lounging, irrelevant conversation and sartorial catastrophe.

In the year before the school opened, Professor Friedman asked me where we might get 60 sets of all the tissues of the body. I replied that this was a major undertaking since not all the normal tissues of the body became available in pathology departments at one time. He therefore asked me if I would phone Thomas Marsland, the excellent histology technician whom we had had at Oxford. It was hard to make Marsland believe that I was calling from Vancouver. I told him that for the first of September 1950, we simply had to have 60 complete sets of all the tissues making up the body, and could he in some marvellous way produce these 60 sets from monkey material. He gasped and said he would. One week before the course was to begin in September 1950, the 60 sets arrived by ship around the Panama canal and the situation was saved. The work in histology was very successful, thanks to the superb teaching ability of Dr. Paris

Constantinides, one of Hans Selye's students from McGill University.

The Crease Clinic research laboratory was incorporated into the university as the department of neurological research and I became a voting member of the council of professors, which directed the early years of the medical school. I suppose a better prepared class never entered any medical school then or since. Most of the students were well–educated veterans who had waited for their chance to study medicine. On one occasion, late in the year, they all dressed up in their uniforms and medals and asked for a formal meeting with the council. One of the fighter pilots plaintively said, "Could we possibly have some time in our curriculum when we might rest?" The ever–verbal William Boyd, professor of pathology and a world authority, replied in his marvellous Scottish brogue, "Laddie, ye can rest in the hereafter."

One class that graduated in the 1950s was led by Dr. James Jameson from the town of Salmon Arm, in the interior of the province. His father was the printer, typesetter and publisher of the local weekly newspaper. Jimmy went on to the Rockefeller University in New York and then accompanied Professor George Palade, a Nobel laureate, to Yale University where he is currently teaching and researching.

The establishing of a medical school in a university where there had never been one before took some stamina. One of the road–blocks was posed by a woman who telephoned the president to say that she had learned that male and female cadavers were being stored temporarily up on the farm in the department of animal nutrition, in the same tank. She said that if this were not corrected by 5 p.m. she would call the newspapers and the radio stations. So the poor beleaguered president had to find an extra tank so that male and female would forever be separated. It reminded me of my one–time landlady in Broad Street, Oxford, who would not allow mixed bicycles in the same shed.

The first year of the medical school's existence was a busy one for everyone. Dean Myron Weaver, who had come from Minneapolis to head up the faculty, was given an office in an unused end of a corridor on the main floor of the physics building, which was partitioned off for him and his secretary. I was able to open my door and shout across the chemistry courtyard to Myron as to how things were going.

The first medical library was set up in the balcony of the Kaye Lamb Wing of the main library. The library committee was chaired by Dr. Sydney Friedman who had been active in that capacity at McGill

University. We were given funds to buy back issues of periodicals, especially long runs, if we could find them.

In 1951 we admitted a class of 80 as against the previous introductory class of only 60, and the laboratories and the lecture halls became very crowded. Eventually, during the night an old tarpaper shack was brought down from the Little Mountain Army Barracks on trucks in five sections. The land up there belonged to the Canadian Pacific Railway and they were anxious to get on with subdivision after the war. Luckily for UBC, our then chancellor, the Honourable Eric Hamber, was a C.P.R. director and was able to keep our housing there for veterans as long as needed. Finally this very large shack was brought down, specifically for radioactive research under Professor Gordon Shrum in physics. He had it placed outside his back door, but before he could occupy it, the professor of biochemistry took 3/5 of it and my laboratory of neurological research took the southern 2/5, leaving Dr. Shrum the toilets at the north end. It was a great time to possess hammers and saws and lots of nails, so without any authority we remodelled the kitchen area of the old army hut for our research, and it was there that Dr. Margaret Kennard, one of my friends from Yale University, came to do her work in neurophysiology. Her prized monkeys were kept by Dr. Alex Wood in a special unit in the laboratories of animal nutrition. He did a great deal to help the medical school get started. Dr. S.E.C. Turvey came to work on a research project in which the arterial system of the human brain could be injected with an alloy that melted in hot water, and on cooling became rigid and gave an excellent idea of the vascular supply of cerebrum and cerebellum. I had known him at Queen Square, London.

When permanent fireproof buildings were constructed for the engineering faculty, the medical faculty was allowed to possess their huts. It was into these that the Kinsmen Laboratory for Neurological Research moved. This enabled us to take in summer students. Two of these were notable in that they both possessed the Doctor of Philosophy degree in chemistry or biochemistry: Dr. Patrick McGeer had taken his degree at Princeton University and Dr. William Brown at McGill University. Despite having this qualification they were required to repeat the biochemistry course at UBC! These summer students came to work in the new laboratory with me and soon Dr. Edith McGeer, a Ph.D. in organic chemistry from the University of Virginia and a former chemist with the DuPont Corporation, came to work as a volunteer. She and her husband spent six years without pay developing some very interesting biochemical studies on the abnormal excretory products of schizophrenics. For a year we had Dr. John Smythies from Cambridge University, who was interested with Dwight Peretz in dementing chemicals. Joining me in microscopic anatomy of the nervous system was Dr. Michael Livingston, also a graduate of Cambridge University. One of our most active medical student researchers was Patrick Bosley, who collaborated with me on a study of the capillaries in the skin at the base of each fingernail. It had been suggested that schizophrenics in mental hospitals in the eastern United States had abnormal capillary networks. To see these capillaries one had only to remove the natural oil at the base of the fingernail using a solvent such as Xylol or Toluol. Thereafter, one placed a drop of clear cedar oil on the cleansed skin in order to give a level plane upon which to focus with the medium objective of a microscope, using light from above, reflected back, therefore, from the capillaries. We were able to show that in 500 consecutive athletes lining up for food at Acadia Camp during the British Empire Games, the capillary networks were not different from those seen in the American publications in a population limited to mental hospitals. In other words, the capillary findings in mental hospitals had nothing to do with mental diseases that incapacitated the patients.

However, in one interesting case the nailbed photographs were so bizarre that we followed up immediately. The capillary network was dilated in such a peculiar way that we looked up the name and origin of the athlete. It turned out that the subject had been a newspaper reporter who had sneaked into the food line at Acadia Camp. I was able to trace him to a Vancouver newspaper and asked if he would come for further studies. He gave me a blast over the telephone that I shall not forget, saying that he was aware that we were finger–printing people and that he wanted nothing to do with these C.I.A. investigations!

Dr. Juhn Wada, a distinguished researcher and a graduate of Hokkaido University in Japan, came from the Montreal Neurological Institute. It was already clear that he would become an internationally renowned investigator in the field of epilepsy and in the little–understood area of sleep disorders.

As the year 1951 proceeded, the status of the faculty of medicine within the university became a hot potato. There had been a long history of lack of development of medical education in British Columbia. As early as 1870 Dr. John Sebastian Helmcken, one of the three representatives of the crown colony of British Columbia who went east to Ottawa to press for adequate terms should the province join in the Canadian confederation, was a physician on the west coast serving the Hudson's Bay Company. He made it clear in Ottawa that one of the desiderata was a marine hospital of sufficient size to permit a medical school to be built in Esquimalt, Victoria, the Pacific base of the Royal Navy. No action was taken and eventually the idea of such a medical school died.

In 1913 a distinguished medical educator and researcher, Dr. Frank Fairchild Wesbrook, became the founding president of the University of British Columbia in Vancouver. He had been both professor of pathology and dean of medicine at the University of Minnesota following his early medical education at the University of Manitoba in Winnipeg. He had three years of postgraduate work over–seas, largely at Cambridge University with his great friend Charles Sherrington. When the Carnegie Foundation sent the sharp–tongued gadfly Abraham Flexner across North America to survey medical education in the first decade of the 20th century, the first state university medical school to be given a class A standing was Wesbrook's at the University of Minnesota. He had hardly become established in Vancouver when the First World War broke out and he was not able to proceed with a medical faculty. He had many offers of competent, young, would–be teachers, one of whom was Geoffrey Jefferson. He was a surgeon and researcher trained in Manchester, who came to practice in Victoria, B.C., with his wife, Gertrude Flumerfelt, a native of the city and an Oxford graduate in medicine and protégé of Sir William Osler.

Dr. Wesbrook had to explain to all who offered to help that the war made the operation of a university very tenuous, not to mention a potential faculty of medicine. The charter of the university included in its remit the development of a faculty of medicine, thanks no doubt to Dr. Henry Esson Young, the minister of health and education in the government of Sir Richard McBride.

In 1919 John D. Rockefeller appropriated a very large sum of money to be made available through his foundation to promote medical education and research, stipulating that Canada and the United States, having fought side by side in the First World War, and as good neighbours, should share in this bounty. As a result, Dr. George Vincent, president of the foundation and a long–time friend of Wesbrook, inspected the existing facilities and suggested to the Rockefeller trustees that they apply some of this munificence to Canada's medical schools. Unfortunately, Wesbrook died in 1918 at age 50, just before the armistice, in the devastating influenza epidemic. The foundation did not find conditions conducive to starting a medical faculty in British Columbia in 1919 so young students from the Pacific coast who wished to study medicine had to proceed east to such universities as the University of Toronto, McGill and other well–established faculties.

In the concluding year of the Second World War, pre–medical students at the University of British Columbia started a campaign designed to produce a faculty of medicine by the time the war would end, when many young veterans would want to take a medical degree. Their views were well received by the incoming president of UBC, Dr. MacKenzie, who had just completed his term as the president of the University of New Brunswick and his work as chairman of the Wartime Information Board in Ottawa.

On coming to the University of British Columbia in 1944, MacKenzie found a distinguished physician, trained in Britain, who was professor of bacteriology and public health. In the top floor of the science building, Dr. Claude Dolman operated the Western Division of the Connaught Laboratories, which were based in the University of Toronto. The president asked Dr. Dolman to make a survey of what was happening in medical schools across North America in relation to the returning veterans. He made a very comprehensive report, but when it burst upon the physicians at the Vancouver General Hospital, there was an uproar. The head of medicine at that hospital, Dr. G. F. Strong, took it upon himself to make a rapid survey in which he visited some of his friends in the American College of Physicians. His report contradicted everything the Dolman Report had said.

As the rocks began to fly, President MacKenzie invited a number of distinguished medical educators to come to the campus and to advise him on what should be done in British Columbia. These scholars included Dr. Alan Gregg, head of the division of medical sciences of the Rockefeller Foundation, a truly wise man. The others were: Professor Wilder Penfield, the internationally renowned brain surgeon from McGill University in Montreal; Dr. Ray Farquharson, head of the department of medicine at the University of Toronto and during the war years head of medicine for the RCAF; Dr. George Edward Hall, president and former dean of medicine at the University of Western Ontario, a protégé of Sir Frederick Banting and wartime director of research for the RCAF; and from the United States, Dean Goodpasture of the faculty of medicine of Vanderbilt University.

The advice given by these seasoned experts in medical education and research was that British Columbia both needed and could support a medical school. It should include, they said, a teaching and research hospital on the UBC campus, and an affiliation with the existing hospitals in the greater Vancouver area.

The B.C. Medical Association, the political arm of the profession in British Columbia, set up their own committee under Dr. K.D. Panton, who was the city of Vancouver police surgeon. Dr. Panton unfortunately told the public that President MacKenzie "will be guided by our advice on technical matters." The president felt otherwise and informed Dr. Panton's committee immediately, "I would like to emphasize again that if a medical school does become an integral part of the University of British Columbia, all of the final decisions will have to be made by the Senate and the Board of Governors and by no–one else."

The University of British Columbia Alumni Association, under the presidency of Colonel W. Tom Brown (recently returned from the war in which he was seriously wounded), presented a brief to the visiting consultants on August 22, 1946. Colonel Brown was not a lawyer to mince words and reported on behalf of his committee:

> It is realized that for proper medical education clinical facilities of several private hospitals will be necessary and working arrangements with these will no doubt be concluded on mutually satisfactory terms. This, however, does not envisage the dependency of the university on any one hospital, and is essentially different from any suggestion whereby large capital sums are expended in a permanent contract with some civic hospital. In other words, any temporary measure taken because of the necessity of getting the medical school established in the immediate future should not be of a nature which will prevent the eventual establishment of the faculty on the campus.

He went on: "The public outside Vancouver would regard a faculty of medicine at the university as less likely to be affected by local conditions and interests than one attached to a Vancouver hospital."

The university senate in November of 1947 unanimously passed a resolution framed by the dean of law, Dr. George Curtis, and by Dr. Garnet Sedgewick, the well–known English teacher, endorsing the development of a faculty of medicine.

As 1951 progressed the university was amazed to read press releases in the city papers of Vancouver to the effect that the government was building the medical school at the Vancouver General Hospital. The fact was that the clinical end of the medical school was being based at one large city hospital boasting around of 2,000 beds. That hospital had employed an expensive consultant from the United States to trumpet its virtues and to declare that in future the Vancouver General Hospital would be "British Columbia's mother house of medicine." The provincial legislature allocated a considerable sum of money to build accommodation for the professors in the clinical subjects of the medical curriculum at the Vancouver General Hospital.

Thereupon the battle was joined and at the senate meeting at UBC on December 12, 1951, I put the matter before a very large meeting of that group. The chancellor of the university, rarely seen at senate, attended to make the case for the Vancouver General Hospital, of which he happened to be chairman. After acrimonious debate, in which the dean of medicine characterized my remarks as "ill informed and inflammatory," the senate passed a motion put forward by Mr. Justice Lord and seconded by Dr. Ian McTaggart–Cowan: "That Senate notes with interest press reports with respect to the intentions of the government concerning the erection of the new building at the Vancouver General Hospital, which will, in part, house the teaching facilities for the faculty of medicine, but hopes that this will in no way affect the long term principle of the ultimate establishment of all medical school facilities on the campus of the University of British Columbia and that the board of governors and government be so advised." Those supporting the motion vigorously included two future chancellors, Dr. Phyllis Ross and Mr. Justice J.V. Clyne. The session concluded, out of breath, at about midnight.

The next morning I called on the president to show him evidence which I had not produced the night before and he was shocked. A local newspaper had reported in its "Real Estate Deals This Week" the fact that the dean of medicine had just purchased the property on the corner diagonally across from the site of the new medical school building at the Vancouver General Hospital for $22,000. I did not pursue the matter further because I had a wife and three children to feed, but the president was forewarned of things to come.

On a happier note, my research was proceeding well and a very good team was being built up at the Kinsmen Laboratory. Occasionally I was confined to my bed with the rheumatic fever problem again. While in bed I was able to do the reading necessary to find medical students who, in the past, while still undergraduates, had made important scientific contributions. One of the very pleasant lectures that I was to give on this subject was requested for the special day set aside at the University of Washington medical school in Seattle to hear students recount their summer researches. The number of undergraduate discoveries in history began to mount and one of these I was anxious to pin down was Dr. Wilder Penfield. When he was a medical undergraduate at Oxford, Sherrington gave him a problem to investigate concerning the pain fibres of the human ureter, the tube leading from the kidney to the bladder. It was well known that kidney stones impacted in their course down to the bladder caused extreme pain. Sherrington remarked dryly to Penfield, "I suggest you limit yourself to one ureter." Later, while a medical student qualifying during the First World War at the Johns Hopkins University in Baltimore, Penfield worked with Professor Howell on blood substitutes that were needed over–seas for surgical cases involving a history of haemorrhage after wounds had occurred.

In a very conservative university setting in Vancouver, I found some things difficult to stomach. In my capacity as senior medical officer for the Air Force Reserve on the west coast, I had had an enquiry from one of our nurses living at a bush station in the north as to whether or not the school of nursing at UBC provided distance education in public health. After enquiring at the school I was told that was unavailable, and when I remarked that I hoped we could have such in the future, I was told that there was certainly no likelihood of such diversionary developments. These were the kinds of things in a developing university that made my blood boil. I had to tell Air Commodore Gordon Corbett at Air Force Headquarters that none was available, but that perhaps through his good offices nursing education for Armed Forces nurses could be considered on a large scale. I said that if horses could be put on the army payroll, as was being divulged by the press, perhaps we could get something for nurses.

My Air Force duties at 19 Wing Auxiliary increased with the development of two unique formations. Under Squadron Leader G.R.F. Elliot, a medical board unit for recruiting was set up in the basement of what was eventually to become the University Club of Vancouver at 1021 West Hastings Street. I arranged that all three Armed Forces recruiting offices could have medical examinations carried out there including electrocardiography and electroencephalography. The latter was an innovation in recruiting procedures and eventually was applied in our research on the rejection of epileptics and fainters from air crew. However, we also put it to work to study the effect of boxing on the brain waves, so that boxing was downplayed and eventually abandoned by the Canadian Armed Forces in 1964.

The other unit was under the guidance of Squadron Leader James Mather, professor of public health in the faculty of medicine at UBC.

This was a very interesting Air Evacuation Unit, which enlisted former flyers who had graduated in medicine, along with nurses who had served in the RCAF. After a great deal of training with American groups in summer vacations, the nurses served on the Hawaii–Vancouver leg of the transport of wounded from the Korean War, some of them going as far as the burns centre of the U.S. Air Force in Texas. Others served on the European runs to Andrews Air Force Base in Washington, D.C. Over the years we built up a very strong group in this field. On emergency runs to some isolated places in British Columbia, the medical and nursing personnel stood out and received great approbation. It was possible in these two reserve units to employ, on a reserve basis, many of the recent British graduates who had settled in Canada, especially at veterans hospitals, so that there would be some income for them over and above the pitiful amounts paid to residents in hospitals at that time. Many became specialists thanks to the opportunities given by the Air Force.

As in the Second World War, in the reserve field I was very averse to putting anything on paper because that tended only to start a laborious and endless discussion. Instead, I used to telephone Ottawa to get things done. In one case we were sent some x–ray apparatus that must have come from the First World War. A telephone call to my friend Brooke Claxton, the minister of defence, soon produced the most modern equipment available.

On one occasion a North Star transport plane containing wives and children being transferred to the west coast to follow their fathers rolled off a banked runway and completely turned over. All the passengers hanging by their seat belts were uninjured. The hospital personnel at RCAF Station, Sea Island, Vancouver, completed 450 x–rays during the day and we were able to advise a surprised Air Force headquarters that there were no injuries to be dealt with. Despite, or perhaps because of, my unorthodox methods I was awarded the Coronation Medal commemorating the Queen's coronation of June 1953.

By 1954 my role as director of research to the mental hospitals of British Columbia came to an end and I was taken on full–time in the University of British Columbia medical faculty. It was my hope that physicians taking their residency training in the provincial medical hospital system could spend a year in research in the Kinsmen Laboratory, but the budget of the mental hospitals was so limited that it was not possible to send interns and residents for even brief periods in the laboratory. Instead, members of the Kinsmen Laboratory carried on their research at the Crease Clinic with the help of Dr. A.M.

Gee, who was succeeded by Dr. Alan Davidson. Over the ensuing years we developed our work there on the biochemistry of schizophrenia, the biochemistry of phenylketonuria or "Pink disease," and the Parkinsonian sequelae of long dosages of tranquillizers.

Our association with physicians in the public service was always harmonious and I hope as helpful to them as it was to us. It was at about this time that members of the clinical staff of St. Paul's Hospital asked me to set up a brain wave laboratory. The hospital in the centre of Vancouver cared for many head injury cases, epileptics who lived in the West End of the city and cases of migraine. My pronunciation of the latter disease "mee–graine" was corrected liberally by referring physicians until I explained to them that it came from a corruption of the old French term "hemi–cranie." I set up an epileptic clinic within the general outpatients at St. Paul's and for many years saw the more chronic cases that needed continual monitoring. I was all too conscious of the case that I had dealt with in the emergency room at the University of Texas Hospital at Galveston, where a woman who thought that the drug Dilantin that she was taking for epilepsy was similar to aspirin. Over a few days she consumed a bottle full of Dilantin and was brought to us in a frightful state of desquamation and bleeding of the gums. She lost all her skin and died in hospital.

On the UBC campus we installed the decompression chamber that the RAF group captain at Patricia Bay, near Victoria, had refused to commission towards the end of the war. We set this up in the university Armouries with the help of Squadron Leader Alex Wood, the professor of animal nutrition. We were keen to see, in actual practice, whether stationing pilots even for short periods well above sea level would significantly reduce the decompression sickness or "the bends." We therefore stationed a group of reserve air crew up in the coast mountains at Alta Lake, where they were deposited by a seaplane. After 48 hours of energetic activities they were flown down by the same plane to the tip of Point Grey, climbed the cliffs to the decompression chamber and were then subjected to very high simulated altitudes. We knew their bends susceptibility from earlier runs and showed in this very brief experiment that there was protection to be gained by stationing air crew at altitudes ranging between 4,000 and 5,000 feet. After these experiments were completed, the decompression chamber was used as a large facility in which the respiratory quotient of young deer could be measured. The experimenters found that deer produced more protein per month than almost any other ruminant.

On the academic political front, I was elected president of the faculty association at a time when people were leaving for eastern universities where the salary scale had kept up with inflation. Walter Koerner, one of the Czech refugees who had developed our hemlock lumber industry where none existed before, introduced me to the Premier of British Columbia, the Honourable W.A.C. Bennett. At an elaborate tea at the Vancouver Hotel, I met the distinguished politician and some of his lieutenants. As our chancellor, Dr. Phyllis Ross, had prophesied, I was given a 30–minute hosing about the alleged lack of interest by the university in the economic future of the province of British Columbia. When that tidal wave subsided, I was allowed to put our case to the premier. I explained to him that I held rather heretical views on university education and that I believed no one should attend university unless the potential student had been gainfully employed for one year. The premier jumped up and shook my hand and then archly looked around at his attorney general, a well–known army type, and said, "Now, Dr., I don't suppose one year in the army would count as being gainfully employed." Finally I came to the point of the meeting, which was that British Columbia, because of the niggardly way they dealt with their professors, was currently losing some to the east and was likely to lose many more. On hearing this the premier set his jaw, pounded the table and said that this must stop. He asked what it would take to make a serious impression on the problem and I replied $250,000. He blinked but then said "You shall have it." He went on to say that he would like the president and the chancellor, Brigadier Sherwood Lett, to understand that this was to be applied to faculty salaries and to nothing else. He had no use for either of these gentlemen, since it was rumoured that they put the story around the province that the premier was a great supporter of higher education because he gave the university four million dollars a year, and provided 40 million dollars a year for highways to get the students to the campus.

Before leaving, the premier asked me about the requirements to increase the size of the UBC campus, a matter on which he had been pressed for some time. When I recounted the true history of the six square miles of federal defence lands that had been meant for UBC in the 1912 property exchange for 2,000,000 acres of near desert in the interior, he whistled. Growing from the original measly 150 acres first offered to President Wesbrook in 1915, to the 548 acres which we currently had, was progress for sure. The premier wondered if a campus of 1,000 acres was a reasonable figure, to which I replied that if we could not do what was required on that total area then we were in the wrong business. He then said that down the road he did not want to be accused of being as mean spirited as his predecessors seemed to have been. Then he added with a smile: "We should not bear grudges against the past. That sort of thing does no good."

At a special meeting of the faculty association called to report on this development, I saw a standing–room only audience in front of me; they were delighted with the results of my visit to the premier. The university administration, of course, were less enthralled, and kept pointing out that the government should not be making university policy. It should be noted that universities in British Columbia are not allowed to run deficits. This is something that generation after generation of students have never faced up to, and they have found it easier to beat up boards of governors rather than governments.

On the fund raising side, I became involved with the so–called Three Universities Development Fund, in which the newly created Simon Fraser University, University of Victoria and the University of British Columbia were to share. The unheard–of goal of 25 million dollars was established and over the ensuing three years this amount was raised with the help of foundations, friends and alumni. This was matched by the provincial government. The executive director in the first instance was a Great Trekker: the veteran newspaper man Aubrey Roberts. Later, Alfred Adams, formerly secretary to Sir Roy Wolensky, the prime minister of Rhodesia, came to take his place.

As I sat in Aubrey Roberts' office discussing the campaign, a long–distance call came from Dr. Neil Perry; my fellow graduate of the class of 1933, who had taken his Ph.D. in economics at Harvard, had been governor of the Bank of Abyssinia and was now vice–president of the World Bank in Washington, D.C. He wanted my advice on some means of returning to the Pacific coast and I asked him to hang on since there was an important opening in the commerce faculty. I ran downstairs to President MacKenzie and told him to pick up the telephone and invite Neil Perry for lunch the following Saturday. The president acquiesced and also invited me to come for lunch. Two weeks after the luncheon with the board of governors, Neil Perry still did not know why it was they had been discussing his work, nor had he heard another word. When I explained this to President MacKenzie he very quickly made it clear to Neil that the board wished him to come back home to the university campus in Vancouver as dean of commerce. He later succeeded Professor E.D. McPhee as vice–president of the university.

During a visit to the Wellcome Trust in London, Sir Henry Dale and I discussed the possibility of a grant being made to the University of British Columbia towards the construction of its much–needed University Hospital on the campus. When I told him that I was seeking one million dollars, he laughed uproariously and said, "Young man, that is the largest amount we have ever been asked for." When I replied that I was not asking for this amount so that it would be the largest they had been held to ransom for, he said, "Now Billy, that is very disarming, but you shall have $250,000." I nearly fell off my chair. Alas, because we did not build the University Hospital within 15 years of that date, the money was withdrawn and used by the trust for other purposes. Sir Henry had already given us 5,000 pounds per year for five years to purchase rare books for our history of medicine collection at UBC.

When he and Lady Dale retired to Cambridge, I visited them as often as possible when in England and used to enjoy his description of how discoveries had been made. I explained to him on one occasion that I was writing a book that would be called "Young Endeavour," detailing the discoveries made by medical undergraduates. I asked if he would write the foreword to it and he readily agreed. His grasp of the history of discovery in the field of medicine was amazing.

On one occasion I was introduced to his daughter Alison, the wife of Lord Todd, a Nobel laureate in chemistry and a man who must have been six feet six inches tall. He told me one of the best stories to come out of the war. He was asked to come from his post at the University of Edinburgh to Aldershot in the south of England as a civilian adviser. He arrived at this large encampment shortly before lunch and noted that the officers were streaming to what turned out to be the officers' mess for lunch. He had been all night on an unheated train and was very hungry. In the mess, however, he found that people were lining up at a counter where a sergeant was dispensing cigarettes. He had run out of cigarettes on the night train and arrived in front of the sergeant, towering over him. The sergeant asked him who he was. He said that he was the professor of chemistry at Edinburgh. Before he could say anything further the sergeant said "Where is your uniform?" Todd remarked that he had come as a civilian to help in the war effort. Still the sergeant was not very sure what he should do. Then the sergeant said: "Well let us see. Twenty cigarettes a week for an officer. Ten for an enlisted man. Here's five."

Committee work at the University of British Columbia increased and President MacKenzie became very demanding in this regard. One of the pleasant surprises in the Three Universities Development Fund was a gift from my old schoolmate of Victoria days, Franc Joubin (or as we called him "Mr. Uranium," because of his mammoth staking with 50 aircraft in one day of vast territories of northern Ontario. Professor Shrum said this would give the world uranium for over 100 years.). Franc Joubin sent a large sum of money to Dean Walter Gage for what he called "intellectual prospecting." This enabled the university to subsidize unusual students at UBC. Over the years Franc Joubin became one of our most discerning contributors and always had wonderfully imaginative targets in mind.

In my reserve capacity in the Air Force, I spent June and July of 1955 with my colleague Dr. Herbert Jasper, electroencephalographer at the Neurological Institute in Montreal. The head of neurosurgery, Dr. William Cone, saw me limping around the institute, put me in a corner, asked me what the problem was, and said "We will do you tomorrow morning." So on the morrow he and the professor of orthopaedic surgery, Dr. Gordon Petrie, exposed my left sciatic nerve under local anaesthesia and, after reproducing the pain I had been suffering from for a couple of years, removed the ischial bursa. They explored the course of the sciatic nerve, in case a tumour was involved, but finding none they concentrated on the bursa. Its removal gave me freedom from pain for 30 years.

Miss Eileen Flanagan, the director of nursing who had always been a pretty tough critic during my residency years, turned out to have a very tender heart and put me in what was the only air– conditioned room at that time in the institute. After a week I was taken by ambulance to Windsor Station, where I boarded the Canadian, the wonderful train that crossed Canada. My sister came from New Jersey to help me on the way, as I was in the peculiar position of either having to lie down or stand up. No sitting was possible because of the surgical incision in my hip. Therefore, as I was standing in the dome car enjoying the Rockies, women would say to their husbands, "Stand up and let that poor injured officer sit down." I had to explain that it was impossible to sit down and that I had not, despite my Air Force uniform, incurred any injury in flying. After two weeks of increasing exercise in the Commonwealth Games pool at UBC, I was able to return to work and never imagined that I could have had such a good result from this surgery.

CHAPTER TWENTY-TWO

Getting Started at UBC

From my arrival on the University of British Columbia campus on July 2, 1949, to my sabbatical year in Marseille in 1958–59, there was an air of expectancy in the new group of professors—all under age 40—as we set to work to build a medical school from scratch. In the intervening four years since the end of the Second World War, there had been mounting pressure on UBC to open a faculty of medicine to accommodate returning veterans whose education had been seriously interrupted, and to study claims for the primacy of the largest hospital in Canada, the Vancouver General Hospital, as the alleged "Mother House of Medicine" for British Columbia and therefore its proposed site for UBC's medical school.

There had been rumblings of this contest before the war ended, and I recall ward rounds at the hospital early in 1945 when I, in my Air Force uniform, was put down firmly for asking embarrassing questions about the future. The reigning clinicians had the strong feeling that I should stay with my teaching and research functions at the RCAF station at Sea Island in the delta of the Fraser River.

It was no surprise, therefore, that early in 1946 the chief of the hospital's medical staff made a hasty survey of selected medical schools in North America from which some remarkable conclusions were drawn. The printed report of eight pages was in reply to a thorough survey of a large number of medical schools, authorized by the senate of UBC and made by the head of its department of bacteriology, who was simultaneously the director of the western division of the Connaught Laboratories of the University of Toronto.

The issue was joined in 1946 and the geographic and other factors affecting the university's medical school are, even today, still very much alive.

The contestants had not reckoned with the remarkable president of UBC, Dr. MacKenzie, nor did they appreciate the fact that he had brilliantly completed the first year of the medical course at Dalhousie University in Halifax as a veteran returning from the 1914–18 war. He subsequently graduated in law and was not about to be told by any hospital spokesman what was good for UBC.

I used to chat with "Larry" MacKenzie about the head-on collisions that erupted almost daily, and I may have convinced him that what was required was a factual statement of the objectives that might be achieved by a new and academically sound medical school. He knew the pressure of veterans who hoped to study medicine. All Canadian medical schools were swamped by applicants hoping to get their discharge from the armed forces. The Pre-Medical Society at UBC, of which I had been the founding president in 1932, surveyed the immediate post-war situation methodically, and did their best to get early provincial action on the proposed school. To their great credit the officers of that society stated publicly on February 8, 1947, that despite their personal disappointment they would, in all likelihood, not benefit from a delayed medical school. "We feel that the benefits to be derived (from our recommendations) by future students, general medical practice, scientific research and the populace of the entire province over-shadow our personal interests." This was the constantly displayed spirit of generations of students at UBC. When they subscribed funds for new campus-wide recreational facilities (which the provincial government rarely supported), there was no holding back simply because those new facilities would not come on stream during the campus life of many contributors.

From the end of the war to the assembling of the medical professors in 1949, the air was full of rockets launched by self-appointed guardians of professional education. As this chorus grew in volume, President MacKenzie in 1946 reminded one persistent purveyor of free advice: "I would like to emphasize again that if a medical school does become an integral part of the University of B.C., all the final decisions that are made in connection with it will have to be made by the Senate and Board of Governors of the University of B.C. and by no one else."

The president clearly was nettled by such statements as the following:

> The statement regarding the advantages of full-time clinicians in the economic saving to the community, is, of course, the well-worn argument in favour of state medicine...It is obvious that good medical students have little time for extra-curricular activity...while every effort should and will be made to maintain

> their health, such measures cannot interfere with their medical studies.

Full–time heads of departments were to be avoided, according to this authoritarian report, because "some departments headed by a full–time man suffer because the interest of those men is directed more toward their consulting work than the activities of their departments." A part–time dean was brought from a nearby medical school for a three–day survey of the Vancouver situation and thought the Vancouver General Hospital was ideal for the medical faculty's base.

Fed up with so much speculation and special interest testimony, President MacKenzie discussed with some of us in the UBC Alumni Association his desire to bring advisors of international calibre in medical education and research to the campus. Years later he wrote of this trying period in a letter to the *Vancouver Sun*, dated December 4, 1976:

> With thousands of veterans returning to the UBC campus in 1946, I sought the advice of a group of medical educators of international stature in connection with the development of a much–needed medical school. This group, comprising Dr. Wilder Penfield of McGill University, Dr. Alan Gregg, chairman of medical sciences division of the Rockefeller Foundation, Prof. Ray Farquharson of the University of Toronto, and President G. Edward Hall of the University of Western Ontario, advised that an early start be made on a medical faculty, with a campus teaching hospital as one of the desired goals.

At the university senate, Dr. G.G. Sedgewick and Dean George Curtis successfully proposed that this become the university's official policy. This was reconfirmed in 1951, a year after the first medical students enrolled, noting that affiliated city hospitals should be asked to assist, but that a campus hospital was essential.

Although President MacKenzie had not met Wilder Penfield, he knew this native of Spokane, Washington, was renowned around the world for his skill as a neurosurgeon, as a researcher in the field of epilepsy and as the director of McGill University's Montreal Neurological Institute. So I made sure that the two met in Dr. Penfield's sixth–floor office, with its walls covered with personal photographs of the world's top neurologists, and with a fine view over the Montreal skyline to the St. Lawrence River.

MacKenzie pressed Penfield to come to the west coast with a team of advisors who could help him get his new medical school started on the right track. Without a moment's hesitation, Penfield said: "Of course I'll come. When?" The elated MacKenzie then went through the institute with me on what came to be known as the rapid "50–cent tour." Before long he had recruited Dr. Alan Gregg: director of the medical division of the Rockefeller Foundation, universally recognized as the "wise man" of that foundation, with experience on all continents, and moving spirit in supporting Penfield's project in Montreal.

Then two of Larry's friends from his University of Toronto days were approached: Professor Ray Farquharson, head of the department of medicine, and just released from the Air Force; and another consultant, Dr. George Edward Hall, who had retired from the Air Force where he had been director of medical research. Pre–war he had been Sir Frederick Banting's right hand in Toronto, and post–war became dean of medicine at the University of Western Ontario. There he showed his administrative zeal by asking each professor for his resignation. Having received that, he re–appointed all but one, who was a conceited obstructionist. Hall was soon made president of the university!

These were among the real experts brought to UBC for consultation, and their reports were a bitter pill for the downtown cabal that sought an off–campus site for the future school. While all of the visitors had wise things to say, a few of the pungent remarks of Dr. Gregg are worth noting:

> I distrust any deliberate mediocrity that begs for approval on grounds of modesty and economy...Experience shows that only when wisdom is matched with courage do long–term plans resist the haste, waste and futility of opportunism. I am convinced that the greatest danger to the medical future of British Columbia lies in the present temptation to launch an unseaworthy craft because there are so many cheering spectators assembled and some available grease on the ways...the patient who is used for teaching is better cared for...No mistake should be made by the university authorities about the value of what they offer the affiliated hospitals...Harvard, Hopkins, Cornell, and California...spend endless time and effort in trying to make up for their handicap of isolation (from their main university centers). And to me at least they have harped on the handicap separation causes them.

The A B C of Vitamins

A

Oh fine and fat was Ralph the rat,
And his eye was a clear cold grey.
How mournful that he ate less fat
As day succeeded day,
Till he found each cornea daily hornier,
Lacking its vitamin A,
"I missed my vitamin A, my dears",
That rat was heard to say.
"And you'll find your eyes will keratinize
If you miss your vitamin A."

B

Now polished rice is extremely nice
At a high suburban tea,
But Arbuthnot Lane remarks with pain
That it lacks all vitamin B,
And beri-beri is very, very
Hard on the nerves, says he.
"Oh take your vitamin B, my dears!"
I heard that surgeon say;
"If I hadn't been fed on standard bread
I shouldn't be here today".

C

The scurvy flew through the schooner's crew
As they sailed on an Arctic sea.
They were far from land and their food was canned,
So they got no vitamin C.
For "Devil's the use of orange juice",
The skipper 'ad said, said he.
They were victualled with pickled pork, my dears,
Those mariners bold and free,
Yet life's but brief on the best corned beef,
If you don't get vitamin C.

D

The epiphyses of Jemima's knees
Were a truly appalling sight;
For the rickets strikes whom it jolly well likes,
If the vitamin D's not right.
Though its plots we foil with our cod liver oil
Or our ultraviolet light.
So swallow your cod liver oil, my dears,
And big bonny babes you'll be.
Though it makes you sick it's a cure for the rickets
And teeming with vitamin D.

continued on page 254

I had occasion to discuss the UBC situation, as well as Harvard's, with Dr. Gregg at the 25th anniversary celebration of the Montreal Neurological Institute in 1959.

Encouraged by such expert opinion, the General Practitioners' Association of Vancouver, on December 10, 1948, passed this resolution:

> Be it resolved that we urge upon our governing bodies and other responsible officials the advisability of building more hospitals with a maximum capacity of 600 beds throughout the city and province. And further be it resolved that one such institution be built as part of the University Medical School, that this hospital be a "closed" hospital, staffed by the university, and that all patients who may choose to participate in care and privileges obtained therein make themselves available as clinical material.

At the same time the profession voted by 104 to 15 not to house its library (started by Sir William Osler with a gift of $100.00 in 1914) in the Vancouver General Hospital, but instead to build its own Academy of Medicine, equidistant from the General Hospital and St. Paul's Hospital downtown, and part way to the UBC campus.

By 1951 a spacious campus building designed to house bacteriology, public health, the Student Health Service, and a 24-bed infirmary, was completed. Larry MacKenzie called me into his office and asked if I would be willing to act as the administrator of the structure, since it was to serve a number of divergent interests. I could not let my good friend down, but it would be futile to try to preside over such a "dog's breakfast." After getting all the cards out on the table I suggested that this handsome structure be called the Wesbrook Building, to memorialize UBC's founding president: a distinguished bacteriologist, public health advocate, pathologist and the first full-time dean of medicine at the University of Minnesota. I had learned of his greatness from my Oxford teacher Sir Charles Sherrington. MacKenzie beamed broadly and said that would be put to senate that night. Larry's habit of prolonging the discussion of minor matters until 11 p.m., and then asking a restive senate to give quick passage to his favourite items, was again in evidence. Dr. Claude Dolman, the professor of bacteriology, remained behind as senate dispersed and asked the president where such an excellent suggestion had surfaced. Larry smiled as he said, "I just ran into Bill Gibson on campus today." There was to be a lot of "running into on cam-

E

Now Vitamins D and A, B, C,
Will ensure that you're happy and strong;
But that's no use; must reproduce
Or the race won't last for long.
So vitamin E is the stuff for me,
And its praises end my song.
We'll double the birth rate yet, my dears,
If we all eat vitamin E.
We can blast the hopes of Maria Stopes
By taking it with our tea.

C.M.A.

pus" over the next 20 years, not only on medical matters but on fund raising, athletics, the government, doubling of the size of the campus and on many unrelated projects.

The opening ceremonies of the Wesbrook Building turned out to be a bizarre comedy of errors in which the key to this glass and stone edifice, planned before World War II, was mistakenly handed by my friend, Minister of Education W.T. Straith, to the dean of medicine, who quickly got rid of it to another dean, who wanted nothing to do with the place. The key was a "hot potato."

It became obvious later why the minister had given the key to the dean of medicine. The provincial government made it clear that the Wesbrook Building was one half of its commitment to the new faculty of medicine, and the final half would be built at the Vancouver General Hospital! As this piece of political finesse began to unravel, tempers began to rise.

The guns opened up again at the General Hospital, this time, however, with an imported and highly-paid public relations expert. When I questioned him on "the third and final building" for the medical faculty (at Tenth and Heather), he replied that the first two were the totally unrelated Biological Sciences and the Wesbrook Buildings at Point Grey. (Forty years later, as I proofread a history of one of the clinical departments for one of my good friends, I found that he, poor fellow, had believed all that the public relations people had told him.)

So much, then, for the rocky road I had chosen to follow. My championing of the kind of medical school recommended by real experts cost me dearly over the years thereafter, but I have survived most of my detractors. It is now time to speak of my research laboratory, the Kinsmen Laboratory of Neurological Research, and the scientists who, by themselves, brought it international acclaim.

Soon after the Crease Clinic Unit for Neuropsychiatric Research began in a disused corridor in chemical engineering's facilities in 1949, I was approached by the eminent paediatrician Dr. Peter Spohn asking whether I would be interested in poliomyelitis research. The 40 or more Kinsmen Clubs of British Columbia had carried on a successful campaign during World War II called "Milk for Britain." There was a very strict rule in this service club: all members must leave at age 40. The graduates became movers and shakers in many social drives, and with those still in the trenches as active members, sought to help polio patients and their families. The idea of research into the cause or causes of polio appealed to them, and their medical advisory board suggested two things: one of the early electron

Nazi Blitz Warfare Expert Dies - Munich - Former Field Marshal Hugo Sperrle, the man who directed Hitler's "obliteration bombing" of Coventry and other British provincial towns, has died in a clinic here. He was 68 and was cremated on Easter Sunday. Sperrle commanded Hitler's "Condor legion", the troops which aided General Franco in the Spanish civil war. His prize achievement was the "experiment" at Guernica, warfare's first example of total bombing. In addition to his "blitz" on Britain he also directed the "air umbrella" which enabled the German battle cruisers Scharnhorst and Guenisenau and the cruiser Prince Eugen to escape through the English Channel to German and Norwegian ports in 1942. The Nuernberg war crimes tribunal acquitted him of war crimes charges.

Vancouver *Province*, April 7, 1953

microscopes be presented to UBC for use by biomedical and other researchers; and that I should be sent to the International Congress on Poliomyelitis that was to meet in late summer in Copenhagen in 1951 to assess what research we might usefully attempt.

The congress turned out to be an historic meeting, with Jonas Salk and others reporting on their basic virus work. It was clear that once the several strains of polio virus were differentiated and could be grown in tissue cultures, there might be renewed hope for prevention of this crippling disease through a vaccine.

En route home from Copenhagen, I visited my Oxford mentor, Sir Charles Sherrington, at an English nursing home at Eastbourne. He was 94 years of age and arthritic. Despite a fine day outside, he had his gas fire turned up high in his room. His first question was: "Look here, Gibson, how many doctors did you say were at those meetings in Copenhagen?" I answered: "Six hundred, Sir Charles." He smiled as he said: "Did any good ever come of getting 600 doctors together?" He then asked if I was keeping "dear Frank Wesbrook's memory green at the university in Vancouver." I replied that I must do that and promised to write our founding president's biography (published in 1973). After much chat about his pupils Penfield, Florey, Eccles, Granit and Cairns, he read me his latest poem with a final chuckle. Sir Charles died a year later, modestly wearing his 90 honorary degrees and fellowships, his Nobel Prize, and the longest entry ever recorded in "Who's Who." I had not realized that Sherrington had visited the west coast of Canada both in 1897 with Lord Lister, following meetings of the British Association for the Advancement of Science in Toronto, and again in 1913 as guest of the Dunsmuirs whose son Jimmy he had tutored at Cambridge.

Back in Vancouver our graduate students were increasing in number. The Kinsmen Foundation, with funds from the annual Mother's March (started in 1953), had set up a professorship in neurological research. We were to be housed in some post–war huts just vacated by the engineering faculty. These white huts were a step up from the 1939 vintage army hut we had been sharing with biochemistry. That massive barrack hut had served the over–flow of students returning from World War II, and was located at Little Mountain, an area of Vancouver that had been given to the Canadian Pacific Railway as part of the 5,700 acres with which the city of Vancouver enticed the newly completed trans–Canada rail line to forsake its original terminus at the eastern extremity of Burrard Inlet in favour of the deep–sea port of Vancouver.

The C.P.R. naturally wanted the temporary army tenancy brought to an end so that a huge subdivision could be created. It finally became necessary to meet their demands, so the huts at Little Mountain had to be sawed into sections and transported to the campus late one night on large flatbed trucks that had once been used to carry aircraft. The next day our hut had its five sections nailed back together. (To run ahead of the story, the same old tarpapered hut was again cut into the original five sections and trucked across campus to serve for years as the school of rehabilitation building, until they permanently located atop the University Hospital, alongside the school of nursing.)

The 600 huts that were pulled onto campus by the MacKenzie–Shrum coalition enabled UBC to take in every student who applied as the war ended in 1945. Suddenly UBC's 1,700 pre–war students became 9,000 and a major transformation was under way. Long before the ink was dry on the transfer of ownership papers for the armed forces' huts, these dark green and black structures were on barges, beating their way down to the Point Grey campus.

Below the cliffs, just off Jericho Air Force station, there were two barges filled with nails, which had been en route to Okinawa when the atomic bomb brought the war to an end. An engineering graduate of UBC, now an Air Commodore, was allegedly in charge of these. He was judged to be worthy of an honorary degree, and UBC magically put the nails to good use in reconstructing those huts that arrived in knocked–down form.

Back to the Kinsmen Laboratory. Distinguished scientists such as Dr. Margaret Kennard of Yale University's primate research group came to join us for several years. She left to become director of mental health research for Washington State next door. Thereafter, Dr. Juhn Wada came from the Montreal Neurological Institute to develop an outstanding group working on the speech centre in the human brain, on epilepsy and on sleep. Dr. James Miller came straight from Clark Fraser's department of genetics at McGill to develop our research on muscular dystrophy. He eventually moved to Japan to study the long–range genetic effects of the atomic bomb dropped on Hiroshima. Dr. Michael Livingston, a Cambridge medical graduate, came to the laboratory for a year's research on the microscopic anatomy of the nervous system. I had known his father, A.V.M. Livingston, DGMS, RAF, the night vision pioneer. Also from Cambridge, Dr. John Smythies worked with me on the brain tracts interrupted by frontal lobotomy and on the psychological effects of lysergic acid; he recommended to the food and drug directorate in Ottawa that it be put on the list of proscribed chemicals.

The Kinsmen Foundation, pleased with the international recognition that the published research from their laboratory produced, eventually agreed to finance half the cost of two floors in the new research tower of UBC's rapidly expanding psychiatry department. This space was designed by Dr. Edith McGeer after consultation with the increasing number of researchers that we had attracted. A sterile operating room was provided for Dr. Wada's work on monkeys, and a neurochemistry suite was included for the internationally renowned pioneer Dr. Judah Quastel, F.R.S., who had just retired at age 65 from McGill. He attracted postgraduate students from China, Japan, Canada, the U.S. and Britain.

All this was accomplished under the firm hand of Dr. Edith McGeer. She had taken her doctorate in organic chemistry at the University of Virginia after being raised in New York City. Her father was a Canadian–born surgeon who qualified at the University of Toronto and then pursued postgraduate studies in Vienna. Edie's career embraced several years in the DuPont laboratories in Delaware. There she met her husband, Dr. Patrick McGeer, who had been a basketball star in his undergraduate years at UBC and a Ph.D. student of Sir Hugh Taylor at Princeton University. Pat's work at DuPont concerned the future winner "Teflon." He literally went from that frying pan material into the fire, as he entered provincial politics!

How and why did this happen? It had a precedent, related to me by my long–time friend Hon. Ray Williston. In the early 1950s, as a high school teacher in Prince George, Ray decided to seek election to the B.C. legislature, which in those days met for only six weeks per year. If elected, he hoped to be able to spend the rest of each year at the University of Washington in Seattle, qualifying eventually for his doctorate in education. This great scheme went awry, however, when he was not only elected to the B.C. legislature, but was made a minister with the important portfolio of education! After a lifetime of service he retired, never having achieved his doctoral degree.

I was beginning to wonder how to find a salary for Dr. Patrick McGeer after his graduation from UBC's new medical school and his year of internship. On the way to a party at the ever–hospitable McGeer home, I learned that the sitting member in the legislature for the Point Grey riding, which included the university area, the Hon. Buda Brown, had just succumbed to cancer. As I entered the McGeer home, I told Patrick this and suggested he run in the by–election that would be called, for I had no method of paying him in the Kinsmen Laboratory. Unfortunately, his wife over–heard me and has blamed me ever since for her husband's meteoric career! So a moribund local Liberal party organization was rejuvenated — against the wishes of the ruling political hack — and McGeer turned on the rhetoric. His lawyer uncle, Gerry McGeer, had been mayor of Vancouver in some of the worst years of the Great Depression of the 1930s, building bridges and a new city hall, reading the riot act, and taking on Canada's bankers and the federal government.

His nephew was an Olympic basketball star, well known to a generation of Y.M.C.A. campers on Howe Sound, and an orator rivalling even his voluble uncle with his Irish wit. Pat's father was a quiet Supreme Court judge who winced through all this notoriety, but his mother was a drama and music critic for the Canadian Broadcasting Corporation and was known for her sharp attacks on all forms of pomposity.

Predictably, Pat McGeer won the seat in the legislature where he sat with Her Majesty's Loyal Opposition for some years. At first he could not believe what he was seeing in the ornate chamber in the parliament buildings in Victoria. He recorded these impressions in a hilarious book, *Politics in Paradise*. Soon, however, McGeer was asked to join the provincial cabinet, first as minister of education and later as the minister for universities, science and technology. He refused to move his family to Victoria and commuted to Victoria on the government planes. He also conducted some of his official duties from government offices at Robson Square in Vancouver. However, on weekends one would find him with his Japanese graduate students at the Kinsmen Laboratory on campus. Many of these Ph.D. candidates have since become professors in Japan.

While this work was in high gear, I began to promote the next stage of the UBC medical school: a university hospital that would pull the health professions together.

By 1915, President Wesbrook had formulated his views, based on experience:

> Proper clinical teaching is only possible if teaching institutions control hospitals which are ready to discharge their double function. This double function involves the care of the patients of today and not less important, the better care of the patients of tomorrow through teaching and research. Hospitals should not be simply boarding houses for the sick but institutions for research, study and teaching. Fortunately both ends are served by the same plan.

> The best results are obtained where the university owns its own hospital which is conducted primarily as a teaching and research institution. This safeguards, at the same time, the best interests of the patient. By arrangement with municipal and other public bodies, university medical schools may assume responsibility for the professional conduct of hospitals, guaranteeing the best possible service, but such hospitals cannot easily be made integral parts of the teaching plant of a university. They will be accessory.

Alas, the Great War robbed Wesbrook and UBC of any chance to provide permanent buildings on the heavily forested site at Point Grey. Wesbrook's death at the age of 50 cost British Columbia a great pioneering spirit, so that no progress was made towards a teaching and research hospital on campus until 1951, when, after an acrimonious meeting of the UBC Senate, the policy was settled, though often honoured in the breach. Finally, 100 years after Helmcken's vision, the provincial government announced a 350–bed hospital at UBC.

A task force was set up under the watchful eye of a member of UBC's Board of Governors, Walter Koerner. With the loyal support of his shadow, Lloyd Detwiller, D.F.C., things began to happen in the one–time agricultural engineering building, which was towed, in pieces, across campus to the 40–acre hospital site that Wesbrook had set aside years before.

During the summer, I visited my sister and her husband, Dr. Hugh John MacKay, in the mountains at Revelstoke, B.C. We were at breakfast one morning when George Hobbs, a six–foot–five locomotive engineer and member of the legislative assembly, hammered on the kitchen door through which he squeezed, his engineer's cap grazing the ceiling. He plunked his lunch pail down and was soon into a large cup of coffee. We discussed the need for a hospital on the UBC campus that would serve as a tertiary or referral hospital for the province. He heard the trans–continental train whistling in the mountains and was soon out the door to climb up into his cab.

Later that year, as the legislature in Victoria was about to prorogue, and paper from wastebaskets was about to be thrown skywards, George Hobbs' great frame rose and he bellowed that he had brought his lunch pail and was ready to spend the rest of the day, if necessary, to get a motion passed saying that Dr. Gibson should get "his hospital" on the UBC campus! There was pandemonium and his brother legislators called for order, shouting that the session was over, or so they thought. However, George Hobbs had an ally in the man in the chair, Deputy Speaker Alex Matthews, a one–time medical student in Scotland. With the support of the leader of the opposition, Ray Perrault, the motion was put on the table and supported unanimously. The members could no longer say they had never heard of a university hospital for British Columbia.

The next character on this amazing stage was Percival Archibald Woodward, whom we have already met as "Puggy." When he learned that the provincial government would match every dollar he put up for a campus teaching hospital and that, thanks to the Hon. Judy LaMarsh, minister of health, the federal government would match those two dollars, he rubbed his hands with glee. He liked four–for–one matching enterprises! When I suggested to Puggy that we could make an early start with a low–rise building for psychiatry, he frowned and said he thought little of those types, but that he wanted to start at once on what was hailed as the P.A. Woodward Health Sciences Centre. Ministers jumped on the bandwagon and construction began "on the farm." Wartime huts were towed away and old apple trees and chicken runs removed.

Then planning began on an 8–storey main hospital, which, alas, was never built. The plans eventually were given to the University of Western Ontario where a modified version was soon built, bringing first–class facilities to London, Ontario, and its environs. With the faint hearts in the provincial government of British Columbia, aided by all the sand that the Vancouver General Hospital could throw into the gears, the main section of the hospital on campus was not only delayed but was cut down to 240 beds. Detwiller was told that he could build a lunch room like one at a 240–bed hospital in the interior. Eventually Walter Koerner wheedled a much larger cafeteria out of the bean counters. Early in the post–war era some American pioneers began to develop health sciences centres, in which all the health professions would be represented on university campuses. The idea was taken up by our new dean of medicine, Dr. J.F. McCreary, and by his hospital advisor, Detwiller, who at a very early age had become commissioner for the health insurance plan of the British Columbia government. He graduated from the University of Minnesota's excellent hospital administration course, and had served thereafter at the new University of California hospital in Los Angeles. His wartime service had been with Coastal Command in Britain, flying submarine patrols through fog and foul weather. This prepared him, I used to tell him, for a pioneering role in developing a whole new hospital on campus. The fog, the false alarms, and the random shots from submarines ai ' destroyers below made his work for the campus hospital hazardous every day of his life in Vancouver. However, he kept at our basic concept and finally produced a 60-bed psychiatric facility, a 240-bed acute care hospital and a 300-bed extended care hospital. I am glad to say that the first of these was named the Detwiller Pavilion immediately after his death from a silent coronary occlusion, which occurred while he was sitting up in bed writing more proposals for the university hospital. The acute care unit was named for our great patron in all this struggle: Walter Charles Koerner, philanthropist extraordinary, and a new Canadian who left his native Czechoslovakia just ahead of the Nazi invasion in 1939. The long-term unit was named for Harry Purdy, a professor, public utilities administrator, and president of the UBC Alumni Association from 1957 to 1958.

CHAPTER TWENTY-THREE

Projects

Instead of pursuing my activities on a chronological basis from herein, it seems more useful to me, and hopefully to the reader, to set out various blocks of my life that occupied me after my first ten years as a professor at UBC.

Soon after I became Kinsmen professor of neurological research in Vancouver, my former McGill teacher, Dr. Francis McNaughton (St. Francis to his Montreal Neurological Institute colleagues), recommended to the newly formed Muscular Dystrophy Association of Canada, on the basis of my research with him on wheat germ oil therapy, that I should be invited to join their Medical Advisory Board. There I met the dean of muscle disease studies in the United States, Dr. Ade Milhorat, a professor at Cornell Medical School in New York and director of the newly opened 10-storey Institute for Muscle Diseases adjoining Cornell in Manhattan. That superb building had been tailored for research only, since there were clinical beds next door. My good friend and fellow Sherringtonian, Professor Derek Denny-Brown of Harvard, resigned over the building of the institute.

Before long, Professor Milhorat recruited me to the Scientific Advisory Committee of the American Association, which met twice yearly at its offices on Broadway. The Hollywood comedian Jerry Lewis took on muscular dystrophy as his philanthropic interest and was the champion of it on his international telethons, which were produced from Las Vegas and New York on Labour Day weekend in September. By 1994 Lewis and two million volunteers had raised a total of one billion dollars for research and patient care. These huge sums include collections by American and Canadian firemen and by U.S. postmen. As might be imagined, this highly successful fund-raising effort has led jealous groups to try to undermine it—so far without success.

When Dr. Milhorat announced his resignation as chairman of the

Scientific Advisory Committee in order to concentrate on the institute, I was made chairman for a two-year period. The committee had on it Nobel Prize winners such as Sir John Eccles, F.R.S., and Ed Tatum, and clinicians and basic researchers from many American universities such as Prof. Roger Williams of the University of Texas. I was not involved in any applications for funds so was seen as a "safe" chairman. However, the closer I came to the economic realities, and to the business, broadcasting and labour leaders who made up the trustees of the association, the more I worried about the funding of our "flagship": the Institute for Muscle Disease. I learned the projects within the institute were not reviewed by our scientific committee and that, even more sobering, the institute received everything it requested. I immediately scotched the idea that I should apply for the directorship of the institute.

I thought it wise to bring together the trustees of the association and the scientists who advised them. To get some perspective on such matters it was arranged that the president of our neighbouring institute, Rockefeller University, should be invited to tell us of his experience. When he told us that only half of his budget came from Rockefeller sources, with the remainder being found in open competition, nationally and internationally, the trustees whistled!

That was just about the beginning of the end for the Institute for Muscle Disease. It so happened that the institute, as distinct from the association, had its own trustees: three in number, all bankers and brokers. When they heard that the scientific committee and the association were thinking of changing things, they resigned. So that settled it and we decided to sell the beautiful Skidmore Owings Institute building to Cornell; to re-locate its research staff to universities in the U.S. and Canada; and to concentrate our major research efforts in "centres" or nodes in nine American universities where muscle research was well developed, and at an over-seas centre at the British Postgraduate Medical School at Hammersmith, London, where many great things were being done by the professor of paediatrics, Dr. Victor Dubovitz, David Hill, F.R.S., and Dr. Richard Edwards.

Once we had invested in updated and dedicated space for research, each of our 10 centres had to apply for research funds in open competition. My concept, as I told the Muscular Dystrophy Association, was to build upon 10 centres and to expand our international research community into a little United Nations of gifted workers. Committees were set up to deal with research fellowships, a search for therapeutic agents, and scientific conferences.

The results were electric. Instead of a few research papers published annually from our institute, we soon had 250 papers produced. Young scientists in graduate schools of our designated universities were hammering at the gates, and the genetic revolution in muscle diseases began. We took 18 neuromuscular diseases into our remit, including myasthenia gravis—a label signifying grave muscle weakness. Dr. Peter Dau's work in San Francisco on plasmapheresis—literally washing the blood, which reversed the symptoms—gave us fuel for the next year's telethon. Some of his patients were provided by Dr. Edward Shev, who in 1949 had been my resident in neurology at the University of California. He had been the great showman who had thrilled the physiology students from Berkeley when we put on a clinic for them at U.C. Hospital on Parnassus.

The toughest part of my two–year term as chairman of the Scientific Advisory Committee was the re–locating of some of the lesser known of our 45 researchers to universities or colleges in need of help. For some months I had to fly from Vancouver to New York on Friday nights, spend Saturday and Sunday at the institute with Dr. Mel Moss interviewing remaining staff, and then fly home on a late plane on Sunday or an early one on Monday. As I was at that time an alderman in the city of Vancouver, I found it hard to stay awake at council meetings on Tuesdays, especially if there was a night session. Living in airplanes was nothing new for me, but listening to endless amendments to by–laws concerning taxi fares or building regulations occasionally put me to sleep. When the vote was called one of my neighbouring aldermen would shake me and say, "Get your hand up, Willie."

For my swan song, the board and the Scientific Advisory Committee met at the Woodward Library at UBC and set up a research fellowship in my name in Britain. While I am still a vice–president of the Muscular Dystrophy Association of America, I have long since dropped off their numerous committees. On the scientific advisory group I was succeeded by Dr. Stewart Wolf, whom I had known over the years at the Cecil and Ida Green Biomarine Research Center at Galveston. The impetus given to researchers in the field of human genetics, such as Professor Kunkel at Harvard and Dr. Kay Davies at Oxford, has paid off handsomely. The next big goal is the application of the discoveries they and their groups have made to treatment and, hopefully, to cures of some of the 40 diseases now covered by the MDA. Looking back, I must say that I have never worked with a more gentle and public–spirited group in my life. Jerry Lewis, whom I knew from backstage at many television productions from Las Vegas, and his shadow Robert Ross, the executive director of MDA, together with their headquarters' staff and their nation–wide volunteers, deserve a front seat in Heaven. Their British counterpart, which originally consisted of a small group of families whose male children were afflicted, has also become a productive organization. When Sir Richard Attenborough, their honorary chairman, produced the great film *Ghandi*, he took it around the world donating the income from its first showings to the Dystrophy Group, as it is known in Britain. They have come a long way from the little audience I found years ago, huddled in a sweaty room in London to hear a sympathetic lecture from Sir Andrew Huxley, F.R.S., the Cambridge Nobelist. The distinguished neurologist Lord Walton has played a great role in the scientific research fostered by the group and, in the early days, by the Canadian Association.

CHAPTER TWENTY-FOUR

The 1970s

In 1970 the barometric pressure was rising in Vancouver civic politics. Three aldermen out of a total of 10 had been elected by a reform group called The Elector's Action Movement. The incumbent mayor, a law graduate of UBC, and six of his aldermen were in the real estate or development business. One of the TEAM aldermen, Arthur Phillips, was a highly reputable stock broker whose mutual fund, held with his business partners, had the best performance rating in Canada. One ally on city council was the urban geographer Professor Walter Hardwick, a graduate of UBC and a Ph.D. of Wisconsin.

The third member of the TEAM group was a developer with a conscience, Brian Calder. The electoral rules dictated that if a sitting alderman ran for the mayor's post and lost, he was out altogether. Thus, if Art Phillips were to run for the office of mayor and lose, the three reform aldermen would be reduced to two.

Their solution was to pressure me to run for the mayor's post against the "law 'n' order" incumbent. I agreed with only one month to go before the November election, and set off on quite a voyage of discovery. Campaigning for three weeks took every hour of the day and I ran into so many vituperative people that the whole thing appeared hopeless. Altogether there were 12 candidates for the mayor's chair—one even wanted "free stores" where people could take anything they liked. An all-candidates' meeting became a zoo.

However, invitations to speak to business or service organizations helped me confront the mayor one on one. By the end of the campaign the TEAM felt I was gaining support. The election canvassing involved standing with aldermanic, school board and parks board aspirants on the bridges into Vancouver, waving large TEAM signs to motorists.

The election night results were surprising to me at least. The incumbent mayor received approximately 44% of the vote, while I received 34%. The remaining votes were scattered over the 10 other candidates. Long after the dust had settled and I had gone back to my work at UBC, the pay–off became apparent: the "victorious" mayor did not run again for public office after his two–year term expired.

By 1972 the scene was set for an over–whelming TEAM victory in all three branches of Vancouver's government. Art Phillips became mayor in a landslide, and his first act was to dismiss the "city manager" who had been hand in glove with land developers. The chap went home to England, reputedly at twice his Vancouver salary.

After two years on city council (1972–74), I decided to run for election to the Parks Board, which is still a rarity in civic government in Canada. Though I headed the poll I could not consider the chairmanship, so busy was I at the university and in disease–related organizations. Though polio epidemics were a thing of the past, thanks to the newly developed vaccine, there were many post–polio cases crying out for orthopaedic and other help. The Western Society for Rehabilitation was organized under the devoted leadership of Dr. George Frederick Strong, whose daughter was rendered paraplegic in an accident. The deputy minister of health, Dr. G.R.F. Elliot (known to us in the Air Force as Gruff Elliot), was the untiring trouble shooter in our early years. The Kinsmen Foundation produced $11,000 to buy a site—half a city block—adjoining Shaughnessy Veteran's Hospital, and the rehabilitation work prospered. As an aside I should mention that though Dr. Strong and I never agreed about the site of UBC's medical school, we agreed completely on the rehabilitation centre. He was a tough American, a graduate of the University of Minnesota who came to intern in Vancouver and stayed. Over the years he rose to be president of the Royal College of Physicians of Canada, in which many of us were enrolled. In that post he was invited to Australia to represent our college at a major bash down–under. One day he called to know if I would lunch with him at a posh restaurant. So I did, all the while wondering what was afoot. It turned out that Fritz wanted to know from my experience in Australia what sort of clothing to take for ceremonial and ordinary wear, considering the season of the year was exactly opposite to that in Vancouver.

I was relieved that was all that was required of me, but almost as an afterthought said, "Could I make two suggestions, which you may think unimportant: do not refer to the origins of Australians and do not mention or strive to imitate their dialect." A month later Fritz was on the telephone again to say he was back in Vancouver and could I join him for lunch. To my amazement he had remembered my earlier warnings and thanked me profusely for them. He told me that an American representative from another professional group had made a fool of himself by launching into a speech on the doubtful origins of Australians and their incomprehensible language!

As a member of the elected Board of Parks and Recreation, I found the work both interesting and rewarding. However, the board had no taxing authority, and for its very considerable budget had to go, hat in hand, to Vancouver city council. That held no terrors for me and I was able to thread the needle there, but always with collisions with the civil servants guarding the public purse. I found that their methods of putting down parks advocates might be very authoritarian, but would not hold water. For instance, an ancient soccer pitch near the centre of the city was leased for a long term to a highway bus company that needed it to build its in–town terminal. The city's finance department claimed that once the rentals, over the years, equalled the book value of the little park, the land passed to the city and was no longer the property of the Parks Board. Even today that battle remains to be fought out, especially as the ancient soccer field is worth many millions of dollars. The chairman of the Parks Board, May Brown, had likewise been an alderman and kept the more turbulent meetings in reasonable order. There was no lack of adrenalin shot off at public hearings where parks advocates would clash with outraged citizens. Emotions still run high when public open space is under threat, especially when some monopoly is sought by a would–be proprietor of a food outlet, or where a user–pay policy is under discussion, usually for 25 cents per hour for tennis courts.

The pride and joy of the parks system in Vancouver has always been the 1,000–acre Stanley Park, set aside by the first city council of Vancouver at a meeting in its tent headquarters a century ago. The land is actually the property of the Department of National Defence. This timbered promontory juts out into Burrard Inlet, and from it springs the high Lion's Gate suspension bridge, built in 1937 by the Guinness interests in Britain. The bridge gave them access to several thousand acres on the North Shore, which they have since developed, at great profit, into a handsome and extensive subdivision. City council's 1935 vote to cut a highway through Stanley Park to the bridge take–off was only six to five. Further inroads into this once pristine area have included an absolutely uncalled for civic works yard of more than four acres and increasing incursions by the Vancouver Aquarium—a world–class institution but the cause of much motor car traffic, parking problems and pollution. At present there is a commission under His Honour Gordon Johnson enquiring into the future of Stanley Park. I have been making some radical proposals to him, which may someday find support. Meantime, I must dwell further on my experience with that noble area. Most Canadians know about the Stanley Cup as the pinnacle of the ice hockey world. Few realize that it was the same Lord Stanley, an early Governor General of Canada, whose name was applied to this great park.

On my flights to Muscular Dystrophy Association meetings in the east, to Wellcome Trust meetings in London or World Health Organization committees in Geneva, I often stopped for a few hours in Calgary, Alberta, to see the officers of the Devonian Foundation. This charity was set up by the late Eric Harvie, Q.C., with capital of approximately $65,000,000 to be spent in 15 years! His son, Don Harvie, and a dedicated staff applied themselves with vigour to this wonderful task and really revolutionized westerners' thinking when it came to preserving their fast–disappearing heritage.

I would dash by taxi from the Calgary airport to the Devonian boardroom, where maps would be spread out with the customary weights applied to their corners, and I would expand on the opportunities that Vancouver offered for parks and preservation. Then I would hurry back for the next plane, leaving the stunned trustees wondering. Finally, the secretary to the foundation came to Vancouver to survey the 55 acres that TEAM had saved from development by its owner, the Canadian Pacific Railway. Poor Jim Fish arrived in the rainstorm to end all rainstorms, so I provided him with rainproof clothes and rubber boots in order that we might trudge over this abandoned area of the former Shaughnessy Golf Course. It was hard going against the wind as we climbed the side of an old reservoir, away up on the height of land over–looking Vancouver. In the end his foundation turned down the project. More must be said, however, of the effect of this "hospitality."

My next visit to Calgary was to try to interest the Devonian in a combined pedestrian–cyclist waterfront walkway around the base of Stanley Park. For three decades a Scottish stone mason in the employ of the Parks Board had been building, when tides permitted, a sea–walk around the periphery of the park—a matter of many miles. Now we wanted to build a hard–surfaced pathway to accommodate cyclists near the bank, and walkers (or wheelchairs) next to the ocean. After several visits to Calgary the plan was agreed, though by then I had returned to city council as an alderman for the period 1976–78. When the good news came from the Devonians that they would give us $900,000 for the water's–edge project, a gasp went round the in–

camera council session. As smiles went around the table the silence was broken by the mayor, Jack Volrich. He demanded angrily, "Is the City of Vancouver being run from Calgary?" We could not believe our ears! I moved, and quickly had a seconder, that this generous offer be accepted. The motion passed, with His Worship still sputtering.

The Devonian Foundation followed up some time later with the $300,000 needed to purchase the land at the entrance to Stanley Park—a garden area now named in their honour.

Reference has already been made to the 55 acres of C.P.R. property that we wished to acquire for botanical gardens for the Parks Board. This once–manicured golf course area is located at the point where diagonals drawn from the four corners of the city boundaries cross on a rising hill over–looking Vancouver and the bowl of mountains in which it sits. The Shaughnessy golf course was part of a highly priced subdivision, with curving roads lined by fine trees and wide boulevards, laid out by the C.P.R. early in this century.

By the time the Save Our Parklands Association was formed, all but approximately 69 acres of the 1910 golf course had been sold off for schools and as building sites. I presided over a band of dedicated conservationists, determined to maintain areas of beauty and utility before progress could over–take them. A small group of us broke off to form the Vancouver Botanical Association, which did the job of wresting all of the undivided property from the C.P.R. to build a public display garden. I exchanged one presidency for another.

The Vancouver city council seemed determined to fall in with the subdividing plans of the powerful Montreal–based company. The president of the C.P.R., Buck Crump, happened to be a British Columbian, so we decided to start with him. A delegation, including Hon. Grace McCarthy, deputy premier, Dr. Robert Long, a tough–minded chiropractor, and ex–Brigadier Theo du Moulin, whose law firm was both public–spirited and powerful, bearded Buck in his office in Windsor Station, Montreal. After reading the crisp brief I am told he looked up and asked in a brusque manner, "Who wrote this?" Mrs. McCarthy was not one to be put down easily and replied with some heat: "It was written by Dr. Gibson, but he was not well enough to come with us." Thereupon Crump shouted, "Tell him to come and work for me. I need someone who can get things across." Sad to say, the president stuck to his original purchase price of six million dollars.

So the delegates came away empty handed, but far from beaten.

On her return from Victoria, Grace McCarthy appealed to Premier W.A.C. Bennett. He hit his desk with a mighty whack as he said: "I will guarantee one million dollars towards your botanical garden: two–thirds of it to go to land acquisition and one–third to improve the land once you have it." With a glint in his eye he said that some time in the future the C.P.R. might want to talk to him about longer "sidings" for their lengthened freight trains that were pulled over the Rocky Mountains by four diesel locomotives–in–line.

With renewed spirits we set out to convert a city council that had turned and twisted to prevent any calamity such as a large botanic garden from befalling Vancouver. Slyly, they had lumped an amount for the purchase of the land in with an impossibly expensive list of public works, in order to defeat the whole lot. In another plebiscite the council urged the voters to shut us up, once and for all. The citizens voted 54% in favour of our gardens, but 60% was required to pass it. However, we realized that we had a toe–hold.

Clearly, we had to get the price of the land down, so we agreed that the golf course land would have 14 acres abstracted from it in order to facilitate an early start on a C.P.R. condominium project on the height of land. However, the six million dollar price tag was unthinkable.

Two key developments then occurred. Theo du Moulin showed that the present city council no longer contained a majority of those aldermen who had voted down the gardens originally. He told us we had an airtight case and that we should keep going. I had recovered sufficiently to go to Montreal on a fund–raising reconnaissance for UBC, and for this purpose met for lunch with the head of the Donner Canadian Foundation, the battle–scarred Air Vice–Marshall Frank McGill. We sat outside in the blazing sun in the courtyard restaurant at Place Ville Marie. He told me how badly one Canadian university had treated one of Mr. William Donner's grandsons when he had visited its campus. I promised to see that UBC did better, and in fact we soon invited all the Donner grandsons to meet at our faculty club over–looking the snow–capped mountains of Howe Sound. The results of A.V.M. McGill's prodding were more than satisfactory.

However, the diminutive mover and shaker, who at the end of World War II had raised 18 million dollars to move the Montreal General Hospital to a new site on Mount Royal, looked at me and said, "You look depressed, what's wrong?" I explained that I was up against an intransigent city council in Vancouver and an equally immovable financial colossus in Montreal. Having heard the details he smiled and told me with a grin: "The new president of the C.P.R. is my next–door neighbour. Leave him to me."

What happened next was stranger than fiction. A.V.M. McGill would wait in his kitchen until he saw his neighbour go out to his garage. Suddenly, the A.V.M., dwarfed by an enormous and bluff chap, would call out, "Good morning Ian, I have just been hearing about you in Vancouver." No response. The next day's encounter would begin, "Ian I was amazed to hear of your public image in Vancouver." This was kept up for a couple of weeks, whereupon Ian retorted, "Come for a drink after five o'clock, will you Frank." There the cards were put on the table so persuasively that the price came down to two million dollars!

Simultaneously, the superintendent of parks in Vancouver, engineer Stuart Lefeaux, was chatting about Vancouver's needs with the quiet philanthropist and timber owner, J.W. VanDusen. I had the pleasure of meeting him at H.R. MacMillan's afternoon chats, and in a few days he was lunching with me at the UBC faculty club. His daughter, Fay, and her husband, Mark Collins, had been student leaders on campus years before. Mr. VanDusen built additions of great value to Union Theological College on campus and helped in its fusion with Anglican College to form the Vancouver School of Theology.

I soon learned that his ancestors were among the first Dutch settlers in New York and that the wall delimiting their land was the original wall of today's "Wall Street" in Manhattan. He liked my reference to the *New Yorker* magazine's story that Manhattan was a corruption of the old Dutch term meaning "the isle of the nuts." He came to the point very cautiously, but finally wanted to know what he could do to forward the acquisition of the 55 acres not far from his home. He was a botanist at heart and as a young man had served as a professional forester (along with his friend Harvey Reginald MacMillan) in the provincial government service in Victoria.

I reviewed the finances of what we were attempting, and he quietly said, "If you could write me that, in a letter, I think I could do one–third of what is required." That was one million dollars, two–thirds of which was to be spent on acquisition and one–third on development, provided that the city would come in on the same basis. He did not want to be thanked by anyone so no public announcement was to be made.

With this anonymous gift we were able to go before a reluctant city council, where a sneering little bean counter stood up and said, as if in pain, "I guess, Your Worship, we can't turn down 33 cent dollars." What a role model for the younger generation: a real cheese parer!

Then cats started getting out of their bags. We found that in one corner of these precious acres, city hall officials had already authorized underground services and had permitted an illegal start to be made on the supposedly certain subdivision.

Thus, a beautiful area, with its neglected fairways and water areas, was transferred to the Board of Parks and Recreation, whose hard-working chairman, Commissioner May Brown, presided over the opening on August 30, 1975. The Botanical Gardens Society has prospered and, thanks to vigorous presidents, now has over 6,000 members; an endowment fund thanks to the foresight of Peter Kaye, the heart and soul of the Vancouver Foundation; an excellent director; a library; a resident artist; and collections boasting wonderful varieties from distant countries. A sculpture contest was combined with the early development of the gardens and internationally renowned figures came to show what they could do. The marble was donated by a contractor who, as he said, "got stuck with a lot of Italian stone." Two nights before the contest was to be judged, the director of the gardens, Roy Forster, called to say there was no provision in the budget for the cement slabs needed to support these remarkable works properly. So I said I personally would go for the pouring of the concrete if it could be guaranteed to hold up the enormous weight of some of the finished pieces. A puzzled public had turned out in summer weather to see what they called "real artists" at work. Since those days, more than 25 years ago, many wondrous things have been added: a fragrance garden for the blind, a Himalayan garden, a restaurant named "Sprinklers," statuary from the Swedish community, a children's garden, and a large Floral Hall for meetings of innumerable societies. Once a year there is a plant sale that halts traffic for a mile around. It is there that I'm able to see my medical friends shovelling manure into bags and, for a change, doing what their wives command. When all the noise of a great city subsides at night, the real botanic garden comes to life: the plants keep growing.

Life as an alderman was always interesting. I was amazed at the variety of civic matters for which answers had to be found. Each of the 10 aldermen (or councillors, as they are now known) was designated to serve on several committees within City Hall, but some of us were given assignments far beyond those limits. I had the good fortune to serve on the board of the Pacific National Exhibition, which once a year showed enough livestock to qualify for federal funds as a tenuous agricultural fair. For the rest of the year it was a stadium, an ice palace for hockey and shows on ice, a racetrack with a lease until the year 2025, a play land filled with noise and the smell of barbecued meat, onions and popcorn. Though the provincial government had given it to the city a century ago as a 160–acre park, it had been turned into a largely black–topped preserve for profit. The best things about the P.N.E. were the British Empire Games stadium in which Bannister passed Landy to win the famous "4–minute mile contest" in 1954, and a magnificent British Columbia educational pavilion in which there is the largest relief map of B.C. that I have ever seen — a wonderful asset for our educational programmes.

The P.N.E. board meetings were often hilarious, beginning with dinner. The board room in which we dined had a broken–down piano at one end, on which Alderman Don Bellamy and I played noisy duets of once–popular songs. However, with dinner over there could be some tense passages. When the board voted, by a majority of one, not to permit an entrepreneur to sell beer at hockey games (always at night), the governmentally appointed chair came close to apoplexy. I still hope that the tawdry "exhibition" will be moved to an agricultural town in the Fraser Valley, leaving the 160–acre Hastings Park to the people. It is located at the eastern extremity of Vancouver where the people need more park space. One of my "lost causes" was to preside over its Restoration Society.

The purchase of waterfront lands along the Jericho beach front that once belonged to the Royal Canadian Air Force was an unusual challenge. Prime Minister Trudeau had sold the city (for one dollar) the 128 acres of the old Jericho Flying Station, where seaplanes had been in fashion since 1922. However, there was another strip of beach on which a fine house had been built, and then desecrated by a public service (which shall remain nameless) for a few years. I was sent to Ottawa to work out the terms by which the city of Vancouver could buy it for park use. When I had concluded the business with the then minister of defence, I was told that never again would defence properties be sold to the city of Vancouver at such rates. He shouted that when the 99–year lease on the beautiful Stanley Park (which was Defence Property) came up for renewal, the city would have to pay 10% of the assessed value. This, of course, would put it into billions of dollars. I replied testily: "By then, I think we shall have had a new minister of defence." Within two weeks he had actually left the cabinet, not because of anything concerning Stanley Park, but over a question of bilingualism. So goes the fight for parkland, which is never ending in an avaricious society.

My final fling at saving parkland took place over a 600–acre parcel on Bowen Island, in Howe Sound, three miles from West Vancouver.

The Union Steamship Company, a British group, at one time allied with a company of the same name in New Zealand, owned large areas of Bowen Island to which it ran regular passenger ships and cruise ships years ago. In some fashion the remaining 600 acres was owned by an American engineer who had built many dams and waterways in Canada. His wife had died of multiple sclerosis recently and he, advancing in age, wanted to divest himself of this excellent parkland on which there was a large lake and a large seafront component. The Parks Committee of the Greater Vancouver Regional District, under the chairmanship of a professor of mathematics at Simon Fraser University, was determined to acquire this but did not have the many millions being demanded by Mr. Crippen's agent. I, therefore, put on a luncheon at the University Club in Vancouver to which the chairman of the district was invited, together with his parks people and the Provincial Parks Authority, so that we might try to resolve this with public funds and stop all further confrontations concerning this once–in–a–lifetime opportunity. The chairman of the G.V.R.D. was the mayor of Coquitlam, a huge man with a beefy fist but an agile mind. As we sat down to lunch the agent for the property kept spouting that he had another buyer on the way with the money from Seattle. I told him to shut up or leave. We then got down to business and instead of 2.8 million dollars, Mr. Crippen said that he would be willing to accept 1.8 million from a public body. Mayor Tonn reached out his enormous hand and shook Mr. Crippens' hand, saying, "You've got a deal at 1.6 million." That settled it and I sent for a bottle of champagne. I wish it were as easy to bring other festering sores to successful conclusions such as that.

The main thing I learned in civic politics was not to make statements, but rather to ask questions. Vituperative and inflammatory statements were a dime a dozen in civic politics, so no one bothered to reply to them. A probing question, however, had to be replied to, in public, or there was a minor insurrection. Occasionally there was an outburst of verbal garbage such as I had never heard before. I realized that the university world was relatively quiet compared with the bull pit of civic politics. However, TEAM made great changes in Vancouver in its 10–year reign, and the city has never looked back.

Another board on which I was happy to serve was that which controlled the city–owned Queen Elizabeth Theatre (2,800 seats) and its adjoining playhouse (700 seats). These facilities occupied a city block and had been designed by a group of Montreal architects, including my friend Hazen Sise. He had survived the Spanish civil war in which he had served as an assistant to Dr. Norman Bethune, the Canadian surgeon and pioneer in a transfusion service using refrigerated blood.

One very attractive aspect of the Civic Theatres Board was the access that it gave me to the four–keyboard Wurlitzer theatre organ. That "gay twenties" behemoth had pneumatically activated notes, so that there was a latent period between pressing a key and the roar or tinkle or whatever in response. The lowest notes were produced high up in the roof of the theatre from bellows a foot square, or actually cubed. The great instrument snored and boomed as one played marches or choruses on it. The Orpheum Theatre was purchased by the city "for peanuts," as one might say. Only half a dozen people were in the audience on the last day of its existence as a motion picture theatre. Today, with a greatly extended stage and a flashy new entry salon, it is the home of the vigorous Vancouver Symphony. Before my term on the board ran out I had an opportunity to make some recordings of my own compositions.

Another board that gave me great satisfaction was that concerned with the Vancouver Public Library, which was a system rather than a single library. Its central branch was the busiest place in town, with adults and children pouring through its turnstiles from morn till night. The business section was heavily used and computer access was just on its way in. Soon the central unit would be surrounded by very large buildings and a new central site needed. The collection of rare books was not large, but as I waited for board meetings to begin I would go through those precious volumes. The major voyages of discovery on the Pacific had been donated by H.R. MacMillan, whose life revolved around books. I was pleasantly surprised to find, in a leather–bound folder of yesteryear, one page from Gutenberg's printing of the Bible in the mid–15th century. It had been salvaged from a damaged and fragmented copy by a well–known bibliographer early in the twentieth century. The heavy German printing was hard to read but to have it in one's hand was a thrill. No record existed of how it came to be in the Vancouver Public Library. We tried to buy it for the Woodward Biomedical Library at UBC, but no value could be put on it. However, it was graciously loaned to us for a display of milestones of early printing which included the riches of the Woodward collection. Years later I borrowed the carefully preserved Gutenberg page to illustrate one of my chancellor's "remarks," which I was permitted to give at University of Victoria graduations. I was trying to impress upon my audience that since Gutenberg's wonderful creation of printing with movable type, there was really no need for students to write down verbatim what a university lecturer was saying. The students most likely wondered, "who is this nut and why is he waving an old piece of wallpaper at us from the platform?" The assembled faculty behind me probably thought: "This guy is dangerous. Of course students should be writing down what we say at lectures. If they take this printing stuff seriously we'll be out of a job." The hierarchy were also not amused by my antics as a chancellor, even if I had once been a professor—in a medical school of all places.

My second term at city hall came to an end on December 31, 1978, much to the relief of some of the civil servants. They had yawned when, as a parks commissioner, I sought a better share of the city budget. As my time was drawing to a close, I learned that the university, to which Dr. "Sandy" Monro had bequeathed an apartment block contiguous to city hall, might wish to sell it off. With the ever–present help of the chancellor, Chief Justice Nathan Nemetz, this was arranged. An adjoining Shell service station was purchased, and the city hall precinct enlarged against future needs. The "bean counters" at first were upset, but lived to cheer.

CHAPTER TWENTY-FIVE

The Woodward Biomedical Library

One never knows where a chance meeting of minds may lead. In 1935, while attending Arnold Carmichael's Bible class at the National Hospital in London's Queen Square—the home of British neurology—I had a lunch of bangers and mash with a Vancouver neurologist, Dr. S.E.C. Turvey. He was besotted with books and read voraciously at the Wellcome Library nearby. Years later he joined me in our dilapidated army hut at UBC to work on the circulation to the brain—one of Christopher Wren's favourite subjects. One day he called me from his office in the Burrard Building, which he shared with surgeon R.E. McKechnie, nephew of the surgeon of the same name who had been chancellor of UBC for 26 years. Sotto voce, "Ward" Turvey said into his telephone: "P.A. Woodward is here in the office and feeling very philanthropic this morning. Did you not tell me, when I worked in your laboratory, that the medical school needed a real library, not a half-baked balcony?" I replied that we were strapped, with next to no space and few books. Soon Turvey had enlisted Bob McKechnie in our campaign and he brought "Puggy" Woodward to see our minimal space. Puggy may never have finished high school, but he was, according to H.R. MacMillan, the best businessman raised on the Pacific coast. He took one look at our pitiful facility and cursed with his usual string of expletives. Things began to move rapidly, so rapidly that to keep President MacKenzie informed was almost a daily routine. Keeping Puggy satisfied that progress was being made each day was a task in itself.

At first he wanted to build a library in which the milestones of medical history would be displayed—the whole to be a memorial to his father with whom he had rarely exchanged a civil word. Charles Woodward, a widower with many children, came from Ontario to found an amazing network of retail stores. H.R. told me he recalls Charles doing the family wash on Sundays. His son Puggy seems to have been a young hellion whose job on Saturdays was to wash medicine bottles in the basement of the Hastings Street department store. Instead of that, Puggy would disappear from the basement, deserting his bottle-washing partner George Cunningham (later a chain pharmacy owner), and jumping on one of the Union Steamships' cruise boats headed for a day's outing at Bowen Island, over an hour away. Puggy would play all day with children his own age who rollicked in the playing fields. When the returning boat docked beside the Woodward store in late afternoon, Puggy would run to the basement and attend to bottle washing. Finally, he found his father waiting for him with a paddle, and that ended his Saturday cruises.

Puggy thought of a better scheme, this time to make money at the nearby wharf. As the vessels from the north coast and Alaska came alongside, miners and loggers hung over the ship's rail to dispatch messages to their respective girlfriends by the quickest method. Puggy would collect a few pieces of paper, and paid in advance, would run as fast as his legs would take him to the scribbled addresses. He told me these were not in the best parts of the neighbourhood and often in dangerous alleys. However, he survived, all the while exhibiting his entrepreneurial brains.

By 1912 some of his friends were leaving by train for McGill Medical School in Montreal, so he decided to join them. As they moved into fraternity houses at McGill, these future leaders in the profession took Puggy in with them. It finally dawned on him that no support or even a letter was forthcoming from his father, so he found himself a job at Henry Morgan's fashionable department store—running the elevator! He used to say, over his late afternoon drink of fortified milk: "Bill, if you want to know what's really going on in a building, run the elevator. People come into a closed space and tell all, especially women. It's the place to be."

When the Great War broke out Puggy was off. No more elevators. By the time the war was over in 1918, his distraught father welcomed him home as a hero. In fact, Charles Woodward told Puggy he would like him to take over the entire lower level of the large department store in Vancouver for any purpose he chose, and to make a go of it.

Whatever possessed Puggy I do not know, but he decided to make the entire area a food floor. When he renovated it he had what we would call today a supermarket. He rejected the conventional way of selling groceries, fruit and vegetables, which was to have little men with black half-sleeves running back and forth behind an oak counter to get things from high shelves, using dangerous ladders. The pandemonium and writing down of orders and accounts with pen-

A good deal of amusement and amazement is to be had very easily by glancing through "Banned Books", an annotated catalogue recently published based on the Junior League exhibition held in New York last spring. Chronologically the authors at one time ot another disapproved of range from Homer (whom Caligula tried to suppress) to various of our contemporaries, and not the least amusing instances are those in which works fell into official disfavor for reasons which it would have been difficult to anticipate. In 1931, for instance, the Governor of Hunan Province in China banned "Alice in Wonderland" on the ground "that animals should not use human language and that it was disastrous to put animals and human beings on the same level." But, then, some quarter of a century before, the English Lord Chamberlain for a time forbade performance of "The Mikado" because it might give offence to "our Japanese allies", and in 1935 a first trombone player in Philadelphia refused to take part in the production of "Lady Macbeth of Minsk" because some of the notes in his part were obscene... But what we like best of all is the letter received in 1933 by the Weyhe Galleries in New York, signed by H.C. Stuart, Assistant collector of customs: "There are being detained... two packages addressed to you containing obscene photo books, "Ceiling Sistine Chapel; Filles - Michael Angelo."

The Nation, January 8, 1936

cils on soft paper, carbon–backed bills was to have no place in the new order. Puggy provided baskets to be carried on each customer's arm. He shouted to high heaven: “”Let the customers at the goods. If their basket gets too full or too heavy let them put it on a hand–pushed buggy. Stop all this handwriting of bills that can't be read. Get adding machines at the exits and let's get this thing done properly.” He was beginning to sound more like his father each day.

So began, according to some, the world's first mechanized “groceteria” or supermarket. Puggy described his encounter with the National Cash Register Company to me. He wired their factory to send 160 cash registers of a suitable type. A telegram came back enquiring whether a typographical error might have crept in, and if his order was for 16 only. He sent back a blast that demanded the 160 be out there fast or he would go elsewhere. So his time as an elevator operator in far away Montreal was paying off, and Percival Archibald Woodward was acclaimed by his family and by the community.

As I sat by the fire in his den listening to this personal history while he raided the kitchen for more milk (which he infused with random spirits en route), I could not help wondering what he might have done had he enjoyed a formal education. Such speculation was cut short by a blow–by–blow description of the donkeys who had tried to block his way. He was not called Puggy for nothing. It was rumoured that if you ever passed his table at noon at the Vancouver Club and said anything more than “Good day,” he would jump to his feet and start taking his coat off, shouting, “Do you want to settle it here?” It is said that he was thrown out of the club three times in his career, but always allowed back.

Puggy was married to a wonderful lady named Marian, who was a daughter of the scientifically minded grain farmer William Douglas of Saskatchewan. Next to his extensive fields was the Federal Experimental Farm at which the famous Marquis wheat was perfected. By shortening the growing season, the scientists were able to push wheat production further north on the prairies. Mrs. Woodward gave me a small metal box containing some of the original seed that the experimentalists had entrusted to her father. The Woodwards' only child, a son, died of Hodgkins disease while a student at Shawnigan Lake boys school. While Puggy was a very lonely man, much undervalued by his associates, Mrs. Woodward was the centre of the women's world of Vancouver until she was struck down with diabetes and multiple small strokes. She was as gentle as her husband was tough, though under it all Puggy was an emotional man. He made sure that while his influence counted in the growing department store chain, no employee of long standing retired without a sizeable holding in company shares.

Once his enthusiasm was aroused, he was a man for instant action. At times this produced unforeseen results. One of his cronies in the feed and grain business told Puggy that there was a new health craze: the incorporation of alfalfa into white bread. Accordingly, the bakery in the Woodward store switched to "green bread" and advertised this phenomenon. The next morning the food floor was mobbed by health "commandos," as Puggy called them, and the place was a near wreck by noon. He wisely arranged for a small bakery nearby to take over this torrential clientele and never ventured into this minefield again.

The day came for the laying of the cornerstone of the Woodward Biomedical Library, and a chilly afternoon it was. A capsule containing a variety of common things was buried under the granite slab, while a white–haired little man struggled to say a few words to the audience. Finally, the beautiful three–storey building was ready, with a superb Memorial Room dedicated to his father, Charles Woodward. It contained the rapidly growing collection of the landmarks in the biological and medical sciences. The design of the handsome high–vaulted room could have mirrored a small Oxford or Cambridge college library, but this one had a fireplace to warm readers' toes. A large bronze plaque over the mantle listed the physicians of British Columbia who had made significant contributions during Charles Woodward's lifetime in B.C., his adopted province. One side of the gallery of this rare book room contained the rarest books (kept behind locked glass doors), and on the other side were study cubicles named for our early helpers. Still to come were two post–war French tapestries. The great day arrived with speeches by the chairman of the senate committee to over–see the University Library. Woodward was the first branch library allowed on campus, and thanks to the distinguished professor of zoology, Dr. Ian McTaggart–Cowan, the holdings in all life sciences were transferred to complement the growing medical constituency. Professor and Mrs. Chauncey Leake, friends from my Texas days, arrived from San Francisco, having sent ahead their superb collection of "milestones," including a first edition of Andreas Vesalius' 1543 version of *The Fabric of the Human Body*. This book had been printed for the Paduan firebrand in Switzerland, possibly to escape the edict of the church against the dissection of the human body.

Percival Archibald Woodward was dressed as never before, and his wife came in her wheelchair. Her close friend, Chancellor Phyllis Ross, graced the proceedings. Our president, straight from Harvard, John Barfoot McDonald, roamed wide-eyed through this new structure. Puggy, falling back on his merchant's experience, wanted everything moveable, so that the pillars to support the tremendous weight of books were spaced 20 feet apart in all directions. When the lights were turned on at night this gem of a building resembled a ship at sea.

The day following the opening, Mr. Woodward returned to see how the library would actually function. He volunteered the observation that it was the only thing to which he had put his hand that he found no fault therein. "What did I think of it?" he asked. Taking the plunge, I replied, "I hate to tell you, but it is going to be too small." Without a second's hesitation he shouted: "We'll double it then. Let's get going!"

When the winter rains subsided, the roof was ripped off and another storey was added, and the entire footprint was expanded to an area 150 feet square. When finished, the building contained 1,000 seats and much more extensive space for rare books, which was located above a new seminar room named for Sir Charles Sherrington, the most decorated man in science. His son Carr had sent out all of his father's 90 honorary degrees and fellowship parchments, his court dress and his Nobel Prize diploma and numerous personal papers. With them came his Chippendale dining room chairs; set around a handsome table made in Ipswich, they now carry the names of famous scholars who sat on them in visits to Sherrington's home in Oxford. Each little plaque carries two names: Osler–Penfield, Sherrington–Adrian, Cannon–Forbes, Ramón y Cajal–Río–Hortega, Eccles–Denny Brown, Cushing–Fulton, Rutherford–Bragg, Wesbrook–Foster, Florey–Lister, Bridges–Dale.

Once the four-storey structure was completed and electronic check-out gates were installed, we began to acquire whole collections of rare books. From Dr. Hugh Sinclair of Magdalen College, Oxford, came 7,000 books. Jacob Zeitlin telephoned from Los Angeles to say he had for sale a three-volume collection, published years ago, of the biological drawings of Leonardo da Vinci. How much? $750! I replied that I would have to see if we had any money left. I called Dr. Noel Poynter, our friend who directed the Wellcome Institute for the History of Medicine in London. He said the Leonardo volumes in mint condition were worth at least £750, so I called Jake back and said we would take them.

Eventually I was able to interest Mr. Woodward in the Crane Library for blind students at UBC, and in research done by an engineering professor on reading machines for the blind. The intensive care ward at St. Paul's Hospital was also pioneered by Puggy at that time.

One of our benefactors, once we had the library up and running, was the dog–food king, Dr. Ballard. He had grown up in Ontario near the home of Sir Frederick Banting, Canada's Nobelist in medicine for his work on insulin. When I asked Dr. Ballard if he would like to donate a life–size head of Banting, created by the Toronto sculptress Francis Loring, he readily agreed — but his wife was not to know about it. On a bright day he came for lunch at the faculty club, guiding his Rolls Royce by peering through the large wooden steering wheel, he was so short. In parking it in a confined space at the club, he tore the rear fender off a bright red Buick convertible. He asked me if I knew whose car it was and I told him it belonged to Prof. Bert Binning, the artist. In a flash he produced his business card and asked me to give it to the professor at once. Eventually we were given permission to have the foundry in Long Island, N.Y., cast one last bust of Banting (five had been the original order). When the Banting bronze arrived, we had an unveiling in the library, with a smiling Mrs. Ballard and members of the family present.

It seemed to me that in my course in the history of the health sciences, the students from medicine, dentistry, pharmacy, nursing and rehabilitation medicine should prepare, in groups of five, displays of our rare books. These displays have taken up a large area in the foyer of the library, though most of the health science schools have given up on assigning academic credit to the displays. The Florence Nightingale material has become a strong point in our holdings.

The first edition of William Harvey's 72–page "bombshell" *De Motu Cordis* (1628), which proved that blood moves in a circle, is housed within the Memorial Room. My search for a first edition had gone on for years. I wrote to institutions in many parts of the world to enquire if their copy of the Harvey classic might ever be for sale. The Bodleian Library at Oxford held three of the world's store of 50 copies, but refused to consider the sale of even the poorest one. Next door, at Jesus College, I called on the master, John Habbakuk, to see if his college might sell or rent their copy. He was very charming but said that their 1628 Harvey was part of Lord Herbert's bequest, and could never be sold. Would he consider loaning it to Woodward or renting it for a few years? He thought that might be possible.

A few days later I attended an excellent conference on medical history at Churchill College, Cambridge. Late at night I encountered a loquacious and diminutive surgeon leaning heavily on the college bar. He asked what brought an American all the way to Cambridge. Once I persuaded him that Vancouver was still in Canada, he asked, "Why Cambridge?" So I told him that I was merely looking for a first edition of William Harvey. He thought me quite mad; there were only 50 in the world all told, and they were all accounted for.

I mentioned casually that my friend Sir Geoffrey Keynes, F.R.S., who was in the process of writing the authoritative biography of Harvey, had recently found not one but two copies of the first edition on the open shelves of his own college in Cambridge.

Not to be outdone, my effusive companion, in a very confidential manner, whispered: "There's a cock and bull story about a Harvey locked up in a bank vault in Belfast! It is held by a bookseller for his children's future."

The next morning I made a call from the London airport to Miles Blackwell, a fellow Wykhamist, asking him to send to UBC the names of the leading booksellers in Northern Ireland. When these arrived in Vancouver, I wrote to each of them the same letter of enquiry. All but one replied, so I called him on the long distance telephone. It was necessary to set my alarm clock for 3 a.m. in Vancouver to catch him at his coffee in Belfast at 11 a.m. The phone was answered in a wonderful Irish brogue. As I started my enquiry I was interrupted: "How is it the best-kept secret in Europe is known to you in Vancouver?" I replied that I would not like to discuss that on the telephone, but perhaps I could come to see him and the book. Eventually he said, "Ye'd better come."

After arranging for bank credit with the Woodward Foundation Chairman, Bruce Samis, I flew to the United Kingdom and, to make the proverbial story short, completed the purchase. The 72 pages that changed the world had been bound, in 1629, into a volume of tracts or pamphlets on how to avoid the plague, how to take a bath and what to eat. The dealer was kind enough to say that the Woodward Library should have the fine vellum binding, and that he would be quite willing to have the tracts back once the UBC staff had separated them out.

This was done by the university's binder, a Cockney whose language I could hardly fathom. He took the matter in hand, and then began a long wait. The trustees of the foundation wanted to see this object in which they had invested so heavily. Finally, the binder proudly brought it to my office in the library. He had stamped, in gold letters, "Harvey—1628" vertically along the spine of this beautiful little volume. He apologized for the delay, but he had needed to visit "every local shop selling used women's clothes," as he put it. He had finally found elbow–length gloves of the same colour as the vellum binding. From these he cut two narrow "ties," which he inserted under the closing edges of the vellum, so that, "as in ancient times, the volume could be closed with gentle knots."

This prize is now housed in the Memorial Room in a bullet–proof glass case, mounted on an oak base that has been weighted down with enough concrete to prevent wild student pranksters from kidnapping it.

The Memorial Room contains two large modern French tapestries acquired from M. Behna, a patron of the arts living in Cher province, south of Orleans. Our first purchase was made by trans–Atlantic telephone from a boutique in Paris. Our friend Dr. Noel Poynter, director of the Wellcome Institute in London, called from Paris to say he had just seen a post–war tapestry in bright colours, so large that it would cover a large oak–panelled wall of the Memorial Room. I called the boutique owner who quoted what Mr. Woodward thought a reasonable price, especially as the tapissier was the young and talented head of one of the Gobelin factories.

Typically, Mr. Woodward could not sleep at night for fear something might prevent its delivery. He called next morning to say: "The French sometimes change their minds. Perhaps it cannot be exported, or the ship may sink." So we telegraphed at his request to instruct the agent to send the tapestry by air mail! In a few days it arrived in a large mahogany box; it was only as Puggy helped to unpack it that we breathed again.

The title of the first tapestry was *Masters of Science*. We could guess the names of the more obvious of the several dozen scientists brilliantly pictured, such as Louis Pasteur. Edward Jenner was shown vaccinating James Phipps, aged 8.

A detective story then unfolded. How had this tapestry reached the market at all? The editors of the widely read *Presse Medicale* wrote to ask if they could feature it on their Christmas number at the end of the year. I went to dine with them when I was en route to a World Health Organization meeting in Geneva and I agreed they should do a cover any time they liked. I drove down to the Behnas' home, which was a jewel of a country house designed by the architect of the Vichy gardens for his own use, and later sold to this charming pair. Their lands covered well over 1,000 acres; they chided me that President Lyndon Johnson's "ranch" was only 40 acres.

These dear people in their seventies lived in another world—one of ease and taste. They laughed, with me, not at me, over my fractured French. After breakfast the next day I was taken out to the cobblestone courtyard, where many tapestries were exhibited on the side of a barn. There in front of me was the very image of the one we treasured in Vancouver. The explanation gradually emerged. An exact copy had been done by the patron's workers, and was given to the niece of the Behna's as a very special present. For whatever reason, the niece had sold it to the boutique in Paris. Then M. Behna made the mistake of showing me an even larger tapestry, entitled *Masters of the Spirit,* replete with philosophers and writers going back to Greek times. It had been created by one of his oldest tapestry makers, who, alas, had suffered a stroke halfway across this wide work of art. One could clearly see the precise vertical line at which his fine work had stopped. M. Behna had allowed the artist to produce this arresting, and arrested, piece at some distance in the country. He wanted the man to finish it, if and when recovery from the stroke took place. The worker likewise was anxious to complete the handsome scene in order to get paid for his labours.

A closer study, out in the sunshine, showed the change in the tapestry that followed "recovery" from the cerebral haemorrhage. The trees, the columns and most of all the faces were distorted, and the honey–comb border was confused in its outline. M. Behna dropped a tear as he related this sad tale. He had protected this worker, and his other workers, during the 1939–45 invasion by the Nazis. Behna invented, in more ways than one, a new process for rendering poplar wood into gasoline—something the German army required. He had stills and furnaces buried deep in his forest as a top secret mission, agreed to by the German occupation forces. The rusted Citroen trucks were still sitting there when we inspected the site. No gasoline was ever produced, but this well–camouflaged pretence had kept his men together.

When we returned to the little chateau he showed me smaller tapestries of great beauty. The only ones he allowed out of France were one given to the Pope and one to President Harry Truman. I still hoped that the Behnas would agree to sell the neurological tapestry to the Woodward Library, and told them how lonely the *Masters of Science* was, away out in Vancouver without the counterpart, *Masters of the Spirit*. The patron still worried that we would laugh at the bizarre picture on the right side of this very large work, and would, in effect, mock the workman disabled by a stroke. I assured him that for neurologists it was an important scientific document, and we would never make light of it.

Finally, it was agreed that as a medical text they would permit it to go to join its complement in Vancouver. By then my French was exhausted, but the family, along with a nephew, Raymond, reassured me that they were amazed that anyone who lived "halfway to Japan" could converse with them successfully. As always, these charming people were generous in their attitude towards Canada and a pleasure to know.

CHAPTER TWENTY-SIX

A Sabbatical Year in Marseille, 1958–1959

With the laboratory going well, I decided to get away long enough to recharge my batteries and to get my family away from the medical politics of Vancouver. The new dean of medicine, Dr. J. W. Patterson, agreed that I should go to work with Professor Henri Gastaut at the University of Marseille in his clinical neurophysiology laboratory. Again, "the luck of the Irish" prevailed as my wife and I spent an afternoon cruising in Howe Sound with Gordon Gibson, "the Bull of the Woods," on his yacht "The Norsal." His guest was the French ambassador to Canada, M. Lacoste. In discussing possible places to live near Marseille, I mentioned two towns picked from an automobile map; one to the west of Marseille and one to the east. The ambassador shouted over the noise of the waves: "The town on the west is filled with oil refineries. The one to the east, Cassis, is a picturesque fishing village and artists' colony. I'll give you an introduction to the wisest man in that little town, Francis Dumon, at his grape farm called Clos d'Albizzi. His ancestors were bankers in Florence but lost out to the Medici family."

So in early September we flew in a "Superconstellation" to Amsterdam's Schipoll Airport, which to the delight of my wife and children (ages 11, 9 and 7) was populated by rabbits. From above they resembled what is known as Brownian Movement under the microscope. A Hillman stationwagon was waiting for us, and we took off for the World's Fair at Brussels, en route south. The most popular feature of this massive fair was a large shallow pool on the edges of which sat hundreds of tired visitors soaking their feet.

By consulting the excellent maps we set off to see the fields on which the Battle of Waterloo was decided. But first we drove through a beautifully treed subdivision that, with its gracefully curved roads, had been the pattern for one built in the Uplands in Victoria, B.C., before the Great War. Even the street lamps were the same.

I called at the Royal Canadian Air Force over–seas headquarters at Metz to which I was accredited by Ottawa. (Already research was being done on what became known in the Falkland Islands war as the Exocet missile.) Then on through the valley of the Rhone River, that amazing fleuve that begins in Switzerland and reaches the Mediterranean through a broad delta. History has been made along the Rhone's course since time began. I was particularly interested in the town of Vienne where the ill–fated Michael Servetus (1511–53) had practised. He discovered the "lesser circulation" (from the heart to the lungs and back, in order to oxygenate the blood), originally described in a manuscript written by him in 1546. In 1553, however, he published this discovery in the middle of an explosive volume on the Holy Trinity. For this heresy he was hunted down by the church and forced to flee to Geneva. There he was caught by John Calvin and burned at the stake! Vienne was also the birth place of Apollos Rivoire (father of Paul Revere), who had to flee to England when the Edict of Nantes, protecting French protestants, was revoked.

To enter Marseille from the north is to look upon a vast spread of city surrounding the hill–top monument of Notre Dame de la Garde. The traffic is ferocious, but long boulevards lined with plane trees soften the chaos. The Vieux Port, the bouillabaisse capital of Europe, is also a busy seaborne circus. The town looks rejuvenated as the sun beats down on the new apartment blocks constructed after the pre–existing structures were dynamited during the war by the occupying Nazis, whose cruelty to the population was an affront to humanity. Over the hill of Genest, on a fine little road, one comes after 10 miles to the village of Cassis (pronounced Ka – Sée) as against Cassis (pronounced Cas – Seese) meaning black currants. This fishing port is protected by a long curving finger of a peninsula on which a pair of boat builders work as in ancient times. As a neighbour they have a modern, low building that houses a casino, thanks to a city edict in Marseille forbidding such establishments within that city's borders. Beyond this area one comes to the extensive beach, which in September was still covered with sun–bathers draped in wild colours, all oblivious to the skin cancer down the road. By the end of the season, due to the lack of tide on the Mediterranean, the sand on the beaches is cluttered with the refuse of months of occupancy.

Our benevolent and wise "patrón," Francis Dumon, whom we dubbed "Saint Francis," telephoned one of his numerous European relatives, who lived near the Swiss border, and arranged that we could rent their century–old house in Cassis for a period of eight months. The owner, the Count de Lombardon, though trained in medicine, had never practised in his life. He and his wife, passionate Royalists, had spent their honeymoon cruising around the island where the pretender to the French throne lived! Their Mediterranean "castle" was a large stone house of four floors plus a tower through which the mistral whistled with hideous sounds in midwinter.

The plastered wall beside the ancient telephone, which needed to be cranked with a handle, bore a galaxy of German words and telephone numbers. Clearly the house had been occupied by German forces during World War II. In the garden we found a machine–gun post that commanded a view of the roadway. At the waterfront we discovered another "strong point" whose guns had a 180–degree range, enough to sink any ship entering the narrow entrance to the little harbour. One could almost throw a stone across to the opposite shore where a monumental lighthouse, centuries old, cut through the black of night with its white flashing.

We all felt that the sooner we got rid of the gun emplacements the better. In dismantling one of these I came close to losing a finger on my left hand. Over the weeks it became infected and swollen, so that Professor Gastaut introduced me to colleague of his in plastic surgery who had an unpronounceable provençal name. Within a short period of time after an operation, the threatened digit regained its proper shape, including a perfect nail.

The education of the three children began when they learned to play "boule." They knew no French and luckily no one in Cassis spoke English. The little school to which St. Francis introduced them was a wonderful place, about four blocks along the waterfront from our house. Every morning, noon and early evening a little "gendarme," with a pill–box hat and a blue uniform, would stop all road traffic while the students paraded in a line from the school yard. His rival in town was the other uniformed official whom we named "Beautemps," because each and every time he met someone he would lift his uniform cap high in the air and say, "Beau temps," even during the foulest weather.

For a while the townspeople were rather unsure of us, because of our mysterious foreign car and our rosy complexions. They thought we were Germans returning to the wartime source of the terror that the Nazis had spread throughout Provence. All the young men of Cassis were rounded up and shot in the town square as soon as the German army arrived. With North Africa under siege they were taking no chances along the French coast of the Mediterranean. Only aged fishermen were allowed out of the little harbour, as they plied their trade in Biblical fashion: a net cast in the dark and only a dim light to attract the fish. Day fishermen came in at dusk.

The children learned some unusual French as they helped fishermen unload their catch. The little fish were classified according to variety and size at a waterside building known as the "co–operatif." Trucks were waiting at the roadside to rush the choice species to the restaurants at Toulon, the large naval base along the coast to the east.

The plumbing and the kitchen reflected the mid–Victorian age of the house and took some time to digest. The drawing room contained an equally old but exquisite little piano, which, according to the neighbours, had been carted "all over Provence" to dances and parties by the Nazis. Some even thought our house had been General Rommel's headquarters! At all events, we had the piano tuned and enjoyed playing the French songs we were learning. My wife was bilingual and greatly admired the hard–working villagers she met on her shopping rounds. When I put the Canadian Air Force flag, surmounted by a red maple leaf, on the car, we were more warmly welcomed in the village.

My job was to do the shopping for such staples as bread, butter and wine between 7:00 and 7:30 each morning. Then off by the faithful Hillman over the hills to La Timone, the neuropsychiatric hospital on whose grounds the medical faculty had recently built the most modern set of laboratories and lecture halls in Europe. The television projector that magically combined colour on the huge screen in the auditorium was far in advance of what we had in Vancouver. Professor Gastaut's clinical laboratory specialized in electroencephalographic study of the epilepsies. He had superb technicians, several graduate students, as well as half a dozen professors–to–be, and an equal number of specialists who came as visitors to his clinics.

Each morning I would stand alongside Dr. Robert Naquet and start "reading" the recordings of the previous day. He was one of the world authorities on abnormal brain waves, especially in the patients with scars and tumours in the brain's temporal lobe. While "Bobie" Naquet rattled off his interpretations, I wrote them down. He had all the expressive French mannerisms, such as wringing his hands on looking at a shocking record, shrugging his shoulders over others, and making a face as if about to spit out a mouthful of pea soup. I learned a great deal from his vivid French phraseology.

By 9 a.m. the corridors and recording rooms were alive with patients, a few of them brought from the gaol system in shackles and handcuffs. All were treated by the sympathetic nurses and technicians as ordinary sick people.

By 10 a.m. Professor Gastaut would hurry in, his bald head twitching and his hands flying. Most of the time he had a slightly husky voice, but when discussing a case his voice would rise while he filled the air with cries of anguish and imprecations on learning what patients had suffered before being referred, sometimes from other countries, to have a diagnosis made.

The neurologists, neurosurgeons, psychiatrists and foreign physicians would sit in a semicircle while cases were detailed to the professor, who would then start a discussion that at times became highly emotional. By noon, however, the participants forgave each other and all went to their own clinics. Often Gastaut would grab my arm and thrust a paper into my hands, saying in his rapid French: "Jibson, another favour I have to ask of you. Could you translate this paper into English for me. It is already over–due. Could you possibly, mon ami?"

It was little enough to ask of me, for here I was, a foreigner returning to clinical work with his patients and his staff of world–class scientists. Translating teaches one a lot about one's own language!

Gastaut had a small research project funded in part by the U.S. Air Force. When Gastaut found that I had spent the war in aviation medical research, he shouted and danced about his office, waving his hands and warning me that I had work ahead. He was interested in the effect on the brain waves (E.E.G.) caused by breathing pure oxygen, and could not believe that my colleagues in the RCAF and I used to sleep in it over–night before going to 45,000 feet simulated altitude.

Eventually we concentrated on the methods we could use to prevent fainters and epileptics from getting into air crew, where they could innocently do great harm. Routine E.E.G.s might pick up some epileptics, but stress tests had to be devised to make any latent brain abnormality "speak," as they said. Fainters posed a different problem and we devised physiological methods of detecting these otherwise normal individuals. One of the ancient methods of causing faints was to press hard on the closed eyes, as in wrestling, or with well–aimed punches, as in boxing. The sensory nerves from the orbital structures and from both jaws were reflexively connected to the vagal centres that, when excited, could slow the heart, or even abolish the heart beat. Acutely sensitive patients soon fainted.

We registered the heart beat and its slowing on a separate channel of the broad moving paper of the brain wave recording instrument.

Once the heart slowed critically, or stopped, the electroencephalographic waves became straight lines and it was high time to resuscitate the patient.

Another method of producing faints in Greek athletes was to compress the two major arteries to the brain by applying pressure to the neck. As a result, the ancients called these carotid arteries "the arteries of sleep." However, at the point of division of the common carotid into internal and external branches, just deep to the angle of the jaw in most humans, there exists a marvellous little pressure receptor: the carotid sinus. One of my teachers at the Instituto Cajal in Madrid had unravelled the neurofibrillary mysteries of this diminutive regulator that literally prevents one "blowing one's top." Too great a pressure exerted on it causes a signal to be sent to the heart by the vagus nerve, causing it to slow down. Because of the "harness" and protective apparatus hung about the neck of Air Force pilots, it seemed wise to seek out those applying for air crew who were sensitive to such pressure. Thus, an examiner would apply pressure while the recruit, or patient, was attached simultaneously to the E.E.G. and E.K.G. recording machinery. While with Dr. Penfield's service in Montreal I had seen a large–framed stockbroker who, on visits to his barber, lost consciousness as a towel was tucked firmly under his collar! The renowned Soma Weiss at Harvard was writing about this in the 1930s, and I vividly recall his demonstration at ward rounds in Boston of the heart–slowing role of the carotid sinus.

Momentary loss of consciousness in allegedly healthy people was a continuous field for research by Gastaut and his circle. Oxygen–poor breathing mixtures were used for very short periods, again to make the brain "speak." Gastaut was at his best in reciting to us the symptoms and the bizarre behaviour of patients who had a lesion in the temporal lobe of the brain. Whether from localized infection (as in the mastoid bone), from post–traumatic scars or from small tumours, these patients had been in mental hospitals or gaols prior to their visits to a modern diagnostic laboratory. Forceps or otherwise complicated deliveries added to these lesions.

One of the saddest things seen in the clinic was the hemiplegia and convulsions that occurred in a few of the children referred to the professor. Sometimes severe mental retardation followed these events. To follow up the history of these combined insults to infants' brains, I journeyed over to Montpellier in the beautiful southwest part of France. The city of 80,000 counted one quarter of its population as students. The medical school was the oldest in the world still teaching. Its superb library was a treasure house of the history of medicine, and before long I had in my hand the graduation thesis of Marc Dax, a "perpetual student" who had lived in the walled city of Aigues Mortes, which was originally right on the Mediterranean and was the embarkation port for Crusaders. Over centuries, in keeping with the Coriolis phenomenon, the silt from the Rhone River turned right on entering the sea and piled up for miles, so that the great "phare" or lighthouse was now far inland.

Dax, in his 33–page graduation thesis, perfectly described the paediatric problem that we were seeing in Marseille. I took a copy of the Dax thesis back to Gastaut, which almost "blew his top." With great gusto he shouted, "You see, Jibson, we French have been at this for a long time."

As an important aside, I found that after his graduation Marc Dax remained a keen observer. By studying wounded veterans of the Napoleonic wars who lived in Montpellier, he found that if the left temporal lobe of the brain had been damaged in a right–handed soldier, speech would be lost. This localization of the so–called speech centre was reported to a medical meeting in Montpellier in 1836. However, it remained in the possession of the dean of medicine and was not published in any widely circulated journal because, it is thought, Dax was ostracized as a "legitimist" in French politics. Whatever the reason, it remained undiscovered until Paul Broca, a Paris surgeon and anthropologist, propounded the same hypothesis in 1861 after having visited Montpellier. Thus, Broca's Area has been the name applied in the neurological literature ever since.

After Christmas we drove to the mountainous area of Les Baux, after which "bauxite"—the ore of aluminum—was named. The ever–helpful Bobie Naquet arranged for us to stay at Baumanière, a former olive pressing mill, now one of Europe's finest restaurants and hotels. The midnight mass held in a quaint stone church high on a hill to welcome in the New Year was a picturesque ceremony. A white goat drew a little slatted wagon through the church, the straw–filled vehicle containing a newborn lamb. A tall taper burned from each corner of the wagon, adding to the oppressive heat in the church, and presenting a fire hazard par excellence. Music was provided by a fife and a primitive drum. Suddenly there was a spine–chilling cry as an epileptic in front of me launched into a seizure. We made way through the crowd to get him out to the chill night air where he was revived eventually. The New Year celebrations at Baumanière were spirited for sure. We were joined by two U.S. submarine crew whose ship was visiting Marseille. One was a Yale graduate and the other a busy shareholder in "West Side Story."

The little Hillman car allowed us to visit the early Greek and Roman remains out to the west. The fortress of Carcassone has been restored brilliantly, and one can see how it was that its high walls kept Charlemagne at bay for five years. The guard pointed to the original Montréal in the distance, which is visited annually by thousands of Quebecois.

From high mountains where solar lenses at Mont St. Louis condense the sun's rays to generate very high temperatures, we descended into the pocket–size country called Andorra. (The chief industry in Andorra is postage stamp production.) Snow made tire chains essential. The fog in the valley caused us to descend in low gear. As we left by the same mountain road the next day, we realized that we had been blissfully driving along the edge of gaping canyons the night before.

Then we followed the Roman routes, enjoying their great amphitheatre at Nimes. (Arles has a competing one). Soccer and bullfights, in which the bull in not harmed, keep these ancient structures full of enthusiasts.

Christmas and New Year celebrations were no sooner over than I received a cable at the laboratory to say that Wing Commander Gibson was to report to the Royal Canadian Air Force base at Zweibrucken in West Germany and that a plane from Decimanimou in Sardinia would pick me up at Marseille's airport. Right on time, an ancient DC–3 dropped out of the azure sky, and I was given a magnificent tour of the Rhone valley and the Durance River dams, built for both power and irrigation for the dry south.

At Zweibrucken I was met by Medical Squadron Leader Dick Wynn, whom I had last seen on Vancouver Island. He swore that he had flown the ancient DC–3 in the invasion. Alas, it crashed the following week in the mountains of Italy, leaving no survivors.

The RCAF station was amazing, with a theatre, large skating rink and many permanent houses for the personnel. I was to give a lecture on my work in the Marseille laboratory and to have consultations with some neurological and psychiatric patients. I recommended that most of these should be repatriated to Canada. I was ready to promote the repatriation of a few officers' wives who complained ad nauseum about the fact that their table silver lay unused in Toronto and they had to put up with issue cutlery, glass and china. None of these complainers had learned a word of German.

The medical group was a welcome change: their families were taking an interest in their surroundings. S.L Wynn drove me over to Heidelberg to see the famous university. We lunched at The Red Ox, where generations of students had carved their initials on the tables, benches, walls and ceiling! Back on the base I was the target for sales pitches by sergeants who, as usual, were trying to unload ancient Cadillacs. One, however, offered me a special deal on what he claimed was Hermann Goering's large Mercedes touring car, which had three horns and five loudspeakers. No sale at $900. My lecture was attended by 80 medical officers from the region, most of whom came out of sheer boredom.

A brief visit taken with the Air Division Surgeon to our fighter wing at Baden Solingen produced a flashback to an earlier century, when Baden–Baden was the watering place of King Edward VII. The bulbous railway station, served by a spur line only, kept the real world at a distance. The opera house, the ballroom and the coffee shops made up a period piece for sure.

The Marseille laboratory observed Easter holidays, so we put the stationwagon on a Turkish ship and went off to Italy. On this voyage through the Mediterranean, my wife was not torpedoed as she had been in World War II, when Canadian medical and nursing units were forced to take to the lifeboats as their former Grace Line ship sank. The wealth of Genoa was in marked contrast to the inhabited ruins of Naples, where the wartime bombing was so destructive. Parts of the latter port could be summarized in four words: "children, flies, garbage and dust."

My medical historical interests got the better of me as I recalled the Neapolitan student who best described sciatica. We visited Amalfi, where Canadian nurses had developed a rest centre. At Caserta we visited the large and beautifully kept military cemetery where, among others, two Canadian nurses and several doctors and stretcher bearers were buried. In Rome it was a pleasure to see Professor Zito, who had been the pathologist at St. Paul's Hospital in Vancouver many years before. I also met Professor Bignami, whose father was the first to inject the malarial parasite into human volunteers. The grandson was a neurologist trained at Queen Square, London.

It was possible to see the Santo Spirito Hospital, with its "wheel" rotating out beyond the wall, into whose little compartments unwanted babies were placed to be raised by the nuns. That bright–eyed Pope, John 23rd, began his pastoral work there, so he had not far to go to St. Peter's basilica. Here we saw him carried aloft as a vast crowd celebrated Easter with pomp but also with thrilling choral music in which the 5,000 in the audience joined.

Then to Perugia where No. 14 Canadian General Hospital was located in a requisitioned tobacco factory. In 1944 the nurses who enrolled for language classes at the University for Foreigners were taken there over the winter roads in army trucks, carrying with them a small stove to heat their otherwise freezing classroom. Book stores specializing in ancient medical texts were all too tempting, but we hurried on to Padua, the ancient university that owed its free spirit of enquiry to the powerful traders of Venice who combed the world for new treasures.

It was no accident that William Harvey (1578–1657), upon leaving Caius College, Cambridge, in 1599, went to study medicine at Padua. The founder of his Cambridge college, Dr. John Caius, had studied in Padua during the period when Andreas Vesalius, the father of the study of human anatomy, was very active in teaching. The Vesalian fire passed to his pupil Fallopius, who transmitted it to Fabricius of Aquapendente. Fabricius, the builder of Padua's great teaching amphitheatre, but most importantly the "discoverer" in 1574 of the valves within the great veins, was to be Harvey's teacher. While Fabricius did not understand the function of these valves, his pupil Harvey did in so far as they promoted—in fact assured—one–way traffic of venous blood from the limbs towards the heart.

As Harvey wrote: "The sole purpose for which the valves were created was so that the blood should not move from the large veins into the smaller ones (thus rupturing the latter or making them varicose), or from the centre of the body to its extremities, but rather from those extremities to that centre."

In the polyglot student body at Padua, Harvey was elected to represent the British contingent. As recently as 1893 his "stemma" or crest was identified on the ceiling of one of the open–air corridors leading to the great hall. My further reason for visiting Padua was to see the research done by the professor of pathology which we were supporting from the American Muscular Dystrophy Association.

So back to Cassis we drove, through Florence, Genoa and Menton. At the French border the customs officials saw the Canadian maple leaf on the car and without getting out of their armchairs called out: "Bye–bye Charlie." At our home in Cassis the packing began for our move to London for the remaining four months of my sabbatical. The children sent off the last of their lessons to the Correspondence School in Victoria, B.C., which had given them a wonderful appreciation of what it is to study by mail. The written comments of their teachers à distance were always received with joy. The teachers must have chuckled when our first son, in describing the port facilities of Marseille, wrote that the city supported 3,000 bars! The second son, born with a hole in his heart, and therefore pale, if not blue, suddenly began to grow as the hole closed spontaneously and the raucous murmur, which previously could be heard without benefit of stethoscope, vanished. The whole family shed a few tears as we drove up the hill from Cassis for the last time. We still regard it as a second home.

While my family spent a few days exploring Paris and Versailles, I flew to Los Angeles to present our Marseille work to the Aero–Medical Association's annual meeting. Professor Gastaut arranged for me to fly with the 659th Special Activities Squadron across the Atlantic. It was a cold flight that I spent strapped into one of many metal seats bolted to the frame of the aircraft. I arrived in time for the session on selection of air crew who must be free of neurological problems, evident or latent. To my consternation the chairman announced the title of our paper but added that clearly no one would be coming all the way from Marseille to give it, so he would go on to the next presentation. I stood up and said I was sorry to disappoint him but Professor Gastaut had sent me by military plane to read our paper, which I would now do—complete with lantern slides. The reception was marvellous, as I told Gastaut on my return next day to Paris. He shouted congratulations over the telephone and confided to me that he suspected that the high–ranking chairman of the meeting might himself be a fainter!

For the four months in the United Kingdom I worked long hours at the Maudsley Hospital in the E.E.G. laboratory of Professor Denis Hill, whose specialty, like Gastaut's, was the assessment of brain abnormalities in patients whose behaviour had brought them into conflict with the law or with their associates. The clinics were less numerous and much less volatile than those I had enjoyed in Marseille. I worked late into the night with Dr. Walter Kennedy, a charming Irishman, as we analyzed large numbers of electroencephalograms, plotting out the nature and location of the offending lesions. Our family had the great privilege of living at West Lodge Park, an historic Elizabethan hunting lodge north of London. By getting a seat on the tube at Cockfosters early in the morning, I could read for nearly an hour on my way to the once–famous Elephant and Castle, and up the hill by bus to the Maudsley Hospital, named after an early British psychiatrist. It was there that I learned the British definition of psychiatrists: "The odd treating the id." It did not apply to the researchers with whom I had the pleasure of working. The strong group in brain pathology, led by Professor Peter Daniel, F.R.C.P., and Dr. Nick Corsellis, the expert on brain damage from boxing, went out of their way to show me their collections of brains, including some under study after lobotomy.

While I stayed close to the grindstone, my family toured England and Scotland, seeing far more of it than I ever shall do. I joined them in Aberdeen to visit relatives and in Edinburgh where I made a broadcast for the Canadian Broadcasting Corporation on recreation as education. From London I did one on medical matters, such as bashed brains in boxers. That matter had occupied considerable time in the House of Commons. Dr. Edith Summerskill, sometime labour minister of health, asked Prime Minister Macmillan what he proposed to do about the slaughter of innocents in the ring. He had no chance to respond as the famous and heavy–set Labour member Bessie Braddock took over the question and with arms flailing defended boxing. It was probably the only time that she had the support of a Conservative member of the House, who had been reported as saying that boxing had not harmed his brain, as his success in elections had amply proven!

As luck would have it I was able to attend the "Commemoration of the Founder" at my old college at Oxford, after which I made these too–lengthy notes for family and friends:

> In 1379 William of Wykeham, high priest, statesman and financier, founded this beautiful college inside one corner of the high city wall of Oxford. He wanted a college to which the graduates of his school at Winchester could go for higher studies. Over the past 600 years or so his ghost must have wondered in what sense "higher;" whether in scholarship, cost, frivolity, pitch, higher on the river, in numbers of cabinet ministers or what!
>
> Certainly, he was not concerned with higher standards of comfort for the occupants of these weathered stone buildings. I truly believe the bedroom I occupied over–night last week was one of the originals. The long climb up a narrow staircase with oak plank stairs, tipped at all angles, led me to a large sitting room and a small bedroom looking out over the beautiful lawns and fortifications of the garden quadrangle. The mound in the centre of the garden, from which King Charles' cannons roared as he defended himself against Cromwell, is greener than ever, and a summer–house type of retreat for fellows of the college has long since been swallowed up by huge trees, ferns and shrubs. The story, when I was a student here from 1935 to 1938, was that this mound had been the rubbish heap of Oxford for centuries and that criminals and Cambridge men used to be

hung there! Things have changed, I gather, and the old gardener now says: "Them studyin' types can say as they likes, but I seen a picture where they was makin' a bowlin' green outa flat lawn as was 'ere first, and I reckon they dumped what they scraped out hup on that side and that's yer mound, an' them gentlemen don't need no long tale like that t'account fer it."

As I looked about the rooms I saw stacks of books, some old some new: one of Stephen Leacock's, a Greek lexicon, and lots about ancient Rome. All the furniture in the place, and the old straw mattressed bed, would bring about $20, but with the little gas fireplace and a few prints on the wall it was home to an undergraduate whose name, painted neatly above the door, was recognizable as one of a long line of Oxford historians. Each door on the staircase had its "oak" thrown back; obviously school was out and there was no one studying for finals behind its heavy thickness. Pinned to each door was a little piece of paper with the name of the intended over-night returning graduate and one's memory started to turn back a lot of pages to the days when these chaps were tearing through Oxford on bicycles with black gowns streaming out behind, as they hurried to lectures in some distant corner.

As I emerged again into the quadrangle I saw confusion at its best. Returning old boys, carrying suitcases, were vainly trying to find stairway No. 9 or No. 12—all protesting that they used to know, but hang it all, they had forgotten their way. One chap came up to me and said it must seem ridiculous but he could not remember which archway led to the old stable full of toilets and he was anxious to find out soon. I should have put him on to Viscount Astor whose name was pinned on the door of his old rooms. Besides carrying a talkative parrot around on his shoulder while he was a student, he was thought to have been the one responsible for buying all the aluminum letters at Woolworths and laboriously tacking them in superbly funny names on the doors of the barn full of toilets. The old dean who had scolded him was now shuffling through the courtyard with his canes, smiling at the return of his former problem child, over whose room a great crest had been emblazoned with a Latin motto "Obey the law."

Scaffolding was all around the quadrangle as masons tore down the weathered stone of yesteryear and faced the old buildings with nice fresh brown–grey cut stone. A gay blade of the pre–war days stopped to look at this substitution of new stone for old. He said finally, "You know, I often wondered what held Oxford together. I used to think it was inertia."

Gradually we gathered for tea in the Founder's Library, a lovely long and graceful room, now happily freed of "death watch beetle" (that fellow who appears on all appeals in England for the restoration of churches, colleges, etc.). At all events this library had been "rebored" completely and served during term for some very important affairs;,such as entertaining the Emperor of Ethiopia for lunch. Most of the books had been moved upstairs to the Wyatt Library, named after the master builder of Oxford who, centuries ago, had made the college his first love. A few of our number came puffing up the stairs late, saying they, too, had been lost in the myriad arches, corridors and masons' tarpaulins.

The new Warden, Sir William Hayter, spent an hour chatting with us. He was a man of 50 or so, of excellent appearance and great composure and recently H.M. Ambassador to Moscow. He had taken the trouble to find out who was coming and he moved easily through the circles of tea drinkers. He showed us a fine painting he had brought of the New College barge on the river, which was the scene of rowing activities for years, but which has now been replaced by a beautiful new boathouse shared with Balliol—a college that seems to be as good at rowing as in scholarship. (I hear Balliol have undertaken to supervise the Martyr's Memorial outside their windows in St. Giles, to prevent any more chamber pots being placed on its high pinnacle. Crockery was alright—it could be shot down—but the joke was felt to be over when some stinker put up a metal one!) The alpinists also seem to have been busy at New College: last week the college awoke to find a bicycle draped over one of the highest pinnacles above hall. Next day a Bristol company was hired to build scaffolding to get it down. When they arrived bright and early the following morning the cycle had disappeared!

I should perhaps mention in connection with the new boat house that the president of the University Boat Club in 1935, the much beloved Ralph Hope, left £5,000 in his will for its construction.

He was shot down in the Battle of Britain after he had accounted for 12 German planes. He was one of that remarkable band at Oxford who belonged to the University Auxiliary Squadron (which had a field nearby), and learned to fly before the war. Richard Hillary, author of *The Last Enemy* was another. This book, by the way, has the best description of Oxford in the year 1937 to 1938 that I have read.

As I drank my tea I was aware of a number of peculiar glances in my direction from all sides. If I smiled at a chap he shook me warmly by the hand and said, “Hello, James. I couldn’t believe you had forgotten me.” This went on and on, and the confusion grew as one fellow insisted that the seating plan for dinner had my initials down incorrectly. In the noise of a large and hearty mob at tea there was no chance to tell them that I was “my brother’s brother” — the phrase that the Rev. Tutor Lightfoot coined in 1935 to meet the situation. Instead, these fellows would rush on and ask for “Old Bates” or “Old Bradley,” and when I would reply, “Haven’t heard of him since we went down,” the usual retort was, “Reckon he’s dead.”

After tea we all retired to our appointed rooms to change into dinner jackets for chapel service, to be followed by dinner in hall. Each staircase, as of old, was provided with a scout who brought up a device like a garden watering can full of very hot water. Washing facilities consisted of a huge china basin sunk into the window ledge, a very heavy china pitcher full of cold water, and a very ingenious old bilge can. A towel and soap were provided, a luxury not heard of in my Air Force days. Of course, the college founder’s motto was “Manners makyth man.”

Before chapel began the members paced around the great path of the garden, under the shadow of Oxford City’s ancient and beautiful wall; with its battlements and half–round bastions; with steps running up to parapets—the better to pour boiling oil on attackers below. Even the top of the wall was being repaired. The ten acres of lawn, perennial borders and beech trees never looked lovelier. Others paced the cloisters, looking at the memorials to the members killed in the Second World War: John Galsworthy, the famous tutor H.W.B. Joseph and so on. Inside the chapel entrance I re–read the familiar lines above the First World War memorial: “Men worthy of all they learned here and an example to those who come after them." A rather constrained Epstein "Madonna and Child" now graces the ante–chapel. Inside the chapel itself there was certainly a dim religious light, and I was startled when the scout "Oliver" suddenly came up to me and said, "Would you like to be in your old seat there, sir?" I said I would, but I thought to myself it's all part of the game; like the greeting I had when I first came up to New College by the lodge porter: "Welcome here, Sir. Well do I remember your father, Sir. Many's the night I put 'im to bed the worse for wear, Sir."

It was an unforgettable scene as 150 or more members came into chapel, took the seats they once had and said their prayers. There were candles by the far altar and a high carved screen, while hooded lights burned over the well–chapped New College hymnals and Bibles all so neatly laid out on the stands before us. Over–head were the great, stained–glass windows, those over–looking the cloisters bearing the Joshua Reynolds glass — all this against a blue and summery sky.

The last of the fellows, Dr. Creed, swept in wearing his bright red and white doctor's robes, followed by the Warden and Lady Hayter. The organist above us in his loft began to play softly and the service started. The boy sopranos, 12 in all, dressed in hard collars and white gowns, supported by six clerks from the bursary (themselves former songsters here), sang Psalm 84: the Magnificat and Nunc Dimittis by Ireland, and Byrd's lovely anthem 86: "Sing Joyfully unto God," which is about 400 years old. The first lesson was read by the Warden, beginning "Let us now praise famous men." The second was read by the chaplain and touched on the familiar subject of college admonitions of old: "But now I am become a man...I have put away childish things." We finished with all eight verses of the hymn, "For all the Saints who from their labours rest." The choir excelled—and we weren't bad either. Next to me was a rowing blue of the 1930s whom I thought, from the way he sang, would burst. The last verse nearly brought the organ down on top of us. The silence after the sound had gone was something to remember. The height of the chapel roof stems from William of Wykham's design, which was "new" in the 14th century; combining chapel and hall as one side of his great quadrangle and sharing a common roof line.

The chapel service re-knit the members together again as nothing else could have done. As we returned to the brightness and heat of the large quadrangle, more men kept arriving from all parts of England. One man told me he had arrived for the reunion from Ghana only the day before.

At 7:15 the choir, now in their grey flannel stovepipes, assembled on the steps to hall and sang a very old song of invitation to dinner. We trooped up the steps, over which undergraduates in dressing gowns had "flown" at one minute to eight in the morning, for the past 600 years, in order to answer roll call. The old scouts were lined up within, smiles across their weathered faces at the sight of so many tamed playboys, radicals and soothsayers filing by, without the proverbial horseplay. The table lamps against the grooved oak surfaces, the spotlighted portraits of former Wardens against tall dark panelling, and the illuminated Latin texts high over–head, made a wonderful setting. The Warden when most of us had attended Oxford in the 1930s had been H.A.L. Fisher, minister of education at the end of the First World War, an early governor of the B.B.C., and best known for his great work on *The History of Europe*. In the red robes of his portrait he looked slightly serious and faintly amused as he peered down over high table. At the other extremity was the portrait of the famous Warden Spooner, with his white hair and a large reading glass, looking down at a book in his lap. People are still coining Spoonerisms, but the originals all concern his lectures to the undergraduates. On entering—"Young man, what you need in Oxford is a well boiled icicle." On leaving—"You have hissed my mystery lectures. You have tasted a whole worm and you must leave by the town drain." To the fellows of the college he protested the poor attendance of their pupils, saying that he was "sick of addressing only the beery wenches."

After the choir up in a little gallery sang grace, we sat down at pre–arranged places, climbing in over the old oak forms. Present fellows of the college were spotted throughout this jam–packed mob: all of us being a little broader than 20 years ago, with a little less hair and constrained to wearing glasses in order to read the seating plan. A chap whom I had taught in 1938 sat across from me. I could not imagine I had ever seen him before—his hair was absolutely white. After I learned what he had been through in the war I was not surprised. I noted five or six others who had been in medicine at the same time. W.D.M. Paton, now a fellow of the Royal Society, had just been invited to come back to be professor of pharmacology at Oxford. Mike Corbett–Ashby had put away his big Aston–Martin racing car and was now a consultant in London, having become famous over–night for his testimony in the Bodkin Adams trial. Another was a chest consultant. Clay, the economist, was now with the Río Tinto Empire. A chap with a fantastic handlebar mustache sat next to me and said he was teaching the history of art in the middle ages to three pupils somewhere. "Besides, it was a terribly hot day to drive to Oxford in the same car he had when he was a student, which had a broken engine block—deucedly cold winter some time back, you know!"

The others within earshot were Peck, now with NATO; Gupta, in chemistry with Imperial Chemical Industries (DuPont); and M.J. Smith, in pharmaceuticals. Two of brother James' friends who were also sure my initials on the seating plan were wrong were Marsden of I.C.I. plastics and Rev. Hayman–Johnson, a parson at Hornchurch: a college "living."

During a long and excellent dinner the choir, accompanied by a cello and guitar, sang some quaint old songs. Then as we toasted the Queen, the shrill voices reverberated up to the roof and back again. Thereupon we broke the cigars out and the din, haze and heat took over.

The first toast was to "Members of the College here assembled," given by the sub–Warden who pleaded timidity, but talked for 20 minutes as he put in odd jibes at the recently deceased Warden Smith's quirks and fancies in the field of architecture. He evidently will be remembered in posterity as "The Warden who left no stone unturned." The new Warden, he said, was literally raising the roof to make room for more undergraduates. From the time the college opened, immemorial Wardens have been telling undergraduates "Do drop in anytime." Recently, the new Warden was caught napping in his study by a man who did just that — he fell through the ceiling he was supposed to have been repairing!

After more songs by the choristers on "Good wine," "Sherry to make us merry," etc., the toast to "The Warden and fellows" was proposed by Major General Hackett—the youngest of that rank in the British Army, and obviously headed for the top! He waded right in, pausing only momentarily to salute Henderson, a former dean who had sent him down before term was over "for the good of Oxford." Then the sub-Warden, Andrewes, caught it. Here was a plaintive letter that had just fallen out of one of Hackett's old books on Roman history, saying: "Hackett you fool. Why have you come up to Oxford without a Greek dictionary? How can I make the best use of my time here if you are so unfriendly as not to provide your next-door neighbour with these necessary amenities?" It was signed by Andrewes. Hackett passed the letter to Andrewes with great gusto. Then Hackett handed over two books on Parsifal, saying that in his post-war rummaging he had found these two books that he had unwittingly borrowed from Andrewes in 1929!

Hackett warmed to his task and said what a pleasure it was to look down from High Table (for the first and undoubtedly the last time in his life) upon such a sea of Wykhamists, full of port and prejudice. The more he travelled, the more he thought that New College men, most of them anyway, learned one thing at Oxford: that was to hold an opinion. They might be the head of the Tory party or, like Mr. Gaitskell, leader of the Labour Party, but everyone had an opinion. There might be a few slackers—"travellers" he would call them—with no opinion, but they were undoubtedly riding "first class" wherever they were. These would probably qualify for Somerset Maugham's description of the group at Oxford that learned only "to talk nonsense with distinction."

Hackett said he was reminded of his old tutors, especially his tutor in logic, the late H.W.B. Joseph, at the oddest moments. He told of "a very unsatisfactory little incident" on the Damascus road during the war when he and a few Free French officers, along with 200 men from every part of the world, were trying to take a Vichy French encampment. After the first firing things were ominously quiet. He looked out of the hole he was lying in and called to a corporal nearby, "who is your senior N.C.O.?" The solder replied, "Sergeant Jones, sir, but he's dead." With a picture of H.W.B. Joseph flashing before him, Hackett replied, "Then Sergeant Jones is no longer your senior N.C.O."

That evening when the Vichy French post had been taken, Hackett asked the captured French commander to dine with him. Hackett was then treated to a lecture by the French officer on strategy, with the knife here and the fork there and on–rushing men represented by spoons, etc. After a lot of this free advice Hackett admitted the British strategy had been very unsatisfactory. After some more free advice by the vanquished, the victor said, "But we did win, you know," to which the French officer said, "Yes, that was the least satisfactory part of the battle."

He brought the house down by repeating Mr. Joseph's everlasting quibble about the idea "If wishes were horses then beggars would ride." Joseph used to say every year, for 40 years, to his students: "Not so, because if wishes were horses then they too would want to ride."

The Warden replied to the toast and told something of the plans for the future. He was concerned at the size of the college—400 students—and felt that there was a danger that things were becoming too impersonal, and that the college tutorial system, which Oxford had given to the world, was being undone under their very eyes. He said that the past year had brought many academic distinctions to the undergraduates, as the waning of college fortunes in rowing suggested! A very cautious experiment was to be undertaken, in the ancient pile known as the "New Buildings," of some of the larger quarters being fitted out as "bed sitting rooms." (Groans from many graduates.) Unfortunately it was mentioned that Cambridge was trying this. A little fellow opposite to me, who had said nothing all evening, burst out with, "Then I say to hell with it." Harvard's plans in this regard were also mentioned, and one of my classmates downstream groaned "Utter rot." Oxford students remain the same till they die.

Eventually we finished with housing problems and the Warden moved the age–old toast for the future good health of the college: "stet fortuna domus."

We adjourned to the quadrangle to cool off and walk around the greying garden wall under a brilliantly blue summer sky—dark blue, of course, "by appointment." One of the older types managed to find the stables but got on to the wrong floor. He called down, "I say, they've got shower baths at last." He was probably a student whose tutor reprimanded him for enquiring about baths by saying, "What? A bath? Term's only eight weeks long, you know."

The Warden had told us that an ancient "beer cellar" had been rediscovered under the Great Hall, having been crammed with junk and lost in rubble for 500 years. It took about 50 seconds for the hearty types to rediscover it on this hot evening and it turned out to be the coolest place in the college. All the stone work had been cleaned up and the lovely arched ceiling gave me the feeling that it had been intended as a baptistry originally. "Total immersion" was the watchword for only the first few minutes, however. It was interesting to see groups of reminiscing men sitting in the Senior Common Room listening with deadly serious faces to stories being told by Sir Christopher Cox about his trying to run the Sudan single–handed, and then suddenly bursting into roars of laughter as he told them the results. This kind of chat went on till 2 a.m., so it was a tired–looking group that sat down next morning to breakfast before saying goodbye to their old friends. It was generally agreed that William of Wykeham should be assigned first–class marks for having founded this useful and enjoyable place to spend some of one's youth. Obviously the already strong ties were made stronger by this pleasant reunion. It was on these ties that Cecil Rhodes said he was gambling when he set up his scholarship scheme to unite the English–speaking peoples of the world. He and William of Wykeham would have felt they had succeeded in producing something valuable and durable if they too had been able to look in at New College gate again.

Flying back to Vancouver over the North Pole, we landed at Goose Bay, Labrador, where the children ran to kiss the runway, glad to be home in Canada again and looking forward to the opening of school in a few days. It had been a good sabbatical year for all.

CHAPTER TWENTY-SEVEN

Libraries

Books, like rabbits, keep multiplying. Even the Bible laments the proliferation of volumes—yet it remains a "best seller." For some people, even for slow readers such as I, books have a fatal attraction and rob one of the desire to face up to the day's work. This agreeable, not to say narcotic, addiction—this happy form of "lead poisoning" latent in the printer's metal—I succumbed to early in my university life. The magnificent library assembled by President Wesbrook at the University of British Columbia during the 1914–18 war was a surprise and a satisfaction to a student coming from the smaller McGill College in Victoria. Wesbrook's first request of his board of governors seemed to them a small fortune, but when he showed them what he had already assembled from friends in medicine and public health across North America, they capitulated. In 1925, when the university moved to its long promised land at Point Grey, the first building completed was a superb library. Beyond its books, it had another educational resource: Bill Tansley, the janitor. He held court in the men's smoking room in the basement, and in Socratic fashion asked "the smart fellows" penetrating questions. (Bill had saved the "library" in the old Fairview huts from a fire in 1916.)

At McGill the medical library was a revelation in expert service given by a helpful but underpaid staff. One woman on retirement was to receive a pension of $28 per month from McGill. It soon became clear to me that there existed a fraternity of student library users who were to become serious students and eventually well-informed clinicians. Across the hall was the fabled Osler Library, sent by Sir William Osler from Oxford to his alma mater. He had died in 1919, but the cataloguing of his 7,600 rare books and manuscripts delayed its arrival until 1929. It was said to have been "the greatest literary treasure to cross the Atlantic" until that time. His nephew,

Dr. William Francis, was the puckish curator: no student ever had a better lifetime mentor in the history of medicine.

At Oxford I found a plethora of libraries, great and small. To stand outside the Clarendon Building at the corner of Broad Street and Parks Road was to be surrounded by libraries: the old and the new Bodleian, college and institute libraries, and that unique "Reader's Rest," Blackwell's Bookshop. Saturday was a "free read" day for the clerics of surrounding villages who were preparing the morrow's sermons. The pile of veteran bicycles outside was a calamity for anyone trying to enter the pub next door. As already implied, their books have multiplied so remarkably that Blackwell's now rent most of the area beneath the lawns of Trinity College next door. Their export division, from which the world's libraries are supplied, occupies a building near the Oxford railway station.

When Sir Thomas Bodley (1545–1613) re-established Oxford's university library, as distinct from 30 or more college libraries, he, a scholar and diplomat, "set up his staff at the Librarie-dore in Oxon" in 1598. He said that all libraries needed "friends" if they were to prosper. For a small amount of money he arranged that a copy of every book printed in Britain would go to the Bodleian.

Sir Thomas clearly over-did it, and thus today the Bodleian system accounts for 4,200,000 books and 50,000 manuscripts. I used its science branch, with its excellent building set among the laboratories on South Parks Road, as much as I could. Today its expansion has had to go underground, below the grassy court of the museums. It was through the latter that Sir Henry Acland, Regius professor of medicine, smuggled science as evidence of the Creator's goodness. Long before that, Oxford's princely benefactor, Dr. John Radcliffe, had left part of his fortune to construct the splendidly domed Radcliffe Camera between the Bodleian and the University Church of St. Mary the Virgin. It was in that circular reading room, during Osler's time, that two bays were financed for the study of history of medicine and science by Dr. and Mrs. Charles Singer.

A London library to which Sir Charles Sherrington introduced me was the comfortable sanctum of the Royal College of Surgeons, in Lincoln's Inn Fields. There, the courtly Channel Islander, William Le Fanu, held sway and provided tea and cookies for Sir Charles and his guests. It was there that Sir Charles developed, on paper, his proposal to integrate the medical libraries scattered over more than a dozen sites in London into a friendly and serving confederation.

One of these was the library of the Royal College of Physicians on Pall Mall, back to back with Canada House. When that building, old

At the south-west end of the drawing room a glazed door leads into the chief glory of the Athenaeum - its library. This is a lofty and comfortable apartment (43ft. long, 30 ft. wide, and 23 ft. high), and lighted by three windows, which overlook the garden. It is completely walled with books, access to the upper being afforded by two light galleries. As illustrating its growth, we may note that on the club entering the present building it possessed nearly 4000 volumes; in 1844 these had multiplied to 20,300; in 1882 they amounted to 48,000; while in 1894 they approximated 61,000. So rapid and irrepressible has been the increase that it has overflowed the space originally allotted. Almost every place where shelves can be erected is occupied, and resort has often been had to the objectionable practice of putting volumes in a second row and packing them behind others. In 1889, however, a store was arranged upstairs with sufficient cases to provide for the overplus literature of some years to come.
In these restless days it is amusing to read that in this room in 1835 'you will find at the fireplace at one end... an elderly gentleman with a cocoa-nut head fast asleep in an arm-chair; and at the fireplace at the other end... a ditto old gentleman, with a ditto head, equally fast asleep in another arm-chair.' Crabb Robinson, a past master of the art of conversation, grew late in life both somnolent and garrulous, so that it became perpetually a disputed question whether it was better to wake him up and endure his talk, or let him sleep on and listen to his snores.

The Athenaeum Club and Its Associations
by Francis Gledstanes Waugh M.A. Oxon

rather than ancient, was offered to Canada House on the north side of Trafalgar Square after World War II, my brother, in the prime minister's office in Ottawa, was deputed to deal with the purchase. The original asking price was $560,000 Canadian, which almost produced an apoplectic fit in MacKenzie King. No building was worth that, etc., so he dithered—his life's trademark—until the price had accelerated to several times that amount. Finally the deal was consummated and the Royal College of Physicians built one of the finest modern structures in London at St. Andrew's Place, in Regents Park. It was constructed around the very large portraits of four centuries of distinguished members. Its library is the gathering place of its erudite fellows and members and, inspired by Professor Peter Daniel and others, it has a continuing series of displays of famous works of the past that affected the way we practice today. On one visit to London I was more than surprised to find that my Oxford friend and fellow neuropathologist had mounted an exhibit of the student contributors to medical discovery featured in my slim volume *Young Endeavour*.

When I became a member of the Athenaeum, I gravitated to the club's library, which dates from 1832, when Sir Humphrey Davy and his friends joined together to form a club for scholars and patrons. While the traffic pours along Pall Mall, one can be ensconced in the depths of this venerable library, totally oblivious. Tea, toasted currant buns and jam are available in the vast drawing room that runs the length of this ornate building along its north–south axis.

There may be a thick layer of dust in the upper gallery's treasures, but that is no hindrance to finding the exquisite first editions of the past—Gould's *Birds*, Darwin's works (to name but a fraction)—all presented by their authors. When I was in London for the repatriation of William Harvey's illegally exported portrait, I took two co-conspirators who aided in its return to lunch at the Athenaeum. As we climbed out of a taxi in the crowded Waterloo Place, a monocled man, resplendent in silk hat and morning clothes, with a red sash on his chest, approached us. Jacob Zeitlin and Dr. Jack Pincus, who had come all the way from Beverley Hills, shot me a glance as much to say, "Here comes one of those mental patients whose day is spent in pretending to be celebrities." Suddenly this handsome figure thrust out his hand and said, "Hello Bill, what are you doing in London?" At once I recognized Sir Miles Clifford, the distinguished soldier, colonial governor and currently chairman of the Leverhulme Foundation.

On meeting my friends he explained that he had just been to a ceremony at Buckingham Palace and was heading home to Kent. Zeitlin and Pincus were sure I had staged all this for them, so I was never allowed to forget it.

As soon as lunch was over, Jake wanted to rush up the stairs to see the library. He was astounded at the size and quality of its contents. I told him to abandon any idea he may have had of offering to buy it "so they can fix this place up." I explained that the club's financial problems would never induce the members to sell the books, although a dozen libraries had been developed in central London since the Athenaeum began. If the club were in financial straits they might do what their neighbour, the Reform Club, had done: admit women members. The odds were, however, that such action was likely to take place only in the next century. I mistakenly believed that they might at least allow women fellows of the Royal Society next door on Carlton House Terrace to join as full members.

The Wellcome Library at 183 Euston Road was home to me, as I worked there on lectures to be given in London. Sir Henry Wellcome, with his large commercial income, had spent millions on the building, its library, museum, an ancient apothecary shop and on some beautiful statuary. Its collection of 400,000 rare volumes sets it apart as one of the country's best selected and best maintained national treasures.

France offered two great libraries where I worked happily: the National Medical in Paris and the faculty library in Montpellier. The library in Coimbra, Portugal, which I visited with my colleague Dr. Alvim–Costa, was certainly the most stunning architecturally, made of ebony and gold. Lisbon was the home base of a book–mobile general library, which the Goulbenkian Foundation financed and which served rural Portugal using vehicles made in England. The executive director of the large and very rich foundation, Pedro Pereira, told me that his boyhood ambition was to sail around Cape Horn and then to navigate the inside passage along the British Columbia coast to Alaska.

He was a welcome change after some of the foundation directors I had met with in America. One of those, in the past, did not even provide a chair for the applicant to sit upon while presenting his case for support. Another was in the business of collecting old playing cards and drawing his salary. When I mentioned that an ancient playing card had been found at Cambridge University after having fallen though the crack in a student's staircase, the alleged foundation director's eyes became like saucers—but he had no money for medical research.

Of North American libraries in which I have worked, my favourite would be the Historical Library in Yale's medical faculty. Its organization and its riches enabled me to prepare 10 public lectures in 10 weeks, the thought of which fatigues me to this day. The main repository, the Sterling Library, and its recent partner, the Beineke (with its alabaster walls that glow at night), are outstanding libraries in a university that began in 1701 when a group of clergymen brought their books together to establish a college. As already mentioned, the Countway Library at Harvard brought together several existing mature medical libraries, thanks to an early morning chat that the ever–alert dean of medicine had in an apartment garage with Miss Countway's chauffeur.

The New York Academy of Medicine library reflects the qualities of the New York physicians who built their cultural headquarters at Fifth Avenue and East 103rd Street, over–looking Central Park. It also reflects the dynamic role played by its librarian, Dr. Archibald Malloch;,born in Canada and the "adopted son" of Sir William and Lady Osler at Oxford after their son Revere was killed in the 1914–18 war in Belgium.

In Bethesda, Maryland, near Washington, D. C., the National Library of Medicine has become one of the world's largest and best–used libraries. In the spring of 1982, Director Dr. Martin Cummings invited me to speak to the staff of this organization on the building and the development of the Woodward Biomedical Library. He had been brought to Vancouver some months previously to advise the Universities Council on library services for the three provincial universities and for the health professions widely spread over British Columbia. He was so impressed with the Woodward facility, which from its birth had been connected to his library's computer by telephone line, that he wanted me to report "from the field."

I recounted the vagaries of the library services from UBC's inception in 1913, interrupted as they were by two wars and the Great Depression. However, their mouths watered as I told the Bethesda audience of the first book in the medical field given to UBC as a present to President Wesbrook from his friend Sir William Osler at Oxford: a facsimile of William Harvey's lecture notes concerning the circulation of the blood, dated 1616. It was not long before Wesbrook obtained, for £21, a first edition of Robert Hooke's *Micrographia* published in 1665 by one of the early members of the Royal Society. (If one can encounter a copy today it is likely to cost £2,000.) To bring cheer to a beleaguered president trying to keep his infant university afloat in the war climate of 1915, Charles

Sherrington sent a Christmas gift of a mint copy of Bidloo's anatomy (1685), which was published in Holland with the first major copper-plate illustrations of the human body. This copy had been the property of Nicholas Hawksmoore, the architect of many noteworthy churches and one of Wren's pupils.

As a special touch, Sherrington had the visitors at his physiology laboratory at Oxford sign their names when they entered: William Osler, John McCrae (the poet of "Flanders Fields"), Gowland Hopkins (the biochemist) and others. Not content with this, Sherrington wrote in the flyleaf the story of London surgeon William Cowper's plagiarism of the text, translated into English. Bidloo won his suit against Cowper and was awarded damages of one shilling.

An even earlier volume, Laurentius Valla's *Elegant Latin Language* (1476), was sent home with me from Oxford in 1938. To these gems I was able to add, using the honorarium from my visiting professorship at Yale, the collection of Osler's publications put together by his pupil in San Francisco, Dr. Cunha. Soon we added the scholarly collection of Chauncey Leake, my old friend from Texas days, and the collection of Dr. Hugh Sinclair of Magdalen College, Oxford (thanks to the generosity of Dr. H.R. MacMillan). From Madrid I had brought the collected reprints of the years 1880–90 by Nobelist Santiago Ramón y Cajal, which I had been given after I left his institute in 1936. The Bethesda librarians wondered if I could stay long enough to collect a few rare volumes for their library. In actual fact the Surgeon General's Library, their forerunner, had been the lifetime creation of Dr. John Shaw Billings. With unused canteen funds from the Civil War, he had built a random collection of 2,300 volumes into the world's largest medical library. Billings used to say to a British enquiry as to how he accomplished so much: "You have only to begin. Do you think there would be any coral reefs in the world if the first bug had sat down and said 'How shall we go about this?'"

During my tenure at the Universities Council in Vancouver, we had Professor Fred Dainton, F.R.S., the former chairman of the University Grants Committee in London, come to advise us. On one of these occasions his time was so limited that the executive director of the American Trust for the British Library, Douglas Bryant, the recently retired librarian of Harvard University, could see him only if he came to Vancouver. Over breakfast I was invited to join the Advisory Committee of the American Trust and ever since have been interested in its remarkable work. In brief, it is to replace the Americana in the British Museum Library that was destroyed in the war by a Nazi bomb. Actually, with the new British Library under way next door to St. Pancras Station in London, the American Trust is likely to do far more than this.

The British Library in its new quarters will have its 150 million items stored on 400 miles of shelving. After its collection moves into the new structure, the British Museum will fall heir to a 40 percent increase in space. For generations the library has been the depository for the Copyright Office, which last year sent over 373,000 items for care and cataloguing. These will be held at Boston Spa in Yorkshire, where a tract of 60 acres has been acquired for this purpose and also to contain the National Bibliographic Service, as well as acquisitions cataloguing.

The net effect on the British Museum of the move is hard to estimate completely, but emotionally there will be a sag in the rope as the Round Reading Room, designed by that genius on horseback, Antonio Panizzi, loses the millions of readers it has had throughout history. The ghosts of Dr. Sun Yat Sen, Charles Dickens, Karl Marx, George Bernard Shaw, Ghandi, Lenin and others will haunt the great domed structure for years. Britain, and in fact the world, will soon have a resource of immense power in the British Library. One is reminded of King George V opening a large library building at Cambridge University and calling it a "power house." All libraries open to the public can be classified, in essence, as power houses of a non–polluting type.

Private libraries may be minor power stations too; over the years I have had the privilege of using or seeing some good examples of these. Wilder Penfield and his fellow pioneers at the Montreal Neurological Institute pooled their classics to form the Fellows' Library. Dr. H.M. Kidd, who entered McGill at age 40 and took the gold medal on graduation, left her library to the Woodward Biomedical at UBC—a well–catalogued collection thanks to her librarian, Jean Lynch. Sir Geoffrey Keynes, the ultimate bibliographer and biographer of William Harvey, had a rich personal library at his home at Lamass House. Roderick Haig–Brown, the fisherman king of Campbell River on Vancouver Island, kept a large private library on the fish of the world and on Izaak Walton's devotees. In addition he had reams of material on water purity, pollution and endangered species. When we sat together with Hon. Justice Tommy Norris, it was Rod who could quote scripture to disconcert commissions of enquiry. Charles and Dorothea Singer, at their home, Kilmarth, in Cornwall, were hosts to a mini–Athenaeum, with classical texts in the history of medicine and science. For voyages of discovery I have seen the best imaginable in the home of Dr. P.R. Sandwell, the international engineer in Vancouver. One might say, and his wife would agree, that their house is supported on first editions. Beware the engineer who is also a bibliophile, for he will collect every milestone in his adopted field. His neighbour, Walter Charles Koerner, collects so many books on political history and its makers that a lorry was needed to take the over–flow to UBC. Finally, another neighbour, the late H.R. MacMillan, had a carefully selected library of Captain Cook's voyages, and those of his successors, along with a well–used copy of the Bible on his yacht, the Marijean.

CHAPTER TWENTY-EIGHT

Awards and Offices Held

It is embarrassing to record the awards that have been made to me, which might better have been given to others who worked just as hard for the common good. This saga of misplaced credit began in high school in Victoria when I won a medal for writing a prize speech on "World Peace." The runner–up was one of my Chinese friends from North Ward school days, and I thought his speech was better than mine both in content and delivery. He asked if he might borrow the medal to take home to show his mother, who was ill. On returning it he said she was as thrilled as if he had won it. I felt so unjustly rewarded then, as I have for the rest of my life when honours and awards that should have been more fairly distributed have piled up.

For good or ill I continued to win essay prizes, music prizes and the life presidency of my medical class at McGill. The theory evidently was that as my classmates there became mentally incompetent, they would be shipped out to me in my home city of Victoria, where age and eccentricity would be less conspicuous, and where these characteristics could be indulged in a mild and soft climate, where snow was considered "disgraceful" and where a summer temperature of 85°F was the beginning of the end of the British Empire. Indeed, some have come west, but they are in good health. The four killed in the war never had this chance.

In brief, therefore, I shall set down the bare facts. I served as president of the Faculty Association at the University of British Columbia and of its Alumni Association. Before it was swallowed up by the Vancouver Club, the University Club of Vancouver elected me president. For reasons unknown (but I suspected my Air Force comrades), I was awarded the Coronation Medal and the Confederation Medal. My rank of Wing Commander was more automatic than earned, I am afraid, but headquarters in Ottawa vacillated between cursing me and congratulating me for the large medical board organization that I put together to do the entry physical examination for all three armed forces in Vancouver, and the air evacuation unit that sent doctors and nurses from Hawaii to Germany.

I suppose my appointment to the chairmanship of the Universities Council, to advise the provincial cabinet on university affairs, could not be considered a reward, but more of a punishment. At all events it brought out all my Air Force methods of persuasion, as I made it clear that each of our three universities, in turn, would put their hoped–for budgets on the table for inspection by their competing institutions in the presence of the independent council, appointed by government, to make recommendations to it annually. President Petch at the University of Victoria sent the minster an unusually warm letter in 1979 saying, inter alia: "Dr. Gibson has been instrumental in bringing about a complete turn–around of the council. What was a time–consuming, ineffective, obstructionist organization is, in my opinion, to play a vital role in the development of the universities during the next decade."

The Alumni Association at UBC and the Graduates Society at McGill awarded me their highest honour for helping to spread the word that both the daughter institution and the mother were doing even better than expected. I was not prepared, however, for the shock of being given an honorary doctorate by McGill, in which the citation stated that I had been born prematurely and had been in a rush ever since. The citation for the honorary D.Sc. at Victoria hinted that I had no time to slow down. That at UBC was widely publicized, alas.

In 1989 a ceremony was held at the Woodward Library to name the Historical Collection in my honour. With the opening of the Biomedical Research Centre, a too–large plaque was unveiled stating that I had helped to develop and build this laboratory. I have since asked that it be removed as my only way of protesting the disgraceful action of its trustees and of UBC's vice–president (research) in dismissing the eminent director without cause.

To be made an honorary fellow at Green College, Oxford, was enough, but to find my name over the door to the beautifully furnished private dining room was too much to contemplate.

CHAPTER TWENTY-NINE

Yale Visiting Professorship, 1960

Once my status at the University of British Columbia as professor of the history of medicine was established, I was able to accept the invitation by Professor John Fulton of Yale University to serve as visiting professor in his department of the history of medicine and science for the first three months of 1960. The salary from Yale went to the struggling UBC Development Fund, for the purchase of the Cunha Osleriana.

Arriving at New Haven in winter weather, after being accustomed to the mild west coast climate, made me grateful for the arrangements made by Fulton's indefatigable staff to accommodate me in the excellent Harkness student residence adjacent to the medical school. My predecessor, Dr. Kenneth Keele, the Harvey Scholar, had chosen to live in one of the superior Yale colleges. My office in the Historical Library meant that I could work from dawn to dusk on the 10 lectures that I had to prepare and deliver in 10 weeks! The staff did not believe it was possible. However, I had become used to working long hours at Yale, having been a graduate student for part of the winter of 1934–35 in John Fulton's physiology laboratory. At that time the security people had told Fulton that since the patrol spotted me in the lab at 7 a.m. and at 12 midnight, they wondered if I had nowhere to sleep. Now this history was to repeat itself.

The Historical Library is one of the greatest collections of the milestones of science available anywhere in the world today. It represents the coordinated buying of the great books underlying medical discovery and progress done by three avid collectors: Harvey Cushing, the father of modern brain surgery; Arnold Klebs of Switzerland, son of the distinguished bacteriologist of that name; and John Farquhar Fulton, a Minnesota and Harvard Rhodes scholar who was inspired by Sir Charles Sherrington's bibliomania at Oxford. Together, their bibliographic knowledge and their love of the great books of the past rivalled that of their "mentor," Sir William Osler. The library itself is housed in an oak–panelled, cathedral–ceilinged wing of the Yale medical library. Over the fireplace is a painting of Andreas Vesalius, the young genius who staggered the scientific world in 1543 with his *Fabric of the Human Body*. (Its woodcuts, done in pear wood, of the first anatomical depiction of the human frame, were carried over the mountains to Basel for printing and revolutionized the orderly study of the body. They were lost in the bombing of Munich in World War II.)

The dedication of the library, carved on the east wall, was written by Rev. George Stewart, who pronounced it at the grand opening on June 15, 1941:

> Here silent speak the great of other years; the story of their steep ascent from the unknown to the known; erring perchance in their best endeavour, succeeding often, where to their fellows they seemed most to fail. Here the distilled wisdom of the years, the slow deposit of knowledge gained and writ by weak yet valorous men who shirked not the difficult emprize. Here is offered you the record of their days and deeds. Their struggle to attain that light which God sheds on the mind of man, and which we know as truth unshared, must be their genius. It was their own but you, be you but brave and diligent, may freely take and know the rich companionship of others' ordered thought.

High up in the gallery, the spirit of the late Harvey Cushing echoed his thoughts of yesteryear on "The binding influence of a library on a subdividing profession":

> There is a spirit–world of books, and the ideas they contain wander forth to haunt and torment those whose grasp they can elude, to solace or stimulate those who have learned the secret of their capture...From the spirit that hovers over some obscure volume, of parentage and birthplace unknown, times forgotten may be reconstructed, the sequence of discovery unravelled, the tendencies of thought traced, the relation of yesterday and tomorrow better understood.

By the sweat of my brow the following 10 lectures were presented at 5 p.m. on the dates shown:

14 January	Scientific Contributions of Medical Undergraduates
21 January	Ramón y Cajal and the Neurone Theory
28 January	Discoveries Made by General Practitioners
4 February	Pioneers in Cortical Localization
11 February	Baron Larrey, Surgeon to Napoleon's Armies
18 February	The Study of Physical Factors in Mental Disease
25 February	Pioneers in Aviation Medicine
3 March	Medical Contributors to Literature and Music
10 March	Doctors and Social Progress
17 March	Some Canadian Physicians: MacCallums, McCraes, Osler, Banting and Tait McKenzie

The anatomy lecture hall accommodated the group of regulars, but there was a standing–room only crowd at the lecture on "Ramón y Cajal, Charles Sherrington, Ross Harrison and the Neurone Theory." Graduate students in biology had trooped across campus once it was known that I was to discuss, among other things, the role of the famous Yale emeritus professor, Ross Granville Harrison, the father of "tissue culture." When he had been a graduate student at Bonn University in 1904, he had perfected a method of growing small amounts of tissue in glass dishes filled with suitable nutrients. This had enabled researchers to study isolated but living cells for years at a time. It was the basis of the Salk Vaccine, to mention but one of the thousands of applications. By inventing the process, Harrison made it possible to study the "building blocks" or single nerve cells that, multiplied several billion times over, make up the nervous system. The lecture was almost a disaster. In order to learn how to operate electrically driven black boards and screens, I had enlisted the aid of a lecturer who was proceeding down the same corridor. He plunked his manuscript down on my lectern while he instructed me. When he left, hurrying to his own classroom, he picked up my manuscript along with his. It took several embarrassing minutes to locate him and to retrieve my papers, while my audience must have thought, "This must be some Canadian nut let loose."

The series of 10 sessions went off well, interrupted at weekends by the hospitality dispensed by Lucia Fulton at Mill Rock, formerly the home of the Whitney dynasty. The house had been the Swiss Pavilion at the Philadelphia World's Fair of 1876. Whitney had it transported to the beautiful hill over–looking New Haven and installed on a previously built stone structure one story high. In World War II this great house had been the meeting place of many of the top Allied scientists; indeed, it was a worthy successor to "The Open Arms," which the Fultons had known in Oxford as Lady Osler's home. Howard Florey, the brains behind the penicillin revolution, was a frequent visitor to Mill Rock where his children, refugees from the Blitz in England, had been cared for by the Fultons for much of the war.

My education began the moment I sat down to a meal with the students in Harkness Hall. Coming from a variety of backgrounds, these students had migrated to medicine and were a constant source of information, sharply dispensed comments and bravado. There was certainly no dull moment. When I had returned to Vancouver, one of the students wrote to Professor Fulton two pages on what it was alleged I had done for the students in the residence. He wrote that:

> In a system of graduate education which purports to further creative, independent thinking by fostering more flexible communication between students and faculty, Bill Gibson is one of the very few people who, to my knowledge, has displayed any interest whatsoever in the views of the present student generation in their education. As a result he had to fence with a steady barrage of conflicting ideas.

At a farewell dinner the students who had stuck out my 10 lectures and still wanted to talk to me presented me with a handsome Yale armchair. Two of the seniors in age or rank were Emeritus Professor Herbert Thoms, the obstetrician who pioneered x-ray pelvimetry, and Professor Paul Beeson, the internist who began his medical career as a student at McGill. He was eventually to become a very good friend and Nuffield Professor of Clinical Medicine at Oxford. (He was offered the Regius Professorship of Medicine at Oxford, as was Wilder Penfield, but Paul turned it down to remain a U.S. citizen. He helped Prof. Richard Doll get Green College started before leaving Oxford.)

One of the pleasant interludes in my otherwise frantic days was a visit to the Yale president, Whitney Griswold. John Fulton and I were received by this tall, white-haired patrician in an impressive office, thanks to a letter of introduction from my own university's president, Norman MacKenzie. I was keen to talk with the author of the short but rivetting book *The Liberal Arts*. By that Griswold meant "the arts of liberty"—never better expressed.

A three–months' association with the professor of fine art, Deane Keller, was of a very different type. Informality and ability were exuded by this gregarious artist. Every Tuesday I was to join his circle at noon at "George and Harry's" spaghetti palace, to eat and chat with Bob Kipputh, the legendary Yale swimming coach and his son DeLaney, the athletics director at Yale. We were sometimes joined by their boon companion Ben Holden, secretary to the university and an ambassador if ever I saw one. Conversation in a noisy atmosphere focused not on the food, but on politics, domestic and international, and, of course, the campus.

I learned of the visiting Japanese dignitary who, on seeing the Yale gymnasium—a great white whale–like structure—named it Moby Dick! Then the story unfolded, embroidered by all present, of the wealthy stock broker in New York who was to be given an honorary degree, with Ben Holden quoting the Bible to us as the story unfolded. The stock broker had been asked, with further malice aforethought, to give the convocation address. He did nothing to prepare for this important role, either in New York, on the 80–mile train journey up to Yale, or in the Taft Hotel in New Haven. As the academic procession entered the vast gymnasium he saw in the distance, in bright blue letters on a white background, Y–A–L–E. "That's it" he said to himself.

When called upon to address "the mob" he launched into his oration "with vigah" as they say at Harvard. "Y" was for youth, "A" for ambition, "L" for loyalty and "E" for enthusiasm. That was fine, but on each of the four letters he spent 20 minutes. The chancellor, in thanking the new honorary doctor, said: "I'm glad our convocation speaker was not graduating from the Massachusetts Institute of Technology." Our humour matched the spaghetti.

Deane Keller was such a joker that I did not take him seriously when he wanted to do a crayon portrait of me while I was at Yale. I laughed at the idea until he gave me a time to appear in his penthouse studio, up innumerable steps in the Fine Arts building. "You come right after Admiral Nimitz so be on your best behaviour!" Each morning I would meet the admiral on the stairs, looking relieved that his sitting was over for the day. Deane absolutely refused to accept anything for the excellent portrait that I took home with me. His firm friend in the Historical Library, Madeline Stanton, had been secretary to Dr. Harvey Cushing when he was professor of neurosurgery at Harvard, and came with him to Yale as he took up his retirement post as professor of neurology. I had known him 25 years before, when I was a graduate student at Yale, and had discussed with him the little notebooks kept by Sir William Osler. He liked the pencilled phrase: "Experience is not to be measured by time served, but by the use made of one's opportunities." Madeline's sidekick was the erudite editor Elizabeth Thomson, who, though greatly incapacitated by poliomyelitis, was the expediter in the very busy department of the history of medicine. Between them, these two women shunted duplicate or triplicate volumes at incredibly low prices (or no price at all) to the Memorial Room of the Woodward Library at UBC.

Professor Fulton's health deteriorated at such a rate that he was not able to appear on Dave Garroway's "Today" television show (a National Broadcasting Company program that was filmed in New York studios), so he sent me. It was arranged that in 30 minutes Garroway and I would discuss the medical ailments of Napoleon, John Keats (the poet physician) and Florence Nightingale. The interview went well and there was no need to shoot any of it a second time. As I was leaving, I remarked to Garroway's assistant, Florence, that probably the first girl in history to bear that name was actually the second Nightingale daughter, who was born to her wealthy itinerant parents at a beautiful house over–looking Florence with its great Duomo. The first daughter was born in Naples and, therefore, was christened Parthenope. No one realized that the microphone was still on, so the broadcast that I saw next day in New Haven had this parting exchange on it.

During my stay at Yale I was invited to spend an afternoon down at Norwalk, Connecticut, at the select library of the history of science collected by Bern Dibner. He was a scientifically minded electric contractor and manufacturer who had grown up as a boy on New York's east side. Bern had designed and built the most beautiful small library I had seen since Oxford days. Even more important than this was the collection of the milestones in the progress of science. For instance, he showed me Dominique Larrey's own copy of his work, *Mémoire de Chirurgie*, complete with its marginal notes for a further edition. Just how Dibner became interested in the surgeon whom Napoleon called "the most virtuous man I ever knew" I cannot imagine. Fulton and Yale attracted many gifted laymen with an interest in science. One of that happy brotherhood was Colonel Richard Gimbel, a retired U.S. Air Force officer who was Yale's curator of aeronautical literature, an expert on Tom Paine (of "Rights of Man" fame), and a former student at New College, Oxford. He was fascinated with Dr. James Parkinson, Paine's benefactor. He came to my lecture on "Pioneers of Aviation Medicine" and thereafter conducted me through the fascinating collection he and his associates had built up over the years. The illustrations of the earliest balloonists were a treasure trove.

The Yale community was an intriguing one. The mystique of Cole Porter and his songs was ever present in the superb colleges that the Harkness family had built. Passing an open window one could hear glee club members rehearsing. At the tables down at Moray's, there was non–stop eating, with students wondering when they could hear the next rendering of the Whiffenpoof song. I was given a dinner in one of Moray's Club rooms where, to our delight, we found a rehearsal in progress next door. The students were keen to come in to entertain us, which they did royally. I still hope to bring the Yale Glee Club to sing at our universities in British Columbia.

Yale's libraries are some of the finest in any university setting. The Sterling Library resembled a cathedral, so much so that the first librarian was greatly troubled by the long line of architects and an admiring public that came to view the building. Finally, in desperation, he placed on the lawn a small sign: "This is not the Yale Library. The Yale Library is inside."

Facilities were on the massive side. In the winter months, when the natural waterways were frozen, the rowing crews practised in a wing of the gymnasium where they learned to stroke against a man–made cataract.

An invitation to visit the editor of a journal featuring medical history and the cultural interests of doctors began a long–time friendship with Dr. Félix Martí–Ibañez of *MD Magazine*. Below his office near Central Park, there was a small, quiet bar where many of our conversations took place. His usual beginning was "Now you must have a Gibson," and we would be off, covering Spain, his native land, and spreading half–way around the world.

His story was an epic that began with his dismissal from his post as deputy minister of health in Barcelona by the General Franco fascists who, with the help of Italian and Nazi armed forces, made short work of Catalonia. Félix plodded over the Pyrennes—as did thousands of Spanish refugees—and made his way to the Atlantic coast of France where he was fortunate enough to find a freighter. Half–way across the Atlantic he heard an American broadcast saying that, from that day on, refugees from Spain would have to have Franco passports. He did not sleep much thereafter, and his heart was in his mouth as he proceeded through the immigration line up.

On producing his passport he was told by the official that it was no longer valid. However, it was clear that when the freighter began its slow crossing to New York it had been so. The official looked at the perspiring doctor, flipped through the pages of the well-worn passport, and handed it back saying "Welcome to the United States and to hell with General Franco."

Félix loved to write, so soon his *MD Magazine*, financed by pharmaceutical companies, was bringing medical history and interviews with famous physicians to the entire continent.

Before reaching my home in Vancouver I was shanghaied by Dean Wendell Macleod, of the faculty of medicine at the University of Saskatchewan, to speak to the first-year medical students on the history of Canadian physicians such as William Osler, Frederick Banting and Wilder Penfield. In the evening I spoke to a neurological group on our research at the Kinsmen Laboratory at UBC. I arrived home a little tired but still enthused by my sojourn at Yale.

I had been back in my laboratory in Vancouver only a few days when a telegram informed me of Professor Fulton's death. It was not possible to return to Yale for the funeral but I learned from Professor Thoms that John's old friend, Rev. Sidney Lovett, had made the service at Battel Chapel one of "praise and thanksgiving." Thus passed one of Yale's (and Oxford's) great scholar scientists, generous to a fault and interested chiefly in helping young people. His bibliography extends to nearly 500 papers and books, and his influence on both sides of the Atlantic was phenomenal. A greatly enlarged second edition of his *Selected Readings in the History of Physiology*, on which I worked with him, was published in 1966.

CHAPTER THIRTY

Travel and Projects, 1960–1978

Even after his retirement as chairman of the Wellcome Trust in London, where I was a privileged beggar for funds for UBC, Sir Henry Dale, O.M., kept me very much in mind when that part of Sir Henry Wellcome's will concerning medical history was being discussed. In fact the medical historical interests of the donor were often over-looked by his trustees, possibly because of a certain degree of ambiguity in the document that may have crept in as his solicitor, John Foster Dulles, drew up the remarkable document.

Sir Henry Wellcome was born in Garden Centre, Minnesota, and began life as a pharmacist representing an American manufacturer of high-grade chemical products in Europe. There he met Silas Burroughs, who was engaged in the same field, and they gave up their American connections in order to found the England-based Burroughs Wellcome. On Burroughs' early death Wellcome expanded the company into a world-wide pharmaceutical concern based on research done by leaders in the fields of biochemistry and physiology. (To date, two Wellcome directors of research have won Nobel Prizes.)

As Wellcome's income grew, he became a well-regarded philanthropist, equipping expeditions to distant parts of the world. He married Syrie, daughter of Dr. T.J. Barnardo, the pioneer in organizing homes for orphans. However, Syrie, Wellcome's junior by many years, is alleged to have run off with Dr. Somerset Maugham, after which Sir Henry applied himself even more assiduously to his special interests. I soon learned from my visits to London that Wellcome had financed the many projects of the Rev. William Duncan at an Indian village outside Prince Rupert, on the British Columbia coast near Alaska. These included a lumber mill and a fish cannery at the settlement of Metlakatla. The natives later became fed up with Canadian federal government interference and decamped into Alaskan territory, styling their village New Metlakatla. Wellcome wrote a book, *Metlakatla,* on this experiment. Understandably, most of the records on it are now to be found in the library of the University of Washington in Seattle.

Another chance Wellcome connection with my home province of British Columbia was revealed to me over lunch by Sir Michael Perrin. He had been born in the Bishop's Close on Burdett Avenue in Victoria, B.C. His parents returned to a bishopric in Britain when Michael was six years old, and he proceeded eventually to New College, Oxford, and thence to the University of Toronto for a master's degree in chemistry. Thereafter he studied at Amsterdam and early in World War II became involved in "Tube Alloys," the code word for the atomic bomb project's British division. He was flown to Canada to seek the uranium ore needed, and on his arrival in Ottawa on this super-secret mission, interviewed Prime Minister Mackenzie King. After 30 minutes of explanation Mr. King said, "I think I heard you say something that related to chemistry," whereupon Perrin, exhausted, quickly agreed. "Oh well" said the P.M.: "We have a man in the cabinet that understands chemistry. I'll take you down the corridor to meet him. He used to be a professor at M.I.T. His name is C.D. Howe." After about 30 seconds C.D. Howe told Michael, "Of course you can have all the uranium you need."

Post war, Sir Michael became chairman of Wellcome and proceeded to make it one of Britain's manufacturing and exporting successes in the pharmaceutical field. I was often suspected by the bureaucracy of the Wellcome Trust because of such underground connections, and I found my aces trumped frequently—but never by the scholarly Dr. Noel Poynter, Wellcome's early adviser on what to buy for his great historical library, and eventually director of his institute of the history of medicine on Euston Road. As already mentioned, Poynter helped us at the Woodward Library to acquire the first French tapestry. He helped us to organize a symposium at Woodward on "British Contributions to Medical Research," but, typically, was not allowed by the Trust brass to attend. However, a handsome volume containing the milestone papers from the symposium was soon published with his help.

When Lord Franks, of Oxford investigative fame, became chairman of the Trust, he decided to set up an advisory committee on the history of medicine segment of Wellcome's will, under the distinguished chairmanship of Lord Cohen of Birkenhead. I was invited to join the group. Henry Cohen had arrived in England as a child refugee, unable to speak English. He became one of England's best known orators, and incidentally, professor of medicine at Liverpool. We often talked of Sherrington's seminal research on the nervous system in the physiology laboratory in Liverpool, as well as the earliest recording of the brain waves by a Liverpool physician named Richard Caton. Alas, Caton became interested in politics, and as was said of the Duke of Suffolk, "his body was never recovered."

Henry Cohen lost no time in appropriating funds for the study of the history of medicine and science at Cambridge. However, a report came back after a time that the lecturer, dressed in jeans, insisted on the students sitting in a circle on the floor as he himself did, the better to absorb the subject. The work there was discontinued. Our secretary reported that there was no interest at Oxford, so I enquired to whom our letter of intent had been directed. It had gone to the dean of medicine, a non–existent officer at Oxford. An offer made to the Regius professor of medicine brought an immediate reply and, under the history board, Dr. Charles Webster initiated a lively unit in a rented house on Banbury Road. It was not long before the number of students and senior researchers over–flowed the premises, so that today, on my visits, I find the Wellcome Unit distributed over two houses. The record of research and publication has been very impressive, as are the students coming from many parts of the world. One of the senior scholars, Dr. Tom Paterson—a plastic surgeon of long experience, including time in India—has brought the inherited interest of his ancestor, Sir James MacKenzie, the early cardiologist who rose from being a busy general practitioner in Burnley, a Lancashire textile town, to being, in Europe's eyes, if not England's at first, the outstanding scholar in this field. In fact, when Osler arrived at Oxford in 1905 as Regius professor, he astounded his listeners by saying that the first physician he wished to see was James MacKenzie in Burnley. Another of his clan, Lord Amulree, made a superb contribution when he turned his medical abilities to the taking over of a Poor House in London and converting it into an exemplary centre for the care and study of geriatric patients. After his visit to us in British Columbia, I was able to send him a patient who, as a mining engineer, had suffered a stroke and wanted to die within earshot of Bow Bells.

In the autumn of 1965 I travelled to the World Neurological Congress in Vienna and saw historical exhibits of the greatness of the Vienna School of the last century.

The social programme was almost as exotic as the scientific. The institute for the history of medicine in the restored academy for army surgeons (called the Josephinum after Emperor Joseph II who founded it in 1785) was a triumph for its director, Dr. Erna Lesky. She had arranged a special gallery exhibition on 200 years of neurology in Vienna for our pleasure. Even Sigmund Freud's first paper, written as a medical student, was there. It illustrated the bipolar nerve cells in petromyzon fish. In addition, there were his works on reflexes and his early interest in brain pathology. The Wellcome Trust had supplied the funds to furnish the spacious room devoted to Vienna's medical past.

My former tutor Jack Eccles and his friend Professor John Szentagothai gave marvellous papers correlating the physiological and anatomical (electron microscopic) details of the spinal cord. I arranged with book dealers to send off some prize acquisitions to the Woodward Library at UBC. The grand banquet and ball at the Konzerthaus was one of splendour rarely seen. Mike Corbett–Ashby, my contemporary at New College, was as dashing as ever, even if he had forgotten to bring the trousers that matched his white tie and tails. So he introduced a new style for the evening: formal attire with grey flannels below.

Henri Gastaut came from Marseille and was as jet–propelled as usual. On the Danube ferry I encountered one of his former students, a military surgeon now at the University of Dakar. Together we visited the large monastery at Melk, and saw Dünsdorf where Richard the Lionheart had been held for ransom.

After that we travelled by ship down the Dalmatian coast where we saw enough limestone to keep the cement companies of the world busy for a millennium. Dubrovnik's old quarter was a jewel, with its ancient walls and cathedral. On the latter there were marvellously carved stone heads, one of which could have been an exact portrait of the Canadian prime minister John Diefenbaker, in a frightful rage with his hair flying and face distorted. In the cathedral shop for tourists I found a five–inch–high plaster representation of this likeness, so I sent it to my friend Mike Pearson, by then Canada's prime minister. He told me later that he kept it in a bottom drawer in his office in Ottawa, but on dull days would place it before him and have a good chortle.

Athens and a tour of the Peloponnesus were both mandatory and delightful. The view from Delphi over olive fields to the sea was unforgettable. By night it was possible to see satellites coursing above, all of which were neatly labelled by a Harvard professor of astronomy who was staying at the Xenia Hotel.

I could hardly wait to see the original stadium at Olympia. This quiet district is said to have one of the most equable climates in the world. The statue there of Baron de Coubertin, who had revived the Olympic Games, was beautiful. It was hard to believe that the running track had not been excavated until 1958, when 20 feet of earth and gravel deposited by a swollen river was removed. The marble starting blocks and finish line were as white as the day they were installed. There were, I should estimate, 20 acres of ruins still to be restored. An echo-hall, designed originally to broadcast the names of winners in seven directions, still exists. It was a fascinating place.

In Athens I had the pleasure of meeting Spiridon Oeconomos, the retired professor of surgery in the Policlinic. This bearded little man bemoaned the fact that if only he could collect one dollar from each of the three million physicians in the world, he could build, on a specially designated area near the Asklepion on the island of Cos, a conference centre as a memorial to Hippocrates, the father of modern medicine, who was born on Cos about 460 B.C. I applauded the idea but had to explain to the man who had devoted his live to making the Hippocratic teachings better known that it would cost more than one dollar to collect a dollar in this fashion. Instead, I proposed the sale of seeds from the great platanus orientalis—a sycamore—under which Hippocrates is alleged to have taught his students, the proceeds to go to the already created International Hippocratic Foundation. I felt that this would give physicians anywhere an opportunity to contribute to the proposed structure.

This rash suggestion catapulted me into one of those lost causes for which Oxford graduates are famous. The saga still goes on as I receive letters and photographs of Hippocratic trees growing luxuriantly in distant parts of the world.

But first I went to see the tree. It graces and invades much of a large town square in the town of Cos, situated at the eastern extremity of the island of the same name. Over the years I have visited the small island many times, gradually learning its unusual history. It is one of the Dodecanese Islands and is closest of all these to the Turkish coastal area, near Bodrum, and near Halicarnassus, the site of the Mausoleum—the so-called seventh wonder of the world.

Cos is said by its historians to have been the site of one of the world's first agricultural irrigation schemes. A great gush of water shoots out of the rocks high up on a line of hills and, since ancient times, has been conducted in a system of channels to the arable land. It is no surprise, therefore, to learn that Cos is often cited as "the tomato capital of the world." (The mechanized plantations near Guadalajara in Mexico today may challenge this view.) Certainly Cos is regarded as the tomato paste capital, with its large factory that produces 10–gallon containers filled with "Hippocratic Tomato Paste," which can be found in distant restaurants.

With the fall of Constantinople in 1453, the island of Cos has oscillated between rulers other than the Greek—French, Italian, Nazi, etc.—until the British army liberated it near the end of World War II. The French brought archaeologists; the Italians, an excellent airport; and the rapacious Nazis, death to every Jew on the island. Today the population of Cos is said to be 20,000, with an additional 20,000 summer tourists. These come on charter flights, complete with bicycles, from cities such as Manchester. An added attraction is the rehabilitation spa and clinic opened near one of the fine hotels by Dr. Christian Barnard, the heart surgeon who is too arthritic today to do surgery.

Back to the tree. It is alleged to be 2,500 years old and is approximately 45 feet in circumference. Much of it is hollow, recalling the plane trees described in ancient times by Suetonius, which reputedly were so large that a picnic could be accommodated within them. For some reason Wilder Penfield, who had spent considerable time on Cos while writing his novel, *The Torch*, held the view that no plane tree could survive for more than 500 years! I could not convince him otherwise, so on one of my visits to Greece I flew over to the beautiful island of Rhodes. There at the castle were plane trees known to have been planted 400 years ago. I measured them and found that they averaged three feet in diameter. The Hippocratic tree on Cos was 15 to 16 feet in diameter, so I have no doubt it dates from Hippocratic times.

Of course, there is more to Cos than the tree. Its harbour is home to fishing and pleasure boats, especially sailing craft from all over the world. Cruise ships stand off at anchor while tourists come ashore by lighters. The crowning glory of the harbour is an ancient fort, surrounded by a moat. Until the Italian health officials drained it, the moat promoted malaria through voracious mosquitoes. The stones of the fort give away their secrets through the many inscriptions chiselled upon them, indicating clearly that they were stolen from the Aesclepion or healing site in the hills.

Years before Hippocrates was born, the Greek temples of healing were catering to patients high above the town of Cos. Only in the early 1900s did a Greek archaeologist, Dr. Jacob Zeraftis, locate the site—since which time representative columns, friezes and other structures have been unearthed and restored. The area of this Aesclepion is immense, much of it still to be retrieved from the pine forest that covers part of it. There is an annual festival of dancers and a chorus commemorating the ancient rites.

My wife converged on Cos from the Turkish mainland where she had been studying the underwater archaeological work of an American group at Bodrum. She had thought that the dozen miles separating Cos from the Turkish coast could be negotiated by boat in an hour or two. No such luck. The "negotiation" was of a very different kind: no Turk would think of travelling to Greece. After much persuasion in French and funds, a sailor was found who would drop her unceremoniously on Cos and then retreat quickly.

The Lord Mayor was aware of her visit and seemed more amused than upset by her late arrival. She was given a warm welcome by his officials and opened the door for my unusual method of raising funds for the projected Hippocratic Conference Centre, high up near the Aesclepion. Since the characteristic seed balls—the size of golf balls—were not ripe at the time of the visit, plans were made with the mayor, the resident agriculturist, the postmaster and the city's gardener to send ripened seed balls to me at the University of British Columbia in late autumn. The precise location of that province was not clear, but nearly everyone seemed to have a cousin in Chicago or Los Angeles.

The gardener, however, had a surprise for me: a rooted cutting from the great tree. It was contained in a stout plastic bag in which a solution of food had been provided. He handed me a few tablets that were to be added daily on my aerial voyage to the Pacific. The agriculturist typed out a long statement in Greek, in purple ink, to certify that the roots were clean and that there was no "golden nematode" infection on the island, and then applied his signature and stamp with gusto. The editor of the local newspaper made notes of all this palaver and the principal of the little Hippocratic School explained it all to his students. His nice white building was situated on the edge of the city where the destruction from a frightful earthquake in the 1930s had been greatest. The ever–present guide, George Soultanous, gave me a racy account of the island's history, explaining repeatedly that he had been Dr. Penfield's guide and friend.

Autumn brought a large container filled with the platanus orientalis seed balls to the customs postal service in Vancouver. Armed with the purple–inked certificate, I went down to what turned into a hilarious session as the officials made the usual jests that it was all Greek to them, and why in the world was I importing seeds from an old tree?

It was all very well to have a bucketful of seeds, but what next? The dean of forestry at UBC sent me to see his professor of forest genetics: a man who used a rifle to bring down pine or fir seed cones, or lassoed them from a helicopter! Dr. Oskar Sziklai, one of our Sopron refugee students from Hungary, was enthusiastic from the start. I thought that enthusiasm might dwindle as time went on, but precisely the opposite occurred. I have never seen a scientist so interested in a genetic problem of another person's making. First the seeds had to be broken carefully out of the neatest golf ball structure I have ever seen: thousands of radially packed, light brown bodies, each fitted with a fuzzy tip to carry it in the wind.

Under a Japanese soft x–ray microscope, one could see that only three percent of the seeds contained any genetic material—understandable after 2,500 years.

We used long tweezers to pick the viable seeds from the stage of the microscope. These were then planted in test tubes bearing a special food, and presto, little seedlings began to develop, which were then transferred to filter paper beds spread under special growth lamps. At first we thought of selling only those seeds that, under the microscope, appeared likely to develop into seedlings. We gave up this idea, and sent out packages of seeds just as they arrived from Greece. Many of these went out to interested physicians and botanists by mail. Then Professor Siklai thought we should try growing Hippocratic seedlings in his so–called rice paddies on the campus. We planted plenty of seed, hoping that the fertile three percent would declare itself. My children helped with the watering and early care of the little plants, and as the years slid by, the little trees that were not shipped out became larger trees. The original tree that I brought by hand from Greece was planted in front of the Detwiller Pavilion of the University Hospital. Wesbrook Mall's playing fields are now bordered by them.

An early UBC–raised seedling, 18 inches high in 1970, was planted at the University of Victoria. Twenty–five years later it was 60 feet high. Another of the same vintage, planted at the Royal Jubilee Hospital in Victoria by my medical colleague Lou Ptak, now covers an entire quadrangle. A similar seedling planted by Dr. Sziklai in the Burrard Street entry to St. Paul's Hospital, Vancouver, now reaches the fifth floor.

Until her death, caused by a rapidly growing brain tumour, Dr. Henrietta Banting kept one outdoors on her patio in summer, and indoors in winter. An amusing situation developed in Philadelphia where I had sent a tall seedling—really a rapidly developing tree—to my friend Henry Watts, Jr., to be planted at the College of Physicians. After being inspected at the American border in Washington

State by an officer who was a university graduate in biology, the tree was air–expressed to Philadelphia's airport, where a paralysing strike was in progress. Watts went to the airport to collect it only to be told that nothing would be allowed to leave the grounds. With his Harvard '25 accent he asked if, since this was a medical emergency and that part of Hippocrates' tree would die for lack of water, he might be allowed to pick up the tree in an ambulance. The gatekeeper convulsed into laughter at this suggestion, but with his help the tree was rescued and has survived the pollution as the downtown traffic crawls past the College of Physicians. It is remarkable how the "platanus occidentalis" relatives have survived the exhaust fumes in London and Paris. Straight–faced, I have occasionally explained to too–eager devotees of art that it was the dappled bark and the fluttering leaves of the plane or sycamore tree that started the Impressionist school of painting in Paris.

With the death of Professor Spyridon Oeconomos at close to 100 years old, his mantle fell upon his son, the distinguished dean of medicine in Athens. The money that we had accumulated in far–off British Columbia and transmitted to Cos was soon dwarfed by the funds now produced from the Greek government and other sources, so that construction finally could begin. Remarkably, the Hippocratic Conference Centre was completed quickly; it opened under blue Aegean skies, with the sun reflecting off the white buildings of Cos, far down the slopes of this productive green island.

With many trumpets and even more dignitaries, this beautiful little palace was opened. I felt a thrill as the Canadian flag was raised along with those of other nations that had participated in the venture. Its first use was for a French vascular surgeons' conference. On a large marble plaque are displayed the names of those individuals who contributed to the structure. Beside mine is the name Oskar Sziklai, M.D., which caused a doctor of forestry from Vancouver much merriment.

One thing that irritated Oskar regarding the care of the Hippocratic tree down in the town of Cos was the cement that had been poured into the hollows of the tree when France controlled the island. He thought that the Lafarge consortium had gone too far. Thus, on his last visit to Cos, he and a biochemist friend from Athens procured sledge hammers and proceeded to smash up the concrete, throwing it over the "Greek–key" fence into the town square! Without a doubt, this attracted considerable civic attention. The poor old tree, at last freed of this burden, soon began to put up new shoots from its root system, a little like the renewal of the base of the ancient conifers in the Garden of Gethsemane, which I was able to see on one of my visits to Jerusalem.

Although I had lived in Acapulco and visited Morelia and Lake Patzcuaro in Mexico in 1939, I had never been in South America until an accident suddenly propelled me there in the 1970s. My wife slipped and fell in the house, breaking her femur close to the hip joint, only a few days before she was to accompany a University of British Columbia group to Guatemala, the Galapagos Islands and Peru. I had to fill in for her, so in the three weeks saw a great deal of interesting country.

Guatemala was a country held in the grip of a dozen powerful families, who had a pitiful record as far as human rights were concerned. There was nothing we could do about that social ulcer on our visit so I concentrated on a minor miracle in the ancient capital Antigua, far down in a valley towards the Pacific.

There, in a town wrecked by earthquakes, I visited a truly remarkable plastic surgical clinic operated by a well–trained father and son team with connections to Stanford University in California. The Rotary Club in the area had become interested in the high incidence of hare lip and cleft palate in the children of highly inbred families living in the valley. I could hardly believe what I saw: a beautifully clean, modern and well–staffed small hospital with surgical facilities that would do credit to any university.

Within a few days of birth, children born with gaping holes in their faces—for lack of a better word—were successfully operated upon. Glass walls separated the newborns waiting for surgery from those in various stages of post–operative recovery. All the staff were diligent about maintaining sterile conditions, and the results of their labours were wonderful to behold. The photographs given to me as I left have haunted me ever since.

Passing through small towns with colourful markets, we drove to one of the world's most beautiful bodies of water: Lake Atitlan, a blue jewel surrounded by hills and old volcanoes. The only jarring note was a bus load of German tourists who wanted to drink the night away in the hotel's flowered courtyard. A tough nurse in our group cried out from a balcony at midnight that we had suffered enough, and threatened them with the fire hose if they kept on!

On flying into Quito, the capital of Ecuador, one collides at once with modern and ancient Andean cultures. As usual in South America, the Independence Plaza is a central civic institution, with palm trees, statues and fountains. The mountain peaks, such as Chimborazo (20,577 feet), accentuate the fact that some of the citizens live at altitudes of nearly 16,000 feet. The early travellers and soldiers who lost fingers, limbs and even their lives in attempting to cross the Andes were described in great detail by Father Joseph d'Acosta in 1590, in his *Historia natural y moral de las Indias*.

In the Air Force I learned that at 16,500 feet altitude, the atmosphere has approximately one half the oxygen found at sea level. As a result, the inhabitants in the high Andes have more red corpuscles per cubic millimetre of blood than do those who make their homes in the Ecuadoran coastal city of Guayaquil. It was reported years ago that llamas, the indispensable beasts of burden in the Andes, have an acquired characteristic of double the usual number of red cells than one finds in other animals raised at sea level. The llamas born in the Hamburg zoo in Germany are said to have kept their high altitude original complement of red cells. The diminished barometric pressure at Quito would prevent the bends in aviators taking off for high altitude flights.

All this apart, our objective was to take a plane from Guayaquil to the Galapagos Islands. The descent by rail from Quito to the coast was one hair–raising ride. Soon after we left Quito the train ran over a woman, which obviously delayed things for several hours. The train's squealing and smoking brakes must have been put to the test a thousand times as we snaked down the cliffs and trestles. There was food to be had at several stops, along with a rush to find toilets, since those on the train were indescribably awful. A little less spent on advertising tourism and a little more on sanitation would seem wise.

Guayaquil was historically once the lair of pirates. I found it to be so still. Because of our train's delay we found ourselves isolated on an unlit railway platform facing half a dozen desperado–looking characters who were deciding whom to tackle first, and whose baggage looked most promising. One of our men pulled out his camera and boldly took a flash picture of them, whereupon they departed sheepishly.

Finally our ground transportation arrived and by next morning we were flying the 600 miles westward along the equator to the Galapagos Islands in an Elctra, eventually to land on Baltra. Since those precious natural laboratories were a national park, the Air Force had been put in charge of all entries and exits by plane. An excellent small ship took us aboard and for four days we visited several of the five large islands and avoided the 70 or so smaller ones into which this outpost of Ecuador had been fractured.

While whalers and pirates knew of the Galapagos group for more than four centuries, there was little evidence of ancient human occupation. There was reason to believe that the huge turtles, tropical marine birds, iguanas and other creatures had been there for a long time. The turtles, weighing up to a quarter ton, had miraculously avoided slaughter by sailing crews in search of live fresh meat that they could hoist aboard and use at sea as the length of a voyage dictated. Turtle farms for the study of these lumbering giants were present at the Darwin Station on Santa Cruz Island. The station was the scientific centre of the islands and the lure that brought many distinguished researchers here. Our guide, José, was at the same time enrolled as a student there. I financed him later for a semester at the department of zoology at UBC, where he was allowed to attend any lectures and laboratories that interested him. Before he returned to the Galapagos Centre he was lecturing to the professors! As a guide and teacher for our group he was superb; the first day out he stopped anyone trying to pick up a stone or a feather as a memento. He told us that if anyone was allowed to collect such souvenirs, all would demand the right and there would soon be nothing left to see.

The first thing that strikes one on these islands is the multiplicity of species—of marine, bird and botanical nature. The large iguanas and sea–lions roar at intruders on the beaches, whereas the dolphins love to put on their air–sea displays and the seals want to swim with their human visitors. There are shrubs that conserve water by turning the edges of their leaves, rather than their flat sides, to the sun. As to birds, one is over–whelmed by the numbers of each species: boobies raising fluffy young beside the trails; pelicans that dive at great speed into the sea to catch puffer fish; soaring frigate birds; and, most importantly, Darwin's finch, which uses a cactus needle held in its bill as it digs meat out from shells.

No islands ever had such an effect as the Galapagos had on Charles Darwin—one of the fathers of the theory of evolution. This student who left medicine at Edinburgh in order to study theology at Cambridge, only to give that up in favour of geology and biology, sailed in The Beagle (Captain Fitzroy) nearly 150 years ago.

Much has been written about how the time spent on The Beagle may have affected Darwin. It is best summarized in the *Dictionary of National Biography*: "It was both his education and his opportunity. He left England untried...and returned a successful collector, a practised and brilliant geologist, and with a wide knowledge of zoology gained at first hand in many parts of the world."

Our plane journey to Peru was interesting to anyone who had been in the Air Force, for many small landing fields were on what had been untouched mountain tops prior to the removal of vegetation and debris. The cloud cover on these must have created real risks for the pilots of small planes, but at least they were a level (or nearly so) port in any storm.

With much clashing of gears in an ancient Lima bus, we reached the mountains where, for several days, we explored "lost" cities that had been plundered after having been discovered by intruders centuries ago. Some climbed the conical heights of Machu Picchu and its neighbours, where they reported fabulous views of the surrounding mountains. My athletic daughter later chastised me for not having climbed Machu Picchu at least, which she herself had done years before.

Back in Lima there were five ethnological museums to be seen, as well as the San Marcos, the oldest in South America. The bustling city presented a danger to women tourists who sauntered along sidewalks too close to the kerb. Suddenly a motorcycle would swoop towards them and while the driver prepared to accelerate, his rider on the pillion seat would wield a long razor, cut through the strap of a woman's shoulder bag and, in a flash, be gone. It was a thief's paradise.

We travelled by plane to a cottage–type beach resort at Paracas, where we spent two days. In one harbour we saw a fishing fleet that had been aided by the Canadian International Development Fund. All in all, it was an interesting three weeks.

CHAPTER THIRTY-ONE

Personalities, Highways and Byways

I would like to agree with Ulysses that "I am part of all that I have met" but one's life is often shaped not by events, but by personalities encountered en route. One's earlier teachers naturally make a lasting impression, but the first to give me an exciting view of university life was Professor Walter Gage at Victoria College. An avid mathematician and a born teacher with an inexhaustible store of energy, he had an abiding interest in students and their welfare—both short term and long term. He had a militant sense of fairness that would boil over if any weak, disadvantaged or unhappy student were put at risk. From his own pocket, often full of cobwebs like Osler's, he would provide emergency help. Some years after he had persuaded Franc Joubin to give up hauling coal sacks up narrow stairs and alleys in Victoria's Chinatown, Walter had the pleasure of receiving from Franc, the then– successful geologist and prospector, a cheque for $100,000 for what they agreed to call "intellectual prospecting."

A quieter and more philosophical professor at UBC was the entomologist Dr. George Spencer. During the Great Depression, when excellent teachers were being lost, George had to take on histology (microscopic anatomy) over and above his already heavy load in zoology. He sized up his class of eight, then on the blackboard divided the term's lectures into eight parts, and put one student's name against each system. I was assigned the nervous system, on which I prepared what must have been a pretty elementary lecture. When it came to demonstrating the silver staining methods to selectively show the minute structures in the mouse brain and spinal cord, I had the luck of the Irish. The slides seen under the microscope were beautiful and I was hooked for life. It was my ability to stain nerve cells that appealed to Wilder Penfield at the Montreal Neurological Institute, so he propelled me into neurological research as a career thereafter. Spencer mixed structure and function, as well as the history and philosophy of evolution, in his discussions. He is, I am happy to say, memorialized in a named lectureship held annually at UBC.

Having dealt throughout this account with Penfield and Sherrington, I shall pass quickly to Warden H.A.L. Fisher, the head of New College. The writer of the eminently readable *History of Europe*, he was one of Oxford's shining lights. In the 1914–18 war he served as minister of education in Lloyd George's cabinet at Westminster. We used to time the speeches he gave in hall; he would invariably mention this duty after about 20 seconds. What we did not know, as a bunch of irascible and bumptious students, was the far more important fact that as the minister concerned with returning soldiers, sailors and airmen seeking a university education, Fisher read every application made by the 27,000 aspirants. Equally important for Oxford University was Fisher's 1917 intervention with the Privy Council at Westminster in the matter of direct grants to the university, necessary because of the rapidly increasing costs of science courses. His submission was based on information supplied at his request by Sir Charles Sherrington, his friendly physiological confrère. Of course, Fisher was also very close to Sir William Osler, whose international reputation, along with Sherrington's, would sway any cabinet. Warden Fisher, a graduate of Winchester School, had two brothers, both admirals. Outwardly reserved, he was inwardly dedicated.

Another Oxford graduate who was committed to the developing world was Alan Lennox–Boyd, who as Commonwealth Secretary put his organizing powers to work after serving in the 1939–45 war. Long before he became a viscount he was a very active member of the Conservative party in the House of Commons. He could analyze a problem or a proposal in short order, which made him an excellent co–chairman of the Guinness empire. When the University Club of Vancouver entertained him, his towering height rather over–whelmed the diminutive Walter Koerner, our honorary president. After the reception, Walter said to me: "I should be his 'beater' when he goes hunting for game. I'm only up to his umbilicus."

One day this quiet peer of the realm told me how he was "commanded" by Churchill to join Britain's cabinet. The prime minister called Alan's mother by telephone at 2 a.m., the day after yet another of her sons had been killed in the armed forces. Alan remonstrated that his mother finally was asleep following a sad and harrowing day. Churchill insisted, however, and on being put through on the phone said to her: "Madam, I am calling to tell you that your son Alan will not be going to sea again. He will be joining my cabinet later today."

When I visited Lord Boyd in Cornwall, his wife Patsy (Guinness) told me the history of the restored Ince Castle in which they lived. It had been the ancestral home of the Crease family, whose descendants were legal luminaries of British Columbia, including a chief justice in the stage–coach days, as well as Dr. Arthur Crease who had invited me in 1949 to head mental health research there. Alas, Alan Boyd was struck down by a speeding motor car as he and his co–chairman, Lord Home, were attempting to cross a street in Chelsea. As his wife wrote to me, "It was a great mercy that Alan was killed instantly." So, one of Churchill's best men was lost, and Saltash, Cornwall, lost a fine citizen.

Still near Plymouth, one thinks of Earl Mountbatten of Burma. He was a fascinating personality: theatrical at the proper time, a hard–driving activist in matters of international peace, and always fair in his assessment of people and their projects, which sometimes became his projects. Clarity and brevity characterized the early meetings held at his London flat concerning the projected United World College in British Columbia. For that reason, the little group bringing the project forward would meet beforehand to plot our strategy at the nearby Hyde Park Hotel. Then, after a half hour's discussion with Mountbatten, the course would be set for immediate action. He never knew how close we were to losing Lester Pearson as our sponsor and "red tape cutter" in the Canadian venture. "Mike," his wife and Robert Blackburn had set out from London by car to drive down to Atlantic College in Wales, the flagship of the consortium–to–be. Stopping for lunch part way on the long drive, the prime minister felt weary and wanted to turn back. His wife insisted on going on, and in the end Pearson was happy that he did. The 200 students at St. Donat's gave him a great welcome, which he never forgot. Some time later, when Mountbatten selected Pedder Bay, 18 miles from Victoria, B.C., as the 70–acre site for the next college, Pearson locked horns with Canada's Department of National Defence, who owned the property, which was about one–millionth of their holdings in Canada. As a matter of fact, according to Professor Peter Oberlander, who was once a deputy minister at Ottawa in the regime of his Harvard classmate Pierre Trudeau, D.N.D. had so much property that there was no inventory of it all. Nevertheless, they would give none of it for a good cause, so the Hon. David Wills, of our London cabal, stepped in and purchased it for what became the justly famed Pearson College.

Once we had land, a resourceful architect named Barry Downs, and a Canadian headmaster who had taught at Atlantic College named Jack Matthews, we were ready for a board chairman. Thanks to my late night phone calls to Ottawa, the scene was set for our enthusiastic supporter, Mrs. Pearson, to drop the brick on the unsuspecting Hon. John Nichol, who was having coffee with her in Ottawa the next morning. For 10 prosperous years thereafter, the ex-senator was a great chairman of the board. Under its present chairman, the very able Galen Weston of Toronto, the college goes from strength to strength. The day Lord Mountbatten opened the college was the last time any of us saw him, but his successor as chairman of the United World Colleges movement around the world, Prince Charles, has visited Pearson College on several occasions, sat in on lectures with the students, and tended by Zodiac his secret "windjammer wreck" in the depths of the nearby Strait of Juan de Fuca.

The vice-president of the United World Colleges was Thor Heyerdahl; he has an interesting connection with Pearson College, near Victoria. As we drove the 18 miles from the capital to Pedder Bay, he recounted his pre-war history. In the summer of 1939 he graduated from Oslo University, winning a scholarship that would take him to Bella Coola on the British Columbia mainland, half-way between Vancouver and Alaska, to study the native Indians.

He had scarcely begun his work when World War II broke out. He travelled back to Vancouver to offer his services to Norway through the Norwegian consul. He was shocked to find the consul was an out-and-out Nazi, who shouted at him that Norway was now a province of Nazi Germany and would remain so forever. Poor Heyerdahl hardly knew what to do. His wife was in St. Paul's Hospital in Vancouver having their second child and he wanted to help in the Allied war effort. Finally he found a job in the large smelter at Trail, B.C., far from the coast that he loved so much. After six months he was able to pursue military training at "Little Norway," on the Island at Toronto, and thereafter was in the Norwegian armed forces until 1945.

In his hand he brought to Pearson College a precious piece of papyrus, made from one of the giant Egyptian reeds, shaped like the Ra—the vessel on which he had crossed the Atlantic. On the piece of papyrus he had drawn a sketch of the Ra, with a thin mast at either end and a piece of clothesline linking the two. Displayed on the line were the "flags" of the multinational crew that made the crossing.

I had the good fortune while at UBC to know two "forest giants," Walter Charles Koerner and Harvey Reginald MacMillan. Walter was short, quick and courtly, and an avid tennis player and horseman. His rival, H.R., was tall and quiet, but nevertheless pretty positive. Walter Koerner was one of four brothers whose family forests ranged from Czechoslovakia to Poland. To escape the Nazi build–up of menacing armaments, they and their families left Prague and settled briefly in England where Walter and Marianne's two sons went to school in the quiet Cheltenham countryside.

The senior brother, Leon, had once visited Vancouver and was able to convince the others that British Columbia was the place to settle in order to keep up their work in forestry. Arriving in Canada they were advised by Prime Minister MacKenzie King to invest what capital they had escaped with in property, because as "enemy" immigrants they might be put in gaol or an internment camp for the war's duration. This never happened. Indeed, before he knew it Walter was telling Ottawa how to produce industrial alcohol from wood waste. However, Walter's chief discovery was that some of our tallest trees, the hemlock, were being wasted in the forests. They were occasionally cut down, but no one wanted to turn them into lumber because the lumber warped once cut. The Koerners knew how to kiln–dry such recalcitrant wood products, so began a very lucrative industry. They chose one of the least–used names for hemlock (Alaska Pine) and were soon major contributors to the economy. With European thoroughness, born of years of tough competition, Alaska Pine mills became show places of industrial safety and its rewards.

However, Walter's real discovery was not hemlock, but rather Indian totem poles that he found lying rotting in the dense evergreen forests. He was shocked to see these cedar creations, done by talented natives, lying in the bush unsung. It was not long before some that could still be saved were riding on top of the booms of logs, towed by colourful diesel tugs to the mills near Vancouver. Over the years they were stored in warehouses. In a shed on the UBC campus, the Haida carver Bill Reid made replicas of some that were decomposing. He and Walter Koerner talked of the day when these and other great works of aboriginal art could be assembled on campus in a suitable setting. Happily a Museum of Anthropology was designed by the west coast architect Arthur Erickson, and built with provincial and federal funds (added to by Walter). A towering glass palace was erected on the cliffs over–looking Howe Sound and its mountains. The adjacent heavy concrete gun emplacements from the war were co–opted, and on one of them there was mounted Bill Reid's masterpiece: a huge clamshell opening and little human figures emerging from it, representing the story of mankind. Walter would tell me of the tribulations and the successes in laminating a block of knotless cedar from pre–cut timbers. Today it is the greatest single attraction in the museum.

Walter and Marianne Koerner then gave their collection of northwest Indian gold and silver jewellery to the museum. The Devonian Foundation provided a handsome lecture hall in the complex where students and the public can learn more of this ancient culture. Without Bill Reid's interest in recapturing the arts of his Haida ancestors, I doubt if we would have the blossoming of native art that we see everywhere in British Columbia. Museums are sprouting in small villages where nothing of this nature was seen before.

As a child Bill had attended the little kindergarten in Victoria that was operated by the sister of the famous painter and writer Emily Carr. After an initiation into university work at Victoria College, he became Canada's much–loved news broadcaster from the Toronto studios of the C.B.C. His voice, like Ed Murrow's in the United States, carried quiet conviction.

By enrolling in night classes at Toronto's Ryerson Institute, he learned the arts of jewellery making. Now there are several generations of his people creating beautiful new, as well as traditional, forms of jewellery.

Walter Koerner just kept on giving to UBC. He began with the science library building and at age 94 completed an annex to the Museum of Anthropology with an addition in which to display all the world–class ceramics he began collecting in Moravia as a boy. His gifts to good causes in his adopted country were legion, but it was his interest in the educational opportunities for young people that occupied his waking hours. (Walter Koerner died in 1995 at the age of 97.)

It is interesting to find a similar driving force in his friendly competitor in the forest industry, H.R. MacMillan. This commanding figure graduated from Guelph's agricultural college only to spend three years in bed in the Laurentians with tuberculosis. After that he took his Master of Forestry degree at Yale. In order to get the prescribed fresh air he became a provincial forester in B.C., as did his friend J.W. VanDusen, another forest "giant" despite his retiring nature. H.R. was so infuriated by the American monopoly that marketed British Columbia timber around the world that he set up a very successful rival company, which he headed for most of his long life.

I met him at his home to give him information on Canada's medical pioneers when he was about to retire from active participation in his empire. He had of necessity become a great reader during his years in the sanatorium. He told me that the Department of the Interior at Ottawa had sent him editorial work to do while convalescing. Over the years he had built up an excellent library, but he was always on the look–out for new ideas. I was invited to drop in any time I passed his fine stone home, which I often did, usually on Sunday afternoons when returning from the provincial gaol at Okalla where I read the electroencephalographic tracings on inmates showing neurological and psychiatric symptoms.

On the other hand, when I would return from scientific meetings in London or Geneva or New York, the first question to be answered was always, "What was the best thing you heard there?" He was a good listener, but sometimes his comments were shocking or comical. He never missed a beat. He gave a graphic description of his encounter with an intruder armed with a large knife. Meeting this maniac at the door he threw the man into a coat closet and turned the key in a flash. The police did the rest.

H.R. had a wonderful secretary for 40 years or more. In fact, many said she ran his empire. At about 10 o'clock one morning she telephoned me with the blunt statement: "Dr. Gibson, Mr. MacMillan is losing his mind and I thought you ought to know." I asked for evidence and was told sharply that he claimed to have been at Bowen Island with me yesterday, which she said was simply nonsense. To these explosions I replied that it was all quite true; we had sat out on the balcony of my log house, looking north over the sea to the mountains, while sipping sherry (all of which could be vouched for by the nurse who had attended). Bang went the receiver and I never heard of his alleged decadence again.

As mentioned earlier, H.R. ordered for the Woodward Biomedical Library a wool tapestry made in Shanghai, which showed the Canadian surgeon Dr. Norman Bethune operating on soldiers of the Eighth Route Army in northwest China. His eight million dollar gift to UBC for library resources was a "blockbuster." It was in part due to the respect he had held for UBC's founding president, Frank Wesbrook. As early as 1915 H.R. wrote to Wesbrook concerning a faculty of forestry. Unfortunately, Mrs. MacMillan's intervention brought an end to Wesbrook's dream of having H.R. as the first dean.

Personalities I have known in the medical profession were sometimes characters, but more often scholars. I think particularly of Sir Richard Doll, F.R.S., the Regius professor of medicine at Oxford, with his full head of white hair, his insatiable curiosity about preventable disease and above all his foresight and determination. With his friend, the late Bradford Hill, he laid the groundwork for the campaign to root out cancer of the lung by eliminating the smoking of tobacco products. With his present colleague, Richard Peto, F.R.S., he informs the world of the abominable invasion of China by American tobacco interests. The American factories in China export their "coffin nails" to all of Asia, while keeping the most lethal for the Chinese. Years ago, with Doll's help, the staid Royal College of Physicians of London (of which I am a distant fellow), dropped a bombshell on smoking as a cause of cancer.

I have had a long and enjoyable friendship with Richard Doll and his medically trained wife, Joan, dating from the early days of his plans for a residential medical college on the 3.5 acres surrounding Dr. Radcliffe's observatory of 1785. Once my friend Cecil Howard Green and his wife, Ida, entered the picture, the mails could hardly keep up with the sketch plans and the written prospectus that ensued. Richard had already prepared the ground with his often reserved board colleagues, who have to agree on new developments at Oxford, and with whose ratiocinations we were long since familiar. We always had the support of our mutual friend, Dr. Paul Beeson, a McGill graduate whom I had known at Yale and who was appointed by Oxford to Lord Nuffield's chair in clinical medicine.

Once the Greens had seen Oxford, and were bowled over by its concentration of ancient colleges, some dating back to the 1200s, things began to happen. I could not fathom how this one man carried the Regius chair and its attendant responsibilities, which most other deans in the world would collapse under. Richard had a quiet, abiding sense of the possible, no harsh language, and a healthy dose of Osler's favourite ingredient: equanimity. Osler's other prescription was work and this is what the long since retired Richard Doll practices. Every day one can see him striding through Green College grounds to the little bun-shaped sighting observatory, which has been transformed into a graceful study where scholars can write in trappist silence. If Dr. John Radcliffe were to look in upon his observatory today, he would see a chorus of medical, not astronomical, observers, trying to understand the diseases that still rule the world. He would bless Richard Doll and Cecil Green for their productive partnership in furthering scholarship in an ancient profession.

Howard Florey, the Australian Rhodes scholar, professor of pathology at Oxford and Nobel Prize winner, provided the first injectable penicillin used in the Radcliffe Infirmary next door to Green

College. I knew him from my first year in Oxford because he had worked, or tried to, at the Instituto Cajal in Madrid where I had spent the spring vacation of 1936. He loved to mimic the officials of that great institute who could not find him rats on which to work.

Florey frequently visited the physiology laboratory, and would look at the silver–stained slides of nervous tissue under my microscope. His close friend, Harry Carleton, was the histologist–in–chief—a genius with his hands when it came to microscopic specimens for his classes, but a man who got awfully frustrated at times by his severe stammer. Nevertheless, he lectured laboriously to his classes, with the help of Dr. Humphrey Leach. (On a few occasions I filled in for them, on the microscopic structure of the lungs and the kidneys.) Florey constantly joshed Carleton about his race–car driving at the Brooklands track. We assumed that because of his stammer Harry could not coordinate his movements very adequately; but in this assumption we were quite wrong. Harry's invective was reserved for university officials, such as the director of the Delegacy of Lodgings, who turned me out of quarters on the Broad and sent me to licensed lodgings in Headington—a long cycle ride in the rain.

The lectures Florey gave to our class of eight clinical students were the best I have ever heard in pathology. As Sherrington used to assure him, what pathology needed was a physiological approach, and that is what we were privileged to have presented to us. As stated elsewhere, Florey's Australian twang was imparted to every word he attempted to stress. In or out of class, he was always approachable, though his humorous asides were likely to put one off the original question. When he slammed down a paper in front of me in my laboratory and demanded "sign this," I wasted no time in getting to it. Only then dared I ask what it was all about. It was a character reference for his secretary so that she could walk her dog in the Parks after public closing time. Florey may have been afraid to sign it because his predecessor had built the Sir William Dunn School of Pathology into a small area of the Parks.

As time and World War II went on, Florey became severely fatigued. He tried to fight back when the Beaverbrook press announced that Professor Fleming in London was shipping large quantities of penicillin to Florey, at Oxford, in order to treat a colleague. They had the story backward: Florey had sent his entire supply of penicillin to Fleming, whose colleague in London was dying. Only Florey's toughness saw the penicillin story through to a successful conclusion. Once, when we were talking in Vancouver, he said: "How wonderful it would be if we could give penicillin by mouth. Injections are so painful for children." Even that was realized in his lifetime.

I was fortunate to have had the pleasure of entertaining Florey in Vancouver. Once I sent him up Howe Sound on Senator McKeen's yacht. Much to Florey's delight we would use the ship's radio phone every noon in order to check with the recuperating traveller. He in turn would broadcast the weather to us. He lived through a hectic period in history, but came to a quiet end as he and his wife were taking tea at the Queen's College garden in Oxford.

Another pathologist who moved mountains was the gifted Cornell professor Cornelius P. Rhoads. I heard him lecture when I was on the wards at the Neurological Institute at McGill. Years later at Vancouver I wrote to him in hopes of getting an outstanding York lecturer who, thanks to Senator McKeen's bounty, could raise the sights of our medical educators. To my surprise, "Dusty" Rhoads said he would be delighted to come. He could not have had any conception, on leaving his Sloan–Kettering Institute's super–laboratories and his presidential suite, of the array of wooden huts he would find at UBC. He revelled in the pioneer atmosphere and sat down between his lectures to chat with graduate students about their work. When he returned to New York, his letters sounded as if he had been to Buckingham Palace. When I was aroused from my bed early one morning by a secretary who said "Dr. Rhoads calling," I suspected my neighbour, an Air Force prankster, but in a moment his distinctive, husky voice said: "Mr. Sloan wants you to come for dinner tomorrow night at the University Club in New York. The tickets will be wired to you if you can come." So I recovered my voice and said I would go. I have written elsewhere in this volume about Alfred Sloan in full flight, tapping his glasses on the cleared table and saying he would like two things: "clarity and brevity." I imagine that is how he presided over General Motors. Years later Dr. Frank Horsfall, a McGill graduate from Seattle, was the head of Sloan–Kettering. He attended a McGill medical reunion held for those living in the Pacific Rim, as did his classmate Paul Beeson, who came from Oxford. The Sloan–Kettering connection was later kept up by its talented head, the writer and philosopher Lewis Thomas. When it was time to return to New York after a sold–out crowd at the Vancouver Institute, he asked me: "How long has this wonderful place been going? We hear so little of you people far beyond the mountains."

Still discussing the pathologists, we have taken great pride in the association that UBC had with the best–known writer of pathology textbooks in the English language, Professor William Boyd. He graduated from Edinburgh in 1908 and then trained in psychiatry. He always maintained an interest in the pathology of the nervous system and the Spanish school of Ramón y Cajal and Río–Hortega. Wartime service in a field ambulance whetted his interest in pathology; after further work in that field he was appointed professor at the University of Manitoba in Winnipeg. He told me over many cups of tea in our combined hut at UBC that he "sweat blood" on the voyage to prepare his first lectures. He managed to keep one lecture ahead of his students. I used to tell him that he over–did it, for his textbooks became literary treasures for students in Winnipeg, then Toronto and "in retirement" in Vancouver. World wide they were acclaimed wherever the English language was read. He had that ability, known to Scottish bards, of being able to make everything spoken or sung into graceful cadences. The hard–pressed medical student, immersed in unpronounceable terms, would have his imagination stirred by reading in Boyd's *Textbook of Pathology: Introduction to Medicine* (1932) that the pituitary gland was the "conductor of the endocrine orchestra." Boyd had what is often lacking in doctors: a basic civility and a respect for great teachers. Thus, he recounted the story of his attendance at a conference of pathologists in Britain. The session was well under way when Dr. Maude Abbott, late as usual, entered the front of the lecture room. At once the audience stood up to show their respect. Bill Boyd thought that showed good breeding. He supported her efforts to create more museums of pathology in which students, even William Osler, could continue their education. Boyd, at age 85, was still revising his student textbook, then in its eighth edition. His Scottish accent was acclaimed by the endless medical audiences he addressed, and whose attention he could hold half the night, if need be. It is a pleasure to record that his name is perpetuated at UBC, and in the naming of the magnificent library of the Academy of Medicine in Toronto.

Neuropathologists have sometimes been thought of as a breed apart. But over the years I have found those I have known well to be normal human beings—in a hurry. Whether in Madrid or in Oxford, Don Pio del Río–Hortega was always busy at his own laboratory bench. When he had achieved a particularly beautiful staining of part of the brain he would command us to come quickly to look down his binocular microscope. When one of us was in trouble and getting poor results, he would sit down, whip his glasses off (his "anteojos") and concentrate on the problem. After which he would go through the staining procedure step by step, and then invite us to see the finer structure of the brain as it should be stained. His microscopes at the Cancer Institute in Madrid were of the best quality.

To watch him at home as he prepared a Spanish omelette was another lesson in technique. He wrote imaginative pieces such as the lecture he gave to the students in one of the large university residences: "Art and Artifice in the Science of Histology." When I showed the colour illustrations in this whimsical masterpiece to Howard Florey, he asked me to translate them for him. I published them in 1993 in *Histopathology*, thanks to the editor, Professor R.N.M. MacSween, and to Don Pio's grandnephew, Dr. Juan del Río–Hortega of Valladolid. I have two regrets about my friendship with Don Pio: one, that I had so little time with him at Oxford, and two, that I was on the Atlantic, returning to Canada, when he and Harvey Cushing, the neurosurgeon, were given honorary degrees. Don Pio died in 1945 in South America, having told General Franco that no true Spaniard would return to Spain under his rule.

There are qualities one comes to admire in one's teachers and one's own physicians. Having already described Jonathan Meakins at McGill, I must write briefly of the cardiologist Paul Dudley White, who cleared the way for me to return to medical school after a year out with rheumatic heart disease. In 1913 he and Professor Meakins had worked in the basement of University College Hospital in London with the British "father of clinical science," Sir Thomas Lewis. Returning to a basement laboratory at Harvard after the First World War, White started to plan a volume on heart disease. During a six–month sabbatical on the island of Capri, he brought together a classic volume that became the touchstone of generations that followed. In conversation he was always quietly hopeful that funds for medical research would some day be adequate for the job that needed to be done. If it took an appearance before a legislative committee in Washington, D.C., to drive home the point, he would drop everything in Boston and speak out in the Capitol, along with philanthropist Ben May and their supporter, Senator Lister Hill.

A philosopher at University College, London, whose seminars and writings I held in high regard, was Professor John Macmurray. He was a Scot who had been gassed in the 1914–18 war. Thanks to H.A.L. Fisher's concern for returning soldiers, he was able to enter Balliol College at Oxford. He told me that in those heady post–war days he would step into his bath wearing his dressing gown, only later realizing his error. He enjoyed the roaring twenties, as the Americans labelled them, and gradually took up university teaching as a career. He became a popular broadcaster for the B.B.C., and was later imitated by his former student, C.E. Joad, who copied John's medically necessary beard and who was one of the characters in the popular broadcast "The Brains Trust." Joad's career came to an abrupt stop as he was found guilty of misusing train tickets.

Macmurray's books, such as *Reason and Emotion*, came out of his participation in Canon Streeter's study group at Oxford. John began lecturing at University College, Gower Street, to droves of British and over–seas students. In Paris a student questioned him at one of his lectures, "Pourquoi êtes vous si optimiste?" to which Macmurray gave one of those economical British replies, "Pourquoi pas?" Eventually he was stolen away by Edinburgh. In April 1942 he wrote a long letter to me saying, in part, "Perhaps you will find that the increasing grip of war begins to squeeze the life out of ideas and convictions." Macmurray had great respect for Sherrington's philosophical statements, as in *Man on His Nature*. He was very attached to his over–seas graduate students.

My friends in the world of entertainment have ranged all the way from George Feyer, the pianist, to Jerry Lewis, chairman of the Muscular Dystrophy Association of America and spark plug of their annual Labour Day telethon. George Feyer loved to come to play in Vancouver for UBC and University Club audiences, and for the sedate Union Club in Victoria. To please his fellow Hungarian Andrew Saxton, he would play to a large audience each summer at his Grouse Mountain chalet, which was only accessible by a ski–season cable car lift. When I was president of the UBC Alumni Association, George came from Cafe Carlyle in New York to entertain 600 dinner guests. On that occasion he played "My Fair Lady" as the old masters would have written it. Every time he came to UBC he admired the sculpture presented by the refugee Hungarian school of forestry, which came to us with professors and students intact, rather than suffer humiliation by the Soviet Red Army. He was proud of his countrymen. Jerry Lewis, on the other hand, was devoted to children suffering from muscular dystrophy. He never stood in the way of my wild idea to sell his new institute for muscle disease and put the funds he so spectacularly raised into top university research laboratories. It was an act of faith on the part of himself and his board; now he gloats over the successes that followed. However, he still has a relentless drive to conquer 40 neuromuscular diseases now under the MDA umbrella. His dedication is not merely oratory. He once told me that in one year he had spent 65 days at home and 300 days on the road. He came to the British Post–Graduate Medical School at Hammersmith in London for the opening of a laboratory built on top of one of the wings of the ancient but active hospital, and named in his honour. When animal activists burned it down, MDA quickly rebuilt it. My only regret is that he sold his waterfront property near Victoria, B.C., because he could rarely visit that lovely part of Canada.

On the distaff side, I encountered many women whose sense of mission set them apart. Two of these—Lady Dodds-Parker, an American, and her running mate Judy Hutchinson (the daughter of the estates bursar of Christ Church College, Oxford)—met at Rodean School in Brighton. I met this pair of benign conspirators at a meeting of the Fairbridge Farm Schools that I addressed in London: I was reporting on the society's valuable property near Duncan, on Vancouver Island, once known as The Prince of Wales Farm School. Like its opposite member in West Australia, the Canadian school, dating from the 1920s, brought orphan children from England for a new life in Canada and gave them some training in agriculture with a view to future employment. The scheme was the brainchild of Kingsley Fairbridge, a Rhodes scholar who came from Rhodesia in the early years of this century. He was revolted by the slums of England, so attempted to develop a plan to reduce those slums' child populations.

With the coming of World War II, it was next to impossible to bring British children to far-away Vancouver Island. Indeed, after the war legislation prevented it entirely. Eventually the Canadian property was sold and the chapel organ—a memorial given by a well-wisher in England—was removed and placed in one of several chapels in Christ Church Cathedral, Victoria. I had hoped it could be rescued for the interfaith chapel at the University of Victoria because it was such a sweet instrument and a pleasure to play. The funds from the sale of the property in Canada were transferred to London where, with much ingenuity (and aid from that tall Oxford oarsman, Sir Douglas Dodds-Parker), a school designed to train young people in nursery and greenhouse techniques is flourishing. The school has trouble graduating enough professional gardeners to meet the demand.

While Lady Dodds-Parker is still active, perhaps even hyperactive, in this work, her friend Judy Hitchinson died recently of a stroke in Cyprus. Her medical history was a story in itself. In an accident during the war she suffered a severe head injury that produced a subdural haematoma. Since she was on General Alexander's staff in one of Britain's most secret decoding establishments, she was worried that under surgical anaesthesia she might reveal state secrets. However, the surgery performed at the head injury centre at Oxford by my old friend, American-born neurosurgeon Joe Pennybacker, went smoothly.

Another dynamo, whether she was in Britain or in the furthest corner of the world, was Barbara Ward, sometime editor of the *Economist*. She had the amazing ability to lecture on world politics and the threatened environment for exactly 50 minutes without using notes, just as she had done at Oxford. I convinced the UBC Alumni Association that if they wanted a large audience at their annual dinner in April 1976, they should invite her to speak on whatever subject she might choose. This initially sounded a bit risky to them, but she managed to fill a very large banquet hall and held her audience spellbound. Her title was "The world is a ship and everyone's in steerage." Before the festivities began she was introduced to the mayor of the city, who said he was delighted to meet the author of *The Zimmerman Telegram* and *The Guns of August*—he had confused her name with that of Barbara Tuchman. He had not heard of her book *The Home of Man*, the working paper for Vancouver's U.N. Habitat conference. The cherubic Allan Fotheringham, another loyal alumnus, burst out laughing and, being no friend of the mayor, retold the story ever after. During Barbara Ward's address a long–haired chap who looked like a hermit began to make his way to the microphone, carrying on his shoulder a garbage bag allegedly full of garbage from the dinner plates. He was halted in his tracks by our speaker, whose invective caused the hermit to retire before any more thunder bolts hit him. She never missed a beat and continued right on, flagellating us as a collection of the over–privileged of the earth who took no heed of its future. As a student at Heidelberg she had seen the Nazis, Mussolini in Rome and Dolfuss in Vienna. She enjoyed her UBC graduation as an honorary doctor.

Unfortunately, Lady Barbara Ward Jackson, to use her correct name, underwent strong irradiation for breast cancer, which affected her oesophagus and hence reduced her to food such as soup and ice cream. However, after repeated passage of a "sound" under anaesthesia—an iron rod that resembles a poker—she began to eat a wider variety of food, so that when I had lunch with her and her secretary near Midhurst, south of London, we all enjoyed fresh lamb from her farm. Our conversation included a preview of what might someday happen to Robert Maxwell, the publisher.

The final personality I want to describe was a quiet but determined woman from Toronto: Dr. Henrietta Banting. I met her with the crusading Dr. Jason Hannah, who was sponsoring her work in the history of medicine at Massey College. She had been in medical school in Toronto in 1941 when her husband, Sir Frederick Banting of insulin fame, was killed in Newfoundland as the bomber in which he was flying to England crashed. On completing her medical studies she taught for a time in Hong Kong and then returned to Women's College Hospital, Toronto. There, with surgeon Marian Hilliard and her friend Cecilia Long, she made a life for herself and became one of those strongly motivated women who saw the need for their unique hospital in the masculine world which existed in Toronto at that time. It was sad and ironic that after a lifetime of work on cancer, Dr. Banting was herself stricken with the most malignant of brain tumours. On the day she was diagnosed by a cerebral biopsy, she nevertheless cooked me a good dinner and gave me directions for her future, which she estimated to be a few weeks—an estimate that proved true. She regretted that her work in the history of medicine could not be finished on time. But that was all she regretted.

CHAPTER THIRTY–TWO

The Athenaeum

In the 1960s, thanks to nomination by Dr. Wilder Penfield and Professor Edgar Adrian, I was made a member of the Athenaeum on Pall Mall in London. I must say that was quite an introduction to club life in England. Humphry Davy and his friends started the Athenaeum in about 1823 as a gathering place in London for scholars living in the British Isles. I was certainly one of the lightweights in this milieu, but I truly enjoyed the experience. The great building with Greek frieze around it, situated at the foot of Regent Street, was across a beautiful open area from the United Services Club. The clubs were called "The Mental" and "The Regimental." Both the inside and the outside of the imposing structure of the Athenaeum were a bit over–whelming at first. Gradually I began to ask friends in the club why the elevators were so long and narrow and I was jokingly assured that this was "to bring the coffins down." I had not realized that there was a slight suggestion of age in the members.

It seemed to me that there were inordinate numbers of bishops stopping over–night in the 20 or so bedrooms on the top two floors. These bedrooms I came to know very well as I shot back and forth over the roof of the world for meetings in London. The mattresses on the bed were remarkable. Carr Sherrington told me that they had been bought as war surplus after the Boer War and had actually been called "biscuits." Each mattress consisted of four transverse compartments so that it could be folded up and carried on a soldier's back. It was hard to tell whether there was hay or horse hair in these remarkable creations; if one awoke in the night due to discomfort, one might hear half the club turning over, so great was the echo. One day I was passing through Aldwich and the Strand when I noticed some fancy single beds with wild pink undercarriages and movable mattresses in a department store. When I returned to the club I told the secretary that I proposed the next day to bring one of these home on the roof of a taxi, since it was on sale for £25. He blanched and said that could never be permitted. I forcibly gave him the £25 and told him to do it the next day, using any back entrance. The bed appeared in room 15 on the top floor and caused an insurrection in the house. Bishops demanded the best, so within a few years all the South African biscuits had been replaced by wild pink beds. My next project was to get rid of the telephones, whose frayed cords suggested that they had come in soon after Alexander Graham Bell's invention. To my great surprise, on a subsequent visit, I found each room fitted with a new green plastic telephone of very modern design.

The Athenaeum Library was superb, and became more of a historical treasure as an increasing number of public libraries developed in London. It contains many dedicated first editions written by members of the club, such as Charles Darwin's works and Gould's *Birds*. My New College friend Dr. Peter Daniel, a medical researcher at the Royal College of Surgeons in London, used to call up and say: "I would like to join you at the Athenaeum for a meal but I find the food intolerable. Come over to the Garrick Club and have a real meal." At breakfast one might hear the most amazing conversations between the slightly deaf elder statesmen sitting together drinking in the sun in the large south windows. On one occasion one called out to the other, "Did you know that the poem was not always, My Love Is Like a Red Red Rose?" The other replied, "No, what was it then?" "It used to be, O Love Is Like a Red Red Rose." The listener said in an astonished voice, "I say, I think that's horrid." The same pair at dinner one evening discussed the excellent collection of periodicals displayed near the bar. One began: "I say, I see there is a castle for sale in Cornwall in which it is said there is a ghost. Now does one have to take the ghost, or would there be a reduction in price if one did not wish the ghost?"

The annual meetings I sometimes attended were made up only of a corporal's guard. In fact it seemed to me that the majority of those attending had come for only one purpose: to prevent membership from being offered to women. This became rather difficult when Lord Florey established the headquarters of the Royal Society nearby on Carlton House Terrace, in the old German embassy where Ribbentrop had held sway before the war. The Royal Society had a number of distinguished women members, but they were not allowed to be members of the Athenaeum across the green. Imbedded in this intervening lawn was the Ladies' Annex, where members could entertain female guests. The entrance to it from outside the club an-

A prospectus was issued, signed by Michael Faraday as secretary; Croker and Davy proceeded to form a committee, and it is through the wise judgement they exercised in sending invitations, and in making selections from the enormous number of applicants, that the success of the undertaking was assured from the outset.

Among the earliest to co-operate was Thomas Moore. He records in his Journal, December 14: 'Received a note from Croker proposing that I should belong to a new Club;' and a few days later he writes: 'Lord L.' [Lansdowne] 'will belong... , but bid me impress upon Croker strongly the necessity of keeping it select, as we shall otherwise be overrun with all the pretenders to literature and the arts, than whom there is not anywhere a more odious race.'

On February 16, 1824, the committee held a preliminary meeting in the apartments of the Royal Society, then located in Somerset House. At this, which is historic in the annals of the club, the following were present: The Earl of Aberdeen, K.T., P.S.A.; Sir Francis Chantrey, R.A.; The Right Hon. J. W. Croker, F.R.S., M.P.; Sir Humphry Davy, Bart., P.R.S.; Lord Dover, F.R.S.; Davies Gilbert, F.R.S., M.P.; Sir Henry Halford, Bart., P.C.P.; Charles Hatchett, V.P.R.S.; Richard Heber, M.P.; Joseph Jekyll, F.R.S.; Sir Thomas Lawrence, P.R.A.; Thomas Moore; Sir Walter Scott, Bart.; and Thomas Young, M.D., F.R.S.

On February 6, 1830, about thirty of those who had served on committees held a dinner to celebrate the opening, and the members entered into possession two days later. In their old domicile a party had been given every week, and these entertainments were now superseded by a series of soirees on a larger scale. Sir Charles Lyell writes to his sister: 'Women fill it every Wednesday evening... and seem to examine every corner with something of the curiosity with which we should like to pry into a harem.'

Another misogynist of the some date also utters his complaint: 'We are now really in our new palace, and we throw open its gates every Wednesday evening to whomsoever, among your gentler sex, are disposed to enter... I, who am a hermit in my own way, and by no means too inclined to sociality, must confess that I never felt a more melancholy pang than when, for the first time, I beheld, from the large chair in which I was "quietly inured," a party of invading Amazons, with bare necks and yellow gowns, sweep across the chambers I had hoped would have been forever sacred to frock coats and the modest virtue of cravats... true, that Wednesday is only one day in the week, but, then, that one day unsettles us for the six others... Besides, what mischief to the tone of our society! Instead of the learned silence hitherto breathing around, of the murmurs of scientific discussion or literary dispute, we hear the *suaves susurri* of 'Last night—charming woman—beautiful eyes—good bust—pretty ankle!"' These reunions were, however, highly appreciated by others. and by no one more than the eccentric Mr. Walker.

We read that in 1834 'The mixture of Whigs, Radicals, savants, foreigners, dandies, authors, soldiers, sailors, lawyers, artists, doctors, and members of both Houses of Parliament, together with an exceedingly good average supply of bishops, render the melange very agreeable.'

In spite of every precaution, however, it was not always the right people who got in, for when it was noised abroad that it was 'the finest thing in the world... to belong to the Athenaeum..., all the little crawlers and parasites and gentility-hunters, from all corners of London, set out upon the creep; and they crept in at the windows, and they crept down the area steps, and they crept in unseen at the doors, and they crept in peers' pockets, and they were blown in by the winds of chance.'

nounced this in Greek letters. I saw an American tourist and his wife and two young children passing by this one morning. The children hung back to try to decipher these unusual characters over the entrance. The father went back to see what was holding them up and told them: "Come on. That's clearly an underground synagogue." Alongside this entrance, and also across at the United Services side of the intervening course, sat elevated horse–blocks made of granite, which it is said were provided for the Duke of Wellington.

The cost of train travel in Britain has caused many retired gentlemen now living outside London to resign, so the membership has been somewhat curtailed. However, the Athenaeum remains a bulwark of academia on the premier corner of Pall Mall. West of it are several other private clubs of great distinction. The Italian style architecture of the Reform Club is very striking. It was from this club that the chef, Alexis Soyer, went out to the Crimean War to try to improve food for the troops. That would have been a miracle in that morass of officialdom and gross inefficiency, as the beleaguered Florence Nightingale found out. Once the *Times* correspondent in Constantinople wrote the truth in his dispatches to London, the British public rose up in horror and anger and tried to give Florence the help she and the soldiers so badly needed. It is fitting that a fine bronze statue of her graces Waterloo Place, accompanied by one of Sydney Herbert, the minister for war who had done everything within his considerable power to aid her mission.

Many Cabinet Ministers of successive Administrations, glad to be free from the shibboleth of party, are wont to take luncheon in this safe retreat, even in a Long Vacation as many as six of those actually in office having been observed at the same time. Theodore Hook relates the following in his 'Elements of conversation' (1836): 'It was the custom with certain of the present Ministers, during their last reign, to have house-dinners at the Athenaeum on the Wednesdays in each week. One Wednesday came, and the names of Lord Lansdowne, Mr. Spring Rice, and a few more were down on the house-dinner card, although they had ceased to be Ministers. The house-steward, as usual, directed the butler to inquire of the proper authority as to the arrangement of the dinner. The proper authority gave the proper direction. 'They have always had a Cabinet pudding,' said Mr. Watson, unconscious of the effect of the observation; 'is that to be the same, Sir?' 'Oh, to be sure,' said the competent authority. Whereupon the other gentleman officially connected with the club added - 'but without the plums, I presume?'

Of the tables, the most historic is, perhaps, the round one at the north-east angle, near the door. At it Hook was accustomed to sit, and from the euphonious designations he gave to the gin-pinch and other stronger potations he so repeatedly demanded - asking the intelligent waiters in his gurgling, deep voice for 'a little more toast - and - water,' 'another tumbler of lemonade,' or 'a cup of tea' - the name 'Temperance Corner' survives to this day. Once, on his bill being brought, he notices he was charged for ten glasses of brandy, and objected, declaring he was positive he had 'only nine.' 'But, Sir,' explained the attendant, 'you forget the one you had before you sat down!' The statement, often quoted from the *Quarterly Review*, that after his disappearance dinners fell off to the number of three hundred a year is an exaggeration.*

This place, in the neighbourhood of the fire, was the favourite resort of Abraham Hayward, the brilliant essayist: thus it came also to be known as 'Abraham's Bosom,' and 'Hayward's Heath.' He alludes to a dinner here, in company with Dean Milman, Sir T.N. Talfourd, Lockhart. Sir Henry Ellis, and Charles Dickens, who was then writing *Nicholas Nickleby,* and of whom he thought 'no great things, a very commonplace talker at best.'

Thackeray, a constant frequenter, usually sat at this table. Dickens dined sometimes at that in the south-east window, but his luncheon (a sandwich or so) was generally taken standing, or while striding about the room. Here Darwin would dine 'like a gentleman, or rather like a lord, for I am sure the first evening... I felt just like a duke. I am full of admiration for the Athenaeum,' he proceeds, 'one meets so many people there that one likes to see.'

*His lines will be remembered:
There's first the Athenaeum Club; so wise, there's not a man of it
That has not sense enough for six — in fact that is the plan of it;
The very waiters answer you with eloquence Socratical,
And always place knives and forks in order mathematical.

CHAPTER THIRTY-THREE

The Cecil and Ida Green Story

The story begins with my introduction to Senator Stanley McKeen, who lived in the waterfront mansion nearest the tip of Point Grey with his wife, who was in poor health. One of my colleagues in internal medicine suggested to the senator that since I lived close by I might be readily available. So it followed that for more than a decade I saw him and his wife and her nurses on an almost daily basis.

I had never, in Canada, seen such a beautiful residence as theirs on North West Marine Drive. It was set in three acres of garden on the cliff looking north to Admiral Howe's Sound and out to the Strait of Georgia, with its fabled islands whose names recalled early Spanish explorations.

I learned from the senator that his three acres and an equal parcel next door, the home of Mr. and Mrs. F. Ronald Graham, had been divided off from the Point Grey lands in 1912 and auctioned by the provincial government.

On my first visit the senator was determined to show me the whole estate: the squash court, the basement with steel beams going way down into the cliff, the diesel auxiliary power plant, the vast pantry and kitchen under Chef Wong's sway, the conservatory full of orchids, the pool full of goldfish and the stables full of Cadillacs, Rovers and Mercedes!

Evidently E.P. Davis, the lawyer whose name still crowns a huge law firm in Vancouver, and Dr. Lefevre, who built the B.C. Telephone Co., went to Victoria to the auction sale in 1912. For the six lots bought they had to bid a total of $96,000—a huge sum in 1912.

By 1913 Davis was writing to President Wesbrook asking him to join in preserving the cliff from erosion by the high seas and the 16–foot tides. Dr. Lefevre built the large house just east of the Davis mansion, only to lose much of his land in the frightful washout of

1936, when a sudden spring thaw unleashed millions of gallons of water from the campus. This flood quickly wiped out the bridge leading from N.W. Marine Drive to the campus and removed a vast tonnage of clay too.

The Davis house had passed from the son, Ghent Davis, to a Mrs. Switzer, an Austrian refugee who lived secluded in it for the duration of the Second World War. At the end of the war she offered the entire property to UBC for a rumoured $19,000. Before the war it was reportedly offered to President Klink at UBC for a sum of $8,000. Due to the state of the university's finances on both occasions, the price might just as well have been $1,000,000! There was no hope whatsoever of buying it.

Then, post–war, the Lefevre home (well known to members of UBC's Letters Club because Mrs. Lefevre, a poet, loved to entertain them) was sold to F. Ronald Graham, the well–known and tough–minded Montreal stockbroker. He was a widower with several children who married a widow, also with several children. They moved to the Lefevre house after an architect had been instructed to remodel it so that 750 people could comfortably pass through it to the gardens. Barbecue and food services were to cater for garden parties of 3,000.

As Mrs. McKeen's health began to deteriorate and the head of one femur crumbled, it became clear that a smaller home on one level was needed. Accordingly, the senator purchased the house built by one of the Gibson brothers (the loggers) on West 33rd Avenue. The senator's agent met with me to tell me of the wild ideas then in the air for disposal of the waterfront McKeen property. A syndicate wanted to tear it down in order to build high–rise homes for old people. Another group wanted it exactly as it stood for a nursing home. Finally the senator and Mrs. McKeen decided to sell the beautiful estate to St. Mark's College as a residence for women students. Suddenly half a dozen people told me that they hoped to be made dean of women of an otherwise austere men's college! The rumours were circulating at a dizzy pace until one morning a distraught treasurer of a large company, who shall remain nameless, called me. I agreed to have lunch with him at the University Club downtown and there I heard a most bizarre story of fund–raising to meet the basic price of $105,000.

The unhappy company treasurer told me how he had sweated to get a down payment of $50,000 together, only to learn that to house students in the residence—25 or 30 of them—the fire regulations called for expenditures equal to far more than the entire purchase price.

I told him that he was lucky in a way to have hit the brick wall so soon, and that UBC would buy the property from him, so that he could then sleep at night. I had researched the financial situation in which St. Mark's College found itself. It was a pitiful reflection of the ambitions of an aging Archbishop. The interest on his building's loan was paid by the excellent fathers of the college signing over their monthly cheques. To this day I do not know how Father Oliver and Father Kerr and others of the college managed to live.

I was now stuck with the property and had to move fast, as I had no authority to commit UBC. On a beautiful Sunday evening in summer, just as the sun was about to set, I picked up Hon. Nathan Nemetz, chairman of the board of governors, from his home nearby and drove him down to the McKeen house. He had never seen anything like it, and could not believe it was for sale for $105,000. Within a few days UBC purchased this magnificent property to prevent its permanent alienation from the campus. I undertook the search for an "angel" to repay UBC the amount of the sale.

Strangely, Cecil and Ida Green of Dallas, Texas, decided to visit UBC about this time—midsummer, when the weather was gorgeous. I had visited them in the south when I was lecturing in Galveston at the University of Texas Medical School (where I had interned in 1941).

On two earlier occasions the Greens had come to the campus, but were so baffled by the post–war development and the feeling that they knew no one any more that they went away unannounced. This time I lodged them in the Royal Suite at the Faculty Club and one morning after breakfast took them down to see the McKeen house and grounds. The view of the Tantalus Glacier up Howe Sound was spectacular. Freighters and sail boats were moving in Burrard Inlet, and the Forbidden Plateau on Vancouver Island was crystal clear. We went through the house in detail and then began to walk west along the cliff towards the president's house. Suddenly Cecil stopped and said, "Ida, that's the stump on which Henry Gunning and I used to eat our lunch when we were engineering students surveying the campus in summer school."

I thought they were both going to weep. Suddenly their long–dashed hopes of 1929 of living in Vancouver came flooding back to them: there was a very poignant silence. When they had recovered, I said that if they were interested the university was looking for someone who would relieve them of the debt incurred in buying this three–acre estate, and who would consider making it the headquarters for all alumni, to which they could return year after year. Then no one need ever feel himself a stranger on coming home to their alma mater.

Cecil looked wistfully up Howe Sound and said, "I see." Ida looked at him with much understanding and said in a mock–authoritarian voice: "See here, Green, don't procrastinate. You do what Bill suggests. He's right. You'll never find anything like this again."

So by noon it was all decided. Ida said: "Look here, Green. We're a–goin' to Alaska and if anything should happen to us this plan wouldn't come off, so you just go right upstairs and you telegraph that lawyer of yours and tell him you're putting $200,000 into this right now. It'll be the best investment you ever made." He replied, "Yes, Miss Ida."

And so it has proven to be. The alumni has had an unrivalled home. In accordance with Mrs. Green's wishes, the entire lower level of the house was given over to the Faculty Women's Club for their painting, music and other forms of activity. The main building became what Cecil Green hoped it would be: a town–meets–gown centre, so necessary when the campus is seven miles from the centre of the city.

The coach house was transformed for the Resources Council under the Greens' good friend Alfred Adams. The very extensive gardens have been greatly simplified and it is hoped that they and the Graham gardens may be put under the UBC Botanical Gardens.

The gift of the Graham house to UBC took place on the death of F. Ronald Graham. The Grahams had been good neighbours from the day they arrived on Point Grey. One of their first good works was to clean up the mess and destruction left across Marine Drive by the pre–war washout. The "Graham Gates" to the campus were constructed, much stonework was done at their expense along the side of the Anglican College property, and planting on that part of the campus began. The rhododendrons and azaleas there date from this time.

Garden parties for visiting congresses and for distinguished university visitors were given with a free hand. At other times their yacht was used, as Senator McKeen's had been, to give UBC visitors a view of Howe Sound and its islands and mountains.

It became obvious to Mr. Graham's physician, Dr. R.E. McKechnie, that circulatory problems were rapidly increasing in his patient. Yet Mr. Graham was determined to be host to all his children and grandchildren once more over the Christmas season, at his Banff home high in the Rockies. Because of my years in the Air Force doing work on oxygen at high altitudes, Dr. McKechnie asked what I would suggest. Eventually we had a number of high–pressure oxygen cylinders loaded on the train. Each could deliver oxygen through a reducing valve in order to fill up a slender "jump bottle" designed originally for parachutists. Mr. Graham kept this little flagon in his gown pocket, with a tube attached to a Queen Anne collar affair, which gave him plenty of oxygen as the train climbed up into the Rockies. They all had a happy Christmas, though clearly it was to be their last at Banff.

I encouraged Mr. Graham on returning to Marine Drive to walk about his home—largely on the deck of the upper floor—using his oxygen continuously. I saw a great deal of him at night or on weekends when Dr. McKechnie was away. The conversations used to be incredible. If Mr. Graham rolled on top of his oxygen line he would start to talk of going to town to make a little money. I would assure him this was impossible, because he had made it all and there was no more to be had in the city. He sometimes told me of his early history and of leaving school to become a messenger boy to support his widowed mother. He swore then he would never be poor again: I think he perhaps over–did it. He was reputedly ruthless in his business dealings in Montreal, but in Vancouver he lived the life of a retired seigneur—full of help and bounty for endless musicians and artists. Movie actors and actresses from Hollywood were to be found at the parties put on by the Grahams or in their absence by their hospitable children.

One evening, while looking out over the mountains, Ronnie started to talk about England. We soon got on to Oxford, Cambridge, the "establishment," and so on; he had just been reading *The Anatomy of Britain*. He reached over to his bedside table saying, "You could use this in your business," and handed me this very terse analysis of the power structure in the United Kingdom. He joked about what an organizational chart would contain for Canada and the United States.

About 6:30 one evening I was at dinner when Helen Graham telephoned in alarm. She said, "Bill, please come over quickly. Ronnie's gone blue." I asked her to have the nurse prepare a syringe of adrenalin and I shot down the two blocks in a hurry.

I gave him a walloping dose of adrenalin into his hip muscles, whereupon he called out "God Almighty." The nurse corrected him brusquely: "No, it's Doctor Gibson." Quick as a flash old Ronnie shot back, "I'm sorry, Doctor," and then smiled benignly to all at the bedside.

As the clock ran down, Dr. McKechnie stayed with his patient over–night. On a Sunday morning at 5:00 he telephoned to say it was all over. He asked if the university, which was to have the great house and grounds, would allow Ronnie's ashes to be buried there. I said at once that I believed they would, so at 7:00 a.m. I called President Macdonald to confirm this. I never heard a president react so fast on a Sunday morning. He thought I was pulling his leg at first, but as I described the situation to him he began to realize what a great gift UBC had received. He confirmed that we would welcome Mrs. Graham's request that Ronnie's ashes be placed in the garden.

In the ensuing struggle to see whose department would be placed in the Graham House, the main point of the gift was forgotten: the last remaining piece of land, alienated from the defence preserve in 1912, had returned to the fold. With Cecil Green Park's three acres, and the Graham three acres that now belonged to UBC in perpetuity, we could stop worrying about some uncertain future use of our front door on Howe Sound.

Once the UBC Alumni offices moved into the upper floors of the McKeen house, we renamed the three-acre property Cecil Green Park. The main floor became a busy social centre, with a Young Alumni Club, seminars, lectures and wedding receptions filling a busy timetable.

Soon the Greens came forward with a new benefaction: $600,000 to endow visiting professorships for the whole university. I was not long in the chair of the president's committee on this matter when I insisted that, situated as we were on the western extremity of the continent, we had to fight the factor of geographical isolation if we were to combat intellectual isolation. Thus, instead of one visiting professor per year, I suggested that UBC needed as many gifted intellects, as visitors, as we could finance each year. The committee agreed. As a result, UBC has had a constant stream of world-class lecturers who would spend from one to two weeks delivering their particular message or research findings to our campus.

At first the Greens wondered if this method was viable, but over the years I think they came to realize that we were trying to give our students a taste of many cultures and views of the world, both contemporary and historical. These visitors brought something of great value to the community as well. Again, I was in trouble for disturbing the status quo as I sought to arrange public appearances of Cecil Green visiting professors before the Vancouver Institute. This body had been put together as an amalgam of small societies by the late President Wesbrook in 1915. After World War II groups still met (though attendance was small) on Saturday nights in a small classroom in the Buchanan Building, amid blackboards that never seemed to be cleaned. With the completion of the Woodward Centre, adjacent to the Woodward Library, there were modern rear-screen projection facilities and seats for 500. After a little hesitation the Vancouver Institute, under the inspired direction of Mrs. Bel Nemetz, moved to Woodward Centre and has never looked back. Five other lecture halls can be connected by television to the main theatre, so that 1,500 can enjoy major lectures, such as those by Dr. Lewis Thomas and Jessica Mitford.

CHAPTER THIRTY–FOUR

The Founding of Green College, Oxford

I found an entry in my diary for 1976 concerning the telephone call that interrupted my siesta one Sunday in Vancouver. The high–spirited English voice was hard to understand at first, but as I became fully awake I realized it was Sir Richard Doll speaking from Oxford. I had known him for some years in his capacity as Regius professor of medicine at Oxford, largely, as I recall, in connection with the hope I had that the history of medicine could be taught or studied at Oxford and financed by the Wellcome Trust on whose advisory panel I was serving.

Sir Richard began the conversation by wondering if I would ask my friend Cecil Green for a million dollars for Oxford University! When I brashly asked "Why?," I was told of the old problem of Oxford students in the last three years (the clinical years) of their six–year medical course being turned out of their respective colleges to make way for succeeding waves of undergraduates.

I reminded Sir Richard that in 1937 I was one of eight medical students allowed to stay in residence at Oxford for the clinical course offered for six months, with what turned out to be tutorial supervision at the Radcliffe Infirmary. I think he was surprised to learn that, so long ago, the Nuffield professors in the clinical fields, along with Prof. Florey in pathology and Prof. Burn in pharmacology, had given us such a wonderful condensed six–month credit course in Oxford.

As the telephone conversation continued, I explained to Richard that I really could not ask Cecil for one million dollars to found a college of any kind. Richard began to wonder if I was still a loyal Oxford man, so I hastened to tell him that the Greens had built a veritable skyscraper for the graduate school at M.I.T. in Boston, and were in the process of doubling the size of the Stanford library, not to mention the building of a large hospital for the Scripps Metabolic Clinic in La Jolla, California. Because there was dead silence on the other end of the line, I added, "But I'll be glad to ask Cecil for a million **pounds** in order to get the derelict Radcliffe Observatory building back into use for medical studies." "Oh I say!" shouted Richard. I told him I would pursue this concept at once, if he could allow me a few days.

Later that fateful afternoon, I sat down to plan an approach to Cecil and Ida Green in Dallas, Texas. I felt flying down to Dallas to see them might be interpreted as inappropriate pressure on my good friends. I was determined not to ask them for money, ever, but to try to act as an informal investment advisor, pointing out good projects that they might consider at their leisure.

So I assembled and classified all the facts bearing on the project. I must say I had to skate quickly over thin ice, since the details of the University of Oxford's involvement in the proposed new project were, to my mind, not entirely clear. I was sure, however, that Sir Richard must have all this in hand or he would not have called me by telephone. By midnight I had written eight pages. Early Monday morning I posted my airmail letter to the unsuspecting Greens.

As soon as I had posted the letter, I called Cecil to say I had been up most of the night writing a long letter to them. He said, "Oh! Tell me more." I went on to ask if he would promise that he and his wife would be sitting down when they opened it. He said, "Oh, a block–buster eh?" I did not disclose its contents.

It must have been on the following Friday that he called to say that they had read my letter several times and were going to book passage by air to Oxford to see this golden opportunity. Neither Cecil nor Ida had ever seen Oxford, though they had often travelled in the British Isles, near Manchester, where he was born.

The rest is history. Their visit to Oxford was marvellously arranged by Richard and Joan Doll, with dinners and luncheons at which the outstanding scholars in Oxford's relevant fields were introduced. After a whirlwind visit the sum of £1 million was promised. An equal amount was given a short time later when, as I recall, the Dolls were asked to fly out to Dallas on the Concorde for further discussions. Some discussions!

My mail became heavier by the week as Sir Richard sent more and more building plans out to Vancouver for my information. I have never been kept so well (and so happily) informed on any endeavour as on the building of Green College.

The factors that transformed an idea into a happy reality were the enthusiasm of the Greens, the friendliness of the Dolls and their successors, the Waltons, and the excellent group of fellows, students and staff attracted to the college. Over and over again Cecil Green has remarked on this wonderful ingredient—friendship—and with good reason. On Lord Walton's retirement, Sir Crispin Tickell was appointed Warden. He took up his duties as soon as he completed his term at the United Nations, where he rendered great service during the Desert War crisis.

After Ida Green died of leukaemia, Cecil began to think about his alma mater even more seriously. He was fond of saying that after seeing most of the world's great cities, he concluded that his home town, Vancouver, was the best situated in the world. The sparkling sea, the mild climate and the mountain background made a great combination. He therefore decided to build an Oxford–type college where graduate students from around the world might come into residence. He wanted the students to be closely associated with the productive and acute minds of faculty members. The target was for 150 such students in residence and several dozen tutors who are already in teaching and research in the university. There are community members and honorary fellows as well. Laying the cornerstone was done on May 19, 1993, and September was set for the opening and for the celebration of Cecil's 92 years of a fascinating and useful life.

CHAPTER THIRTY-FIVE

Wilder Penfield as a Physiologist and Pathologist

Perhaps, gentle reader, I may here intercalate my paper read to the McGill students' Osler Society at the Montreal Neurological Institute, January 26, 1983.

Mr. President, Ladies and Gentlemen,

It is an honour on Dr. Penfield's birthday to be asked to address you on the development of this great McGill institution. Having arrived on its opening day, September 27, 1934, as by far the youngest of its research fellows, after one year of medical studies, I am erroneously thought to be its omniscient historian. Perhaps, however, because I was treated by Dr. and Mrs. Penfield as the fifth child in their family, in sickness and in health, I may have learned, at close quarters, something of their hopes and fears for the institute, its ups and downs, and its truly great contributions to healing and to neurological science the world over.

I often think of Louis Pasteur's dictum, "Fortune favours the prepared mind." Much of what I will tell you today concerns the preparation of Wilder Penfield's mind. Let no one think that this magnificent institute was some felicitous accident, nor was it an automatic product of the times.

On that auspicious opening day in 1934, with a beaming Mayor Camillien Houde rubbing shoulders with Sir Herbert Holt and the chancellor, Sir Edward Beatty, and with Harvey Cushing and Gordon Holmes describing the brain's unsolved mysteries, Wilder Penfield spoke with feeling of the debt he owed to two great teachers:

> For any constructive ideas that I may have contributed I have to thank the guiding influence of the men under whom it has been my good fortune to work. Most important was the initial influ-

> ence of Sir Charles Sherrington. In his laboratory at Oxford to search for the hidden truths of neurology became a habit of mind, a colouring to all of one's thought. There was also the early influence of McGill's great teacher Sir William Osler. Following him on the ward I discovered something of the human idealism and romance of medicine at the bedside. It is unnecessary to elaborate the importance of that contact. I see many others here today who also belong to the free masonry of the Osler tradition.

Penfield went up to Oxford in 1913 as a Rhodes scholar after completing a liberal arts education at Princeton University, where he had been an outstanding athlete and one of the group of students urging Woodrow Wilson to run for the presidency of the United States. With the Great War on, Sherrington's small class was composed largely of Rhodes scholars from distant countries. Wilbur Davison, later dean of Duke University's new medical school, and Emil Holman, later professor of surgery at Stanford, were in the same class.

Penfield found Sherrington to be a bird–like man, short in stature but mighty in mind, with a bright eye and an international reputation. His Silliman Lectures at Yale, published in 1906 under the title *The Integrative Action of the Nervous System*, were to the brain what William Harvey's *De motu cordis* (1628) was to the heart.

Strangely, Sherrington was a pathologist strayed into physiology. Like Osler he had been a pupil of Berlin's great Rudolf Virchow, the father of cellular pathology. Sherrington loved to tell of his visits to the Reichstag with Virchow to listen to the threats and rantings of the professor's arch–enemy Bismarck.

Wilder Penfield could not have chosen a better time to study at Oxford. His gifted teacher changed the medical world through his writings and his disciples. Not only did Sherrington win the Nobel Prize; three of his pupils were Nobel laureates also: Eccles and Granit in neurophysiology, and Florey, the Rhodes scholar who made possible the clinical use of penicillin. When Sherrington died in his 95th year his greatest distinction, the Order of Merit, was soon bestowed on Wilder Penfield, I am happy to say.

To go back to the Oxford of 1915, it is necessary to recall that histology—the microscopic study of the tissues of the body—was part of physiology. Thus, Penfield found in Sherrington's laboratory an accomplished and jovial microscopist, Harry Carleton, a pioneer in staining techniques for nervous tissue. He was always experimenting with new methods which he later described in his textbook of histological technique. When Dr. Penfield sent me off to Oxford, 20 years later, I found Carleton still keenly interested in new silver methods. Those which I brought back from Spain in 1936 fascinated him and he spent hours looking at my slides.

If ever there was a group of Oxford students enjoying day-long tutorials it was the 1915 class in physiology. Sherrington, himself a poet, loved to quote Keats—"the surgeon poet"—and Shakespeare to his students as they gave their anaesthetized cats a "breather" and everything stopped for tea. When his medical friend, Robert Bridges the Poet Laureate, published the "Testament of Beauty," Sherrington would quote long passages of it to the unsuspecting students whom he was assisting. In 1935 I found that the "lab boys" who anaesthetized the cats in an ether-filled side-room were not quoting poetry, but were singing, in wildly robust fashion, revival hymns learned in the Boys' Brigade. This was an allowable respite from the stern disciplinarian, the major domo George Cox who had been Sherrington's original lab boy in Liverpool days. Cox frequently recited to me a list of neurologists he had taught such as Harvey Cushing, Wilder Penfield, Denny-Brown, Alex Forbes and Hugh Cairns. In time Cox was succeeded by Giles (pronounced "Joils"). I had no sooner arrived in Carleton's histology laboratory than Giles accosted me thus: "Yew tell that goi Penfield I haint forgiven 'im fer gettin' me to sniff that bottle uv pyridine wot 'e was usin' in them silver stains." In 1935 Sherrington retired. I inherited his little operating room as a place to study my silver stains under high illumination, and his scrub sink, which was about the size of an inverted mortar board.

Amid all these attributes of higher education what was it that Wilder Penfield absorbed at Oxford? He may have been surprised, initially, to learn that medical science was in the making there, and that it was not all cut-and-dried as North American students believed. The workings of the nervous system were being unravelled by Sherrington the great teacher—a human biologist with an early training at Cambridge under Michael Foster. There, C.S.S. had worked in a laboratory surrounded by such fellow students as Horace Darwin; William Bateson, who gave us the word "genetics"; W.B. Hardy, in low temperature physics; Almroth Wright, the pathologist who later taught Alexander Fleming; William McDougall, the psychologist; George Adami, the pathologist who came out to McGill; Humphrey Davy Rolleston, a future Regius professor of medicine; W.H. Gaskell, the pioneer in electrocardiography; and closest friend of all, Frank Wesbrook, pathologist and later dean of medicine at Minnesota and founding president of the University of British Columbia.

As professor at the Brown Institution in London and as professor at Liverpool until 1913, the Sherrington that Penfield and his fellow Americans found at Oxford was the most sophisticated and yet the most informal medical scientist in Britain. In the 10 years between the Silliman Lectures at Yale and his appointment to Oxford, Sherrington had published 77 scientific papers! It was not his accomplishments which made him the right man in the right place as far as these privileged students were concerned—but rather his attitude to learning and to research. This is best summed up by Alan Gregg of the Rockefeller Foundation, writing years later. Gregg had asked Sherrington what Oxford stood for in education. The reply was a classic:

> After some hundreds of years of experience we think that we have learned here in Oxford how to teach what is known. But now with the undeniable upsurge of scientific research, we cannot continue to rely on the mere fact that we have learned how to teach what is known. We must learn how to teach **the best attitude** to what is **not yet** known. This also may take centuries to acquire but we cannot escape this new challenge, nor do we want to.

In 1917 Sherrington wrote to H.A.L. Fisher, minister of education in the War Cabinet, "stating the urgent needs of the university for a parliamentary grant." Years later, as Warden of New College, Fisher told C.S.S. "The claim that you set out was so strong that I had very little difficulty in convincing the Chancellor of the Exchequer and the (War) Cabinet that parliament ought to come to the rescue of the ancient universities."

All this suggests the stature of the man with whom Penfield was to spend two precious formative years. The breadth of Sherrington's interests may suggest itself to you when I tell you that the record shows that he was the "best benefactor in modern times" of the British Museum in gifts of incunabula and other rare books. He contributed also to the Osler Library here at McGill.

An echo of Sherrington's reply to Gregg's enquiry was heard on the McGill campus in 1922 when C.S.S. and his pupil Harvey Cushing opened the New Biological Building. C.S.S. concluded his address: "Do not, o my brothers, forget research. Science calls us all to it—and the call is from humanity as well." Surely this was Sherrington's spiritual legacy to Wilder Penfield.

Wartime service by W.P. as a hospital volunteer in France was followed by the two final years of the medical course at Johns Hopkins, and this by a surgical residency at the Brigham at Harvard. Peter Bent Brigham, like Johns Hopkins, was a merchant who believed in medical science as a harbinger of health and happiness for mankind. Harvey Cushing had just returned to Harvard Medical School from the war, and with Colonel Thomas Salmon, Professor Lewis Weed of cerebrospinal fluid fame, and other U.S. Army physicians, was trying desperately to gain support for "The Establishment of a National Institute for the Investigation of Disorders of the Nervous System." Cushing with great foresight had put this before John D. Rockefeller's General Education Board in May of 1917, just before Cushing sailed with Base Hospital No. 5 for France. Two years later, with the war over, the project was still being reviewed to death by foundations, the armed forces and the federal government. All the while the neuropsychiatric and neurosurgical cases were being dispersed to the far corners of the United States and a great opportunity to study disorders of the nervous system was lost. Cushing had originally hoped that his teacher of Liverpool days, Sir Charles Sherrington, could be induced to join such an institute, post–war.

It is unlikely that a struggling surgical intern at the Brigham was cognizant of his chief's plans for a national institute that was to be or not to be, depending upon a large number of imponderables. It was, alas, ahead of its time. Just before the Montreal Neurological Institute opened in 1934, Cushing, who was to give one of the opening addresses, asked Alan Gregg of the Rockefeller Foundation if the M.N.I. was an echo of the 1917 proposal. Gregg replied:

> Your account of the project to start a National Institute of Neurology was new to me, and so far as I know, did not have a traceable connection with the development at Montreal...Thus it was not merely a request from Penfield and Martin [McGill's dean of medicine] coinciding with a special desire on our part to help neurology which decided the matter: there was a conviction that it is men that matter, especially in a new undertaking. I thought Penfield a good bet (and I think so now) and my colleagues agreed. I could wish that the end–result of your address [at the opening of the M.N.I.] would be a heightened appreciation of the meaning of persons—of the importance of finding them, training them thoroughly, and backing them generously and thus liberating their energies.

I wanted to document this for you since much nonsense has been talked in some cities about our origins here.

To retrace our steps to the autumn of 1919, we find the Penfields with a son and a daughter, in Oxford. W.P. was soon immersed in neurophysiological research with another Sherrington pupil, Cuthbert Bazett, on decerebrate rigidity and in neurohistology with the ever–friendly Harry Carleton. "The professor"—Sir Charles—was, alas, obliged, as president of the Royal Society, to travel frequently to London. He told me that sometimes he had to go to London twice in one day, so onerous were his presidential duties. Penfield's Rhodes Scholarship ran out after its third year, but C.S.S. sponsored him for a Beit Memorial Fellowship.

The year 1920 found W.P. at Queen Square's National Hospital for the Paralysed and Epileptic. With the help of Gordon Holmes in the clinics and of Godwin Greenfield in the pathology laboratory, our Beit Research Fellow made good use of his opportunities. As a result he arrived back in the United States with an excellent clinical background in neurology and competence in neuropathology, both gross and microscopic.

There was lacking, however, to his way of thinking, the glue—or should I say "glia"—to hold clinical neurology and neurophysiology together in any clinic. It is hard for us to realize that research was almost a hobby in hospitals, and W.P. was listened to by administrators as if he were talking a foreign language.

The early years of practice at the Presbyterian Hospital in New York were trying times. One bright ray of hope was to be found in the benevolent Professor Allen Whipple, a master surgeon and a productive thinker. He opened doors for enquiring minds. I hope we shall never forget in this institute what he did to permit a hard–pressed clinician to go for six–month periods of study to Madrid in 1924 and to Breslau in 1928. What he did for Wilder Penfield was to be repeated over and over again here in Montreal where our director opened doors for dozens of us to new opportunities in teaching, research and patient care.

The six months in Madrid I would view as one of the major turning points in Wilder Penfield's plans; not just for himself, but for neurological science in general. Hidden away for centuries behind the Pyrenees were enquiring minds, but from the days of the Inquisition there was a stagnant air of authoritarianism which suffocated all but the most gifted and most determined.

In Ramón y Cajal, Spain found its Leonardo—a wayward but enquiring youth of Aragonese stock. Through Sherrington, as foreign secretary of the Royal Society of London, through von Kölliker and Krause in Germany and Van Gehüchten in Belgium, Cajal came to the top in the world of microscopic anatomy, especially that of the nervous system. He richly deserved his Nobel Prize awarded in 1906. His greatest protagonist, Charles Sherrington, had to wait until 1932 for his Nobel Prize. By then he had been nominated by 130 scientists!

In marked contrast to Cajal the peasant was the gifted and nobly born Pio del Río–Hortega from Valladolid. Like Sherrington, he was interested in poetry and art, but his pre–eminent devotion was to neuropathology. His work on the oligodendroglia—the linemen on the power cables of the nervous system—was revolutionary. His experimental work on the microglia—the scavengers of the brain tissue—was unique, and we still speak of them as Hortega cells.

How fortunate was "el doctor Penfield" therefore to be able to work with Don Pio with revolutionary new silver stains devised in Madrid, but almost totally ignored abroad. The straight morphological approach by Cajal to the most complicated of all the body's systems was a revelation but it was static. Río–Hortega's techniques were throwing open a whole new chapter in brain disease, and were dynamic. Galen may have said that he had "seen a wounded brain healed." That was easy. It was left to Río–Hortega and Wilder Penfield to show **how** it healed.

With this precious information in his possession, Wilder returned to New York for another four years. He clearly was over–doing Osler's policy of a "quinquennial brain–dusting" since by 1928 he was over–seas, studying this time with Otfrid Foerster in Breslau. There he saw a neurologist and self–trained neurosurgeon removing the post–traumatic brain scars that seemed to cause seizures in war veterans. W.P. has recorded his pilgrim's progress: "As I sat there at my bench in Breslau, I was free at last to turn back to neurophysiology, to study the living processes that lead to epileptic discharge and to study the changing circulation of the brain."

At the same time, his magnum opus, *Cytology and Cellular Pathology of the Nervous System* was taking shape. Though this three–volume set, beautifully produced and including Penfield's finest personal work, did not come off the press until 1932, its early planning and editing further clarified Penfield's thinking on the kind of institute he must develop. Its form and function were his daily preoccupation. But "Where?" was the question.

There is no need to review here the long and short of the many opportunities presented to a discerning medical scholar on his return home to New York. We used to discuss the realms of the "what might have been" openings. They were always on someone else's terms, not to say turf. Any number of alleged openings existed, but they all fell short of the broad spectrum approach sought by W.P., and they all sought to use him, not to serve his great plan for the study of the brain and its problems. The only salty phrase that I recall from his recounting of those days was the then "corrosive influences of the New York Neurological Institute" built in the 1920s. This was no reflection on the neurosurgeons there, Charles Elsberg and Byron Stookey, who were always supportive. The problem was at an organizational level, that most lethal plane of medical politics! All these factors were important guideposts to a future director of an institute.

It was against this background that Edward Archibald, the uncrowned king of surgery at McGill, entered the picture. I sometimes wonder if McGill really knew what a genius they had in Archibald—cultured, a scholar strayed into surgery, perfectly bilingual, father of thoracoplasty in 1912, neurosurgeon of great sagacity, and with a realistic appreciation of its problems. In his large volume on the brain in the *American Practice of Surgery* (1909) Archibald wrote: "There is perhaps no department of surgery which is so difficult and at the same time so thankless as that of the brain."

Above all, Edward Archibald had perspective because he knew the history of his subject. When describing to students the problem of mounting intracranial pressure, he always referred to the case of the beggar in Paris who went about asking people to place their contributions in the top part of his upturned skull which had been removed and which he extended confidently to prospective donors. Why his bony cap had been excised no one knew, but probably, as the medical literature prefers to say, "it was removed in another city." At all events, as Archibald recounts:

> And he would frequently permit experiments to be made for a small trifle of money. Upon gently pressing the dura mater with one's finger, he suddenly perceived, as it were, a thousand sparks before his eyes; and upon pressing a little more forcibly, his eyes lost all their sight; by pressing the hand still more strongly on the dura mater he fell down in a deep sleep, which was attended with all the symptoms of a slight apoplexy, merely by this pressure with the hand, which was no sooner removed than he gradually recovered from the symptoms as they were brought on, the apoplectic systems first vanishing, then the lethargy, and

> lastly the blindness, all his senses recovering their former perfection.

The ever–altruistic Archibald wanted to hand over all neurosurgery at the Royal Victoria Hospital in Montreal to a younger man, and in June of 1927 Archibald visited Wilder Penfield in New York. He was possibly over–whelmed by the plans outlined by W.P. Archibald commenced negotiations which brought Penfield here in 1928, with his "right hand" William Vernon Cone, to found an institute—so far unauthorized, unplanned as to detail, and certainly unsung. In six short years this institute in which we meet today was opened.

I have already indicated "Why" and "Where." The only question remaining—and a large one—was "How?"

If Harvey Cushing could not convince the Rockefeller group in 1917 and again in 1919 that a neurological sciences centre was needed, and his pupil Wilder Penfield in 1929 could not do so, how was this desired goal to be reached? The key to it all materialized in 1931 in the person of a new broom at the Rockefeller Foundation in New York, Alan Gregg. Who was he and what did he do?

His life has been gracefully chronicled by Penfield in that most satisfying biography entitled *The Difficult Art of Giving: The Epic of Alan Gregg*. As a first–year Harvard medical student aged 19, Gregg had been exposed to such exotic minds as Freud and Jung at the camp in the Adirondacks owned by the medical brothers Putnam and by Henry Pickering Bowditch. One of Bowditch's physiology students at Harvard was Alexander Forbes, who in time went on to study with Sherrington in Liverpool. Eventually Forbes found himself teaching physiology to his young Harvard friend from the Adirondack camp, and soon thereafter Gregg joined Forbes in a research project in neurophysiology.

By 1931 Gregg was in the saddle as director of the Division of Medical Sciences in the New York headquarters of the Rockefeller Foundation. From McGill's perspective, Gregg was the right man in the right place. Any applicant for a grant who had been associated intimately with Sherrington, Osler, Ramón y Cajal, Río–Hortega, Gordon Holmes and Foerster, was surely on the inside track with Gregg the one–time neurophysiologist. One informal meeting with Penfield in New York concerning everything but grant applications was followed up by a visit by Gregg to Montreal.

This wonderful visit by the scintillating Gregg made it clear to McGill what the university, for its part, would have to achieve in funding for capital and operating. That day has been well described by Dr. Penfield in his autobiography. What no one seems to have recorded, however, is Dean C.F. Martin's humorous account of the incredible 48 hours of fund raising which he personally undertook. When I finally left the institute in 1947 I was given a dinner by my colleagues at the Faculty Club and to my great surprise and pleasure Dean Martin came to tell "the true history of the founding of the M.N.I." His account was preceded by a musical number which brought the house down. Professor Boris Babkin, one of Pavlov's brilliant pupils, played on the balalaika a composition which he had written at age 17. The title of this delightful number was appropriately "The Pussy Cat Gavotte."

With this warm up over, Dr. Martin launched into his description of his whirlwind campaign to raise the one million dollars required for operating funds for 20 years. First, Dr. Martin went to see his old friend Camillien Houde, the indestructible mayor of Montreal. He told His Worship that if the wife of the mayor or any alderman had a brain tumour she would have to go to Philadelphia in future. McGill was in danger of losing Penfield. Then a few case histories were rattled off to Houde, who said brightly, "Dr. Martin, I want you to come with me to City Council in a few minutes and tell them this." The dean wisely deferred to Camillien but agreed to accompany him into the Council Chamber.

As the meeting began, Houde explained who their distinguished visitor was, and said they would amend the agenda to discuss at once a medical emergency that concerned the whole of Montreal. In a few seconds Houde had the aldermen spellbound as he threatened them with having to take their wives with brain tumours to Philadelphia. "Mon Dieu," they cried, "Philadelphie!"

The mayor told them that a poor woman came all the way from Vancouver to see Penfield because she had gone blind. The good doctor had taken out both eyes, washed them, put them back, and now the woman could see—and she prayed for him every night!

Soon the dean's remaining hair was standing on end as Houde demanded an immediate vote of $400,000 spread over 20 years. There was instant unanimity, so Martin rushed to Quebec City to ask Premier Taschereau for an equal amount. Taschereau blew up on learning of the Montreal City Council's pledge. They were millions of dollars in debt to the province, he shouted, and to hell with them! So Dr. Martin looked out of the window and saw a large limousine and chauffeur–in–waiting, and commented on the cost of keeping large cars and 24–hour chauffeurs, having one himself in Montreal. He neglected to mention that he personally had a Rolls–Royce, thinking this a bit abrasive. Reluctantly the premier settled on $15,000 per year for 20 years, a total of $300,000.

Thereupon Martin entrained for Montreal, having summoned an emergency meeting of the governors of the Royal Victoria Hospital. When all were seated in the board room he locked the door and asked that $300,000 in pledges be put on the table. In a remarkably short time these gentlemen got the message and the dean got the money. There were, of course, families such as the Refords, Hodgsons and Stewarts who gave generously to the building fund from the beginning.

In the darkest days of the Great Depression, the detailed preparation and eventual construction proceeded, with many hard decisions to be made along the way. But on the great day, September 27, 1934, all was spick and span and we crowded into the foyer to witness the opening ceremonies which brought to fruition almost 20 years of imaginative planning and teamwork.

Little wonder that Alan Gregg could later say at the second Foundation of the M.N.I. in 1953:

> If I were asked to name a single grant that the Medical Sciences Division of the [Rockefeller] Foundation has made since 1931 that I consider ideal in purpose, in performance, in local response and in national and international influence, and in the character of our relationships maintained from the very beginning, I would say without a moment's hesitation the grant to the Neurological Institute of McGill University.

As we contemplate the inspired concept that has characterized this undertaking, I think I can hear Wilder Penfield saying, with Tennyson: "I am part of all that I have met; yet experience is an arch wherethrough gleams that untravelled world."

It is in this untravelled world of research that we hope this institute will "adventure on" for centuries to come.

CHAPTER THIRTY-SIX

Lectureships and Broadcasts

My life seems, at times, to have been one long series of lectures: to university students in courses, but also lectures designed for specific formal occasions, often to a wider audience than just medical listeners.

One of the first of these was the Rhoads lecture given at Boston University memorializing a brilliant medical student by that name who had died before graduation. Of a choice of subjects offered, the committee thought that the students would like to hear about scientific discoveries made by medical undergraduates, some of them in Boston. I could not believe the size of the audience that gathered. There were students, professors, clinicians, librarians and others packed into the auditorium. After the adjournment, the professor of medicine took a group of us to his home where we took turns playing the piano and singing into the early hours of the morning.

Soon the news spread up to McGill, where the undergraduate Osler Society invited me to do likewise. So on March 27, 1958, I addressed the very formal annual banquet of students and their teachers at the Ritz-Carlton in Montreal. The menu and toasts were a knock-out. To see my teachers again, all bearing their age well, was an unexpected pleasure, with the majestic Jonathan Meakins, retired dean and army general, and Wilder Penfield, still teaching neurosurgeons world wide, in great form. Osler's nephew, Dr. Willie Francis, slipped into the menu an old phrase from one of Sir William's little day-books: "Experience is not to be measured by years but by the use one made of one's opportunities."

The lantern slides carried most of my lecture, as usual. One student, Allan Sherwin, wrote to me afterward that he had enjoyed hearing from a neurological researcher, since his student research was on allergic encephalitis. He has since gone on to a distinguished research career. The annual report of the Osler Society recorded that "A quartet composed of Dr. Gibson and three of his former associates at the Montreal Neurological Institute added to the fun of the evening." We had sung the ditty I had written years before, "The Old Dilantin Pill," set to the tune of "My Darling Nelly Grey." We sang only the English version. (I had composed the French, German and Spanish verses as I waited for the traffic to clear every morning at the crowded Bondi Junction on my way to the University of Sydney.)

An early McGill College (Vancouver) graduate, Colonel Harry Logan, on hearing of my lecture, wrote to say that when he was a Rhodes scholar at Oxford he was reminded by Lady Osler of her husband's advice to his students: "First, get an education; then a library; and then, and only then, a nursery."

Thanks to Sir Charles Sherrington, I became interested in Christopher Wren, his early work at Oxford on blood transfusion and his intravenous injections in dogs. His beautiful drawings of the human brain and its major components are startling in their clarity. Gradually I built up a great deal of information about him, and when asked to give the Monckton–Copeman Lecture in London, I chose as my subject "The Biomedical Interests of Christopher Wren." The lecture was given in London at the Wellcome Institute of the History of Medicine—the mecca of historians of medicine and science. I had no sooner begun than the projection lantern blew all the fuses in that part of the building, and the large audience had to sit in total darkness, telling stories and gossiping to each other for a good 10 minutes. The lecture was an eye–opener for many and I was pleasantly surprised when one of my listeners arranged for me to repeat it at the Clark Institute for 17th century studies of the University of California at Los Angeles. I still think of Wren's sorrowful remark concerning his favourite dog, which was used in experiments such as the injection of white wine into the veins: "He waxed fat and was stolen."

A weekend symposium was held at the new medical faculty of the University of Washington in Seattle to hear student reports on research problems that had engaged them during their four–year course. This well–attended meeting was brought to a close with another student banquet, at which students proposing toasts were liberally heckled. However, they gave me a good hearing as I spoke on the subject of my first published book *Young Endeavour*. I suspected that Dr. Dean Crystal, my assistant in animal surgery at Oxford (where he was a Rhodes scholar), was behind the invitation to speak to the students in Seattle.

When I was next in Britain I lectured to the Abernethy Student

Society at St. Bartholomew's Hospital, one of London's oldest and most distinguished. Since the time of William Harvey, the discoverer of the blood's circulation, Cambridge students have been heavily represented there. The Great Hall is a splendidly adorned area where physicians on staff were once required to see London's poor on prescribed days of the week. My lecture tilted towards London medical students who had made significant contributions, such as Victor Horsley on the intervertebral discs, on his way to neurosurgical triumphs; James Paget, who first described calcified parasites in cadavers in cases where uncooked pork had been eaten; or Thomas "Phenomenon" Young, who on his first day's dissection of the fresh eye of a bullock showed that the intrinsic muscles of the eye could, by contraction, change the shape of the lens.

On a later occasion I spoke to the medical students at University College Hospital, London. Since Quakers were not allowed to attend Oxford or Cambridge in the middle of the 19th century, Joseph Lister, of later surgical achievements, published at University College Hospital his first student paper on the microscopic structure of the ciliary muscle of the eye, and a subsequent one on the muscles within the skin that cause one's hair to stand on end occasionally.

On a visit to Edinburgh to inspect the books in the students' ancient Royal Medical Society that had been offered for sale to Dr. Jason Hannah and his foundation in Toronto, I spoke to a pleasantly rowdy student assembly on discoveries made by their predecessors. The list was very long and the supremacy of the Edinburgh school during the 19th century could not be doubted. From Black's discovery of carbon dioxide and his pupil Rutherford's discovery of nitrogen, to the undergraduate work of William Withering, who later gave us digitalis for heart disease, the record is a long and glorious one. Alas for me, the fog was so thick that no golf was possible at St. Andrews, and the Humber car sent to transport me to the trans–Atlantic airport at Prestwick had to proceed at a snail's pace as far as Glasgow.

Since my undergraduate days in economics, banking and the mathematics of finance and investment at UBC, I had been interested in a cost/benefit analysis of medical care, but principally medical research. An invitation to address the Medical Society of London, that breath of fresh air created 200 years previously by Dr. John Coakley Lettsom of Little Jost Van Dyke Island in the British West Indies, was a chance to try out my views on the economics of research today. I was already an honorary member, thanks to Professor Peter Daniel, the neuropathologist at the Maudsley Hospital, but I thought I had better approach my subject gently. This idea was agreed to by the society's president, Dean Geraint James of the Royal Northern Hospital Medical School. Over dinner at the Athenaeum he kept shouting, "Give it to them. You've come a long way." He was an exuberant fellow, married to one of the world's best-known liver experts, Dr. Sheila Sherlock.

So I gave it to them good and proper and the response was so explosive that I could hardly believe I was speaking to a British audience. Of course we must invest in medical research if we ever hoped to cure disease! The noblest Roman of them all, Dr. Thomas Hunt, a famous rugby player at college, was most vociferous, and I wondered if he was about to lead the charge down to the Houses of Parliament.

On the strength of that reception, it occurred to me to be ready to blast a hole in the defence against medical research in North America. The opportunity came from an unusual direction: through my old Stanford University friend, Dr. Josh Lederberg, by then president of the Rockefeller University in New York. Would I speak to my fellow members of the large council of that great research institution? I was to be brief and to the point, for the donors and potential benefactors had not come out for a morning of platitudes. They wanted an "executive summary." My title was, for some of my listeners, enigmatic: "The Cost of **Not** Doing Medical Research." With lantern slides and invective I held up the mirror to what was going on in hospitals, clinics and in doctors' offices for lack of knowledge of the true basis of so many illnesses. I thought that 10 percent of the cost of illness was surely a conservative amount to be put into research to find out the causes of diseases that would make up the other 90 percent of our financial burden. I finished by saying that I would like to see a bumper sticker on every car, reading, "If you think medical research is expensive, try disease." There were howls of delight and the applause was rather unrestrained for that establishment. David Rockefeller was out of his chair like a shot to congratulate the unknown, itinerant rebel from British Columbia.

Again to London for meetings of the Wellcome Committee on medical history, but this time to give the Fitzpatrick Lecture before the Royal College of Physicians—an honour that comes rarely to one of its Fellows. The lecture was to be part of a symposium on the work and influence of Sir William Osler (1849–1919). For variety, in discussing the influence of Osler, I thought it best to offer the fellows a lecture on "Three Canadian Internationalists: Dr. Frederick Banting, Dr. Norman Bethune and Dr. Brock Chisholm." I was able to illustrate my remarks with slides made from paintings by Banting, by the H.R. MacMillan tapestry of Bethune, and the portrait of Brock Chisholm that graces the board room at the Geneva offices of the World Health Organization (of which he was the first chairman). The triumvirate had graduated from the University of Toronto's medical faculty, at whose predecessor, Trinity College Medical School, Osler had first studied. However, my emphasis was on the international views of each as they matured and gained world acclaim. Banting had told the annual meeting of the Canadian Medical Association in Victoria, B.C., that medical research was the one thing on which no customs duty was ever imposed by any country. Bethune's volunteer work as a surgeon, first with the Republican Army in the Spanish Civil War and then with the Eighth Route Army in China against the Japanese invaders, made him an international figure revered by millions. Brock Chisholm's organizational skills, developed as director general of medical services in Canada's wartime army, as well as his training at Yale as a psychiatrist, helped him after World War II to bring together disparate governments in support of a new international concept: a World Health Organization.

When the symposium concluded and the Oslerians retired to their respective hospitals, the cultured Alfred White Franklin, the doyen of paediatricians at Great Ormond Street in London, was left with the unenviable job of editor and, hopefully, publisher. I offered him my stipend as Fitzpatrick Lecturer, but I knew that this would not go very far. As I sat in my office in the great Woodward Library in Vancouver, I felt sorry for quiet little Alfred, so I telephoned him to say that we would guarantee the cost of publication. He nearly wept and insisted that I choose the title of the little volume. So I said "Let's call it 'An Oslerian Occasion,'" and that wrapped it up.

A very delightful lecture to give was that at Bonn University on the Rhine. The rector, to be addressed as "Your Magnificence," was the professor of the history of medicine. The hospitality offered by the students was heart warming. What a change from my 1937 visit!

On the North American continent I had two major speeches to prepare: one, the Penfield Lecture at the Montreal Neurological Institute, and the other, my presidential address to the American Osler Society meeting in Philadelphia. The Penfield lecture began with Liddell Hart's tribute to the Duke of Marlborough: he was a true leader with "the power of commanding affection while communicating energy." My aim was to chronicle Wilder Penfield's life as a conscious preparation for a role in bringing together, in his neurological and neurosurgical career, both research and practice, in a setting conducive to the continuous development and application of both. The locale was less important than the realization of the goal.

I thought it wise to downplay the heartbreaks and temporary reverses suffered en route, but I thought the large audience would appreciate the views of the lay director of the Ford Hospital in Detroit. An attractive offer had been made to Penfield as he worked away in New York—attractive, that is, from a bean–counter's perspective. Research, he told Penfield, was whatever he did after five o'clock: before five there was to be neurosurgery and no nonsense!

I beamed a few sharp remarks to the president of Canada's Medical Research Council who was sitting in the front row at my lecture, but he regained his composure when I challenged the federal politicians to get behind him financially and help him to carry on the late Wilder Penfield's work. I reminded McGill that it was their principal, Sir Arthur Currie—the 1914–18 wartime commander of Canada's army over–seas, and the former school teacher from Victoria, B.C.—who entered the lethal medical battle on campus to give Penfield's dream the bricks and mortar that were needed.

In the presidential address to the American Osler Society, I chronicled the influence that the great teacher had demonstrated in British Columbia through his favoured pupil, Dr. Henry Esson Young. It seemed fitting to describe to an audience in Philadelphia the son of a Presbyterian manse in Quebec who had followed Osler from Montreal to the University of Pennsylvania as a summer student. As minister of education, and as the father of every good cause in British Columbia—including the university—Young was truly an Oslerian hard at work. Only with a strong scientific and cultural background, to which William Osler contributed, could one man have achieved so much for a pioneer province the size of France and Germany combined, or, for my American audience, larger than Texas.

Lectures were one thing, but radio and television broadcasts were another. Whether the subject was the Mothers' March for the Kinsmen Rehabilitation Foundation or the history of medical discovery, the demands seemed interminable. The talk shows held when I was running for a seat on the Vancouver Board of Parks and Recreation were hilarious. Until then I had no idea how many people existed only to jump on radio station hosts and their guests every day! Strangely, one gravel–voiced host who had a large following of unusual listeners was a strong advocate of our parks system, so when one of his daily brawlers would succeed in getting on a line, the distraught host would hold up a card on which he had scrawled "Kook," and would shut the well–known crank off. We had a good laugh when an unidentified (I was about to say "undiagnosed") caller set out to prove that my name was not Gibson, and that I was a foreigner masquerading as a Canadian, and that Ottawa was not my birthplace. I was reminded of the title of one of Sigmund Freud's essays: "The psychopathology of everyday life."

For the Canadian Broadcasting Corporation I did a dozen television shows on the history of medical discoveries, going over–seas with a small crew to film the settings in which the great advances began. We did the penicillin story at Oxford, with Dr. Norman Heatley describing Florey and Chain's pioneer work, which was done with a £25 grant from a miserly Medical Research Council, who later rebuked Florey for accepting a vital grant of $5,000 from the Rockefeller Foundation. The crowning indignity was when the M.R.C. declared that it would be immoral to patent the substance and the process used to produce it. The result was that it was patented outside of Britain, so that patients in Britain then had to pay royalties to companies abroad, instead of being able to build up a huge fund for medical research in the United Kingdom, which is what Florey and Chain had hoped for.

In France we photographed the home and early laboratory of Louis Pasteur. We were able to film the beautiful gardens surrounding Florence Nightingale's home high above Duomo and the art capital of Italy. In Paris there was Baron Larrey's great hospital. In Canada we featured William Osler's home in Dundas, as well as parts of McGill University. In a short 21 days our group covered a great deal of history and geography. The series was well received in Canada and some viewers were irate when hockey replaced history on their screens.

CHAPTER THIRTY-SEVEN

China Pilgrimage, 1973

I travelled to China in the summer of 1973 with seven members of the Norman Bethune Foundation from Montreal. Our object was to visit the scene, in northwest China, of the battles against the Japanese invaders, in which the Eighth Route Army and their Canadian-born surgeon Norman Bethune served.

The "Long March" that took the army all the way from south China to the province of Hopei is one of the military epics of modern history. Our little group could not follow the route of that volunteer army as it struggled to cross the Yangtse River gorges before the regular army of Chang Kai Shek could pin them down. So we concentrated on the area in which Bethune had set up his operating room in a disused Buddhist temple to the west of Peking (Beijing).

Bethune, born in Gravenhurst, Ontario, in 1890, had graduated from the University of Toronto medical school in 1916, along with Frederick Banting. After wartime service he studied in London to be a paediatric specialist, and took surgical training in Edinburgh, as did his grandfather. He shared this ancestor's unorthodox views, as well as many of those of his father, who was a Presbyterian minister whose congregations, seriatim, could not accept the social gospel dispensed by him for very long. After suffering tuberculosis and being hospitalized at the famous Trudeau Sanatorium at Saranac Lake in New York state's Adirondack mountains, Bethune gravitated to McGill's Royal Victoria Hospital in Montreal to train as a chest surgeon with Professor Edward Archibald, a pioneer in that field.

In the depths of the Great Depression, Bethune's social-medical gospel was too much for his English-speaking colleagues, so he transferred his surgical work to the Sacré Coeur Hospital across the river. One of his assistants there joined our group in China.

Bethune was outraged by the 1936 German and Italian aerial attacks on the five-year-old Republican Government of Spain, and resolved to take a blood transfusion service to the front. He was assisted by Hazen Sise, the son of the president of the Bell Telephone Company in Montreal, and Dr. Paul Weil, of the blood bank recently set up at the Royal Victoria Hospital.

After battling with the Canadian government over his transfusion equipment and its transport, Bethune arrived at the Madrid front where he established a refrigerated blood transfusion service that began to change the way in which war wounds were handled. Once that was going well, he returned to Canada to raise funds for an even larger blood supply unit, and had progressed as far as British Columbia when he learned of the Japanese invasion of China. He left others to carry on the mobile transfusion service in Spain, and crossed the Pacific on the great white ship "Empress of Asia." He made his way to the northwest frontier zone, at first using the caves of Yenan as hospitals, much as he had in Spain. On arriving at Mao Tse–tung's headquarters, he explained what he wanted to do to reorganize the primitive care facilities and to write the curriculum for a field–helpers' training school. After 18 months of heroic surgical work he contracted blood poisoning from a wound and died. Mao's tribute to him was published in a thin little book that every child in China received and memorized. As we proceeded through the countryside we heard children in schoolrooms reciting this memorial, over and over again.

Our progress out to Hopei was first by train (with coal–burning locomotives) and then by high–board army "G.P."s, which crossed streams and rough terrain in an amazing fashion. Often villagers would hear the four–wheel–drive vehicles coming through the hills and would line the roads to cheer. One of our party was a red–haired, red–bearded nephew of Sir Frederick Banting who stood six feet four inches when he was not trying to fit into a "G.P." or go through a door. Whenever we stopped the Chinese would cautiously come up to scrutinize this giant. Similarly, the Chinese women wanted to touch the hair of the wives in our party. Dean Wendell Macleod, of the University of Saskatchewan medical faculty, and an old friend of Bethune, had taken the time to learn some elementary Chinese greetings, but whenever he used them he was embarrassed by a volley of Chinese reciprocal greetings he could not translate. However, the army supplied us with good interpreters.

Our first objective was to see a large coloured globe of the world, set upon a large monument that marked the burial place of Dr. Bethune. Three times it had been demolished by Japanese machine–gun target practice. Eventually Bethune was buried in the courtyard of a large military hospital closer to Peking. Nevertheless, the original site was kept in exemplary manner in a clearing on a ridge.

Our second stop was at a beautiful stone and wood home, one floor high, with an elegant courtyard in which a long low table had been set, with little wooden stools around it. On the table there were baskets of apples and nuts. The family invited us to sit down and drink wonderful green tea from little bowls, while the grandfather related the events of Bethune's last days and the care that they had provided. There was not a dry eye as the bearded old man described the scalpel wound that had festered, and the over–worked surgeon who would not look after himself until his fever over–came him. We were shown the tiled bed on which he was nursed while they burned straw under it to try to stop his shivering! The grandfather had been a 16–year–old boy when Bethune died on November 12, 1939. The family had no Canadian flag, so they draped his coffin with an American one. The photographs taken at that time showed an emaciated and prematurely aged 49–year–old man. In fact, a photograph of Bethune operating in the little Buddhist temple during his busiest period depicted a man worn out trying to do too many good things with too few tools.

The gentle nature of the three generations of the family who cared solicitously for a surgeon from the far side of the world was something we all remember. It recalled to us Bethune's words when he addressed his ragged but steadfast army brethren at the opening of his rustic school for surgical assistants and nurses, set up in the hills beyond the reach of all but Japanese planes:

> The eyes of millions of freedom–loving Canadians, Americans and Englishmen are turned to the East and are filled with admiration of China in her glorious struggle against Japanese imperialism...Do not consider it strange that people like yourselves, thirty thousand li away, half way round the globe, are helping you. You and we are internationalists; we recognize no race, no colour, no language, no national boundaries to separate us.

I was reminded of the words of his classmate at the University of Toronto, Frederick Banting, whom I heard speaking in Victoria, B.C., in 1929, when he described medical service as "the most truly international commodity we possess. It knows no protective tariff, no embargo, no boundary line to prevent its free dissemination for the good of all. At present it is the common language and common spirit among the nations."

We were taken to a rest house—a small conference centre—where a dozen of Bethune's former assistants and patients had been assembled for two days. One was a former physician who had lost vision in both eyes due to a penetrating shell. One of the real characters was a very young stable boy whom Bethune called "Little Red Devil." One of his tasks was to teach Bethune to ride a mountain pony. Each morning the boy would lead the horse to a position between two large piles of sawdust, so that the novice rider, if thrown, landed gracefully.

We talked long into the night, tape recording the conversations with these survivors of what had been a cruel war, with Japanese planes flying bombing sorties far inland. It was during these sessions that we learned of the pressure Bethune had to endure as he, a Canadian missionary doctor and a nurse carried out 110 surgeries in 25 days.

Whether it is by the marble tomb at the hospital at Shih–chia Chuang, or the Jackman statue in Montreal, or the illustrated booklet memorized by every Chinese school child, Bethune is deservedly honoured by a billion people. I had no sooner arrived home to Vancouver than I had a telephone call from the aging industrialist and university philanthropist, H.R. MacMillan: "Come in when you can, and tell me about Bethune in China." I arrived as Senator Wallace McCutcheon was leaving.

H.R. had partaken in a long chat on the telephone earlier in the day with his friend, Rt. Hon. Harold Wilson, in London. I thought, therefore, that what I had to say would be cold porridge. No such thing! The man with the menacing eyebrows wanted to hear everything I could tell him about Dr. Norman Bethune. He filed this away in his remarkable memory, to be produced years later when he told me to order a large tapestry of Bethune operating in China.

The impact our voyage by air, train and army vehicle made upon us will last as long as we will. The outgoing and friendly spirit of the people in China confirmed my experience of Chinese students, doctors and professors in Canada. Their adaptability was key to their survival.

CHAPTER THIRTY-EIGHT

Second Visit to China

One day in 1984 I was sitting in London at the Wellcome Foundation headquarters when the chairman told me he was just back from China, where he had found no market for their new human Interferon. It was being made in 5,000 gallon steel tanks at Beckenham, Kent, from frozen cells of a young girl who had died of Birkett's lymphoma in Uganda.

I brashly suggested that with Vancouver's interest in China we would like to carry out clinical trials using Interferon against viral hepatitis, of which China had 100 million cases. My argument was that if the chairman felt that there were no markets visible for the new therapeutic agent in China, he might be willing to have the Terry Fox Foundation in British Columbia, of which I was chairman, try its hand at the very challenging hepatitis problem. The result was that we were given the rights in China for 15 years. Interferon, "christened" over a cup of tea by Alic Isaacs and Jean Lindenmann at the Medical Research Council laboratories in London, was theoretically of potential use in interfering with the growth of viruses, of which the world was increasingly aware.

So a small group of physicians was organized in Vancouver to study the problem, and a forerunner, skilled in infectious diseases, was sent off to Beijing to make arrangements for our visit. Within a few weeks our small group was en route and we were met at the Beijing airport by Professor Ho, of the Second Infectious Diseases Hospital, and many of his staff, bearing traditional Chinese gifts. This remarkable man was fluent in French and English and was a dynamo day in and day out. Under his supervision the postgraduate medical training in infectious diseases for all of China was concentrated in his research hospital. His staff and the hospital facilities were excellent, but the road to them was a mixture of ruts and bumps that invigorated our team as our minibus plunged through them daily. Dr. Ho arranged for us to be gathered in the courtyard at noon one day for the planting of a maple tree, which represented Canada at the institute.

The patients, many of them young women, had enlarged livers that pushed their abdominal walls out in grotesque fashion. The protocol laid down was for liver biopsies before, during and after treatment with Interferon, and this is still going on as a China–Canada co–operative study.

Towards the end of our stay, the physicians and wives were invited to visit the Great Wall, some miles from the capital. The air–conditioning in the van had to be turned off in order to get us over the highest hills en route. When we arrived at the Great Wall—the successor to lesser walls of ancient times—we found a crush of buses, animal carts and tourists, which dispirited my wife, who was going to be pushed up the wall in a wheelchair. The crowd pulled back in awe as this shiny contraption was unfolded and young people rushed to help us up the sometimes steep incline. The chair was a six–day wonder, which children ran alongside to touch. With a few bumps we made it part way up the slope to an observation post of yesteryear, from which we could see this incredible 2,000–miles–long structure straggling off into distant hills. No wonder the astronauts thought they could see it from outer space.

My wife, already ailing from the cancer that was to take her life, rested on some days, only to be waited upon by the women doctors from our adopted hospital who showed sisterly concern. Our farewell dinner, an endless round of unusual (for us) dishes and numerous toasts, had a wondrous finale. Our host, Dr. Ho, who had been trained in his pre–medical days as an actor in Chinese theatre, put on a side–splitting performance, which I wish his patients had seen. It would have rejuvenated them, despite their fatal illnesses.

CHAPTER THIRTY-NINE

The University Club, Vancouver

The Reserve Air Force was being phased out in Canada in 1958, so the downtown headquarters in Vancouver became available for a re-instituted University Club open to graduates of any university in the world. The building had been the original Quadra Club but had gone under in the depression of 1929. Now a group of 16 of us undertook to revive what had been the University Club of Vancouver, which failed to survive World War I. We collected 200 signatures on a petition to the Honourable Ralph Campney, the Vancouver lawyer who was at that time minister of national defence in Ottawa. Our committee scouted many possible locations but finally determined to procure the former Quadra Club on Hastings Street, which has a wonderful view of the harbour and mountains. This became a very tricky business because it seemed to me if it was loose on the market it would be picked up very quickly. Three of us converged on Ottawa and through our ever-helpful friend Senator S.S. McKeen made an appointment with the Honourable George Perks, V.C., who had served in two wars and held a generals' rank in the Second World War. We outlined our proposal to the general, who asked what we were prepared to pay for the property. I replied that we really did not know. He thought this was a very peculiar way of doing business, until I explained to him that we wished to pay for the building and small lot exactly what the Crown had put into it, not a cent less and not a cent more. We made it clear that we did not want to steal from the Crown, nor from anyone else. This amused the general and he slammed his hand down on his desk and said, "I think you should have that building." To make quite sure that there was adequate support from other British Columbians in the federal cabinet, we lurked outside the revolving doors of the House of Commons chamber and waylaid the Honourable Howard Green, minster of external affairs, and the Honourable Davie Fulton, minister of justice. As British Columbians and University of British Columbia graduates, they were delighted with the idea and gave their full support. We were received at about 6:00 p.m. by the minister dealing with the disposal of Crown assets after the war, and on the grounds that we had to fly back to Vancouver that night he was kind enough to see us ahead of several dozen of his constituents. He was slightly amazed to hear the details of our purchase, but said that if the three cabinet members were for it he would expedite the matter.

The armed forces, however, became concerned with this manoeuvre and sent a brigadier by air to Vancouver, presumably to delay the proceedings. He was staying over the weekend at the Air Force Base on Sea Island and came into the Officers' Mess as I was playing the beautiful grand piano that somehow had entered that unusual area. He recognized my insignia as a medical officer and asked if I would stop playing long enough to come to the hospital and help him with his haemorrhoids problem, which had troubled him all the way out from Ottawa on a military plane. He confided to me that he came to investigate the matter of the sale of a building downtown to an unheard–of University Club. After applying the standard medication, I explained the facts of life to him, how the building had been acquired, and how a grateful patient could expedite things on Monday morning. The brigadier bravely went through with his side of the bargain and the club was off and running.

Since we lacked funds, we rented the ground floor to the Air Force Medical Board Unit for one year. One department store gave the Three Universities Development Fund $50,000 "in kind." This presented a problem to the Development Fund, but I suggested that the University Club would be glad to use up the $50,000 "in kind" on furnishings; paying it off in cash over a five–year period to the fund. The competitor of this large store, hearing of this deal, rushed to make sure that they had their furnishings in at the same time. Gradually we made it uphill and developed a very excellent meeting place for university graduates, while at the same time providing a downtown headquarters for many of the activities carried on in development work by the University of British Columbia and later by Simon Fraser University.

At about the same time that these negotiations were going on, I was asked to be president of the UBC Alumni Association. This involved a great deal of organizational work but I think that it was well worth doing. Since my undergraduate days from 1931 to 1933 at UBC, I had been impressed not only with the students' drive for the development of their new university, but also by the help rendered by members of the original classes from 1915 on, who had attended

UBC in the Fairview shacks and had never really enjoyed the new campus, "The Promised Land," out at Point Grey that opened in 1925. It was one of these early graduates, Phyllis Ross, that I dared to put forward as the first woman chancellor of the university. In the hotly contested election, where the rival candidate was also a woman graduate of great distinction, some amazing statements were made. However, Mrs. Ross had been in a high administrative post during the war years in Ottawa and brought a great deal of organizational capability to her work as chancellor. She had been one of my firm supporters on the question of building the medical faculty on the campus and eventually the construction of the University Hospital. Her eventual illness with Alzheimer's disease brought her son, the Honourable John Turner, also a UBC graduate, to the support of neurological research in the Kinsmen Laboratory and across Canada.

For 20 years the University Club of Vancouver flourished, but eventually was controlled by a theologian president and a retired lawyer as secretary, and fell on allegedly hard times. Though I addressed the members on the value of selling off our valuable unused air rights or development rights, I was put down as a "nut" who knew nothing about business. The club was taken over by the neighbouring Vancouver Club, which soon found that our property and its air rights were worth six million dollars.

CHAPTER FORTY

Lester Pearson College of the Pacific

During my visits to England in the 1960s, I became acquainted with the group in London House that had established Atlantic College, about 40 miles west of Cardiff in Wales. One of the moving spirits in this development had been Admiral Desmond Hoare, at the Paris headquarters of the senior military officers who were concerned with the maintenance of peace in Europe. When he and his wife came to Vancouver we had many conversations about future colleges. His wife's father had designed the beautiful St. James Anglican Church in the lower east side of Vancouver. It was said to be a 1/5 scale reproduction of the Anglican Cathedral that existed in Cairo. Late one afternoon we went to visit this beautifully crafted church interior, to be met by a down–and–out vagrant who had clearly been on the bottle. He said proudly to our British friends, "How do you like our church, lady?" She said, "I like it very well; my father designed it."

Eventually I was able to accept Admiral Hoare's invitation to pay a visit to the castle at Atlantic College, which was all of 600 years old, perched high above the waters of the Bristol Channel. It was said that no structure interfered with the view of Boston and New York from that point right across the Atlantic. As I understood it, the castle had been refurbished by William Randolph Hearst, the American publisher, for his friend Marion Davies, but that after spending one wet Welsh weekend there she had said to her protector, "Honey, I'm goin' home." He then built her an imported Italian castle in California. He had evidently gone to every church auction and demolition and used the interiors thus acquired to make his castle in Wales outstanding. On the top floor of the main tower was "The Hilton Suite," and I must say it was astounding in its furnishings and its outlook over the ocean. The night I spent there saw one of the wildest electrical storms, complete with wind and sloshing rain, that I have ever beheld. Once I understood that the students there came from all parts of the world, and that no one could buy their way in, I thought that North America must soon have such a college catering for students in the British system's Forms 6a and 6b, or in North American equivalence, the final year of high school and the first year of college.

I was invited to join a committee in Canada, centred in Toronto from the Canadian side and in New York from the American side, chaired there by Malcolm Muir, a white-haired prince of the publication world.

Eventually, Earl Mountbatten of Burma became head of the organization to be known as The United World Colleges. President Nixon invited him to come to a dinner to explain and popularize his concept at the White House on Thursday, November 5, 1970. There I joined two other Canadian representatives, Senator Donald Cameron of the Banff School of Fine Arts (and many other things), and George Kitching, a retired major general of the Canadian Army. Immediately after the dinner I recorded the account, which appears in the next chapter.

The hope of a joint American–Canadian College went out the window when the American committee was shanghaied into believing that a New England private school was about to be donated to the cause. As I understand it, a heavy mortgage was found to be part of the alleged donation, which caused that initiative to come to naught. The Canadians, however, pressed on and when Prime Minister Lester B. Pearson was visiting London, it was arranged that he should drive down to Atlantic College in Wales to get an idea of what it was we were talking about. He was simply astounded at the wonderful surroundings and the college itself, but even more so at the concept. He went back to Canada a great supporter of the proposal that we should build one of the United World Colleges on the Pacific coast of Canada. Then negotiations began for property. On one of his visits to the west coast, Lord Mountbatten was shown an area near William Head where the trans–Pacific liners used to put in for quarantine examination. A very junior naval officer accompanied his Lordship, who was showing a very considerable interest in this fine beach and forest property. The officer mentioned that this area would probably not be available for any potential college because it was reserved for "combined operations," of which Lord Mountbatten might have heard! There was much merriment in the party as the great advocate of combined operations digested this remark. Other waterfront property was offered by an entrepreneur who merely had an option on it and wanted to sell it to the proposed college for four times what his option was. This was denounced and abandoned very quickly. Finally, the prime minister took on the department of defence and had to be very aggressive to get even 70 acres out of their vast preserve in British Columbia. Happily, it gave access to a World War II defence area of about 1,500 acres of hill country. The treasure lay in the acreage on Pedder Bay—a long inlet of the Pacific with quiet water suitable for a marine haven for something paralleling the seafront activities of Atlantic College in Wales.

The actual acquisition of this property was achieved through our good friend the Honourable David Wills, an Oxford graduate who was determined to put his Bristol–based ancestral company, and its profits, to good public use. In the same way the French shipping magnate, Anthony Besse, had participated in the acquisition of the Hearst castle for Atlantic College.

Eventually, what was to be known as the Pearson College of the Pacific began to take shape in our minds. An imaginative architect, Barry Downs, and his friends and associates produced a plan for a college to accommodate a total of 200 students. There were to be 100 students in each of two years, and they would come from many parts of the world. Prime Minister Trudeau, Pearson's successor in Ottawa, guaranteed a certain fraction of the places for Canadians, but he was determined that the rest of the world would take up most of the places. From the beginning the policy was that no one would be able to buy his or her way into the college as a student, and that local committees around the globe would nominate students, after competitive interviews, who would attend free of financial encumbrances. This has meant an annual solicitation of funds in order to bring these students to Pearson College, situated about 18 miles southwest of Victoria, British Columbia. In fact, the Pearson College campus must be one of the most southerly points of Vancouver Island as it juts down into the Strait of Juan de Fuca. From the college one can see clearly the northwest coast of Washington State, not much more than 15 miles away. The students often come even closer to the American shore as they go out in their zodiacs.

The actual opening ceremony at Pearson College attracted many people, including the board of governors from all parts of Canada under the able chairmanship of the Honourable John Nichol. A large bronze plaque memorializing Lester Pearson was mounted on the cross–section of one of the very large Douglas Fir trees removed during construction of the main building. The plaque records the words of Nobelist Pearson: "How can there be peace without people understanding each other, and how can this be if they don't know each other." Lord Mountbatten asked if I could get him another round from the same tree. Before doing this I questioned the British Consular authorities as to the problem of getting such a thing into the United Kingdom. After some investigation they told met that it would be quite impossible to certify that wild life was not hiding in the bark.

CHAPTER FORTY-ONE

Memoir on Mountbatten

I met the Earl Mountbatten of Burma at the British Embassy in Washington along with Senator Donald Cameron and General George Kitching when the three of us went down from Canada to the dinner in the White House being given by President Nixon for Lord Mountbatten's United World Colleges. This visit I have detailed at the end of this chapter.

Following that remarkable evening when Mountbatten held 100 guests spellbound, some time passed before it became clear that the Canadians were going to have to go it alone if we were to establish a North American college comparable to Atlantic College in Wales and the United World College in Singapore. About a year after the White House dinner, Lord Mountbatten decided to visit the southern–most tip of Vancouver Island near Pedder Bay as one of several sites selected out of about 50 for critical review. At the same time I arranged that he should speak to a meeting of the Men's Canadian Club, a thousand strong, in the Hotel Vancouver.

I was writing at my desk in the Woodward Library at UBC at about 3:30 in the afternoon when the phone rang. I expected that it was news from the control tower at Sea Island to say that the Fabergé jet bringing Lord Mountbatten was in the circuit. Instead, it turned out to be an American voice saying, "Doctor, this is Capt. Porter, Lord Mountbatten's pilot. We are just leaving Palm Springs now." To be quite sure that I had understood Capt. Porter properly, I said, "This is about the time I expected you in Vancouver." He laughed heartily and explained that they had eaten a very late lunch with Frank Sinatra and Bob Hope and that I would probably understand why they were so late leaving Palm Springs. It was agreed that they should pull into the industrial side of the Vancouver airport about two hours later, as they estimated.

By that time it was getting dark, so I went across to the industrial side with an old olive–green Cadillac sedan that I was driving. Pulling in to a temporary shed in which Customs and Immigration were housed on that side of the airport, I was met by a gruff officer who asked me if I were sure that this was really Lord Mountbatten coming. He said this because he had been troubled in the middle of the night to admit to Canada someone claiming to be Howard Hughes, the recluse who eventually settled in the Bayshore Hotel here. Clearly the officer was not sure that he had been talking with Howard Hughes at any time during the admission procedures. I assured the officer, however, that this really was Lord Mountbatten and I would introduce him if he could just wait a few minutes.

The plane rolled in—a most handsome and beautifully equipped jet—but down the stairs came a terribly haggard man with a frightful cold. He shook hands with me and asked how far it was to the hotel and could he get to bed right away. I assured him that all was in readiness and we would get him to the hotel quickly.

On entering the Royal Suite at the Hotel Vancouver, he was stunned by the spaciousness of the place and he turned quickly around and said, "Bill, who is paying for this?" I assured him that the Men's Canadian Club were delighted to be paying for it and we wanted him to be absolutely quiet and get a decent rest before his speech to us at the following noon hour.

I got him some medicine for his extremely sore throat and he went off to bed.

Next morning after he had finished breakfast, I went in to see him at the hotel, only to find him with a terribly husky voice, a flushed face and feeling very miserable indeed. I called across the street to the medical dental building to my friend Squadron Leader Badger of yesteryear, now an ear, nose and throat specialist. He said he could see His Lordship if we would come over, which we did very soon, because it seemed to me that unless something radical were done for his throat there would be no speech to the Men's Canadian Club. Badger had a good look at his throat and his sinuses and it was agreed that he should spray his throat with some local anaesthetic so that he could get some rest from the terrible coughing, and take some medication that would get him through his speech at least. In going down to MacDonald's Pharmacy on the ground floor to collect these prescriptions, the man behind the counter jumped when he saw to whom the prescription was made out. He filled the requisite number of bottles and then bringing the prescription forward with the medication, asked Lord Mountbatten if he might retain the prescription. Lord Mountbatten said of course he should do that, he would be very happy to have him do that. As we returned to the hotel he said,

"Bill, what is this building?" I replied that it was Christ Church Cathedral and that he had better say good–bye to it. "Why?" Because, I said, the dean was determined to take it down and build a skyscraper, with the church either in the basement or the top. By renting out the office space in the tower he thought he could support the cathedral in perpetuity. This enraged Mountbatten and he stopped and said: "No he is not going to do that, and you are going to see that he does not. Do you understand?" I said that I would do my very best at city council as an alderman to make sure that this did not happen, whereupon Mountbatten repeated his charge that it must not happen and that he would hold me responsible.

We arrived back in his room and he felt much better and went down quietly then to speak to the Men's Canadian Club. There was a model of one of the destroyers he had known so well during the war and a lot of naval people to meet him, including some from the Bowen Island Canadian Legion of which he had long been a member. His speech was really fantastic and was recorded with all the wonderful jibes and witticisms that he used to lighten his message. But his message was very clear indeed, and that was that only by working hard now could a third war, involving the whole of mankind, be prevented. He got an excellent reception: three aging men sitting at a table sent up a note to say that each would contribute $100 there and then for the college that he proposed to build on the Pacific coast. At the end of his speech he gave, at my request, a wonderful imitation of Winston Churchill encountering Bessie Braddock in the corridors of the House of Commons in London, which brought the house down, as it had previously in Washington.

The same evening we went to dinner, where he presented his case for a west coast college to a distinguished group of business and professional men. He wanted to talk half the night back at the hotel but I assured him that he must get some rest or he would be in trouble again. The next day we went to Victoria to see a potential site at Pedder Bay. He did not like the first site that was offered because it was mixed up with a commercial marina, but he determined on a site closer to the ocean on Pedder Bay and, of course, this site belonged to the Department of National Defense. On the way out we had called on the commanding officer of Royal Roads, the armed forces college in the old Dunsmuir residence, Hatley Park. The commanding officer was rather non–plussed at the visit. He provided us with coffee, but wondered why we looked in such detail at all the buildings and the grounds. We admired them greatly and persistently as we chatted with him and then left. Mountbatten said as we drove out the great curving driveway up to the highway, "I do not think we could pay for even cutting the grass in this establishment. It is far too expensive for us." So that settled the matter of whether or not we would try to get Royal Roads for the Pacific College. Going on to Pedder Bay it was clear that he was still dogged by high temperatures but insisted nevertheless on climbing the cliffs and settling on where the college should be. It was after that journey that Mike Pearson did such good work with the army, having them release 70 acres along the waterfront for the college.

When the Royal Yacht Britannia arrived in the inner harbour of Victoria to meet the Queen and Prince Philip at the end of a Canadian tour, I had the privilege of taking the captain of this beautiful vessel, Admiral Trowbridge, to see Pearson College. We were driving through some National Defence lands in an unauthorized entrance when he spied some cream-coloured dogtooth violets under the oak trees. He asked if he was allowed to pick a few for the Queen's cabin. When I assured him that this land belonged to the Queen of Canada, he whipped out a pair of surgical scissors and carefully cut a few. To satisfy me that they really were for the Royal Suite he gave me a tour of the yacht. Little did the royal party know that a few days later they would sail, at sunset, into Victoria harbour to be greeted by a naval band playing "Strangers in the Night."

White House Dinner

Thursday night, November 5, 1970, Washington, D.C. Midnight, just back from the White House after one of the most interesting dinners, in honour of Lord Mountbatten.

About 7:45 p.m. General George Kitching, Senator Donald Cameron and I went to the southwest gate of the White House in black tie and showed our invitations to the guard. Our car then drove very slowly through the lawn which surrounds the beautiful trees of this large area set in the centre of a big city. We entered the reception foyer under a large marquee beneath which a number of plain clothes detectives stood with their hands in their pockets. At the door we gave up our passes and checked our coats.

We found we were there early enough to be ahead of the crush but soon a steady stream began with three retired admirals and eleven retired generals, most of the Cabinet, all of the present heads of the armed forces, many retired ambassadors and fifty or sixty top business leaders. We were ninety-three in all. The first man to walk up and shake my hand was General Omar Bradley. He was wearing a most handsome dark mess kit with miniatures covering his chest. I told him how much I had enjoyed and learned from his television interview when General Eisenhower died and he told me how it had been made, partly in Hollywood and partly in the east. He went back over some of the material for me, reminding me that he had been a classmate of Ike's through military college.

Next came General Norstad and General Alfred Grueunther and a youthful looking General Lawton Collins. And so they mounted the stairs, Maxwell Taylor and so many of the Second World War leaders, full dress uniform leading the way past a huge portrait of Eleanor Roosevelt. We were ushered into the large reception hall on the south end of the White House where every one of the ninety guests fraternized freely and trays of drinks were passed around. There were no noisy bars set up and no distractions to mar the excellent scene. A bright military band in scarlet struck up familiar music and played beautifully.

It was not long until I ran into Stephen Bechtel, Jr. of San Francisco who had once lived in Vancouver and is still a member of the Vancouver Club. I had been in touch with his father about visits to the Ford Foundation where he still remains a Trustee, but the father was away in Russia just now. Richard Scaife, one of the Mellon grandsons came up to chat. He had been the room-mate of Harold Foley's son at Notre Dame University in Indiana, the boy who had been killed in a car accident just before graduation in 1955. Robert Maes of the Independence Foundation in Philadelphia also started to chat along with McGeorge Bundy of the Ford Foundation and Thomas Watson of IBM. It was an incredible gathering of diplomats of the post-war era including John McCloy, Jock Whitney and others. Malcolm Muir the head of the United World Colleges group in the United States was on hand of course, because that was what the dinner for Lord Mountbatten was all about. His fellow publisher DeWitt Wallace of the Reader's Digest was also there.

After about twenty minutes, the band struck up "Hail to the Chief" and in the archway stood President Nixon with Lord Mountbatten on his right. The guests soon formed into a reception line and moved forward to greet the President and his guest of honour. They shook hands in turn with each of the guests and had a brief but sometimes hilarious conversation with them.

Paired with me in the line as we moved up was Colonel Frank Borman the astronaut. I reminded him that I had seen him at "Hello Dolly" about a year ago in New York when Pearl Bailey and her all-Negro cast tried to get onto the stage at the end of the show a pair of Russian astronauts who were visiting New York that night in charge of Borman. He told me that though they were very shy about going up on the stage on their first day in America they did not want to go home at all after three weeks in the country.

As I approached the President, Lord Mountbatten came forward and presented me as coming from Victoria and Vancouver. The President was very affable and well-tanned, looked rested from his campaigning, and said that he and his wife had enjoyed part of their honeymoon in Victoria when he was in the U.S. Navy.

In a few moments dinner was announced and each took his place quickly, which it was possible to do because a miniature seating plan which was handed to each of us in an envelope as we entered the original reception room. The food was simple and excellent and the dinner was punctuated at intervals by marvellous music. The first group of musicians came in bright red costumes and tricorn hats playing a fife and bugle arrangement. Then later on a military choir came in and sang "Rule Britannia" and "Hearts of Oak" as I have never heard it sung before. Lord Mountbatten beamed at this one-time heretical music being sung with such determination by this choir in the White House in 1970.

The President spoke for about fifteen minutes on what his fellow sailor Mountbatten had done in fifty years of service to the Queen. He certainly spoke from the heart when he dealt with Britain's role in preserving freedom when she stood alone from 1939 to 1941. He spoke very quietly and reminiscently and made and excellent effect.

Then the other "Dickie" spoke in a charming way about his association with the White House going back to 1922. He told about having his ship the Kelly shot out from under him and coming to Norfolk, Virginia to pick up the aircraft Illustrious early in 1941. While he waited for his new ship he managed in some way to get out as far as Pearl Harbor and on coming back to the White House to report to the President he was informed by Franklin Roosevelt that he was the most expensive visitor he had ever had at the White House! The President had asked him then what he thought of Pearl Harbor and Mountbatten had said that the U.S. Navy headquarters should be put underground with the least possible delay. Alas, none of this was ever done. You could hear a pin drop as he described this situation.

Then Mountbatten went on to tell of Winston Churchill sending him back to Washington after Pearl Harbor, to try to persuade Harry Hopkins and the President first, that all the political hue and cry in North America for a 1942 invasion of France was just going to lead to diaster. He urged them to invade North Africa and possibly the soft underbelly of Europe first, and to postpone until 1944 the Channel crossing which it was hoped would finish off the Nazis completely. This was not very popular evidently in Washington at that time but he made the case so well to the armed forces that when his role of John the Baptist was over he said, Winston Churchill could come and clinch things.

He then took off on some mimicry of Winston Churchill which had the people in the aisles. He spoke in such staccato bursts that we missed some of the best parts of it but he told a wonderful story about a depressed Winston at the end of the war, turned out of office by a grateful public, etc. Dining for too late and on too much brandy in the House of Commons he was weaving his way through the corridors when he encountered a woman member of the House not noted for her beauty. She roared at him, "Winston, you're drunk". He shot back "Bessie, you are ugly". As he moved off again down the corridor he called, "Tomorrow I shall be sober". This brought the house down as did many more marvellous sallies by Lord Mountbatten. The President at the end of his remarks had toasted Her majesty the Queen, and Lord Mountbatten did the same for the President as he closed his remarks and explained that he must be off in a U.S. Navy plane to New York and there to pick up a jump seat in the belly of an air freighter so that he would be home in time for tea with the King of Sweden the next day!

CHAPTER FORTY-TWO

Christ Church Cathedral, Vancouver

Shortly before the end of the 19th century, a group of Anglican church members and adherents in the young and booming city of Vancouver decided that they should have a centrally located mini-cathedral. They purchased five lots, at the intersection of the rutted Burrard and Georgia Streets, from the transportation monopoly known as the Canadian Pacific Railway. Despite its history of political scandals, the C.P.R. behaved as if it were divinely guided when it came to dealing with the hard-pressed parishioners. However, the churchmen hung on and finally built a stone edifice about 40 feet high. The hammer beam construction of the roof is still of great architectural interest. The light shade of wood used throughout the interior is beautiful.

Over the years the little cathedral has been the centre for marriages, baptisms and funerals of rich and poor without prejudice. The organ music at religious services and at noonday public recitals has been superb.

Imagine, therefore, the effect on the stalwarts of the congregation when they learned that their dean was well into negotiations with developers who wanted to tear down this landmark, replacing it with a skyscraper. His plea was that by the 1970s his flock had abandoned the centre of the city, with the result that Sunday offerings had dwindled seriously.

Congregation meetings, which raised a lot of temperatures, led to charges and countercharges with little Christian forbearance. As a city alderman I was peppered with briefs from both sides, and my telephone wires glowed in the dark. I was amazed by the outpouring of strongly held views from the parishioners, but most of all by the senior citizens and their all-too-forgiving spokesmen. Ranged against these dear old people were smartly dressed lawyers and supposed businessmen. The doughty Harry Verney Warren—one of Canada's premier geologists, athlete, Rhodes scholar of the gay '20s, and a distant relative of Florence Nightingale—led the opposition to the dean's plans for the little church on the corner. He was an excellent and polished debater and not to be downed lightly.

As I mention elsewhere in this meandering memoir, I was given sharp instructions by Mountbatten to take it up at city–council level, so I went to see the TEAM members of council individually to brief them on the pitiful arrangements being made by the dean. The Electors' Action Movement had come to power on a platform of downtown civic betterment, not civic exploitation. The UBC professor of urban geography Dr. Walter Hardwick knew the zoning laws affecting downtown properties and hammered the shortsighted council members. Alderwoman May Brown heaped scorn on the "quick buck" artists, so that soon we had quite a fire going.

I assembled the preservation forces for a lunch at the University Club, and invited the dean's official legal advisor to lead us through his plans. It was disappointing to find that the long–sacrosanct plans were utter rubbish, financially, and were about to lead the dean and his vocal backers into a fiscal wilderness.

Sobered by this tale, I telephoned John Gibson in Toronto, where he represented the large Hammerson Group of London property investors. He agreed to come for lunch the next day and caught the late non–stop plane to Vancouver. Over lunch I reviewed the alternatives and with the help of my colleagues convinced him that there had already been one case of the transfer of "air rights," or of "development rights" in Vancouver, several more were pending, and that Christ Church Cathedral owned rights 150 feet in height that it would never use.

I rattled on about the transfer of such rights within a few blocks of their origin in New York and in Chicago, where the banking of excess development rights for distant use was common.

Our visitor agreed that he could add the cathedral's spare rights to his projected office building on the lot next door, producing a skyscraper by Vancouver standards. All this was eventually agreed upon. By a 7 to 4 vote in city council, the cathedral was classified as a heritage building in perpetuity and therefore beyond the power of anyone to tear it down.

This produced two sermons castigating this emissary of the Devil—called Gibson—but the old people just smiled. While the legal and construction mills ground in low gear, the financial wizards came to the conclusion that the transferred rights were worth $300,000 per year for 105 years! Even before they were able to announce this publicly, I had a call from the Hon. Grace McCarthy to know if a sum of money could be advanced to provide an urgently needed new roof. Finally the financial bonanza was announced, whereupon my friend the dean called to say, "Bill it is the will of God." I told him it was merely a 7 to 4 vote of city council and I regretted I must hang up.

My work on Sir Christopher Wren's contributions had taken me to see several of his 50 London churches, which were built after the Great Fire of 1666. In the process I came upon sad remnants of some of them evidence of the Nazi bombing raids on London. There were a few solitary towers left where the remainder of the church had simply disappeared. In the midst of an appeal in Britain for massive funds to renovate the damaged churches, including St. Paul's Cathedral, I saw a chance of moving one of the derelict towers to the entrance of our little cathedral in Vancouver, with the generous help of H.R. MacMillan. He dropped a few tears every time Wren was mentioned in our far–ranging conversations, and would quote, with a voice filled with emotion, Wren's epitaph in St. Paul's Cathedral: "Si monumentum requiris, circumspice."

Through Sir Michael Perrin, the son of an Anglican bishop, married to the daughter of a bishop, I began enquiries. It was impossible to get the several church authorities in England to agree on anything, so we eventually gave up.

CHAPTER FORTY–THREE

New Projects

There is nothing that promotes a sound circulation of the blood better than a few uncompleted or new undertakings. You win some and you lose some, possibly one win for 10 losses—at least that is so in the fund–raising game. On the public awareness campaigns resulting in positive action, one's record may be slightly better, but there may be a longer waiting period for success. Sometimes a victory is short lived, as when governments or autocrats move the goal posts.

Campaigning for better legislative protection of parklands used to be a lonely business, unless one had the cultured Roderick Haig–Brown or the bluntly spoken Tom Norris, the Supreme Court justice, on one's side. When the future of Strathcona Provincial Park was in the balance, those allies were a marvel to behold. No sooner were they dead than mining claims of yesteryear were turned into mines and electrically powered ore–grinding mills. Soon, however, the environmentalists' blood pressure began to rise and remaining claims were bought out. The hidden agenda was pursued in a different direction, as parts of the park's boundary areas were lopped off. In the run–up to an election, more acres were added to the park. And so it has gone for decades. The moral to be drawn from this and other contests is, "Beware, and never give up the fight."

Still on parks, my hope is that the moribund Pacific National Exhibition in Vancouver can be booted out unceremoniously from the 160 acres of Hastings Park, which it has blacktopped and wrenched from the City of Vancouver Parks Board. I trust that Stanley Park will be recovered from the non–parks uses that infest it. A pathetic zoo should be closed and the animals given to a zoo already started in the Fraser Valley. As public protests concerning the acrobatic use made of whales increase, it is my hope that the highly educational aquarium can be moved out of the Stanley Park Defence lands entirely and relocated on the Devonian area at the entrance to the park that is totally under the jurisdiction of the city, and is on non–polluting electric bus routes and, therefore, accessible to families with children or invalids. This will free Stanley Park of a great deal of local motor traffic. The Naval Reserve area, H.M.C.S. Discovery, on Deadman's Island, should be joined to Stanley Park and tripled in size by a wall built from low tide level. Its buildings should become an athletic community centre for the whole of the park. From the ancient lighthouse on the northeast corner of the park, a breakwater should be built in a southeasterly direction on top of the so–called Burnaby Shoal, whose boulders can be seen clearly at low tide. The breakwater would add to the walks and trails of the park, at the same time protecting small craft moored in Vancouver harbour.

The long–term effort to make a pedestrian pathway along the waterfront from Hastings Park to the airport should be continued by stopping through motor traffic along Point Grey Road, in exchange for a water–level walkway at the foot of the high bank and out of sight of the residents.

Speaking of the Vancouver International Airport, there comes to mind the need for a third major runway for a "flying field" as crowded as YVR is today. The federal department of transport was pictured as an ogre in its post–war campaign to clear all farms and farm buildings from Sea Island, a diked island in the broad Fraser Delta. Now, however, there should be space forever, as the airport can be extended for at least a mile out into the shallow shorelands of this section of the Gulf of Georgia. This extension would require a prodigious amount of fill, perhaps garbage pounded flat as in San Francisco.

The problem, however, is that the west wind, coming in from the Pacific, prevails, or the reverse occurs, often with rain from the coast range to the northeast. A linear extension on the east–west axis would produce only longer runways. What is officially sought is a new one parallel to the existing main pair, but placed towards the S.W. Marine Drive area of Vancouver. Better still, in my view, would be a very long one based on Swishwash Island in the middle arm of the Fraser River. I became interested in this mile–long uninhabited island during the war, when my high altitude and survival laboratory was nearby. Since then small trees have started to grow on it. It is made up of "the topsoil of British Columbia," as the writer Bruce Hutchison called the non–stop run–off borne by the mighty Fraser River. (It has its source in the Rocky Mountains less than a mile from the headwaters of the Columbia River and of the Mississippi–Missouri system.)

The thing that has long appealed to me about Swishwash Island is that, though long and narrow, it runs in an east–west axis and could be reached from the Sea Island airport by a short–span, low level bridge, which would in no way upset the flow of fish up or down the Fraser. When the president of B.C. Packers, Chancellor John Buchanan of UBC, asked me to examine it as a potential rowing course for our crews, I had to report, unhappily, that it was too exposed both as to winds and tides. It could, however, serve as the runway for large planes landing from across the Pacific or over the North Pole, thus establishing an intercontinental terminal to reduce the stacking of planes in the air and to speed the arrival and customs clearance of weary passengers from abroad.

In my hometown, Victoria, I hope to convert the derelict St. Ann's Academy, behind the Empress Hotel, into a civic cultural centre. These six precious acres, recently saved from becoming a 600–seat beer parlour and amusement park, must remain in the public domain, unused, until a first–class future is found for them.

In the field of university education, I have one piece of unfinished business that I am anxious to conclude. It concerns the concept of a "Weekend University," and it may have general application. Extension courses for credit have been offered for generations by colleges and universities in many countries. "Open Universities" and "Knowledge Networks" have flourished with the development of television, telephone and computer connections, and with the public correspondence courses from high–school level to university entrance that my father, John Wesley Gibson, pioneered in North America in the Great Depression.

However, my economics background causes me to listen to the critics when they attack the waste of public funds involved in the closure of universities on two days out of every seven–day week. They are outraged as taxpayers. But what they and most people fail to understand is this: (1) most people work in industry of whatever kind, for the five days of the week that universities are open; (2) exactly when the "workers of the world" could attend university, on Saturdays and Sundays, the universities are closed, except for their libraries; and (3) Most graduate students working for a degree beyond their bachelor's have to finance the rapidly increasing cost of their advanced courses by assisting in undergraduate laboratories or seminars, or in some cases lecturing. If some could earn their way by assisting with weekend laboratories and classes, in concentrated form, they would be free for the five day week to concentrate, unhindered, on their research, which is, in large measure, the content of their future master's or doctor's degree. When I was working for my D.Phil. degree at Oxford and serving as a demonstrator in microscopic anatomy, I found that five days each week were interrupted by the scheduled teaching I was required to do, and only on weekends could I concentrate on the research I had undertaken for my degree.

Some day I hope, in summary, that it will be possible for those who earn their bread on five days of the week to take weekend courses on university campuses for credit towards a first degree, and that graduate students who assist in the weekend teaching will be able to spend five complete days on their own research. It is not likely that at first there will be many applicants for either role, but eventually there will be a tax–payers' revolt against the shutting down of universities on weekends.

While I am in full flight as a disturber of academic tranquillity, I might as well drop a brick on the subject of "lectures as a deterrent to learning." Since Gutenberg began the use of movable type in the year 1455, there has been little need to transcribe, seated in large lecture halls, what is already in printed form in libraries and university book stores. When I was chancellor at the University of Victoria, I was telephoned by a generous friend who was interested in universities. He said, with some force, "Have you not something more important for your professors to do than lecture? What about research for a change?" I told him that he must stop reading my convocation remarks, "forth bloody with," as the Australians say. I agreed! He went on to say that if the Russians could embrace a market economy, perhaps professors could as well—and replace the publicly despised tenure by five–year contracts, renewable if both sides were satisfied. With that the university telephone exchange started to smoke. He was, in my amateur's view, right on.

I am in the early days of a campaign to get a small change made in Canada's income tax law, which would bring freedom from the capital gains tax to those who have contributed to universities, properties or other assets that have appreciated in value since purchased. Then we shall have some real support for universities by private citizens, as has been the case in the U.S.A. for generations.

One project that is far too large for one physician to handle is the development of one or more botanical gardens in which each of the flowers, plants and trees bears the name of a physician. The list is long, but would be limited by the climate, the setting and possibly the regional association with medical pioneers.

The most obvious names of such plants would include: Dahl, Wistar, Zinn, L'Obel, Magnol, Fuchs, and Garden. Other physicians memorialized in botanical names include: Fothergill, Lettsom, Valerius Cordus, Linnaeus, Bigelow, Eschscholtz, Sarrazin, Colden, Kuhn, Marshall, Barton, Mead, Hosack, Torrey, Asa Gray, Parry, Howe, Hippocrates, Rauwolf, Monardes, Malpighi, Bouvard, Weigel, Gloxin, Rudbeck, Gaulthier, Euphorbus, Freese, Gerard, Menzies, Paeon, Kaempfer and von Bunge, to name but a few. So that project awaits physicians everywhere.

CHAPTER FORTY-FOUR

The Open Arms

A little more than a century ago there was completed at 13 Norham Gardens, in Oxford, a house so fashionable that its architect, William Wilkinson, featured it in his book on English country houses. It was to become, after a year of modifications, the home of William Osler, Regius professor of medicine, and his wife, Grace Revere Osler. During the enlargement of the house—including, by English standards, an unusual number of new bathrooms—the Oslers and their son Revere lived at No. 7, Norham Gardens, in a furnished house rented from Professor Max Müller.

From 1906 to 1919 hospitality was dispensed by the Oslers on a scale unknown before or since in Oxford. Trans-Atlantic visitors, in particular, were entertained at what soon became known as The Open Arms. After Sir William's death in December 1919 the stream of visitors abated, but for another 10 years the warmth of Lady Osler's friendship with Oxford students persisted. She left this great brick mansion to Christ Church College, to which the Regius' chair was always attached. My old teacher, Professor Gardner, as Regius professor, persuaded Christ Church to give it to Oxford University in the hope that future Regius professors of medicine might live in it. He had himself lived for many years on Boar's Hill, having taught bacteriology to our small clinical class with the assistance of Dr. Roy Vollum, an early Rhodes scholar from Vancouver. When that perceptive neuropathologist and Oslerian Dr. Alastair Robb-Smith saw a tree growing out of the roof, it was agreed that the time had come to act.

The house had suffered occupancy by an Institute of Mathematics and by the pre-St. Anne's College group known as the Society of Home Students. On Sir George Pickering's election to the Regius professorship, it was wisely decided to make him a suitable house embracing the delightful rooms on the main floor and on the first floor, while areas not thus needed were to be subdivided off as future small apartments.

Upon Sir Richard Doll's retirement from the Regius professorship, to become Warden of the new Green College, a new Regius, Professor Harris, was appointed, but he, like Gardner, already owned a house in Oxford and did not wish to take on anything of the size of 13 Norham Gardens.

I had hoped that the excellent Wellcome Unit in the history of medicine might inherit The Open Arms, but Oxford City's town council ruled against any further institutional use of the large homes in the Norham Gardens area. They felt that the housing stock within the city was being eroded daily. By the same token a computer facility of the university was ruled out as a potential user.

Then Sir Richard and Lady Doll conceived a plan to save 13 Norham Gardens as a residential property by attaching it to Green College on a lease basis for 21 years. Green College, a tutorial and postgraduate medical college, was founded in 1979 by the Manchester–born electrical engineer Dr. Cecil Green, one of the founders of the electronics empire known as Texas Instruments. His college is situated on the three acres immediately north of the Radcliffe Infirmary. It consists today of beautiful quadrangular residential, administrative and educational units surrounding the massive Radcliffe Observatory. Thus, Green College is but a very short walk from Norham Gardens.

The Open Arms now enters upon a new life with its fabric mostly renovated, but with a few basic structural problems remaining (for example, the severity of the winter of 1979–80 was disastrous for some of the slates and the brick work). Oslerians around the world have still an opportunity to contribute to another of those productive "lost causes" for which Oxford is allegedly famous.

Oslerians will be interested in the ingenious scheme that the ever–patient and hard–working Dolls have devised to keep 13 Norham Gardens a viable entity. The main floor contains two fine rooms for the display of Osleriana that was contributed by his followers around the world. The remainder of the floor, including the kitchen and drawing room, is used by the Newcomers Club—a voluntary organization that has been in existence for many years. It receives a small grant from the university for its work in welcoming the wives and families of new members of the professorate, as well as short–term visitors such as those on sabbatical leave. The catalytic role of the Newcomers Club in helping new arrivals to get the best out of their time in Oxford is really a continuation of the very practical hospitality and counsel dispensed by Lady Osler in her time. The City of

Oxford authorities were very keen on this aspect of the renewed life of 13 Norham Gardens. Next floor up, one finds an excellent large flat for the use of future Regius professors of medicine should they wish to use it.

Quite separate from the above features, one finds four apartments for married students in the field of medicine. Three of these flats contain one bedroom and one sitting room, kitchen and bath, while one has two bedrooms. All are situated high enough in the mansion to provide good views over the Parks or North Oxford. Under Lady Doll's constant supervision the builders produced these very comfortable quarters.

Green College contributed £25,000 towards the renovations, which was matched by the university. Thereafter, a residual requirement of £30,000 remained to be found. Many individuals, led by the ever generous Dr. John McGovern of Houston, have contributed. A small number of foundations, usually headed by Oslerians, have helped as well. There still remain some pretty basic requirements—such as a renewed heating system and repairs to the outside of the building—so that well-wishers around the world can still help. Contributions made to Oxford University for this designated purpose qualify for income tax deductibility in Canada and the United States. Members of the Osler Club of London and of the American Osler Society were generous contributors even when it was not certain what the future held for this historic home. Now, however, a multi-purpose role has been negotiated successfully by the Warden of Green College, so that all that remains is for devotees of the Oslerian tradition to support this imaginative new venture in old and hallowed surroundings.

Perhaps, in conclusion, I might say a word about Oxford medicine today, for I constantly marvel at the number of physicians and others who doubt that there is anything of a scientific nature going on up the Thames! They have long since forgotten the association of Harvey, Wren, Willis and Boyle with Oxford. They may have heard of Sherrington and his three Nobel laureate students, Florey, Eccles and Granit, but probably not of Nobelist Rodney Porter and the potent Enzyme Group, nor of Sir Rex Richards, of nuclear magnetic resonance fame and sometime vice-chancellor of Oxford University. Cancer of the lung in heavy smokers may ring a bell, but they may be unaware of Sir Richard Doll's role in this saga, or of his great success in the founding Warden's post at the innovative Green College.

The fact is that the 100 students in each year of Oxford's six-year medical degree course are the most fortunate students in the world. The accomplished teachers and the enquiring minds to which these students are exposed have made Oxford a medical mecca. The extension into the clinical years of Oxford's unique tutorial system has been one of the goals of Green College. Another has been the bringing together in its refectories and common rooms of medical scientists with engineering and social scientists. The neighbouring Wellcome Unit in the history of medicine would have pleased Osler, whose last speech at Oxford in 1919 dwelt so cogently on "The Old Humanities and the New Science."

Let Oslerians everywhere be assured, therefore, that The Open Arms is back in service, with several new roles, but basically in its old role of felicitous hospitality in the tradition established three-quarters of a century ago by William and Grace Revere Osler, in an edifice whose construction began about the time William Osler embarked upon his medical studies at Trinity College, Toronto. Thus does history repeat and renew itself.

CHAPTER FORTY-FIVE

Unfinished Business

Parkland and its preservation continue to occupy my working hours. The mail never ceases and there will, I suppose, always be a need for vigilance against developers in search of a quick buck. They destroy and move on. Few developers ever live in the areas whose riches they have exploited for gain. They are not to be confused with real estate agents who try to find the housing most suited to their clients.

However, wintering in California has shown me that some local governments prefer to keep public and private open land in public use. The total cost to taxpayers of the servicing of new developments including schools, fire and police protection, has become excessive.

Efforts to save once-dedicated parks have brought me and my friends into inevitable collision with mining and forest interests. Alas, the workers who carry the heavy, daily physical load in these industries have been talked into an alliance with exploiters—always in the name of jobs. Those harmed by this siren song never stop to ask what jobs will be left for them and their children when the clear-cut logging and the extraction of ore is finished.

In his advancing years, H.R. MacMillan, the forest giant, used to shake his head as he said to me, "I hope someone will come along, after I have gone, who will do something other than chop it down or dig it up and ship it out!"

For the most part our laws for the protection of parks have been diluted by elected bodies, rather than strengthened or enforced. There is, however, too much handwringing and too little positive political action today, except by women's groups. Men have certainly failed. It is frightening to see the exhaustion of coal resources, simply because coal will burn. It can be the starting point for chemicals and pharmaceuticals for the future. Solar power can yet save our earth.

It seems to me that the transfer of air rights (development rights) that exist over our city parks can do two things: keep buildings off those sacred lands in perpetuity, and bring, through the sale of those rights, money into a foundation dedicated to the acquisition of more civic parks in areas currently deficient in them.

Wrecking our planet, however, is the silent but ticking time bomb of over–population. It is destroying the undeveloped areas of the world, while populations in the developed are nearly stationary. My wife's solution would be to include a handful of the French pill RU 486 in every sack of food sent to famine–ridden areas.

Despite what right–wing politicians claim in their ignorant ramblings on the sins of alleged revolutionist professors, the academic world remains frustratingly averse to internal change. Gradually the outreach to the community is being sanctified, and "open" universities, rather than closed, are slowly becoming acceptable. It has not occurred to some, however, that the annual traffic jam as students try to enrol for the courses they want and need could be relieved by advising students to take courses, equivalent in every way, through open university offerings, with their tutors, video cassettes, excellent texts and so on. In fact, the texts are likely to have been written by distinguished scholars, too often dismissed with a sneering dose of provincialism. Some day short–changed students will protest about barriers to learning, instead of scrapping with administrators about matters of extra–curricular turf. The great teachers are those who open up a subject, not close it off. Only a system of external examiners will get fresh air, and room for fresh ideas, into our universities. Too many institutions are run as high schools. Sooner or later the best institutions will forget tenure and move to five–year contracts, renewable any number of times, if both sides are happy. Then rewards will match effort, and the notorious few who retire at age 35 and coast until age 65 will disappear.

Stanford's great president, David Starr Jordan, the first student to graduate with an advanced degree at Cornell, regarded graduate students as "the crown jewels" of any university. Having written a volume, *Young Endeavour*, on discoveries made by medical undergraduates, I agree with his view entirely. Our future hinges on getting enquiring minds to stay in university research settings for as long as can be afforded.

Which brings me to the subject of fund raising for research in our universities. The double Nobelist Madame Curie said it best for all listeners:

> Take an interest, I urge upon you, in these holy dwellings to

Forests precede peoples and nations; deserts succeed them.

Francois Rene Chateaubriand, 1840

The power of population is infinitely greater than the power in the earth to produce subsistence. Population when unchecked, increases in a geometrical ratio. Subsistence increases only in an arithmetical ratio.

Reverend Robert Malthus (1766-1834),
Fellow of Jesus College, Cambridge

> which the expressive name of "laboratories" is given. Ask that they be multiplied and adorned. They are the temples of the future, of wealth and well-being. It is there that humanity grows bigger, strengthens and betters itself. It learns there to read in the works of nature, works of progress and universal harmony, whereas its own works are too often those of barbarity, fanaticism and destruction.

I suppose the first foundation to benefit the world of learning specifically came from the excess funds raised to free Plato from his captors abroad. Thus, his academy was financed by his friends in Athens who over-shot the amount needed for his ransom. During my life I have sought funds for universities, and for medical research, with some surprising results. One is fortunate, I have found, to be able to interest one foundation in ten in a substantial way.

Years ago I was invited by Cecil Green to address a small group of his multimillionaire friends at the Petroleum Club in Dallas on the subject of fund raising. He introduced me as his "most expensive friend." I confounded his compatriots by telling them that the best way to raise money for a project was never to ask for it! That amused them no end, until I explained that asking for money could have one of two outcomes: an outright refusal, or a token amount, grudgingly given. In either scenario the door was closed irrevocably for the future. The only sure way was to put a project before a potential donor in such a way as to arouse his interest, and gradually his participation—on his terms, not on those of the mendicant. If the case had been made quietly, without hysterics, but with back up information supplied, and time given to digest the idea—years, in Dr. Penfield's proposal to the Rockefeller Foundation—then a sound understanding could be mutually developed, with real, not imaginary, results. Cecil persists in telling his philanthropic friends about this approach and has, at great cost, supported my thesis.

Looking ahead, investments in research will pay off handsomely when the stakes are large, as in the case of Alzheimer's disease. The silent annual financial haemorrhage that this one illness causes in the United States is in the billions of dollars. When, in 1905 and 1906, Dr. Alois Alzheimer reported the changes found in the brain to his neuropathologist colleagues in Germany, there was no discussion as the reports of the meetings record.

Now, under the microscope, the reactive cells—the microglia discovered by Río-Hotega—are implicated. Their role may be central or peripheral, but today research is in high gear on this devastating problem. We are back to Harry Hopkins' statement to Roosevelt: "Research is spending to save." In this case it is not merely money, but useful lives.

Social priorities today loom large in public financial policy everywhere. We are shocked to learn that the cost of a prisoner in a "long stay" gaol may far exceed the cost to the taxpayer of a student at university. The cost to the taxpayer of a recruit in the military forces may seem exorbitant if there is no educational element involved. A new type of international peace corps seems necessary, with the enemy being the widespread degradation of the earth's atmosphere and its environment.

Thus, in conclusion, I see so many projects that need personal support that I wonder how best to focus my efforts. I have learned, above all, that to get into the fray is health–giving. Too many of us are reduced to inactivity by being cowed by the feeling that one person's effort can make no difference. Only when this depressive ghost, this self–delusion, is laid to rest will the fruits of democracy become manifest. Recently the University of British Columbia president asked, "When are you going to slow down?" My reply then, and today, is simply "I have no time to slow down."